A Family Business Publication

Family businesses encounter a unique set of challenges, ranging from strategic growth to succession planning to communication between colleagues (and relatives!). The books in Palgrave and the Family Business Consulting Group's family business series provide guidance on how to overcome them and achieve continued growth and success. The authors are experts in the field, sharing practical, effective, and time-tested insights from their many years running their own family businesses.

Wendy Sage-Hayward · Gaia Marchisio ·
Barbara Dartt

Own It!

How to Develop a Family Enterprise Owner's Mindset at Every Age

Wendy Sage-Hayward
The Family Business Consulting Group,
Vancouver, BC, Canada

Gaia Marchisio
CARE for Family Enterprise,
Atlanta, GA, USA

Barbara Dartt
The Family Business Consulting Group,
Laingsburg, MI, USA

ISSN 2947-3985   ISSN 2947-3993   (electronic)
A Family Business Publication
ISBN 978-3-030-20418-1   ISBN 978-3-030-20419-8   (eBook)
https://doi.org/10.1007/978-3-030-20419-8

Cover credit: saemilee

This Palgrave Macmillan imprint is published by the registered company Springer Nature Switzerland AG
The registered company address is: Gewerbestrasse 11, 6330 Cham, Switzerland

To All Generations...
For What You Bring Separately and Collectively

To our Previous Generation

To John L. Ward and Craig E. Aronoff, founders of The Family Business
Consulting Group and The Cox Family Enterprise Center and thought
leaders in the Family Enterprise field. Your vision and contribution are
evident in today's organization, twenty-six years after you imagined a future
that would outlast and surpass any of us. You exemplify the owner's mindset
by leading, shaping, teaching, and then, at the right time, gracefully letting
go. We are proud to add our small part to perpetuate the dream.

		Nonna Cicci, Zionno
Mom, Dad, and	*Dad, Mom, Grandpa Cook, and*	*Alfredo, Papi, Mina, and*
Anne	*Jim*	*Marjorie*
Wendy	Barb	Gaia

To our families, mentors, and clients—who are sometimes one and the
same—we are grateful for the many selfless hours of listening, encouraging,
and exhorting us. You have been and continue to be a huge part of shaping
who we are today.

To our Generation

Ian, Jessica, Heidi, Kathy and the Hayward Family	Brian, Mike, and my FBCG partners	Riccardo, Roberta, Anna, and all my Cousins
Wendy	Barb	Gaia

To our significant others, family, colleagues, and friends. Thank you for being a core part of our team in our own development journey. We have benefited from you supporting us as we strove to continually be a little better, even when it meant last-minute changes in family and personal lives.

To our Rising Generation

Blake, Koshi and all 13 Sage and Hayward nieces and nephews	Alex, Connor, and Quinn	Andrea, Francesco, Elisa, and AnnaChiara
Wendy	Barb	Gaia

To our rising generation family members. Too often we mistakenly think that our relationship with you is a one-way learning street. In fact, it is quite the opposite! Your untainted and unassuming view on the world gives us fresh eyes with which to approach our days and our work. You are an inspiration for us to be the best we can be each and every day. Thank you for continually challenging our ability to adapt and evolve. Our hearts are full.

Foreword

The special nature of ownership of family enterprises has occupied academics and practitioners in the field of family flourishing since its beginnings with writing thousands of years ago. Aristotle opined that he felt it relatively easy to make a fortune but very difficult for a family to retain one. Many other authors in other cultures have opined the same.

We know this pattern in Western cultures as the proverb "shirtsleeves to shirtsleeves in three generations" and in China, in one of its many forms, as "rice paddy to rice paddy in three generations." Why this should be so is unknowable as each family, as its bonds of affinity dissolve, as Tolstoy observed, does it in its own way. Each reflects the second law of thermodynamics, energy to matter to energy, as entropy works its will.

Despite this reality, those of us who seek to help families flourish and postpone this outcome attempt to find answers that work for each such family. We seek to help them define "when" this will happen to them and help them try to postpone this inevitable outcome for at least seven generations. Their humility that the proverb cannot be avoided and their willingness to try is heroic in its own way and is to be applauded.

Such families form the core of Dennis Jaffe's great book *Borrowed From Your Grandchildren*. Families in this book had to have achieved their third generations of flourishing members to get into the book and then often had fourth-, fifth-, and sixth-generation members flourishing together. These families exemplify the quality of affinity and their awareness that their purpose is to enhance the journeys of happiness of each of their family members toward the entire family continuing to flourish. Or if you like, that all family members' boats will rise. They each vow to seek to help each member's boat to rise. All so the family flotilla sails on safely, anti-fragility, and flourishingly far into the future. The members of each generation in turn making the same vow and being given the help each individually needs to attain a flourishing life and strengthen the bonds of affinity each individually shares with his or her family members.

Each of the families of affinity described above shares resources far beyond their individual needs. The creation of their original resources almost always lies in the actions of a single person whose life was about this act of creation. Often, such persons are regarded as the "Founders" of these families and their stories form important parts of the positive myths of such families.

However, the core genesis of such families lies in whether their second-generation members decide to seek to become a family of affinity and seek by doing so to avoid the proverb's edict for at least seven generations into the future.

Among the questions such second-generation family members face is, "Are they willing, as owners de facto or de jure, to work together to 'dynamically preserve' the resources they receive from the Founder?"

If they can answer the previous question affirmatively:

- Can they imagine that their family resources are much larger than their Financial Capital?
- Can they see very early on that their family assets consist of five separate and collective capitals and seek to dynamically preserve each and all of them?
- Can they see that their assets consist of Human Capital, Intellectual Capital, Social Capital, Spiritual Capital, and Financial Capital?
- Can they see that the role and purpose of their Financial Capital, their Quantitative Capital is to grow all four of their Qualitative Capitals, Human, Intellectual, Social, and Spiritual?
- Can they see that a focus on their Financial Capital alone, as history teaches, will condemn them to fail to hinder the proverb coming true?
- Can they see that focusing, as their highest purpose and practice, on growing their Qualitative Capitals supported by growing their Quantitative Capital is the path to success?
- Can they adopt dynamic preservation of each capital as their purpose going forward?

I add that only this awareness and then the consistent persevering development and growth of each capital has enabled the families, mine and all those I have helped and studied, avoid the proverb's edict.

Great dynamic, conserving, stewarding, stakeholder ownership and its principles and practices, as consistently and perseveringly applied to all five Family Capitals (Human, Intellectual, Social, Spiritual, and Financial), by a family, over multiple generations, as the wonderful book you are about to read proves irrevocably, lies at the core of families of affinity's success.

Such strategic owners understand the power of dynamically preserving all five of their capitals to enable all family members to benefit fully from them.

Each family member finds him or herself positively attracted to the family and its continued flourishing as each person finds his or her own "self" growth and flourishing at the core of the family enterprises' governance and evolution.

With this awareness of how others are helping them individually, members much more easily seek to help all the other members achieve their flourishing—as this process unfolds and evolves, all boats rise and the proverb falls farther away; the "when" of the "shirtsleeves to shirtsleeves" adage falls farther away.

Thus, the core of the work of a family at every stage of every member's life is to learn how to dynamically preserve and thereby grow all of its five capitals. How to be a dynamic conserving stewarding stakeholder owner of all five capitals. Why? Because without learning how to do this and then forever practicing what is learned as each capital's growth is continuously challenged by its own risk of entropy the proverb and its description of entropy and the families' dissolution must inevitably occur.

In this book are important truths about the nature and practice of strategic and tactical ownership of all five capitals and at all of the various stages of life of a family's members. This book contains two books. First, the why of ownership is described. As I have noted, dynamic, conserving, stewarding, stakeholder ownership is at the core of every family of affinity. Second, the book contains new, practical insights about how to develop these special, essential owners. It is the first work I have seen that describes developmental stages with both comment on the challenges faced in each stage and then a multitude of hands-on approaches so you can map your own family's work.

I welcome you to the book's journey and the great vision and wisdom it contains for your families' journeys to avoid the proverb and to flourish for at least seven more generations. My blessings on your journey.

Thank you to Wendy, Barbara, and Gaia for sharing your vision and wisdom of what makes a great ownership of a family enterprise.

Namaste

Aspen, Colorado   James (Jay) E. Hughes, Jr.
2022

Preface

How are you successfully managing the dynamic preservation of your family enterprise over generations and thus averting the well-known proverb: "*The first generation builds it, the second generation maintains it, the third generation squanders it?*"

As family business owners, consultants, and researchers, we asked this question repeatedly to our own families and to our clients. We lived the journey to becoming owners and understand well the complex nature of this path—emotionally, relationally, and financially. We were all nervous, intimidated, and yet also excited and proud to be part of our families' businesses. One had been operating for more than a century! Sometimes we struggled to find our own voices among the older family members, particularly those who had deep experience in the business. We felt non-operating owners too often had very limited voices. Our families suffered from the same affliction that our clients often do—a lack of knowledge and dialogue about ownership. In fact, this is more common than not. This complex and challenging journey is what inspired us to write this book.

Unfortunately, very few enterprising families focus on building an owner's mindset in their families. They are busy working and growing their enterprises—and rightly so. In addition, too often family enterprises prioritize and value the management role over the ownership role and thus don't view it as a critical skill. Finally, many rising generation family members do not choose the path of ownership; they are simply born into it. Therefore, it's not surprising that there is little focus on valuing and building an educated owner to steward the family's assets for future generations. Yet, the importance of this role is staggering. There is much more at risk than the financial losses that could arise. The loss of the family itself and relationships within is our greatest risk and most devastating losses.

As much as we loved writing this book and sharing our experience and expertise, once we completed it, all three of us realized that we needed this information decades ago! As in other aspects of life, we learn from our mistakes more than our successes. After we witnessed our clients' successes—and felt their anguishes as well as our own—we concluded that someone needed to define a better journey to ownership. This book is not only born out of our education, dedication to continuous growth, and experience. It also reflects years of working with business families and learning *with and from* them how to avoid the same mistakes we witnessed and experienced.

There is no one-size-fits-all model for the path to ownership, but there are some key principles that provide a guiding light. Our goal in writing this book is firstly, to advance the claim that ownership is a critical role in a family enterprise which needs to be intentionally and strategically developed. Secondly, we want to set out key principles by age and stage of life and provide practical examples of *how* development happens both formally and informally.

We are excited to share the insights we've gained from our evolving experience with family-owned organizations in building an owner's mindset.

Vancouver, Canada   Wendy Sage-Hayward
Atlanta, USA   Gaia Marchisio
Laingsburg, USA   Barbara Dartt

Acknowledgments

Writing this book has been an incredible learning journey for the three of us. Our collaboration has been a blessing *and* there are many people who helped bring this book to fruition. To them, we wish to extend our heartfelt thanks. To Sachin Waikar for your skill and aptitude in bringing our multiple voices and ideas into one, as well as sticking with us through thick and thin. To Stephanie Brun de Pontet for your time, energy, and insights as our FBCG Reviewer. To Otis Baskin, David Lansky, and Craig Aronoff for your honesty and direction. To James Hughes for being a true wisdom keeper and for so generously sharing your guidance and sagacity. Not only did you offer incredible perspectives into the why and how of building an owner's mindset, you have also been an amazing champion for us and this book. To Ian Hayward for your sharp wit and discerning feedback. To Michael Mok for your patience and talent in graphic design. To Tim Foss for bringing Zoe, Zak, and their families alive. To Stephanie Edsall and Jenna Berry for your diligence in ensuring the important and tedious details were accurate and organized. To Karen King for your creativity and continuous encouragement. To Eric Kushins for helping add rigor in our tools. Deep thanks also to those who have been part of our getting "here." To Judi Cunningham for sparking passion in others, advancing our vision in this field, and approaching everything with a tenacious spirit. To Guido Corbetta, Pietro Mazzola, Daniela Montemerlo, and Salvo Tomaselli, because we never forget roots; and to Marjorie Blum for offering wings, by inspiring and mentoring with care and wisdom.

Finally, we put our minds and hearts in these pages. And, as you can see from these tributes, this book is a true team effort. That said, any misspellings, misrepresentations, or missed opportunities were merely an effort to make sure you were reading closely. And, they're the authors' mistakes.

Praise for *Own It!*

"Throughout the book, Barbara, Gaia and Wendy, have masterfully crafted a path that empowers families to explore the multi-faceted and complex arena known as 'ownership' – supporting families to envision their own unique approach to ownership and the development of competent owners within their desired framework. This will be a cornerstone of every family business library."

—Margaret-Jean Mannix, *G4 Owner, Chair, Mannix Family Foundation – Canada*

"This forward-thinking book provides practical strategies for learning and development at all ages and life stages. It refreshingly, uniquely, and successfully addresses "how-tos" and "things to watch out for."

—Monica Walter, *Vice President Family Governance and Development, G4 Family Office – USA*

"This is the first book I read that gives a spot-on practical toolkit to help multi-generational business families develop the right ownership mindset. The Authors' experience working directly with families all over the world, combined with their teaching background, make this book an invaluable resource for every multi-generational business family in the world that want to develop strong lifelong learning practices. Every member of my family should get a copy of this book when they turn 18!"

—Edouard Thijssen, *CEO & Founder, Trusted Family – Belgium*

"This book provides answers to pertinent questions that I have heard from the many business-owning families I have networked and worked with over the last two decades around the world, especially from the perspective of developing the human capital of the family. Read it, self-reflect on it, and use it as a group-learning discussion tool!"

—Dr. Johnben Loy., *G2 Owner, YPO Certified Forum Facilitator + Family Therapist – Kuala Lumpur*

"The book is not about business, it is about how business learning has a special place in business families, through each stage of the life cycle. We see how ownership learning takes place at each stage of children's development, and how organically addressing and teaching ownership early on can anticipate and prevent difficulty, conflict and lack of preparation later on."

—Dennis Jaffe, *Founder, Wise Counsel Research – USA*

"In this excellent book, developed using many relevant theories in a genuine effort of interdisciplinarity and the experience of many families in the world, everyone will find ideas and tools useful to catch opportunities and reduce risks associated with ownership. This process is a long one, and Wendy, Gaia, and Barbara help us learn how to manage it at different ages."

—Guido Corbetta, *Chair "AIDAF-EY of Family Business Strategy in memory of Alberto Falck," Università Bocconi. | Vice President at Wepartner SpA. – Italy*

"OWN IT! does a fantastic job communicating the key technical, legal, and organizational concepts of ownership in the context of the multi-generational family enterprise (and does so in a way that is comprehensible to family members that are not well versed in the concepts and language of business). More importantly, though, [this book] articulates a clear framework with practical starting points that families and advisers should use in educating family members at each stage of development, and also identifies common issues and pitfalls that should be considered and avoided. An invaluable read for family members and advisers working in the multi-generational family enterprise space."

—Thompson Turner, *Esq., G5 Owner, Chair of the Advisors Committee of the Family Council, and Estate Planner – USA*

Contents

List of Exhibits

1

Why a Book About Ownership Development—An Overview

W. Sage-Hayward et al., *Own It!*, A Family Business Publication,
https://doi.org/10.1007/978-3-030-20419-8_1

We believe you're reading this book because you see family enterprise ownership as a critical area and one that deserves a comprehensive approach to development.

We couldn't agree more.

Family enterprises matter—not only to the families who own them, but to the communities in which they operate and the broader global economy. Family-owned firms are foundational to the global economy. Their health and growth have a large impact on every country's economic welfare. Consider the numbers: the top 500 family firms equal the world's third-largest economy, employing about 25 million people, with total revenues of almost US$7 trillion.[1]

And, **family ownership development matters**, but it is often ignored especially in earlier stages of succession. Effective owners have a material impact on the outcomes for their enterprises and, by extension, on the lives and economies they impact. Since its inception, both family firm theory and practice have focused on the overlap and interaction between family and business as the key to understanding why they are different. Despite the major contribution that Tagiuri and Davis[2] made in 1978 when they added ownership as a third overlapping independent system with their famous 3-circle model, the field's attention has been predominantly focused on the business and family circles, and in particular, on the impact that family management has on business performance.

Ownership is often overlooked, and here's why: At the founder stage, ownership and management are the same. The distinction between these roles and related responsibilities emerges only in subsequent generations. As family ownership progresses through various stages, such as founder to sibling partnership to cousin consortium and family dynasty, there is growing separation between management and ownership. However, a strong bias—the desire to concentrate control in the hands of a few family members who work in the business—persists. This bias stems from our tendency to over-privilege the management role. This, combined with the fact that management-level decisions are more frequent and urgent, directs more attention to the business and away from the owner's role. The bias toward consolidation of control in family members working in the business perpetuates the lack of focus on developing non-operating owners. In addition, it is confusing when the rising generation is asked to choose if they are "in or out" of the business because

---

[1] EY and University of St. Gallen Global Family Business Index. (n.d.). Retrieved from http://family businessindex.com/.

[2] Gersick, K., Davis, J. A., Hampton, M. M., & Lansberg, I. (1997). *Generation to generation: Life cycles of the family business*. Harvard Business Review Press.

this limits the option to participate in one type of ownership: operating owner.

Ownership-related matters are typically complex, highly technical, and require the support of external advisors such as lawyers, estate planners, CPAs, and others. Therefore, owners often abdicate these decisions to their expert advisors who act as their agents, frequently reducing their visibility and influence especially on critical decisions. Furthermore, ownership-related decisions are addressed by advisors primarily from a tax planning perspective, especially during generational transitions, leaving the impression that the owner role does not necessarily wield critical influence, particularly on the non-operating owners.

Non-operating owner decisions are often relegated to a few topics related to creating shareholder agreements, large acquisitions and debt, the sale of the business, and dealing with prenuptial agreements. These topics are intertwined with complicated feelings around money and love, mortality, and equality, which can lead to difficult conversations, or not having these discussions at all. Although ownership decisions are less frequent, more complex, and potentially more difficult, they also have deeper, broader, and longer-term implications than management decisions do.

Undoubtedly, the **ownership role in a family enterprise is pivotal**. Lansberg suggests ownership is "the key to understanding where true power lies in a family company."[3] Ultimately, they can decide where to invest their financial assets, and whether to keep, grow, or sell the business. Owners provide an enterprise with overall direction—setting its fundamental purpose and targets for profitability, risk, growth, and liquidity. An owner's direction is much like a helmsman providing continuous adjustment and correction to keep the ship steering straight.

According to Hughes et al.,[4] owners have the power to influence successful long-term wealth preservation when they focus on the growth of their family's human, social, intellectual, and spiritual capitals. When owners are successful, they influence wealth preservation across generations both in the business and in the family. Conversely, when they are not successful, they destroy not only financial resources but also facilitate the tragic end of dynasties (Renkert-Thomas, 2016).[5]

[3] Lansberg, I. (1999). *Succeeding generations: Realizing the dream of families in business.* Harvard Business School Press.

[4] Hughes Jr., J. E., Massenzio, S. E., & Whitaker, K. (2017). *Complete family wealth.* John Wiley & Sons.

[5] Renkert-Thomas, A. (2016). *Engaged ownership: A guide for owners of family businesses.* Wiley.

In light of this perspective, our goal is twofold. First, we want to bring more attention to the critical role and function of ownership. Second, we want to explore how to intentionally develop owners, individually and collectively, so that they can contribute to family resilience and enterprise performance. By shaping an owner's mindset and skillset across all ages and stages of life, we believe enterprising families can increase the likelihood of thriving and avoiding disastrous endings.

What is Family Enterprise?

In this book, we intentionally focus on family enterprise ownership, not family business ownership. A family business consists of operating assets only. A family enterprise, on the other hand, consists of a variety of assets beyond the operating business. It may include financial assets such as stock and bond portfolios and cash, real estate assets of any kind (i.e., commercial, residential, or industrial), and philanthropic assets such as a family foundation. Family enterprises often own heirloom assets such as jewelry, art collections, cars, or a variety of other precious (to the family) material or immaterial items that hold significant emotional attachment and value. Some real estate, such as a family cabin or recreational property, may be considered an heirloom asset for some family members and not others. Family enterprises may also have deferred assets such as insurance, annuities, and specific types of trusts that are monetized after passing. Finally, family enterprises have non-financial human assets consisting of intellectual knowledge, a network of strong relationships and leadership capabilities, among others.

The Family Enterprise Model in Exhibit 1.1 illustrates a sample of a family's assets.[6]

---

[6] Family Enterprise Asset model based on work by Judi Cunningham. For additional contributions on the concept of Family Enteprise, see: Davis, J. *Family Enteprise*. Retrieved from https://johndavis. com/family-enterprise/; Hamilton, S. (2020). *Taking the Long-Term View*, Family Office Exchange, Chicago.

Exhibit 1.1 The family enterprise model—sample assets

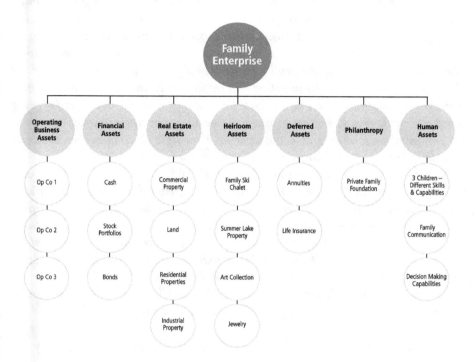

Not all family enterprises own every asset class. Some families may own operating businesses while others have primarily financial and real estate assets. Each family enterprise is unique in what it owns and manages collectively. This model is useful in helping families understand that being an owner may extend beyond just the operating business, and often may not include an operating business at all. When family ownership groups map out their assets using this framework, it creates a common understanding of what the family owns, and which assets may be transitioned to future generations.

Focusing On Ownership

Family enterprise owners **are family members with an ownership stake** (either current or future) in their family enterprise, which includes more than just the legal and economic aspects. By law, owning one share defines a shareholder and its related rewards such as increased stock **value**, dividends, and **control**, manifested in decision-making authority. However, ownership in the family enterprise context is more complicated than possessing shares that can be freely traded on a stock exchange. Aronoff and Ward[7] suggest that *"while owners are investors in the sense that they have at-risk assets tied up in a business, an investor and an effective family business owner are not the same"* (p. 6). They provide us with a much deeper and more meaningful understanding of ownership in a family enterprise: *"ownership, at its best, means stewardship— protecting and nurturing the family business and preserving it for the benefit of the next generation of family members and employees, customers, and the community. As such, ownership can be a vehicle for adding purpose to one's life; for being a better parent, spouse, brother or sister, son or daughter, uncle or aunt or cousin; for enhanced performance as a manager or a strategic decision-maker inside or outside the business; and for providing an opportunity for service."*

The stake family members have as owners builds on Hughes'[8] concept of a steward, conservator, and stakeholder owner: *"a steward as inheritor is someone with an obligation to his or her family and to the world at large to responsibly increase for the good of all, his or her inheritance; a conservator is one who turns over what he or she inherits and what it grows to be to the next generation of his or her family in equal or better condition than it was received; a stakeholder is an active, caring participant, as opposed to a passive, disinterested investor."*

We recognize **not all owners are created equal**.[9] As generations progress, we often witness the coexistence of different types of owners as follows:

- *Operating*: An owner-manager or employed owner involved in the day-to-day operations
- *Governing*: Full-time overseer not involved in day-to-day operations. For example, a chair of the board
- *Involved*: Not employed but takes an interest in operations
- *Investor*: Like a passive owner; if satisfied with returns, makes a conscious decision to retain ownership
- *Proud*: Not involved or knowledgeable about operations but takes pride in ownership
- *Passive:* Collects dividends or distributions and makes no effort to contribute or remain an owner

---

[7] Aronoff, C., & Ward, J. (2016). *Family business ownership: How to be an effective shareholder.* Springer.

[8] Hughes Jr., J. E. (2007). *A reflection of the path of the stakeholder owner: Organizational and management science.* P. 5.

[9] Aronoff, C., & Ward, J. (2016). *Family business ownership: How to be an effective shareholder.* Springer.

A shareholder can fall into more than one type. A host of differentiating factors such as time, commitment, emotional attachment,[10] participation in governance, involvement in management, expectations, legacy orientation, and level of expertise distinguish the various owner types. An inclusive concept of ownership embraces both the typical, more technical aspects (possession, decision-making, and economic returns) as well as the inspirational pieces (stewardship of legacy, contributing to the community and world, support of family, caring, and active participation).

A broad definition of ownership includes the trustee and beneficiary roles related to a trust. A trust is a legal arrangement among three key players: (1) a grantor (settlor) who transfers the legal ownership to a trust; (2) a trustee who manages the property in the trust with the decision-making rights; and (3) beneficiaries who receive distributions from the trust. In the case of trust, there is a clear separation between who has decision-making power (trustee) and who receives distributions (beneficiaries). We believe there is great benefit to developing beneficiaries to be caring, responsible, and active recipients of the powers they are given (i.e., power of appointment, trustee succession, removal and replacement).[11] When ownership is held directly or as a beneficiary, it can cross the various owner types. If ownership is held as a trustee, it falls within the operating or governing types (see Exhibit 1.2 Types of Ownership).

Exhibit 1.2 Types of Ownership

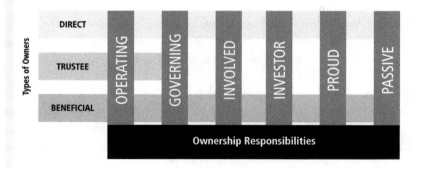

---

[10] Emotional ownership (EO), a term first coined by Nigel Nicholson, is "a natural state of mind in a healthy family, but it needs to be nurtured from quite early on and can be easily disturbed by bad parenting and lack of engagement".

[11] For more information about trust, roles, rights, and responsibilities see Angus, P. (2015). *The trustee primer. A guide for personal trustees.*

Enterprising families who understand that ownership may contribute to an individual's life purpose and personal growth, allow the rising generation to choose the type of ownership to which it aspires. The appreciation and inclusion of different owner types in a family enterprise fosters greater alignment and leads to the development of effective shareholders. Some families may not know who the future owners will be. This should not be a barrier to grooming the rising generation of potential owners. Understanding the nuances of the different owner types enables family enterprise leaders to create alternative ways to participate and clearly guide individuals who want to calibrate their level of involvement.

Generally, regardless of ownership type, owners have some common responsibilities including:

1. *Establishing ownership vision and goals*: Who are we? Where are we going? How do we generally want to get there?
2. *Creating and electing accountability structures*: Who do we want as directors and advisors? How do we support and integrate family and business governance? How do we measure success?
3. *Identifying ownership targets*: What are our profitability, leverage, growth, dividends, and liquidity goals?
4. *Establishing policies defining the relationship among the family, the owners, and the business*:[12] What roles do family members play in our enterprise? How do we compensate family members? What are the employment standards and practices we want to have for our family? How do we manage conflicts of interest?
5. *Planning for continuity*: How do we want to transition leadership and ownership to the rising generation? How do we select the next leader? Under what circumstances would we sell the company?

Owners think and act in ways that help all stakeholders in the family enterprise evolve toward a collective and shared vision while maintaining strong, active relationships. To accomplish this effectively, they need to develop a core base of knowledge and skills[13] *across their life span*, with progressively more depth and sophistication at each life stage. Enterprising families may believe that ownership skills will develop naturally over time or be absorbed

---

[12] See Appendix B for examples of policies.

[13] Aronoff, C., & Ward, J. (2016). *Family business ownership: How to be an effective shareholder*. Springer. Astrachan, C., Waldkirch, M., Michiels, A., Pieper, T., Bernhard, F., (2019). Professionalizing the business family. The five pillars of competent, committed and sustainable ownership. *Family Firm Institute Research Report*.

from other owners through osmosis. That is simply not true. Instead, the complex and dynamic owner role must be planned for and developed through education, experience, and mentoring, regardless of whether a family member works for the firm. Ideally, ownership becomes a deliberate choice, not a random gift with the potential to destroy its recipient.[14] In every family's continuity timeline, some of the most pivotal moments are when decisions are made on how to pass ownership down to the rising generation. This decision involves two important and distinct components of ownership: value and control. With the help of experienced advisors, families create complex ownership structures to figure out how value will be shared and who will have control and decision-making authority. While splitting value among the rising generation is a common and relatively easier decision to make, figuring out who will have control is far more challenging. We regularly experience a bias in families and their advisors toward concentrating control in the hands of one or a few individuals. This assures unity of command and less impact on the business if there is shareholder conflict. Marchisio (2020) named these different options: "We-Family Enterprise" (We-FE) for when both control and value are shared by owners; and "I-Family Enterprise" (I-FE) for when control is concentrated in the hands of one family member and value is distributed among all of the shareholders. We have seen success in both ways and one option is not necessarily better than the other. However, it is important for families to appreciate that if next generation family members share control, more time and effort to build alignment, communicate perspectives, and make decisions is required. When properly built, this approach results in greater engagement, satisfaction, and meaning as the owner team builds and experiences success together. Being intentional and open in discussing whether sharing both value and control, and then preparing future owners for the associated opportunities, is an important step in owner development.

Developing an Owner's Mindset

While knowledge and skills development are necessary, they are not sufficient to realize the gains from truly effective ownership, especially in the case of shared control. We advocate for purposefully building an *owner's mindset* in all owners and prospective owners. A mindset is *a set of beliefs, which drive and shape what we do, how we engage with others, and how we behave*

---

[14] Massenzio, S.E., Whitaker, K. & Hughes, J.E., (2012). *The cycle of the gift: Family wealth and wisdom.* (1st ed.). Bloomberg Press.

in every moment and situation[15] (p. 12). A mindset profoundly impacts our results because it shapes every action we take. Those who attempt to improve by changing their mindset instead of changing their behavior are four times more likely to succeed.[16] A simple illustration of a family enterprise owner's mindset is provided in Exhibit 1.3.

Exhibit 1.3 Family Enterprise Owner's Mindset

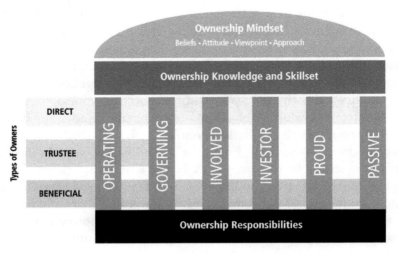

All owners have a mindset but not all mindsets are created equal. We introduce below the key elements of a *family enterprise owner's mindset,* which fosters a greater chance in operating and transitioning a family enterprise over the generations.[17]

The following beliefs characterize a family enterprise owner's mindset (which we will now refer to as an owner's mindset):

• *Development is a continuous individual <u>and</u> collective process:* Development is not just an individual endeavor, but also a collective process that builds a family's human, intellectual, social, financial, and spiritual capitals.[18] It happens at every stage and has no finish line. Developing an owner's

[15] Arbinger Institute. (2016). *The outward mindset: Seeing beyond ourselves.* Berrett-Koehler Publishers.

[16] Boaz, N., & Fox, E. A. (2014). Change leader, change thyself. *McKinsey Quarterly,* 11.

[17] For additional readings about mindsets: Shickler, S., & Waller, J. (2011). *The 7 mindsets to live your ultimate life.* Roswell, GA: Excent; Dweck, C. S. (2008). *Mindset: The new psychology of success.* Random House Digital, Inc.; Covey, S. R. (2013). *The 7 habits of highly effective people: Powerful lessons in personal change.* Simon and Schuster.

[18] Hughes Jr, J. E. (2010). *Family wealth: Keeping It in the family* (Vol. 34). John Wiley & Sons.

mindset is a process that can feel slow, and even ineffective at times, in a family enterprise. Therefore, creating this mindset requires persistence in order for individual family members and the family as a whole to adapt successfully to adversity, division, and setbacks.[19]

- *Ownership requires deep commitment and responsibility.* Those with an owner's mindset understand this is an important role that requires time and investment from which they derive personal satisfaction and energy.

- *Proactivity is paramount.* An owner's mindset entails being proactive and resourceful: it involves learning, engaging others, tackling challenges, and actively taking steps to get things done. Owners take initiative by anticipating and preparing for future challenges.

- *Abundance rather than scarcity.* Individuals and organizations have a worldview as "inherently resource-rich or resource-poor, or somewhere in between. A scarcity mindset assumes that there are limited, insufficient, non-renewable resources, and access is always limited, therefore triggering the fear of "not having enough" and a desire for control. An abundant mental model views resources and power as shareable assets."[20] Those with an owner's mindset believe that there is always more available, expect openness and trust, think big, are thankful, and learn from others.

- *Win—win solutions.* An owner's mindset is characterized by understanding the importance of thinking and acting "together" to become linked as a "we" while becoming differentiated as a collection of "me's."[21] These owners intentionally and continuously manage the delicate balance between individualism and collectivism. This tension assumes critical importance for families who share economic interests, especially for those belonging to individualistic cultures.[22] But instead of leaning toward one at the expense of the other, those with an owner's mindset design creative solutions resulting in mutually beneficial outcomes.

- *Diversity and inclusion matter.* Diversity comes in many forms: gender, race, religion, sexual orientation, age, culture, socioeconomic background, generation, personality type, intelligences, etc. Decision-making, when

---

[19] Southwick, S. M., Bonanno, G. A., Masten, A. S., Panter-Brick, C., & Yehuda, R. (2014). Resilience definitions, theory, and challenges: Interdisciplinary perspectives. *European Journal of Psychotraumatology, 5*, Article 25, 338.

[20] Freebairn-Smith, L. (2010). *Abundance and scarcity mental models in leaders* (Doctoral dissertation, Saybrook University).

[21] Siegel, D. J. (2010). *Mindsight: The new science of personal transformation.* Bantam.

[22] Jaffe, D. T., & Grubman, J. (2016). *Cross cultures: How global families negotiate change across generations.* (1st ed.). Create Space Independent Publishing Platform.

made with diverse viewpoints, has been shown to increase business objectivity, analytical thinking, innovation, and financial performance.[23] In a family enterprise, transitioning from a single or small group of owners who operate informally to a larger ownership group with broader views and greater formality can be anxiety-provoking. Individuals with an owner's mindset recognize natural human tendencies to associate with "similar" people—so they actively seek diverse perspectives, even if this results in increased formality and governance. In particular, those with an owner's mindset embrace people with a variety of intelligences.[24] They appreciate that different brains process information distinctively which adds important value to problem-solving and decision-making processes. In short, they see diversity as a tremendous strength.

- *Stronger together than apart.* Those with an owner's mindset understand they can't do it all themselves. More importantly, they don't want to do it all themselves. Instead, they are interested in collaborating in work and decision-making. They value both independence and togetherness[25] and sincerely appreciate being in business with other family members.[26] In his foundational work, Hughes highlights how *"the ability of siblings and cousins to learn to work together is critical to long-term wealth preservation"* (Hughes, 2010: 20). This idea reminds us of the wisdom contained in the African proverb: "If you want to go fast, go alone; if you want to go far, go together." A properly managed, inclusive approach thus kicks off a virtuous cycle that benefits the enterprise and everyone within it. See Exhibit 1.4 showing the impact of an owner's mindset.

Exhibit 1.4 Impact of an Owner's Mindset

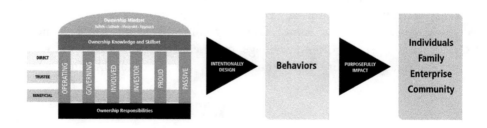

---

[23] Gompers, P., & Kovvali, S. (July–August 2018). *The other diversity dividend.* Harvard Business Review.

[24] Gardner, H. (1983). *Frames of mind: The theory of multiple intelligences.* Basic Books.

[25] Olson, D. H. (2000). Circumplex model of marital and family systems. *Journal of Family Therapy,* 22(2), 144–167.

[26] Adapted from Arbinger Institute. (2016). *The outward mindset: Seeing beyond ourselves.* Berrett-Koehler Publishers.

These beliefs become powerful because they drive constructive behaviors, described in Exhibit 1.5.

We're trying to provide a specific, hands-on road map for developing an owner's mindset and related skillset. Intentionally shaping an owner's mindset across all family members is a complex endeavor and takes time. A mindset is the result of both nature and nurture, and it is trained, by default or by design, from an early age. That is why we recommend getting started early. Even if you don't know what future ownership structure looks like, it is a vital "runway" necessary to create effective owners. If those individuals never become owners of your family business, the beliefs and skills can help them become successful in any endeavor they undertake.

An important disclaimer: we are not suggesting you impose choices on minds too young to understand. However, we recommend being intentional in shaping constructive and purposeful experiences that build attitudes and capabilities, always leaving the rising generation the option to follow its unique calling. Think about developing an owner's mindset as planting and nurturing the right seeds to "harvest" highly capable future owners, optimizing decision-making for the family enterprise and its stakeholders. And, remember that ownership development isn't just for younger family members; it's for everyone, at any age, as each life stage presents us with new priorities and challenges to overcome.

Your family should be asking questions such as: "How are we attracting our family members to want to be owners?" and "Do we foster appreciation and respect for the individual's needs and talents while promoting the power of belonging to the collective?" On some level, family members need to have had experience of being stronger together than apart. This positive attraction within families will inspire and encourage the siblings and cousins to devote their time and energy to building their capacity as owners. Otherwise, why would they engage in this hard work?

Exhibit 1.5 Owner's Mindset Beliefs and Behaviors

BELIEFS	BEHAVIORS
Development is a continuous individual and collective process	• Recognize that the individual, family, and enterprise are always changing so the knowledge, skills, and mindset required to be an effective owner will also continuously evolve • Seek to expand competencies at every age • Create learning opportunities for the individual and the family as a whole • Create initiatives to grow relationships within and outside the family • Cultivate an appreciation for the family's legacy as part of the spiritual capital
Ownership requires deep commitment and responsibility	• Seek to develop passion among all the owners • Cultivate the talents individuals bring to the table • Invite educated perspectives
Proactivity is paramount	• Design policies in anticipation of possible challenges • Create plans for possible different scenarios • Seek emotional maturity and invest in its development • Ensure decision processes include proper notice and preparation
Abundance rather than scarcity	• Share key information before it's requested • Delegate responsibility to others • Listen to different perspectives • Commit to fair process • Work toward ensuring all boats rise • Celebrate everyone's success • Focus on what can be given rather than what can be gained • Seek opportunities, even within challenges

Win-win solutions	• Get to know others well over time
	• Intentionally develop a deep shared understanding around four dimensions:
	  o How individuals learn
	  o What work they are called to do
	  o How they prefer to work
	  o How they prefer to communicate and interact with others
	• Balance individual, family and enterprise needs when making decisions

Diversity and inclusion matter	• Embrace and engage diversity in professional calling, personality type, intelligences, race, sexual orientation, nationality, etc. • Adopt additional formality in governance due to increased diversity • Foster emotional and social intelligence
Stronger together than apart	• Embrace differences to create synergistic teams • Support initiatives that foster motivation and interest • Minimize comparisons among owner team members • Create engaging and inclusive processes

Development as a Lifelong Process

We take a broad view of development.[27] Family members with an owner's mindset treat learning as a lifelong process. They constantly assess their capabilities, improve their awareness, consider their role and responsibilities, and set goals to maximize their contribution to their family enterprise. A wide range of activities and experiences contribute to developing owners' skillset and mindset, which can occur at individual and collective family levels. For example, family members individually take courses, attend conferences, and complete on-the-job training. Likewise, the family can develop its collective capacity through focused discussion, workshops, and skill-building activities to deepen its relationships and advance its capability as a family.

As an ongoing process, development at each stage of life brings new challenges and therefore requires new thinking and new skills for navigating the complex journey of family enterprise continuity. Each stage has developmental goals that define the behaviors, skills, knowledge, and experiences for growing and enhancing an owner's ability to take on new responsibilities over time. In each chapter, we offer developmental goals on four levels:

- *Individual*: This involves increasing self-awareness, forming a healthy identity, developing talents to achieve goals, as well as building the capacity to function well in the complex ecosystem of a family enterprise.
- *Family*: This involves creating a healthy culture in the family that values togetherness, fosters family values, and cultivates shared responsibility and collaboration, as well as the ability to resolve conflicts constructively.
- *Ownership*: This focuses on understanding the structures, processes, and systems that facilitate effective decision- making and stewardship of the family's assets, including the non-financial ones. This level is the most technical of the four levels as it includes understanding shareholder agreements, trusts, ownership roles, risk management, liquidity, and succession, to name just a few.
- *Business*: This centers early on a positive attitude toward the business and basic understanding of the same, followed by more specialized business, industry, and governance knowledge and capability based on the roles(s) the owner seeks to have within the firm.

---

[27] Field, J. (2000). *Lifelong learning and the new educational order*. Trentham Books, Ltd., Westview House.

Owners at every life stage can continuously develop competence in each domain.[28] To support that, in the following pages, we provide ownership development concepts, frameworks, and practical tips in these four domains across the six specific life stages as depicted in Exhibit 1.6 below.

Exhibit 1.6 Six Stages of Ownership Development

Lifestage	YOUNG CHILD	ADOLESCENT	EMERGING ADULT	EARLY ADULT	MIDDLE ADULT	LATER ADULT
Ages	0 - 12 Years	10 - 20 years	18 - 30 years	25 - 40 years	35 - 65 years	60 - 100 + years

To help you access the ownership development advice most relevant to your family situation, our chapters are organized sequentially by the aforementioned life stage. Within each chapter, you'll find development ideas and tools based on research from fields such as psychology, education, family systems, leadership, neuroscience, and more. We've also incorporated many real-life family examples and we are grateful to the families who have provided written permission for its inclusion.

Family members around the same age will generally benefit from similar development tactics. However, the overlap between the stage-based ages reflects fluidity and differences in the pace of growth. Any given family member may advance earlier or a bit later than others of similar ages, so please use the ideas here flexibly.

Some concepts and development categories presented in different stage-focused chapters build upon previous chapters, assuming concepts become progressively more sophisticated as the stages advance. This "spiral curriculum" approach has proven to work well for multiple kinds of learning.[29]

Development is a process that, at times, may feel slow, cumbersome, and even ineffective. Growth takes place incrementally, often invisibly. Mistakes and missteps are inevitable. Each represents a new learning opportunity. The most realistic approach is that the family commit to development and try not to obsess over exactly how much growth occurs in a given period or seek perfection. Trust the process, as it will yield greater outcomes over time.

---

[28] Astrachan, C., Waldkirch, M., Michiels, A., Pieper, T., & Bernhard, F. (2019). Professionalizing the business family. The five pillars of competent, committed, and sustainable ownership. *Family Firm Institute Research Report.*

[29] A spiral curriculum is designed so that key concepts are presented repeatedly throughout the curriculum, but with deepening layers of complexity, or in different applications. For more on the spiral curriculum concept see Bruner, J. (1960). *The process of education.* Harvard University Press.

Who Will Benefit from This Book

We wrote this book for multiple, related audiences.

Family enterprise owners and prospective owners are the most logical readers. This includes owners of an operating business or families who continue to own assets jointly even after the sale of their business. Building an owner's mindset relates to members of any generation: *elders* (typically more senior family members who have relinquished business, governance, or ownership roles or will soon), *leading* (family members currently in decision-making roles in the business, board, and ownership group), and *rising* (members likely to have future decision-making roles).

Non-family executives, independent directors, family office professionals, and family enterprise advisors will also benefit from learning what makes for effective ownership. They work closely with enterprising families on issues ranging from ownership vision to risk management to family employment and often serve as mentors to the rising generation. The ideas in this book will help them become more effective collaborators, mentors, and supporters of individual owners and prospective owners and owner teams.

How to Make the Most of This Book

All ownership skillset and mindset development happens in a context specific to your family enterprise: family size and dispersion, stage of ownership (founder, sibling, and cousin), business size and stage (start-up, growth, and mature), the family's culture and values, and many other factors. These will affect development in terms of resources, potential obstacles, where to get started, and other considerations. We call out contextual factors where possible in the chapters, but remember the specific situation in your family, or in one you work with, and how it might affect development. For example, while one family may own a highly complex global real estate development business, another family may own a less intensive residential property management company with lower risk and complexity. Ownership development for these enterprises will look significantly different. We provide practical how-tos throughout the book to adapt to your specific context. We advise starting from where you are and not letting your context become a barrier to starting at all.

We provide ideas and tips for every stage of life. While the material here has a potential impact across the total life span, starting early with prospective owners is ideal. Development is a layering process, with each learning event building on a base of prior knowledge and learning experiences. When starting early isn't possible or hasn't occurred, don't despair since change is possible when intentionally pursued. We have observed prospective owner groups come together effectively as adults, which we address in Chapters 5–8.

Structure of This Book

In this initial chapter, we've explained our motivation for writing this book and have also provided foundational information about why ownership is essential, how we define it, the different types of owners, the beliefs behind an owner's mindset, and why starting early is so important. In the next six age-based chapters on ownership development—from Young Child to Later Adult—we include these sections:

- *Opening example*: A real-life illustration of ownership development from a family enterprise.
- *The stage and why it matters*: Introduction to the life stage and why ownership development is important within it.
- *Central theme:* A key, core-distinguishing feature of the stage.
- *Development goals*: Specific goals for ownership development in the stage on the individual, family, ownership, and business dimensions.
- *How to develop owners*: The "How-Tos" of building ownership knowledge and skills for that stage, as well as who might be involved in implementing development activities along with a sample development plan.
- *Where to start*: Simple steps or starting points to consider for ownership development.
- *What to look for*: Typical pitfalls of development in that stage.

The final two chapters discuss how to develop the *team* of owners, shifting the focus to collective development, and where and how to start on ownership team development.

We encourage you to use the book as a reference and comprehensive guide. For some, especially those dealing with large, multigenerational family enterprises, that may mean reading it cover to cover. Others may wish to learn about development in a specific stage or cohort. Use it in the way that is best for you.

We are excited to help guide you on your ownership development journey. We aim to help you gain real value across ownership dimensions for generations to come.

2

Starting a Family Enterprise Owner's Mindset Early: Young Child (Ages 0 to 12)

W. Sage-Hayward et al., *Own It!*, A Family Business Publication,
https://doi.org/10.1007/978-3-030-20419-8_2

Zak and Zoe—Young Child Stage

Meet Zak and Zoe, two composite example future family business owners. To set the stage, both are in elementary school and come from families that own agricultural businesses—grape production. Zoe's family business focuses on winemaking and is larger than Zak's, with about $50 million in annual revenues. There are eleven members in Zoe's generation, the grandchildren of the founders. Alongside their business, the family runs a private foundation that donates mainly to hospitals and other organizations focused on children's health and well-being.

Zak's family and business are smaller: Zak and his cousin are the only two third-generation members. The family's farming operation brings in about $5 million in annual revenues, and they sell their grapes for producing jam and other food products only. The founding generation was against winemaking due to a history of alcoholism. Protecting the family was more important than profitability. The family also owns a bed-and-breakfast and some undeveloped commercial real estate near their farmland. They donate to charitable causes but not through a private foundation.

Zak and Zoe will help illustrate some of the stage-related challenges and opportunities that a proactive approach to ownership development can address, throughout the book.

This chapter explains how to develop the youngest potential owners—those up to about 12 years old in a family enterprise. We present an ownership development perspective from a real-life family, describe why this stage matters, present specific development goals for the stage, discuss practical steps to take toward development, then help you think about where to start, and potential pitfalls to watch out for in this stage.

Start Early: A Father's Perspective

"Start as early as you can."

This is the guiding principle for Riley Senft, a Family Director of Canada-based Tricor Pacific Capital.

At the time, his four children ranged in age from 6 months to 6 years, so he's trying to take his advice to heart, motivated by his early experience. "We never really spoke about money growing up because Mom thought we shouldn't. But Dad's dad talked to him about business all of the time which got my dad involved early teaching us about it. That way, it wasn't this big mysterious thing we learned about when we were older."

Though Riley's parents started the family business after his childhood, he recognizes how vital ownership development is in early life. "Some things you learn at school—reading, writing, and math—and some from your family, like how to read a financial statement if it's a business family," he says. "But you have to make it relevant to the kid's life, so there's a connection to something they understand." For example, Riley has been teaching his 6-year-old son Connor about the value and meaning of money. "Connor loves money," he says, "and recently he went to the golf course for lessons and earned 'Bighorn Bucks' which he can redeem for things like ice cream at the clubhouse." Connor quickly learned that giving up money for things he wanted meant less money in hand. "He wanted another golf lesson so he could earn more bucks to get more ice cream. However, when it came time to pay, he did not want to give up his money—so he thought for a moment and asked his grandma to buy it for him instead! Smart kid!"

The family reinforced the lesson that it is important to think carefully about how to spend your money. They also helped Connor find opportunities to make money at home and encouraged him to share with his younger siblings. For example, Connor had an opportunity to earn some money by participating in a health survey at their local hospital. Afterward, when he went to the store to buy a toy, his father asked him to buy something for his younger sister too. "He ended up spending about half of what he earned, so he was happy to get back 'more money' (in change) while still getting something for his sister!"

In this way, the family has helped Connor think about and make decisions related to money more consciously while encouraging the idea of sharing within the family. These are critical skills for future owners.

The Young Child Stage (Age 0 to 12) and Why It Matters

As Riley suggests, it's never too early to start thinking about development. The basic building blocks of good ownership are established in these youngest childhood years. So, our first stage of ownership development involves children—from infancy up to about 12 years old.

Of course, *how* to develop ownership skills at this stage will differ significantly from development for older family members. Although this isn't a parenting book, in these early stages, there is indeed overlap as building a family enterprise owner's mindset requires intentionally promoting and supporting the emotional, social, and intellectual development of a child.

These are the most critical years to form a positive image around family ties, business, and wealth because young people will carry this emotional connection into their adult years, often at an unconscious level. Here are several reasons this earliest owner-development stage is critical:

- *High receptivity of the brain at this stage*: Our brain is shaped by interpersonal relationships at the earliest stages of life.[1] That means early periods of development lay the foundation for life and that our brain is more receptive to key development activities during this stage.
- *Opportunity to create a foundation for success*: Most family firms do not make it through multiple generations.[2] Research has shown that over half of transition failures are caused by breakdowns in communication and trust.[3] Poor development of the rising generation on both family and ownership dimensions is a core source of these dissolutions, including what happens in the earliest years.
- *It is a time of significant influence*: Family business members talk about how their childhood experiences influence their later involvement (or lack of) with their family's enterprise. Therefore, it's critical to act with awareness and intentionality around children, especially regarding family values and attitudes you share about the enterprise. Later in the chapter, we discuss providing children with exposure to the enterprise without setting expectations for their future involvement.
- *It sets the stage for strong sibling and cousin relationships*: Sibling and cousin rivalries are very real phenomena that can threaten the well-being of any family and enterprise in the future. Comparison and competition among siblings are natural and form in their earliest years as they compete for scarce family resources, time, and attention. Each child adopts a unique role, personal style, and identity in a family (e.g., one is funny, one is athletic, one is smart and serious, etc.). Parents may unknowingly contribute to such rivalries by overtly comparing children or encouraging competition. Research shows that adult sibling relationships are more positive when parents did not favor one sibling over another during childhood,

---

[1] Siegel, D. J. (2015). *The developing mind: How relationships and the brain interact to shape who we are* (2nd ed.). The Guilford Press.

[2] See for example Jaffe, D. (2019, January 28). *The 'shirtsleeves-to-shirtsleeves' curse: How family wealth can survive it*. https://www.forbes.com/sites/dennisjaffe/2019/01/28/the-shirtsleeves-to-shirtslee ves-curse-how-family-wealth-can-survive-it/#2a4994e46c8d.

[3] Williams, R., & Preisser, V. (2010). *Preparing heirs: 5 steps to a successful transition of family wealth and values*. Robert Reed.

but rather celebrated diversity.[4] This is a time to help your children understand that while time is a finite resource, parents' love is not, and they shouldn't be fighting for that love. Focusing on ownership development, particularly at the individual and family level, can set a strong and positive foundation for these relationships and appreciation for the value of "stronger together" as a family. Be mindful that they will observe and learn consciously or unconsciously based on how you talk and relate to siblings, cousins, and your own parents.

It may be counterintuitive, but childhood is a critical time to think about the development of a family enterprise owner's mindset. Even the simplest communication of values has profound, far-reaching effects on prospective owners. Intentional development of a healthy owner's mindset has the best potential outcome if started in childhood. Creating positive early experiences and memories matters most.

Central Theme: The Importance of Diversity and Inclusion

The earliest stage of ownership development is a prime opportunity to focus on issues related to diversity and inclusion. Shifting norms about race, family, marriage, parenthood, sexuality, and gender have created wide variation in the definition of family and how people of all ages identify themselves and wish to be identified. Increasingly, children are being raised in single-parent, blended, and other family types.[5]

These trends mean that families with young children will likely face more complex social issues than their past-generation counterparts did. Developing skills and comfort in embracing diversity and inclusion will cause more engaged, capable family members—many of whom are potential owners.

Further, family relationships are some of the longest and most impactful in individuals' lives. Allowing early opinions and family prejudices to color beliefs about future co-owners' competencies makes joint ownership challenging. The more accepting you can be, the more likely you will end up with an aligned, effective owner group. Diversity is a strength, not something

---

[4] Boll, T., Ferring, D., & Filipp, S.-H. (2003). Perceived parental differential treatment in middle adulthood: Curvilinear relations with individuals' experienced relationship quality to sibling and parents. *Journal of Family Psychology, 17* (4), 472–487. https://doi.org/10.1037/0893-3200.17.4.472.

[5] For more statistics on the shifting nature of American families, see Pew Research Center. (2020, May 30). 1. *The American family today*. Pew Research Center's Social & Demographic Trends Project. https://www.pewsocialtrends.org/2015/12/17/1-the-american-family-today/.

to fear or avoid. This is one of the core tenets of the family enterprise owner's mindset.

Looking into a family's future, diversity is real. Think about who in the family may become an owner one day. Many families allow shares to pass only to lineal descendants or have shareholder agreements which stipulate that stepchildren cannot be shareholders. We are not suggesting that every family member should be considered a potential owner in every circumstance, but rather that families must navigate inclusion issues with care, to ensure everyone feels valued, no matter their future ownership prospects. Indeed, supporting a culture that promotes or condones significant exclusion can tear at the fabric of the family, impede supporting the development of the youngest generation, and ultimately harm the enterprise. Increasing research shows the value of diversity, in general, so failing to support it can be counterproductive.[6]

Development Goals

Developmental goals identify the knowledge, skills, and experiences that individuals need to build a family enterprise owner's mindset over every stage of life. In each chapter, we present general development goals relevant to age and maturity, organized by the four main development dimensions: individual, family, ownership, business. This box explains the different mindsets during each stage of life.

---

[6] For example, diversity has been shown to improve group creativity and discipline; see Phillips, K. (2014, October 01). How diversity makes us smarter. https://www.scientificamerican.com/article/how-diversity-makes-us-smarter/.

Exhibit 2.1 Owner's Mindset: Development Goals for Young Children

OWNER'S MINDSET: DEVELOPMENT GOALS FOR YOUNG CHILDREN	
AREA	**DEVELOPMENTAL GOALS**
INDIVIDUAL	**Promote a healthy sense of individuality, especially on these dimensions:** • **Self-esteem and confidence**: Feeling assurance in one's own worth and abilities. • **Trust**: Being able to count on others for care and support. • **Curiosity**: A desire to learn, explore, and discover. • **Independence**: A sense that one can accomplish things without help from others; a growing sense of capability in areas like self-care and learning. • **Delayed gratification**: Ability to wait to receive a reward later. • **Boundaries**: Understanding and respecting our own needs, and being respectful and understanding of the needs of others.
FAMILY	**Promote strong sense of belonging to a larger family with an appreciation for its history:** • Aim for positive family experiences that helps the child get a sense of "together we are stronger" and "we have fun." • Help them understand who family members are and how everyone is related. Simple things like stories about family members living your values have great impact.
OWNERSHIP	**Promote basic understanding of the responsibilities of being an owner (of anything):** • Importance of taking care of what one owns, such as treating toys and books with respect. • Value of giving back to community (such as through early volunteer experiences). • Learning what money is and how to save and spend wisely
BUSINESS / INDUSTRY	**Promote a positive feeling about the business and its contribution to the family and global/local community:** • A basic understanding of the business and industry, especially for older children in this stage. • A positive association with the business. Ideally, kids will see the business as "where special things happen," rather than as a major stressor or "the place that takes my parents away."

How-Tos

This section presents tips for creating a family enterprise owner's mindset in young children, members of the rising generation. We emphasize being *intentional* in promoting ownership development at this earliest stage while being careful not to "pile on too much." This often means exposing enterprise elements without creating any specific expectations or requirements for involvement in the future. We hope children will gain an appreciation of different aspects of their family enterprise—including the business, governance, philanthropy, and others—without being made to feel obliged to take on any particular role in the future. For best results, we suggest emphasizing broad *involvement* rather than a predestined fate.

In 1968, a Senegalese forestry engineer, Baba Dioum, made a compelling statement concerning natural resources management, which applies to enterprising families: "*In the end we will conserve only what we love, we will love only what we understand, and we will understand only what we are taught.*" This is the time where you have the opportunity to set up "love and understanding" in a sustainable way which sets the stage for reaping the benefits for decades. Use the following ideas to think about what may work best for the younger members of your family, based on the resources and time available.

- *Help them know your family and all members.* "You can only love what you know" is a maxim that many family enterprises hold dear. While family members in the same household have many opportunities to spend time together, more effort may be required with larger extended families. Families can create a "Guess Who" board game with family pictures and clues so kids can get to know relatives they may not see often. Santiago Perry, President of the Family Council of the Group Espinoza, in Colombia, shared a creative, fun, and effective tool. His family professionally designed their "family trading cards" booklet, similar to those popular in sports. First, they distributed a few copies among different generations of the multiple branches. Then they got together to trade cards. The gathering became a great opportunity to talk about the people pictured, and make sure people met the "players" behind the cards, creating great bonding experiences across generations.

- *Develop an appreciation for the family enterprise and the time magnet it is.* Sit down early on when emotions are positive to recognize the time demands of running your own business. If you are an owner-operator, acknowledge that your responsibilities will most likely stretch beyond "regular" business hours. Talk through to find solutions that work for your family. Keep this conversation open as the business grows and evolves, so you continue to be thoughtful about how time is being used in your family. But also decide, with the kids' help, which events are most important to attend. Once children reach around eight to ten years of age, they can certainly help you decide—start by asking them! Some specific actions for mitigating the time magnet include:

  - Have regular conversations with your significant other. This will help you understand whether the lack of presence is an issue, which is a sentiment that can easily but inadvertently be passed along to your children.

- Set aside protected time for family activities. Agree on the time each week you will protect as "family time" (e.g., dinner together three nights per week). Make this commitment immovable and recognize the occasional one that may be missed.
- Strive to accommodate each other's needs. Each person has unique wants and needs in a relationship and a family. Seek to appreciate, and meet those needs balanced with the time required to operate and grow your enterprise.
- Manage feelings of guilt. Operating owners often feel a sense of shame and guilt about not being home more with their families. These feelings may lead them to compensate in less constructive ways, such as overspending on gifts or not setting healthy boundaries.

- *Identify and promote values.* So much of development in children is about understanding and appreciating values. This is important for family enterprise members as their values will eventually influence how they steward the enterprise for other shareholders, employees, customers, suppliers, and the broader community. Values begin at home and form early. There may be different interpretations of the communal values held by the nuclear families that are part of that larger family unit. In a multigenerational family enterprise, it's essential for all members of the broader family to define their shared common values and to discuss how families representing different branches might guide their kids, so it is consistent with these values. Respecting diverse viewpoints and experiences when convening to define how family and future owners will interact is critical to building a strong team of future owners. To transmit values within his nuclear family, a senior family business leader consistently provided the rising generation with a full range of experiences from an early age: doing chores (though hired help could have filled that role), volunteering (serving food at homeless shelters), and going camping with zero amenities (the kids had to set up tents, cook, and clean the dishes). The children, now adults, relate how those early experiences helped them gain critical values, including empathy, compassion, resourcefulness, appreciation, and perseverance, while teaching them to not take things for granted. There are other ways to transmit values, including helpful tools and exercises in books like Mitzi Perdue's *How to Communicate Values to Children So They'll Love It*.[7] To transmit values, senior generations must understand *their own* values. We have found the Family Enterprise Values Exercise in Exhibit 2.2

---

[7] Perdue, M. (2017). *How to communicate values to children so they'll love it* (2nd ed.). CreateSpace.

useful in our work with family enterprises for helping members of all ages understand and consciously promote their values.

Exhibit 2.2 Family Enterprise Values Exercise

<table>
<tr><td colspan="3" align="center">FAMILY ENTERPRISE VALUES EXERCISE</td></tr>
<tr><td colspan="3">Family members can review a list of fifty values (below) and identify the ten that best define their family today. Values can be added to the list as needed. After they choose their top ten, they are asked to choose five that should be a priority for the family, and to share both lists (top ten and top five) with other family members while identifying overlapping themes, patterns, and surprises. The family can also discuss whether its members want to identify specific aspirational values for the future. Recognizing and talking about these values in action will help the youngest family members learn, appreciate, and live them.</td></tr>
<tr><td colspan="3" align="center">LIST OF VALUES:</td></tr>
<tr><td>Adaptability</td><td>Fairness</td><td>Power</td></tr>
<tr><td>Aggressiveness</td><td>Family</td><td>Principled</td></tr>
<tr><td>Authority</td><td>Forgiveness</td><td>Professionalism</td></tr>
<tr><td>Autonomy</td><td>Friendship</td><td>Prosperity</td></tr>
<tr><td>Caring</td><td>Fun</td><td>Quality</td></tr>
<tr><td>Caution</td><td>Hard work</td><td>Rationality</td></tr>
<tr><td>Challenge</td><td>Harmony</td><td>Recognition</td></tr>
<tr><td>Change</td><td>Honesty</td><td>Respect</td></tr>
<tr><td>Community</td><td>Humor</td><td>Security</td></tr>
<tr><td>Competition</td><td>Independence</td><td>Self-control</td></tr>
<tr><td>Consensus</td><td>Innovation</td><td>Stability</td></tr>
<tr><td>Courage</td><td>Knowledge</td><td>Teamwork</td></tr>
<tr><td>Creativity</td><td>Merit</td><td>Tolerance</td></tr>
<tr><td>Democracy</td><td>Nature</td><td>Tradition</td></tr>
<tr><td>Diplomacy</td><td>Obedience</td><td>Transparency</td></tr>
<tr><td>Equality</td><td>Peace</td><td></td></tr>
<tr><td>Experimentation</td><td>Perseverance</td><td></td></tr>
</table>

- *Share family stories:* Family stories are a powerful way to illustrate family values related to the business and other areas. Narratives passed down over generations or the story of something that just happened can reinforce family values while bonding members with a shared understanding of the past, present, and future. Research has shown that knowing key details of their family history is correlated with children's well-being, resilience, and other positive outcomes.[8] The twenty "Do You Know Questions" Box provides a set of questions for families to explore their family and enterprise history with the rising generation. Some families professionally

---

[8] See Duke, M. P., Lazarus, A., & Fivush, R. (2008). Knowledge of family history as a clinically useful index of psychological well-being and prognosis: A brief report. *Psychotherapy Theory, Research, Practice, Training, 45,* 268–272.

develop their own children's book (or book series) based on the history of the founders and their business-related adventures illustrating family values and culture across generations. This approach is particularly effective for imparting family values to children from large multigenerational families.

"DO YOU KNOW?" QUESTIONS

When children in late elementary school and older can answer yes to more of the items below, it has been shown to correlate with positive outcomes in later life. It's not just the knowledge itself, but the process of emphasizing such information and sharing it across generations that helps explain the association. Use the list as inspiration to share more family stories at dinner, reunions, and other times.

1. Do you know how your parents met?
2. Do you know where your mother grew up?
3. Do you know where your father grew up?
4. Do you know where some of your grandparents grew up?
5. Do you know where some of your grandparents met?
6. Do you know where your parents were married?
7. Do you know some of the major events that occurred around the time you were born?
8. Do you know some the major events that occurred around the time your brothers or sisters were being born?
9. Do you know the source of your name?
10. Do you know which person in your family you look most like?
11. Do you know which person in the family you act most like?
12. Do you know some of the illnesses and injuries that your parents experienced when they were younger?
13. Do you know some of the lessons that your parents learned from good or bad experiences?
14. Do you know some things that happened to your mom or dad when they were in school?
15. Do you know the national background of your family (such as Japanese, Irish, Canadian, etc.)?
16. Do you know some of the jobs that your parents had when they were young?
17. Do you know some awards that your parents received when they were young?
18. Do you know the names of the schools that your mom went to?
19. Do you know the names of the schools that your dad went to?
20. Do you know any funny or interesting stories about your parent's life together especially early in their relationship?

HERE ARE SOME QUESTIONS TO CONSIDER SPECIFIC TO FAMILY ENTERPRISE:

1. Do you know who founded the business?
2. Do you know how it all started?
3. Do you know why the founder (dad or mom or grandparents) started the business?
4. Do you know what the company does?
5. Do you know why it is important to be in business together?
6. Do you know who works in the business?
7. Do you know who owns the business?
8. Do you know what customers the business serves?
9. Do you know the benefits of having a business?
10. Do you know some lessons that your family learned by working together?

- *Foster healthy emotional development while respecting children's natural temperament:* Talking about emotions, helping children understand their own feelings and the impact of these, and facilitating their ability to express emotion without harming others are key goals.[9] Many adults struggle with emotional expression too. Any approach to emotional development should account for the child's temperament. Temperaments are set early in life from how much individuals enjoy problem-solving to how quickly they become irritated. Try not to take a "one-size-fits-all" approach. Rather, tailor approaches to each child's temperament and style, such as not overburdening a kid who struggles with patience.

- *Find the right level of involvement for each young family member.* Not every potential future owner may be interested in or capable of playing a hands-on role in the business, its governance, or elsewhere in the future. However, *all* rising members will benefit from an effort by others to understand their unique interests, and the opportunity to participate in the enterprise, if even at simpler or symbolic levels. So, when in doubt, promote acceptance and inclusion over rejection and exclusion.

- *Build a healthy relationship with money.* Many family enterprises struggle with money-related matters. Children benefit from gaining a basic understanding of how to use money from an early age (see *Promote financial literacy* bullet below) and developing a healthy attitude toward money, including how to comfortably talk about it. This process involves parents first understanding their own relationship with money, and passing along related values, ideally through discussions, exercises, games, and modeling behavior around money. A key resource of learning for children is observing how adults act around money. It is also important to help children understand how difficult it can be to make money—that is, to highlight the link between hard work and financial reward. That's especially important in a family enterprise, where children often experience the rewards of financial success without understanding the effort that goes into it.[10] The chapter's opening example of Connor, a 6-year-old family enterprise member, provides a great illustration of fostering healthy relationships with money. Resources for younger children with important money-related lessons are listed in Exhibit 2.3.

---

[9] Psychotherapist Michael Gurian's books are especially relevant to emotional development in children, including Gurian, M. (2017a). *Saving our sons: A new path for raising healthy and resilient boys.* Gurian Institute. Gurian, M. (2017b). *The minds of girls: A new path for raising healthy, resilient, and successful women.* Gurian Institute.

[10] For more on teaching children about money, see Peck, S. J. (2007). *Money and meaning: New ways to have conversations about money with your clients—A guide for therapists, coaches, and other professionals* (1st ed.). Wiley.

Exhibit 2.3 Resources for Money-Related Lessons

RESOURCES FOR MONEY-RELATED LESSONS
Several movies, books, board games and apps are listed below that convey lessons and values related to money and can be discussed with kids who are part of family enterprise. **MOVIES** • *Toy Story 2* (importance of relationships and loyalty over fame and money) • *Charlie and the Chocolate Factory* (importance of honesty) • *Aladdin* (being true to oneself, regardless of economic background) • *The Frog Princess* (saving to accomplish your dream) • *Beauty and the Beast* (importance of giving back) **FAIRY TALES AND CHILDREN'S BOOKS** • *The Milkmaid and Her Pail* by R.F. Gilmor (not counting on money you don't have) • *The Grasshopper and the Ants* by J. Pinkney (importance of hard work) • *The Goose who Laid the Golden Eggs* by V. Mastro & A. Wells (the cost of greed) • *Bunny Money* by R. Wells (pitfalls of not looking after your money) • *Lemonade in Winter* by E. Jenkin & B. Karas (a parable about persistence) • *The Go-Around Dollar* by J. Adams (explains symbols and numbers on a dollar bill) **BOARD GAMES** • Cashflow for Kids • The Allowance Game • Money Bags – A Crazy Coin Counting Game • Exact Change Monopoly **KIDS APPS (available at the time)** • PiggyBot (6-8 years) • Renegade Buggies (6-11 years) • Savings Spree (7+ years) • PennyOwl Allowance (8-12 years)

The box "Zak Learns to Value Money" presents a story about the rising young owner from the chapter's opening.

ZAK LEARNS TO VALUE MONEY
An avid hockey fan, 10-year-old Zak wanted a "professional" hockey stick. But Geoff, his dad, was concerned about letting Zak have such an expensive piece of sports equipment without earning it. So, he struck a deal with his son: Zak would work several hours every Saturday picking weeds at the farm, sweeping up, and doing other odd jobs. He would earn $7 per hour for his work and place 20 percent of what he earned into his savings account. "If you work six Saturdays in a row," Geoff said, "you'll earn enough for a hockey stick of your choice." Naturally, Zak wanted to earn money, so he eagerly took on the work. Of course, there were Saturdays when he would have much preferred to play with friends, but the thought of buying the hockey stick kept him focused. After putting in the hard work needed, Zak bought his dream stick and showed it off to his friends on the ice. "I earned all the money for it!" he told them proudly. Zak even slept with the stick propped by his bed every night, a reminder of the value of hard work and saving for something you want.

- *Promote financial literacy.* Helping children gain basic financial literacy early on is critical. For younger children, that means recognizing the value of money and its relation to survival and well-being. Older children in this stage may understand more abstract financial concepts, such as how invested money earns a return over time. At this level of maturity, we want children to be comfortable with the idea of spending some money on themselves, saving some for the future, and spending money on others (whether for gifts or philanthropy). Resources such as Joline Godfrey's *Raising Financially Fit Kids* and Paul Lermitte's book series called *Allowances, Dollars & Sense* can help promote early financial literacy.
- *Involve them in giving back.* In many families, children witness their family's values through their contributions to the community.[11] Take your children to charitable and other community activities, including volunteer work and fundraising efforts that expose them to invaluable learning opportunities. For example, a family in the manufacturing industry regularly involves its youngest members in activities such as breast cancer walks and making items (bracelets and keychains) to sell at the annual family barbecue to raise money for specific causes. Afterward, they celebrate and discuss the importance of giving back. Remember: giving some of their time and talent, more than just money, is particularly impactful in this early stage.
- *Promote ownership literacy.* Don't expect children to understand the full implications and complexity of ownership. However, kids can gain a basic understanding of what it means to own shares in a family enterprise. Beyond discussing ownership responsibilities with younger family members, you can expose them to specific terms related to ownership using a brief dictionary or glossary, as explained in the box "Create a Kids' List of Ownership Terms." You can find a comprehensive list of ownership words in Appendix A: Glossary of Terms. Remember to make it as fun and playful as possible.

---

[11] Lieber, R. (2015). *The opposite of spoiled: Raising kids who are grounded, generous, and smart about money.* Harper Collins.

SAMPLE KID'S LIST OF OWNERSHIP TERMS

Create a list of ownership-related terms to help children understand ownership better at their age level. The list below could be taught to kids from about ages 5 to 10.

- **Business** – The act of making, buying, and selling things or services that people want, or a place where goods and services are exchanged for money.
- **Owner** – A person or group that has something that belongs to them, whether a stuffed animal, toy, book, or business, and they take good care of it.
- **Philanthropy** – An idea, event, or action that is done to help the world, usually involving the donation of something such as money, talent, or time volunteered for a charity or research.
- **Stewardship** – Caring for something you value over time, such as a pet or special item like a baseball from a championship game.
- **Values** – What matters to a person in life such as "family," "respect," and "honesty."
- **Vision** – The dream of what the family would like to achieve or accomplish in the future which will help them understand what they have to do now in order to achieve their dream.

- *Foster a simple understanding of entrepreneurship.* Entrepreneurship is a core value and activity in a family enterprise, so aim to expose young children to the concept of "being entrepreneurial" rather than pushing a dictionary definition of "entrepreneur," which can be difficult for kids to understand. Stimulate them to see opportunities when they play, encourage them to figure out alternative solutions when something doesn't work, and seek alternative routes. Consider explaining the concept in a kid-friendly way, as we suggest in the box "Explain Entrepreneurship in a Kid-Friendly Way."

ENTREPRENEURSHIP IN A KID-FRIENDLY WAY

Here are some child-friendly ways to describe the kind of people entrepreneurs are.
1. Entrepreneurs set out to build something they are excited about and put all their heart and soul into making it work.
2. They dream big and see opportunities others cannot see.
3. They really listen to their customers.
4. They are passionate—and some might say to an extreme—with their work.
5. Before they succeed, they fail, a lot.
6. They are curious about everything and ask questions.

You can also simulate a small business with kids to help them understand the financial side of business-building. For example, Santiago Perry and his family organized an experience for their next generation members ages 6 to 12. With the help of a Professor, they designed a game to simulate an actual "start-up" to bake and sell cookies.

They got a loan from a designated "banker" (the Professor himself), who explained that they were receiving money to start their venture, but they had to return the whole amount plus an additional fee for the "cost of having the money available" ("interest"). The young cousins understood it and started working with great enthusiasm. They used these funds to plan their bakery which included buying ingredients, making cookies, and selling them at a prime location. They had great fun working together, exploring their talents, and successfully managed to sell all of their cookies. As they were celebrating their profits, "the Banker" reminded them of their agreement and claimed his part. Although originally they all agreed to give back the money borrowed with interest, once in action, some of the younger children didn't understand why they had to pay their "banker" back. They were disappointed seeing the fruits of their labor given away. Understanding the concept of borrowing became a new topic of discussion, judgment-free, in the family and a memorable learning experience. This example demonstrates the power of explaining concepts by creating real-world opportunities to guarantee the lesson shall not be forgotten. Books and other resources focused on entrepreneurship can also be helpful, such as *Entrepreneurs in Every Generation* by Allan Cohen and Pramodita Sharma, as long as you can make it age-appropriate.[12]

- *Expose the rising generation to your business.* Aim to foster an appreciation of your family enterprise and what it brings to your family, employee families, and the community. This might include high-level activities such as tours of business facilities, informal interactions with managers and employees at events (e.g., holiday parties and summer BBQs), and passing along stories of how the business came to be. Make sure to create positive and fun experiences connected to the business, as those feelings (or lack of) will stay with the kids for a very long time. Depending on other members' involvement, it might be more challenging to expose children to the business, above all in companies that have reached later stages. For example, a large agribusiness family had almost no family employees by the time the fourth generation arrived. So, family leaders developed a program to give the younger generation a taste of what the business does, including having older children raise livestock. Children in this stage are too young for formal internships, but having them do small things such as picking grapes, cleaning up a development site, or photocopying papers for the business from an early age can help fulfill our "exposure without expectation" principle and give them a sense of pride in contributing to the family. Finally, make sure they do not associate working in the business with any sort of punishment, like going to unload trucks of materials because grades are bad. Be intentional in the connections you want to create; so,

---

[12] Cohen A. & Sharma, P. (2016). *Entrepreneurs in every generation: How successful family businesses develop their next leaders* (1st ed.). Berrett-Koehler.

rather frame, for example, the work in the warehouse as the opportunity to appreciate the discipline and the hard work needed in those areas.

- *Involve them in family governance.* While children cannot contribute much to family governance, they can still attend family meetings and participate in personal updates, family stories, discussions of charitable activities, or short games about the family enterprise. Many families provide exposure by having the kids attend meetings for brief periods and then go off to enjoy a fun time together. Building bonds through fun and enjoying each other's company is among the most important goals at this stage. This fosters a sense of the family's culture, such as showing up regularly to meetings, and promotes a positive association with the enterprise and a sense of belonging.

- *Build family-wide relationships.* The quality of relationships children have with their parents and extended family is critical for their future relationships with each other as owners. Look for structured but informal ways to promote bonds among family members. Many families hold regular reunions, whether in their hometown or a fun destination. Grandparent camps with all grandkids ages 5 to 12 on annual vacations are powerful experiences. Events like these provide quality time and help build connections within and across generations, hopefully contributing to the ability to work better together later in life. To create bonding opportunities, some families also come up with some special names for the gathering of grandparents and grandchildren, like "Oldies and Youngies." Each family culture will have its own style.

- *Promote healthy self-confidence.* It is important to promote self-confidence and self-esteem in children. Instilling confidence will serve them not only as owners but across life domains. For example, treating children's ideas and contributions as important is a must. Ask their opinions. Validate their intuition when accurate, even when they may raise difficult conversations. Listen to what they say. Explain your actions when appropriate. People in general, and especially children, become their best selves within such positive environments. As evidence, note that the opposite of valuing children's contributions—overcontrolling parenting, often called helicopter parenting—during the toddler years results in children less able to manage their emotions between ages 5 and 10.[13] Promoting self-confidence also means being aware of and addressing challenges such as "Black Hole Syndrome," where the founder's vision, ideas, or personality can engulf

---

[13] Perry, N. B., Dollar, J. M., Calkins, S. D., Keane, S. P., & Shanahan, L. (2018). Childhood self-regulation as a mechanism through which early over controlling parenting is associated with adjustment in preadolescence. *Developmental Psychology, 54* (8), 1542–1554.

the needs and interests of other family members. You also don't want to place unrealistic expectations on children, such as preparing them for the Ivy League admissions process well before they enroll in high school.[14] In short, helping children gain perspective, capabilities, and confidence is the most critical priority in this stage.

Sample Development Plan: Young Child

We present a sample development plan for Zoe, our family enterprise owner from the opening.

Scenario: Zoe is now a third-grade student attending a French immersion elementary school. She plays electric guitar and loves a variety of sports, including soccer, swimming, and volleyball. She recently underwent psycho-educational testing based on her school's recommendation. She ranked in the 95% percentile for intelligence but also displayed some borderline attention issues. Zoe's family created the development plan for her (Exhibit 2.4) with the goals and ideas in this chapter in mind.

---

[14] Hughes Jr., J. E., Massenzio, S. E., & Whitaker, K. (2014). *The voice of the rising generation: Family wealth and wisdom* (Bloomberg) (1st ed.). Wiley.

Exhibit 2.4 Owner's Mindset: Sample Development Plan for a Young Child (Zoe)

SAMPLE DEVELOPMENT PLAN FOR A YOUNG CHILD (ZOE)	
AREA	**DEVELOPMENTAL ACTIVITIES**

INDIVIDUAL	• Starts walking to school on her own when appropriate.
	• Takes on new chores with the motto of "many hands make light work."
	  o Starts making own lunches for school two days per week.
	  o Helps with dishes three nights per week.
	  o Washes car on the weekend.
	• Participates in a variety of team sports—parents emphasizing the team—"None of us is as strong as all of us together."
	• Gets a hamster for her birthday which (ideally) she is completely responsible for.

FAMILY	• Joins a parent-child book club with her mom which meets one time per month. • Attends "Grandpa Camp"—a one-on-one weekend with her grandfather where they work and play together. • Attends annual family reunion and participates in group activities with cousins. • Helps family assemble personal care kits for a local homeless shelter. • Picks money-related movie (Charlie and the Chocolate Factory) and watches them with family, then discusses. • Creates a family "Guess Who" game made up of family members (for larger families).
OWNERSHIP	• Cares for toys she owns and doesn't get immediate replacement for those that are lost or neglected. • Receives a small allowance—put equally in three buckets: spend, save, and share/donate.
BUSINESS / INDUSTRY	• Visits the office with Mom—sometimes helps assemble report booklets and clean up; meets non-family managers and learns to shake their hands and treat them respectfully. • Attends the tour or demonstration portions of the annual family meeting. • Plays business-related board games and uses money-related apps. • Creates fun games with her cousins that involve the company (color the logo; create a name contest for new products). • Visits places that have been important for the business growth in the past (e.g., first vineyard site). • Helps give employees turkeys at Thanksgiving. • Sets up a lemonade and cookie stand; parents promote understanding that earnings less costs=profits.

The sample development plan is offered as an example only and includes a variety of ideas—some of which you may already do in the normal course of development in your family. Our goal is to inspire you to take a more

intentional approach to development by building a coordinated plan for your family appropriate to your specific circumstance and context.

Development Influencers

In the youngest family members, effective ownership development requires self-aware and capable influencers with an intentional focus on development. Parents and others are key drivers of this process and thus need to have the capacity to foster it. Exhibit 2.5 shows the wide range of influencers in this earliest stage, with details on each group presented afterward. The influencers closer to the child often have a more significant impact on them.

Exhibit 2.5 Influencers of Young Children

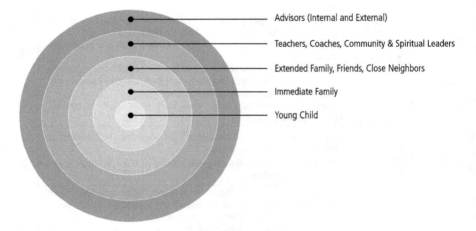

- Advisors (Internal and External)
- Teachers, Coaches, Community & Spiritual Leaders
- Extended Family, Friends, Close Neighbors
- Immediate Family
- Young Child

- *Parents:* Parents or other guardians are front and center as influencers for young children. Children usually spend much of their time with their parents and take direct advice and indirect cues such as modeled behavior. Greater development happens when parents are self-aware, proactive, and intentional about how to talk about the enterprise. Effective influence involves taking great care in how to set boundaries, such as how to talk about money and wealth constructively and how to prioritize quality family time among other areas.
- *Extended family:* Extended family members exert significant influence in this stage too, including grandparents, aunts, uncles, siblings, and cousins. These influencers shape and model the family's broad values and culture, and develop strong relationships with young children. Children can gain

much from extended family, especially as they reach the end of this stage (10 to 12). At the same time, extended family influencers can sometimes be sources of disruption, as described in the box "Handling Grandma Ruth and Other Disruptive Family Influencers" below.

HANDLING GRANDMA RUTH AND OTHER DISRUPTIVE FAMILY INFLUENCERS

Grandma Ruth, founder and matriarch of a diversified retail business in the Midwest, was always known for her toughness. She fought gender stereotypes to become a rare business and industry leader in her generation. However, at one point, her interactions with her grandchildren too often reflected a lack of respect and support. "With grades like that, I'm not counting on you to lead this business," was the type of thing she said, sometimes claiming to be joking. As a result, her children became increasingly uncomfortable with her interactions and needed to find solutions which included the following:

1. *Create alignment on expectations of behavior:* They developed a code of conduct to align all family members around how to treat one another. This process allowed each person to voice how they wanted to be treated by others in the family.
2. *Put the Fish on the Table (even though it stinks!):* The extended family found the courage to talk to Grandma, who was at the center of the issue, to better understand her thinking and make her aware of its effect on the family. Sometimes this can be enough to resolve the issue; often it's not. "Straight talk" has a high value in a family enterprise, as it gets issues on the table, prevents sidebar conversations, sets expectations, and models healthy behavior for all.
3. *Get outside help:* Dynamics around respect and conflict are often difficult for families to address. Many families don't have the skills to unpack interpersonal issues on their own. This family got help from an outside advisor which allowed them to discuss challenges in a safe and supportive environment.
4. *Be patient:* Dealing with these dynamics almost always takes time and rarely offers a speedy resolution to everyone's satisfaction. However, it is always worth the effort to create shared understanding, values, and direction. The Nelsons have been working on this part of their continuity process for several years already.

We recommend that families create a code of conduct on how they will interact, which helps foster a positive environment in the family. A simple sample code of conduct is provided below.

We are stronger together than apart. We each commit to the following principles in our family:

1. Respect all family members—this includes the dog and cat!
2. Be kind to one another.
3. Tell the truth.
4. Be on time.
5. Be positive and encourage each other.
6. Help out—do your part.
7. Share your thoughts and feelings with each other.
8. Love each other.
9. Be generous.

10. Address issues quickly—don't let things fester.

- *Guides or mentors*: Teachers, coaches, religious leaders, therapists, and others outside the family and enterprise can be highly influential. At this stage, children spend significant time with such potential guides and mentors. The themes can be similar to parent–child interactions in helping children develop self-confidence, perspective, knowledge, and interpersonal skills. In addition, these influencers have an arms-length relationship to the family and its enterprise, which helps them provide more objective input and influence on younger family members that may not be accepted as readily if it came from family members themselves.
- *Advisors:* Internal or external advisors may not take a central role in developing children who are owners or future owners but can definitely be of value. Advisors may be brought into teach children basic ownership-related concepts, such as financial literacy. Make certain you hire advisors who had some training and experience working with children. If the instruction isn't age-appropriate and fun, the risk of creating a negative experience and then having to undo it is high. Advisors can also play a role in resolving complicated family dynamics that affect young members, such as conflict between members or branches.

The "Key Influencer Capabilities" box highlights the capacities necessary from these folks to help young family enterprise members develop most effectively as owners.

KEY INFLUENCER CAPABILITIES

When seeking help from key influencers for your family and enterprise, consider the capabilities below. Strong influencers will use these skills to guide ownership development most effectively, while promoting the same qualities in the children they influence.

- Empathizes with others.
- Demonstrates patience and understanding.
- Actively listens to others.
- Sets boundaries within and across the family and enterprise.
- Builds confidence and self-esteem in others.
- Effectively communicates without shutting others down.
- Self-regulates.
- Demonstrates commitment to the family and the tasks at hand.
- Always shows care and respect to others.
- Have sensitivity to kids' needs and stage of development, so that they are exposed to learning that is age appropriate.

Where to Start?

We emphasize throughout this book the need to "begin with the end in mind," which is a core principle from Stephen Covey.[15] Key questions to ask in your family enterprise include: "What kind of family do we want to be?"; "What skills and capabilities do we want our children to develop early on?"; and "What do we want our *family to be like* when our children are young?" This upfront, intentional thinking will lay the foundation for all that comes after.

We encourage you to start with *simple* steps in the development of children—it will serve everyone in the system much better than unveiling a complex, rigid development program or doing nothing at all. Hope is not a strategy! Assess where you are today in terms of development goals and activities, recognizing it is still early. Be proactive by talking about important aspects of being a multigenerational family enterprise. Focus on values and cultural elements, and how best to articulate and live these as a family. Modeling them yourself is a powerful learning tool. Inspire a sense of fun around the development to get the children excited and focus first on relationship building.

Things to Look For

In this chapter, we have examined some of the pitfalls and problems related to the development of young children as future engaged owners. Among the most common difficulties to look for:

- *Beware the business "time magnet"*: In a family enterprise, especially at the start-up stage of a company, one or both parents are likely to devote most of their time to the business. That was the case for Zoe, our rising young owner introduced at the start of the chapter. She felt like she rarely saw her mother, who was a leader in the family business. Not only is parental absence felt by the youngest family members, but it can strongly color their perceptions of the enterprise. "I don't want my life to be 100 percent work like my parents," many rising-generation family members say. The parent staying home to take care of the kids may also have growing resentment toward the partner managing the business. One extreme example, yet not uncommon, is a third-generation family member who, in his forties, sued

---

[15] Covey, S. R. (2013). *The 7 habits of highly effective people: Powerful lessons in personal change (Anniversary)*. Simon & Schuster.

his uncle because he felt his uncle's decisions about the family enterprise kept his father away from home for extended periods when he was a child. In other cases, parents try to make up for their absence by buying children extravagant gifts or coddling them, creating a sense of entitlement or dependence. While privately held businesses demand a great deal of time and attention, be mindful that your children don't internalize the message that the business is the "favored child" and more important than they are.

- *Violating the "exposure without expectation" principle*: A major theme has been the need to provide exposure without expectation of children around involvement in a family enterprise. We recognize that being completely without expectation is not easy. However, too many well-meaning parents and other older-generation members impose overt or implicit expectations on young enterprise members, likely leading to either long-term disengagement or a sense of entitlement that a critical role is their "due." Take the exposure without expectation principle to heart and look for a range of ways to carry it out in this stage.

- *Enabling (or denying) bias in parents or other relatives*: "Why can't you be more like your sister/brother/cousin?" is a question often posed in many families. We unwittingly or sometimes intentionally promote competition among siblings and cousins or think that being hard on a child for perceived shortcomings will motivate change. We can expect too much of children, especially those who show early promise. Any bias toward a child can raise barriers to development in general and as owners specifically. Learn to recognize sources of bias in yourself. Sometimes these prejudices exist because you see a child as similar to you. Be willing to identify and address biases in yourself and others first by naming them. We cannot make ourselves completely bias-free, but we can work to mitigate those we have and help others do the same.

- *Failing to recognize and value different intelligences in your family*: We tend to value people who are highly logical and articulate. Most of our focus, particularly in schools and culture, is on linguistic and logical intelligence. However, people with other intelligences enrich our culture and the organizations in which they operate. The creative artists, musicians, dancers, naturalists, architects, designers, therapists, inventors, and others enhance our world. Unfortunately, children who have these gifts often don't get recognition for their unique ways of thinking, learning, and contributing. Placing value on the diverse set of collective learning styles and intelligences in your family enterprise not only cultivates inclusiveness but also potentially offers ways of thinking and doing things that may amplify your competitive advantage.

- *Losing the middle*: Since this stage represents a wide age range, it may be easy to pay more attention to those on either end of it—babies and toddlers require seemingly constant parental attention, while many 8–12-year-olds have the intellectual capacity and maturity to understand more subtle family enterprise issues. Maintaining a consistent focus on development needs across the age range is important. This is also the case if there is a large number of cousins within a tight age range. Make sure not to let those at lower or higher functioning levels get the vast majority of attention. Do your best to focus on everyone's needs.

Your focus should be to take a simple approach to foster self-esteem, confidence, and a small but important foundation of ownership knowledge and skills in your youngest enterprise members. This information is in the chapter summary in Exhibit 2.6, Young Child Stage Summary.

Exhibit 2.6 Young Child Stage Summary Table

<table>
<tr><td rowspan="2" style="writing-mode:vertical-lr">WHY</td><td colspan="2">WHY YOUNG CHILD STAGE MATTERS</td><td>INSPIRING WORDS OR KEY MESSAGE</td><td>KEY INFLUENCER CAPABILITIES (THESE APPLY ACROSS ALL SIX STAGES)</td></tr>
<tr><td colspan="2">

- Brain is highly receptive at this stage
- Childhood offers an opportunity to create a foundation for success
- Childhood is time of great influence for parents
- Formation of strong sibling and cousin relationships occurs early
</td><td>

- During childhood, even the simplest communication of values has profound, far-reaching effects on prospective owners.
</td><td>

- Empathy
- Patience
- Listening skills
- Ability to set boundaries
- Ability to build confidence and self-esteem in others
</td></tr>
<tr><td rowspan="4" style="writing-mode:vertical-lr">WHAT</td><td>DOMAIN</td><td>DEVELOPMENT GOALS</td><td>HOW TOs</td><td>SAMPLE DEVELOPMENT PLAN FOR ZOE</td></tr>
<tr><td>Individual</td><td>

Promote a healthy sense of self, especially on these dimensions:

- **Self-esteem and confidence:** Feeling assurance in one's own worth and abilities
- **Trust:** Being able to count on others for care and support
- **Curiosity:** A desire to learn, explore, and discover
- **Independence:** A sense that one can accomplish things without help from others; a growing sense of capability in areas like self-care and learning
- **Delayed gratification:** Ability to wait to receive a reward later
- **Boundaries:** Understanding and respecting our own needs, and being respectful and understanding of the needs of others
</td><td>

- Share in household responsibilities
- Understanding self and personal values
- Participate in extracurricular activities
</td><td>

- Start walking to school on own when appropriate
- Participate in chores—with motto "many hands make light work"
  - Start making own lunches for school 2 days per week
  - Help with dishes 3 nights per week
  - Wash car on the weekend
- Participate in a variety of team sports—parents emphasizing the team—"None of us is as strong as all of us together"
- Get a hamster for birthday which (ideally) she is completely responsible for
</td></tr>
<tr><td>Family</td><td>

Promote strong sense of belonging to a larger family with an appreciation for its history:

- Aim for positive family experiences that helps the child get a sense of "together we are stronger" and "we have fun"
- Help them understand who family members are and how everyone is related. Simple things like stories about family members living your values have great impact
</td><td>

Help them get to know your family history

- Build family-wide relationships
- Identify and promote values
- Share family stories
- Expose them to family governance
</td><td>

- Join a parent-child book club with her Mom which meets one time per month
- Attends "Grandpa Camp"—a one-on-one weekend with her grandfather where they work and play together
- Attends annual family reunion and participates in group activities with cousins
- Helps family assemble personal care kits for a local homeless shelter
- Picks money-related movie (Charlie and the Chocolate Factory) to watch and discuss with family
- Creates a family "Guess Who" game made up of family members (for larger families)
</td></tr>
<tr><td>Ownership</td><td>

Promote basic understanding of the responsibilities of being an owner (of anything):

- Importance of taking care of what one owns, such as treating toys and books with respect.
- Value of giving back to community (such as through early volunteer experiences).
- Learning what money is and how to save and spend wisely
</td><td>

- Teach them to care for what they own
- Create understanding of entrepreneurship
- Introduce idea of money and practice earning, spending, sharing and saving it
</td><td>

- Expected to care for toys she owns and doesn't get immediate replacement for those that are lost or neglected
- Divide small allowance into three buckets: spend, save, and donate
- Participate in breast cancer walk; raise $100 from neighbors and family members
</td></tr>
</table>

DOMAIN	DEVELOPMENT GOALS	HOW TOs	SAMPLE DEVELOPMENT PLAN FOR ZOE
WHAT Business/Industry	Promote a positive feeling about the business and its contribution to the family and global/local community: • A basic understanding of the business and industry, especially for older children in this stage • A positive association with the business. Ideally, kids will see the business as "where special things happen," rather than as a major stressor or "the place that takes my parents away"	• Expose them to your business without expectation • Understand concept of starting a business • Teach them to care for what they own; Create understanding of entrepreneurship; Introduce the idea of money and practice earning, spending, sharing and saving it	• Visit the office with Mom—sometimes help assemble report booklets and clean up; meets non-family managers and learns to shake their hands and treat them respectfully • Attend the tour or demonstration portions of the annual family meeting • Play business-related board games and use money-related apps • Create fun games with her cousins that involve the company (color the logo; create a name for new products) • Visits places that have been important for the business growth in the past (e.g., first vineyard site). • Helps give employees turkeys at Thanksgiving. • Sets up a lemonade and cookie stand; parents promote understanding that earnings less costs=profits.

	SAMPLE STORIES, EXERCISES AND TOOLS DESCRIBED IN THE CHAPTER	KEY INFLUENCERS	THINGS TO WATCH OUT FOR	KEY OWNERSHIP TERMS FOR THIS STAGE
HOW TO	• Start Early: A Father's Perspective story • Family Values Exercise • Joshua Reads during Family Meetings story • 20 'Do You Know' Questions • Stories with Money-related Lessons • Zak Learns to Value Money story • Money Games and Apps list • Sample Kid's List of Ownership Terms • Explain Entrepreneurship in a Kid Friendly Way list • Influencers of Young Children figure • Handling Grandma Ruth and Other Disruptive Family Influencers story • Key Influencer Capabilities list	• Parents • Extended family • Teachers, Coaches, Community and Spiritual leaders • Advisors (internal and external)	• Business • Entrepreneur • Expenses • Money • Owner • Philanthropy • Profits • Steward • Values • Vision	• Beware the business "time magnet" • Violating the exposure without expectation principle • Enabling or denying bias or favorites • Failing to recognize and value different intelligences • Losing the middle (leaving out the children that fall in the middle of an age range)

Suggested Additional Readings

Aronoff, C., & Ward, J. (2011). *Family Business Values: How to Assure a Legacy of Continuity and Success* (2nd ed.). Palgrave Macmillan.

Cohen, A. R., & Sharma, P. (2016). *Entrepreneurs in Every Generation: How Successful Family Businesses Develop Their Next Leaders* (1st ed.). Berrett-Koehler Publishers.

Godfrey, J. (2013). *Raising Financially Fit Kids* (Revised ed.). Ten Speed Press.

Gurian, M. (2002). *The Wonder of Girls: Understanding the Hidden Nature of Our Daughters* (1st ed.). Atria Publishing Group.

Gurian, M. (2006). *The Wonder of Boys: What Parents, Mentors and Educators Can Do to Shape Boys into Exceptional Men* (10th Anniversary ed.). Tarcher Perigee.

Hausner, L. (1990). *Children of Paradise: Successful Parenting for Prosperous Families* (1st ed.). Tarcher Perigee.

Lermitte, P. W. (1999). *Allowances, Dollars and Sense: A Proven System for Teaching Your Kids About Money* (1st ed.). McGraw-Hill Education.

Lieber, R. (2015). *The Opposite of Spoiled: Raising Kids Who Are Grounded, Generous, and Smart About Money*. HarperCollins Publishers.

Morris, R. A., & Pearl, J. A. (2010). *Kids, Wealth, and Consequences: Ensuring a Responsible Financial Future for the Next Generation* (1st ed.). Bloomberg Press.

Perdue, M. (2017). *How to Keep Your Family Connected: Templates, Techniques and Resources for Strengthening Your Legacy (How to make your family business last)* (2nd ed., Vol. 2). CreateSpace.

Siegel, D., & Hartzell, M. (2003). *Parenting From the Inside Out* (1st ed.). Tarcher.

3

Forming Identity and Building Relationships: Adolescent (Ages 10 to 20)

W. Sage-Hayward et al., *Own It!*, A Family Business Publication,
https://doi.org/10.1007/978-3-030-20419-8_3

Zak and Zoe—Adolescent Stage

Zak and Zoe, the youngsters from two families that own farming businesses, are now both 15 and in their second year of high school (10th grade). They lead busy lives, with commitments to school, sports, hobbies, friends, and family. Zoe has continued to swim and play volleyball while Zak is on the high school hockey team. Zak is a member of the debate club; Zoe helps edit her school newspaper. Both have active social lives—but aren't yet dating.

Zoe and Zak have also become increasingly exposed to their family enterprises. Both participate in family meetings, mainly by observing, although their parents have started asking them about future plans, including their possible interest in the enterprise. Neither is particularly excited to learn the specifics of the businesses, though Zak worked as an equipment operator for his family enterprise the previous summer.

Zoe's family established a three-week internship for all next-generation family members. She was frustrated that she had to take time out of her summer to participate in this "unpaid make-work project." Though she didn't voice that opinion out loud, it spilled over into how she participated in the learning process, with a lack of curiosity and a negative attitude. Her mood was evident to the non-family employees. During her internship, a few employees made remarks within her earshot about how "…the only reason she had a job was because of her last name." Zoe was taken aback by this disapproval, which furthered her reluctance to participate.

A Founder's Mentality in Every Generation: The Vander Horst Family

The Vander Horsts know a thing or two about raising future owners—and cattle.

The founders of 360 Ag Management, a commercial dairy farm based in central Texas, Alan and Becca Vander Horst have five children ranging from ages 13 to 22, at the time of this writing. From the start, the couple took a proactive approach to help the kids develop as people and prospective owners. The business started in Texas, but as the kids grew, Becca and Alan worried about the potential constraints of growing up in a small community. "We saw that the kids might be defined by their last name in a small farming town," Alan says. So, they relocated to San Luis Obispo, a larger but still agriculturally focused community in California where Alan had grown up and attended college. They maintained their Texas operation through Alan's regular travel and expansion of their management team. Alan and Becca shared several lessons about development they've learned along the way.

- *Foster familiarity with the business*: By the time the oldest children were adolescents, the operation had grown too large for them to be involved in age-appropriate chores such as feeding calves or taking a milking shift. But the parents ensured they had opportunities to understand the business and industry. "We had them presenting Jersey heifers in shows and created a grazing facility behind the house," Becca says. "We took them to farming and youth conferences and had them participate in animal husbandry and livestock judging contests." In addition, until age 19, each child is expected to spend a specific amount of time every year working within the Texas operations. As the children got older, this time commitment increased to three months during the year following their high school graduation. Alan adds, "We wanted them to understand that the business and industry are rooted in care for the animals. And, we wanted to be sure they understood the nature of the business that had afforded them their current lifestyle."
- *Let them be who they are*: "At the same time as ensuring they knew where they came from, we made sure they knew they would never be forced to return to the farm as a full-time career," Becca says. "We encouraged them to find their own interests and passions. Now they seem interested in the business and understand there's no expectation to work there." Their 18-year-old son now enjoys spending summers at the Texas farm.
- *Aim for broad exposure*: The Vander Horsts created several traditions and expectations related to the kids: an 8th-grade trip with the parents; an over-seas trip on their own; a mandatory post-high school gap year, including several weeks working at the Texas farm. "No wimping out," Becca says. "We want them to value exploration, independence, and experience," Alan says.
- *Approach development deliberately*: As the lessons so far suggest, the Vander Horsts take a very intentional approach to development. "Deliberate is our key theme," Becca says. "We think about communication and the example we're setting for them. We explain differences in how we parent them and work hard to support each child's uniqueness." For example, their youngest learns in a way that is best suited to homeschooling, in which Becca is taking the lead.

Driving the Vander Horst's development approach is the idea of instilling a "founder's mentality" in the next generation. "We don't want them to define themselves as second-generation, but as G1s," Becca says. Alan agrees, adding,

"We want them to have the mentality of finding what they want to create, embracing the hard work of innovation, and recognizing the journey is often better than the destination." "It's about providing opportunities and encouragement," Alan concludes. "We want to help them avoid entitlement while understanding that learning never ends. You're never done with it."

The Vander Horsts' approach reflects the ideas in this book about taking a proactive, deliberate approach to developing adolescents in the family enterprise.

The Adolescent Stage (Ages 10 to 20) and Why It Matters

Current or prospective owners in the adolescent stage will range from late elementary school to early college years. Since the previous (Young Child) and next (Young Adult) chapters overlap with this range, we will focus on development for family members roughly ages 13 to 18, the teenage years. Adolescence is a time of transformation, so paying careful attention to ownership development is essential, as roles, mindsets, and expectations change rapidly for those in this stage.[1] Some specific stage-related factors include:

- *Defining one's identity*: Differentiation or forming one's own independent identity is a priority in this stage. Young family members strive to figure out who they are in relation to their family, friends, classmates, and other social dimensions of their life. Adolescents often distance themselves from their family's and community's norms and culture. They push limits of all kinds—including those related to activities and relationships. Differentiation will proceed at a different pace for each individual.
- *Exploring new roles and responsibilities*: Adolescents are typically learning to wear new hats. Most already function as a son or daughter, brother or sister, grandchild, friend, student, and teammate, but they're likely to add roles as employee, romantic partner, volunteer, etc. Many adolescents today are *overloaded* with roles and responsibilities, as discussed in the next section.
- *Developing brains*: Teenage brains are not yet fully developed. In adolescence, the prefrontal cortex, the part of the brain implicated in more complex behaviors including planning and personality development,

---

[1] For a research-based take on the importance of development in adolescence and young adulthood, see Benson, P. L., Hawkins, J. D., Hill, K. G., Oesterle, S., Pashak, T. J., & Scales, P. C. (2016). The dimensions of successful young adult development: A conceptual and measurement framework. *Applied Developmental Science, 20* (3), 150–174.

remains a "work in progress," leading most youth to struggle with impulse control and judgment. However, individuals at this stage of development often demonstrate greater innovation and creativity, generating "outside-the-box" ideas and insights adults are less capable of delivering.[2] They may act inconsistently across social dimensions, including family, school, and peer levels, which has implications for how to approach teens regarding their role as rising owners.

- *Heightened sensitivity*: Adolescents are highly sensitive to how they are perceived, which explains why they seem to care deeply about appearance, image, and social group. Sensitivity can be even more significant for teenagers of enterprising families, especially if the family is wealthy or prominent in the community or region (see the "Responding to the Visibility of Wealth" in Exhibit 3.1). As a result, people make assumptions about rising generations of such families, including having a stress-free life, living a lavish lifestyle, having it "all," and the like. People may approach them for money or other material gain or befriend them because of their economic and public status. Teens and young adults may also sometimes struggle with sharing in wealth they did not create themselves. Ownership development can help them keep perspective, find ways to respond to others' perceptions, and explore their sensitivities constructively.

---

[2] For an overview see Rothenberg, A. (2016). Adolescence and creativity. *Psychology Today*. https://www.psychologytoday.com/us/blog/creative-explorations/201611/adolescence-and-creativity.

Exhibit 3.1 Responding to the Visibility of Wealth

RESPONDING TO THE VISIBILITY OF WEALTH		
During a conversation about the purpose of money and wealth, a third-generation, 13-year-old future owner of a highly successful auto-group dealership sat silently with tears streaming down his face. When the family advisor invited him to share his feelings with his family, he said that he was often teased about being wealthy and constantly asked for money or a deal on a car. He said he was embarrassed and did not know how to stop it or respond to it. The family then spent the next hour brainstorming with Burt about how he (and the other members of G3) could respond in a way that felt strong and not sarcastic, but also empathic and kind. Ideas they identified included:		
COMMENT	**WHAT CAN WE SAY?**	**WHAT CAN WE DO AND THINK?**
Wow! You got it all but don't seem to appreciate it!	Yah, I get why you might say that. I know that I am lucky. We do recognize our incredibly good fortune and that is why we set up a foundation to help others who are not so fortunate. It is also why I volunteer each year. Hey—you want to go play basketball? I love the hoop at your garage	Recognize and support an important rule of life which is "to whom much is given, much is expected." Empathize and show you understand your peers. Appreciating that those who make these types of comments may have their own struggles financially. Try to see things from their perspective.
I wish my parents spoiled me by buying me a car, like yours.	I may or may not get a car—who knows?! But you know what I am most proud of is our family does the Alzheimer's walk every year (or insert other).	Refocus the conversation on something other than wealth or being given material things
Hey—can you get me a good deal on a car? It's not like you guys need the money!	I can't get a deal for you but I can make a connection with someone who I know will take great care of you.	Don't need to feel responsible for their desire to get a deal. Provide a referral to a sales manager which would be helpful.
You guys have more money than pretty much everyone! Lucky!	Oh gosh, we don't have a lot compared to some!! And, I feel really lucky (fortunate) to have the opportunities that I do!	Be down to earth and trustworthy and don't flaunt your wealth.
You went on an African safari over spring break and I just went on a stupid hiking trip!	It was a great trip! We are fortunate to have the chance to travel. Mostly, we just like spending time together! I hope you had a great break too.	Recognize their comments are not about you as much as they are about discomfort with differences.

- *Passion and potential*: Adolescents often show passion and potential for driving real change. Teenagers worldwide are leading important changes in areas ranging from education to environmental protection, often making a difference where adults have been unwilling or unable to. Helping adolescents understand and harness this potential—rather than dismissing it, as adults sometimes do—will promote capable ownership. It's also important to recognize that passion may quickly shift for adolescents, and they sometimes struggle with nuance on complex issues. Younger teenagers often see things in black or white terms. This stage is a rich, complex period of development for adolescents and their families. Boundaries will be tested, communication will be challenging, and emotions will run high. Still, there is an unparalleled "magic" to this stage as youth transition to adults while uncovering their deeper passions, values, potential, and creativity. As adolescents gain self-awareness, maturity, and voice, they will grow into adults who may contribute significantly to the enterprise as owners. The challenge is balancing influence with the independence adolescents need to become their own people. Failing at this may slow their development and result in undifferentiated young adults who struggle figuring out their career and place in life.

In this context, one overarching theme we'll examine in this chapter is *engagement*. More than in other stages, adolescents need to feel invited into development activities, rather than having them imposed, because they already have so much on their plates and need to feel some control over how they spend their time. Practically, that means fostering engagement and fun, so ownership development happens more *implicitly*. For an example, read about how Josh spends his summers in the box "Building a Platform for Listening: Summers with Grammy."

BUILDING A PLATFORM FOR LISTENING: SUMMERS WITH GRAMMY

Josh, a 15-year-old from a family enterprise, spent several summers living with his grandma on an island, working at the local grocery store, pumping gas, and bussing tables at the local café. During the evenings, his grandmother would cook a big meal, and they would read or play cards together after dinner and talk about the day's events. This experience fostered a deeper relationship between grandmother and grandson, which allowed for a more natural mentoring process. It became easier for Josh to take advice from his grandmother than from his parents!

It's important not to assume that development will just happen, but to actively seek opportunities to let young people lead and feel they're making a real contribution to the enterprise (see the box "Teens Lead Charitable Giving Decisions), building an emotional connection to it and, in turn, creating a greater sense of psychological ownership.

TEENS LEAD CHARITABLE GIVING DECISIONS

Charlie and Helen Davis, founders of a successful food business, had been making a significant donation to their local Children's Hospital for over a decade, but they had never involved their three children in this process. At a recent family meeting, Dan, their youngest son, age 14, asked if their family could donate some money to the local homeless shelter, which he had been studying at school. After some discussion, the family decided that each family member could make a $1,000 donation to their charity of choice, with the children working to make some of that money, or to give up something they normally would have bought for themselves.

The family would also collectively donate $5,000 to one charity they all agreed on. During the discussion, they spelled out several criteria for selecting a charity including:

- **Alignment** – The charity goals and objectives needed to align with the Davis' family's mission, vision and values
- **Population** – The charity supports people who are vulnerable
- **Regional** – The charity is located in their city or local region
- **Accountability** – The charity provides some level of reporting and has a desire to have an ongoing relationship with Davis family
- **Short-term Impact** – The charity has a direct, immediate impact on the population it serves

Over time the family donated to multiple organizations, including those devoted to children's health and education, food insecurity, and the environment. The family was excited to develop longer-term relationships with several of these nonprofits.

Parents and other influencers must walk an often-challenging path: fostering interest and engagement without forcing it, helping adolescents find their way by balancing limit-setting with freedom and encouraging creativity. Foundational to building trust in the relationship with a teen is the idea that while their behaviors may be judged, they themselves will not.

Central Theme: The Overstressed Adolescent

Today's overscheduled adolescents haves classes, homework, basketball practice, dating, volunteering, debate team research, test preparation, college applications, social media, part-time work, friends, video games, exercise, internships, etc. This stage of life also comes with enormous physical, social, and emotional change and pressure.

Today's adolescents are often busy and stressed while dealing with many more commitments, goals, responsibilities, and expectations than similar-aged cohorts did in the past.[3] A recent American Psychological Survey showed that teens experience stress level as high as those of adults—and *even greater* during high school years.[4]

This high level of stress means that today's youth are struggling with sleep issues, substance abuse, food-related disorders, and turbulent concepts of self-worth. Furthermore, increasing dependence on smartphones and social media has compounded the issue as youth are more distracted than in the past, prone to (cyber) bullying even when alone and constantly bombarded with information that allows for easy, often esteem-depleting social comparisons. The box "Top Eight Stressors for Teens"[5] presents a list of factors making the lives of teens today highly challenging.

TOP EIGHT STRESSORS FOR TEENS
1. **Depression:** Clinical depression affects an estimated three million teens, with many more suffering from associated subclinical symptoms of sadness, low self-worth, and others.
2. **Bullying:** Whether physical, verbal, or emotional, bullying affects an estimated 30 percent of all adolescents, including through cyberbullying.
3. **Sex:** Nearly half of all teens are sexually active and only a small minority talk to their parents about it.
4. **Drugs:** Rates of marijuana, opioid, and other drug use are rising in North America, especially among teens.
5. **Alcohol:** Alcohol use has dropped among teens in general, but rates of abuse and binge drinking remain high.
6. **Obesity:** About a third of children between ages 10 and 17 in the U.S. are obese, placing them at greater risk for heart disease, diabetes and other health conditions.
7. **Academics:** Some youth struggle with getting higher grades and test scores and feel pressure to perform academically—from parents, peers, and themselves.
8. **Media-related:** Social media has fueled stress for youth through addiction to smartphones, cyberbullying, easy social comparison, sexting and other sources.

Therefore, the goal for parents and other influencers is to be aware of the challenges adolescents face and to provide support and resources, recognizing that today's teens face challenges that previous generations did not.

---

[3] See for example McVeigh, T. (2016). It's never been easy being a teenager. But is this now a generation in crisis? *The Guardian.* https://www.theguardian.com/society/2016/sep/24/teenagers-generation-in-crisis.

[4] American Psychological Association. (2014). American Psychological Association survey shows that teen stress rivals that of adults. http://www.apa.org/news/press/releases/2014/02/teen-stress.aspx.

[5] Items and supporting content from Morin, A. (2018). Top 10 social issues teens struggle with today. *Very Well Family.* https://verywellfamily.com/startling-facts-about-todays-teenagers-2608914.

Unfortunately, we routinely see parents, grandparents, and others ignore these trials and tribulations, and *add* to their teens' stress with high expectations regarding grades, test scores, college admissions, work, and contributions to the enterprise.

While these pressures may be common in an entrepreneurial high-achievement family, such expectations create stress, discord, and emotional distance. They may ultimately turn off a young person from being involved in the enterprise and family. Our recommendation is that you aim to foster interest and engagement in ownership rather than forcing it; voice under-standing of the challenges adolescent family members face; be wary of adding enterprise-related commitments or expectations to their plates; and give them space to develop at their own pace, while guiding them gently.[6]

Development Goals

Adolescents are less likely to have formal responsibilities related to busi-ness, governance, or other enterprise activities than their older counterparts. Therefore, developmental goals for this stage are about becoming healthy, functioning young adults with positive connections to family and the enter-prise and developing a solid foundation for ownership-related knowledge and functioning. The main goals to aim for are described in Exhibit 3.2.

---

[6] For more see Shellenbarger, S. (2017). Step away from your overscheduled high school student. *The Wall Street Journal.* https://www.wsj.com/articles/step-away-from-your-over-scheduled-teen-151 1282108.

Exhibit 3.2 Owner's Mindset: Development Goals for Adolescent Stage

OWNER'S MINDSET: DEVELOPMENT GOALS FOR ADOLESCENT STAGE	
AREA	DEVELOPMENTAL GOALS
INDIVIDUAL	• Promote identity development including a well-formed sense of self related to interests, preferences, and passion. • Encourage an understanding of how the "real world" works — especially for those with few resources. This can help avoid a sense of entitlement.
FAMILY	• Promote development of strong interpersonal skills, including effective communication with family members. • Help youth appreciate the family's strength and bonds, while understanding the need for and value of boundaries.
OWNERSHIP	• Promote building business fundamental knowledge. • Early in the stage, that might mean helping them understand what the business and industry do, along with fun visits to the office or facilities. Later, it may include summer work or internships, along with ensuring young people understand family employment policies and the rationale for these.
BUSINESS / INDUSTRY	• Promote an understanding of the basics of ownership, such as the difference between ownership and management, obligations and responsibilities of ownership, formal and informal roles owners take in the enterprise, and the beginnings of a working knowledge of ownership terms (see our Ownership Glossary). • Foster a healthy understanding and relationship to money.

How-Tos

Here we present a list of ownership development opportunities for adolescents. The idea is not to take on all of these at once, but to assess which best align with your family situation. Then craft intentional, engaging development opportunities guided by the motto of "foster, don't force."

- *Foster friendship and goodwill among siblings and cousins*: This continues to be a crucial time to encourage strong relationship development among younger family members across sibling groups or cousin branches as they will likely be making ownership decisions together in the future. Differences among branches on interests, values, geography, lifestyles, and other dimensions may create challenges. The "Create Meaningful Family Time" ideas in Exhibit 3.3 provide tips on making precious time together count.

Exhibit 3.3 Create Meaningful Family Time

CREATE MEANINGFUL FAMILY TIME

- **Play sports:** Athletics can be a great forum for interactions. Choose team sports, ideally with family on the same team, to foster collaboration and light-hearted competition. The key lesson is that everyone has a specific, important role, and that together you are stronger. Avoid competing within the same family; instead, try to challenge some external teams to build collaboration.

- **Create a Private Facebook Group or "WhatsApp" or "GroupMe" chat:** Families can share funny stories, updates, achievements, and questions through such groups, no matter their distance from each other. More secure platforms, like Trusted Families, have been created for enterprising families to have protected shared space.

- **Take trips together:** Traveling the world or just visiting local destinations can provide a meaningful, fun experience and creates important memories. Hiking or camping can be an especially good bonding experience.

- **Create a mock business challenge:** Have adolescents brainstorm about a real or bsimulated usiness challenge such as a marketing exercise. Make it fun and risk-free. Ask them to present their ideas in a creative way, such as musically or through a humorous skit. Get a facilitator who works well with adolescents. You may be surprised by the quality of the ideas they generate.

- **Do community service work:** Working side by side as volunteers again brings the family closer together while contributing to the community. (More on this below.)

- **Let them decide:** Give the adolescents in your family a chance to plan a fun family activity, whether a dinner out or a hike. Give them a budget and some basic criteria (such as how far away it can be), then give them the space to decide.

- **Use games to promote fun and learning:** Learning key skills by playing games is a low-pressure, enjoyable way to build capacity as a family. For example, try using a survival exercise that promotes the value of team versus individual decision-making. Some board games both build business skills and offer a fun activity a family can complete together.

- *Expose them to the "real world"*: Many families struggle with how to ensure younger members understand the world beyond their family experience, especially when the family is wealthy. Beyond talking regularly about the broader world—such as the challenges those without resources face—you can foster real-life experiences that offer windows into a wide range of external realities. That includes encouraging younger family members to responsibly support the family and home with chores, seek volunteer efforts, internships, travel opportunities, and others. "The Lee Family's Big Move" box that follows describes one family's unique strategy to ensure real-world exposure for adolescent members.

THE LEE FAMILY'S BIG MOVE
An Asia-based business family took drastic steps to ensure their adolescent and younger members learned about real-world issues. The mother moved with the children from the family's large, luxurious compound to a modest apartment in the city. "We wanted them to understand what it's like growing up without maid services or people constantly doing things for them while still being responsible with their school commitments," the mother said. The children were also transitioned from an exclusive private school to a public school with primarily middle-class peers. Not surprisingly, the move took some adjustment; still, the children quickly acclimated to their new life. "They have adjusted very well and enjoyed many aspects of this life, such as walking to friends' houses—something they couldn't do in our original neighborhood." The Lee family's strategy may be a more extreme example of exposing younger family members to the real world, but it's one that drives the point home that such exposure is important to pursue in a way that makes sense for your family's situation.

- *Create a rite of passage*: Cultures around the world have various rites for the adolescent stage, celebrating the transition from childhood to adulthood. In families, it's a moment that can be honored by a longstanding tradition involving the participation of multiple generations. It can be done with little means but much meaning. For example, an adolescent may receive a special gift (symbolic coin, ring, or anything representing family or business history or values) at a birthday milestone (such as 16) or be included in specific meetings such as those for adult family members (at age 18). See the Box "A Colombian Family's Rite of Passage" for a real-life example.

A COLOMBIAN FAMILY'S RITE OF PASSAGE
In Colombia, the nearly twenty teen members of a prominent fifth-generation business family regularly receive a semiannual formal, printed invitation to attend exclusive meetings with the five remaining members of the third generation and members of the executive team. The meeting invitations are sent once the family member reaches age 13, making them an official teenager. Everyone takes the meeting very seriously. The senior generation puts significant effort and planning into what to discuss and how to celebrate the newest invitees, such as bestowing a special gift on them that matches the teenager's interest. During the meeting, the senior generation provides business updates and stories from their past, emphasizing the values they gained from the first-generation founders. They also take the time to learn about their grandchildren's interests and activities. As a result, everyone comes away from the meetings feeling enthusiastic about the family and enterprise. The newest, youngest members feel especially important because they are now treated more like "partners" than children.

- *Undertake family charitable activities*: Philanthropy and volunteer work present rich opportunities for involving younger or prospective owners in the enterprise. Such work helps youth see the family's values in action and understand the legacy they are part of, while boosting planning, decision-making, and leadership skills. Ideally, we recommend involving youth in choosing causes meaningful to the family or aligned with the business (see the Box "Building Toilets in Laos—and Other Community-focused Efforts" that follows). In addition, some families with junior family councils task this group with making key decisions about the focus of volunteer work and provide junior members with a small philanthropy fund to allocate.

BUILDING TOILETS IN LAOS—AND OTHER COMMUNITY-FOCUSED EFFORTS

One enterprising family spent a recent spring break building toilets in a remote village of Laos, where the lack of such facilities is a major cause of disease and mortality. The work inspired both sons to engage in further community-focused efforts, including fundraising for local charities, a high school trip to build a kitchen and greenhouse for a Peruvian school, and work with Habitat for Humanity to build affordable housing for low-income populations. Along the way, they gained a more profound sense of commitment to the community, along with organizational teamwork and leadership skills. Consider these other community-focused options as part of ownership development:

- Fundraisers such as silent auctions, cancer walks, and sponsored runs
- Volunteer work with local hunger relief organizations (like food pantries) or those that provide clothing and other essentials
- Volunteer teaching or coaching with underserved youth
- Assembly and distribution of backpacks for homeless people or holiday baskets for families in need
- Habitat for Humanity builds or similar community efforts

Look for opportunities in your community and engage adolescent family members in choosing how to get involved (based on their passions and skills). Projects that allow many family members to participate together are ideal. Once completed, take the time to discuss what was gained from the experience, and how this might relate to their goals for future ownership, such as continuing a family legacy of giving back.

- *Encourage activities outside the family enterprise*: The reality is adolescents will be busy mainly with activities outside the family and its enterprise, such as school, extracurricular activities, and peer networks. In this context, encourage youth family members to seek diverse learning opportunities through sports teams, arts and cultural experiences, community service, or church groups. Take advantage of occasions to discuss what they're gaining from the experience and challenges they face. Consider asking questions to draw subtle links between such activities and skills related to ownership responsibilities. "Subtle" is the key word here!
- *Develop a family code of conduct*: As adolescents push boundaries, it's crucial to develop a family code of conduct that sets expectations of children and adults. A simple but thoughtful code may be built on the family's existing

or newly articulated values and will reinforce the culture the family is trying to promote. It also enables members to "call" other members on challenging or hurtful behavior by reminding of jointly developed standards, rather than their own guidelines. ("What you did/said doesn't seem to fit with the idea of mutual respect in our code of conduct.") Involving youth in creating a code of conduct can be an informative experience for adolescents and one that sets the stage for a similar approach to ownership dynamics in the future. If you already have one, take the time to review and update it for this stage of life. See the "Sample Family Code of Conduct" in the Young Child Chapter.

- *Tell and discover stories:* Story is one of the most powerful mediums for fostering shared values and understanding.[7] This is especially true for family enterprise, where stories of early generation struggles and success can power a strong sense of belonging and stewardship among future generations. Thus, sharing stories with adolescents is critical, as is discovering the stories they tell about themselves, which provide windows into their thinking and perspectives. Researchers Robyn Fivush and Marshall Duke have shown that children who know their family's stories have higher levels of self-esteem and greater academic and social performance. They created a 20 Questions exercise to help families share specifics of family history[8] (see full set of questions in the Young Child chapter). This exercise, and more formal approaches, help families share, celebrate, and discover family stories with adolescent family members.

- *Foster a constructive emotional environment*: Too often, senior generations move into ownership development without first establishing a resilient emotional environment in the family: values-driven behavior, open communication, constructive expression of emotion, appreciation for the diversity of skills and interests, and others. Promoting ownership development amidst chronic, widespread conflict or broken relationships is unlikely to yield hoped-for results. If your family has struggles with interpersonal dynamics, strive for needed improvements here first. See the box "Build a Strong Family Dynamic" characteristics for specific tips.

---

[7] For an overview of the power of story see The power of stories. *Psychology Today*. https://www.psychologytoday.com/us/collections/201106/the-power-stories.

[8] For the full 20 Questions exercise see Fivush, R. (2016). The "do you know?" 20 questions about family stories. *Psychology Today*. https://www.psychologytoday.com/us/blog/the-stories-our-lives/201611/the-do-you-know-20-questions-about-family-stories.

BUILD A STRONG FAMILY DYNAMIC

Here are six essential behaviors of family members committed to strong family relationships:
- They are attuned to each other's needs and wants.
- They are committed to repair relationships when conflicts arise or trust breaks down—where disagreements are around ideas and not between people.
- They encourage individuals to express their feelings, concerns, and desires and members listen to one another.
- They continuously demonstrate respect and appreciation for one another, work to foster one another's success, and choose to spend time together.
- They behave as collaborative problem-solvers in the face of adversity.
- They choose to define a positive meaning for experiences and stressors that individuals, the family, or the business go through.

TIPS FOR BUILDING AND MAINTAINING A STRONG FAMILY DYNAMIC INCLUDE:

- Learn and hone communication skills together as a family so you are using the same language and frameworks (e.g., have a skilled facilitator teach you as a group).
- Establish family traditions together especially around holidays and special days such as birthdays and anniversaries.
- Promote discussions while eating regular meals together such as dinner. Ask everyone to "share one thing that was great today, one thing that was hard today, and a blessing for today I can be thankful for" (or any similar question that is stimulating for your family).
- Take holidays as a family. As the children grow, ask them to participate in planning efforts.
- Use "round robins" (each person gets a turn) during conversations to provide all family members an opportunity to share thoughts and feelings.
- Don't try to address specific problems when family members are upset or angry. Wait until tempers are calmer to restart a conversation around difficult topics. Advance your family's capability in managing differences of opinion and conflict resolution.
- Seek counseling if you can't get past an issue.
- Check in periodically to ask for feedback about how to improve how the family operates together.

- *Establish clear personal boundaries*: Similar to the previous point, this tip is about creating the right environment for the ownership development of adolescents to take place. Defined personal boundaries within the family go a long way to fostering growth. Personal boundaries are the physical, emotional, and mental limits and rules we set for ourselves and in our relationships. Boundaries act as filters that permit what is acceptable and unacceptable in our life and promote appropriate self-care and self-respect while protecting us from being manipulated or violated. The box "Establishing Clear Boundaries" provides more information on making boundaries a reality for family members. Share these ideas with adolescent members, who are often struggling with boundaries of multiple types.

ESTABLISHING CLEAR BOUNDARIES

Use the ideas here to work toward understanding the boundaries in your family enterprise and to establish unambiguous boundaries at all levels

WHAT ARE BOUNDARIES?

Guidelines, rules or limits in relationships.

Define interpersonal responsibilities and rights.

Are intangible, can change, are unique to each individual, and define the distinction between individuals and others.

Clarify what types of communication, behavior, and interaction are acceptable.

TYPES OF HEALTHY BOUNDARIES IN A FAMILY ENTERPRISE

Relationships – Awareness of the significance of relationships and demonstrating respect for others' ideas and an awareness of appropriate discussion topics; managing one's status needs and insecurities; listening and being respectful during conversation.

Time – Awareness of how a person (or you) use their time for each facet of life such as work, relationships, and hobbies; showing up on time; respecting others' time; being present and available (appropriately).

Privacy and Transparency – Awareness of how much and when to share information about the business and family matters; awareness of what is appropriate to ask and not ask; understanding of when transparency is beneficial and necessary between family members and as it relates to the business.

Roles and Responsibilities – Awareness of the need for clear roles and responsibilities within the family enterprise which helps mitigate conflict and tension as well as manage expectations; moving from family role dynamics (child, parent, sibling, cousin, etc.) to adult-to-adult communication and business roles.

Money and Material Things – Awareness of limits on money and possessions such as what you will share, and with whom; creating appropriate accountability; suitable giving (and taking); not using money for power and control.

Decision-making – Awareness of whose voice and vote are appropriate to what decisions as it relates to the family, enterprise, and ownership systems; understanding when consensus is important and when to utilize other forms of decision-making such as majority or unilateral; making decisions wearing the appropriate "hat" (family, business, owner).

TYPES OF HEALTHY BOUNDARIES IN A FAMILY ENTERPRISE

Creating appropriate boundaries is empowering. Here are some examples of how families set them within the context of their enterprises:

1. **Protect family time:** don't talk only and always about business at the dinner table—no matter how tempting.
2. **Establish accountability:** create guidelines for minimum entry standards for working in the business (e.g., outside work experience + university/vocational training).
3. **Clarify decision authorities:** identify who gets to have a voice and who gets a vote in decisions.
4. **Provide appropriate compensation:** too often families pay all of the next generation the same amount.

Boundaries often get blurred in a family enterprise. Identifying boundaries is a good first step to better boundary management.

- *Provide family employment opportunities*: Adolescents may spend time with the business, informally through office visits or formally through summer jobs, internships, or special projects. There's no "formula" for the right opportunity. The idea is to create engaging experiences proactively. One way to help manage family interaction in the business is to draft formal policies spelling out rules of employment for family members. For example, a Midwestern U.S. manufacturing family has created opportunities in the business based on age, including gaining early exposure to the factory in preteenage years, working summer jobs there in mid-teenage years and completing formal summer internships between ages 18 and 20. In general, start small by involving young people in the mailroom, washing cars, picking or sorting grapes, or similar activities. Don't use make-work activities in the business as a punishment of any sort which sends a negative message. It's also important to prepare non-family employees for the arrival of young family members, as outlined in "Prepare Non-Family Employees for Youth Involvement."

PREPARE NON-FAMILY EMPLOYEES FOR YOUTH INVOLVEMENT

It's important to anticipate challenges when family members become involved with the family business in any capacity. That includes being respectful and proactive in preparing non-family employees for this reality. Here are specific tips:

- Share the family employment policy with managers and other employees as needed, to help them understand the family's thinking and decisions around this vital area.
- Reemphasize that all family employees or interns must follow the business code of conduct.
- Talk about the possible different roles family members will have and lay out expectations for their performance (which is often higher than for non-family employees).
- Discuss the formal and informal performance evaluations expected for family employees.
- Prepare the business for the idea that a small percentage of family employees' time may be devoted to learning about the family business. Emphasize that resources will be provided to affected areas to help deal with this potential burden.
- Avoid having family members report to other family members when possible.
- Consider instituting a "safety valve" such as an ombudsperson or a development committee to settle emergent issues, particularly between working family members and their supervisors.

- *Offer dynamic business updates*: Business updates (like detailed financial updates) may be considered "boring" by youth (and some adults for that matter!) or—if presented without context—may risk creating a sense of entitlement. However, exposure and repetition are foundational for development. Therefore, livening up dry content and creating interactive discussion is critical to maintaining engagement. Describe industry trends or stories about specific business decisions to expand a product line, get new clients, or change a particular technology in fun and engaging ways. In particular, adapting your own business situations to games or story problems can create active participation in a "real-life" business scenario. This approach can lead to engagement, loyalty, and pride in younger prospective owners. With financial information, it is useful to expose teens to different concepts illustrated in the reports before getting into specific numbers. Numbers without context may create more entitlement and expectations around lifestyles. In particular, without an appropriate explanation, younger owners may confuse revenue with profit or otherwise develop false expectations about the wealth in their family. Based on your kids' knowledge level begin by sharing the context and explaining the content. Actual numbers can follow. At one family enterprise, the CFO (a family member) presents a high-level but consistently formatted financial report at every quarterly family meeting, including a "word of the day." Prospective owners in this family now begin this session by shouting out prior financial words of the day: "ROA! Retained earnings! Fixed assets!" The ability to have fun with the concepts encouraged younger prospective owners continued attendance and helped them retain complicated financial concepts.

- *Conduct "future" ownership meetings*: It's easy to avoid going deep on ownership-specific topics with adolescent family members, or simply asking them to sign a revised trust document without explaining the paperwork's purpose because we sometimes assume they don't understand or care anyway. Instead, take the opportunity, in small doses, to help them gain familiarity with key ownership concepts; see the Box "Build Basic Ownership Knowledge for Adolescent Stage" for tips on topics. Formalize short discussions that help them engage with ownership-related concepts in a meaningful way and explain why this stuff matters. For example, a real estate development family conducts brief ownership meetings on their site walkarounds. The mother in this family brings a summary of interesting facts about a particular development site related to the family's commitment to the environment. She shares these facts during the semiannual tour of their development sites (e.g., the cost of using geothermal heating or how many EV car stalls the building will have and why).

BUILD BASIC OWNERSHIP KNOWLEDGE FOR ADOLESCENT STAGE
Work to provide adolescent family members basic ownership knowledge in these areas and others as needed: • Ownership terminology (see Appendix A: Glossary of Terms) • Stages and types of ownership (see Chapter 1) • Ownership rights and responsibilities • The value and benefit of business ownership • Distinction between management and ownership roles and responsibilities • Types of ownership agreements • Types of legal business structures including trusts • Types of ownership policies (see the ownership policy appendix) • Basic definition and understanding of risk management • Concept of continuity and succession planning.

- *Implement regular family governance*: A fourth-generation Netherlands-based business family is reorganizing its family council to accommodate next-generation adolescents. They will not only attend council meetings but also participate actively. Other families have started junior family councils that include members as young as their early teens working on issues such as charitable giving activities. Other families include everyone over age 16 in formal family meetings. Family governance offers rich opportunities to involve adolescent members in the enterprise. However, it is important to expose younger members to what constitutes effective family governance. It is not just getting together and talking or hearing business updates but practicing focused discussion and decision-making on issues like family employment, prenuptial agreements, reunion-planning, conflict resolution, and family cohesion building. If you have no formal family governance body or process, now is a good time to start.[9] In a few steps, based on your family's size and needs, a more structured family governance approach may create a "safe space" for families to talk calmly about what's working and not, with adults setting the example of rational, respectful discussion. The Box "Four Cornerstones of Family Meetings" lays out key areas of focus for family meetings. The "Sample Family Meeting Agenda" provides example meeting topics.[10]

---

[9] For more on family governance steps and tools, see Eckrich, C., & McClure, S. (2012). *The family council handbook*. Palgrave-Macmillan.

[10] Sage-Hayward, W. (2014). *Four cornerstones of family meetings*. Presentation.

FOUR CORNERSTONES OF FAMILY MEETINGS

The purpose of family meetings is to advance the family and foster individual development. Use these four main areas of focus for such meetings:

- *Family development:* An opportunity for the family to learn and grow together around technical (e.g., financial and philanthropic literacy) and behavioral (e.g., empathy, conflict management, and listening skills) topics. This includes assessment, learning, planning, skills training, policy creation, and philanthropy.

- *Family cohesion:* An opportunity to build connections in the family by doing things like setting vision, values, and purpose as well as understanding each family member's interests, hopes, and dreams. This includes vision, mission, and values; history and traditions; hopes, dream, and aspirations; support, care, and love; and fair process.

- *Family enterprise understanding:* An opportunity to learn about the family enterprise, including the operating businesses, real estate management, investment choices, and others. Some families will share size and value; others wait until later stages. Do what is appropriate for your family while recognizing the messages you are sending to the rising generation. Other ideas include: entrepreneurial focus; information sharing; tours and internships; meeting with directors; innovation; connection to ownership and business.

- *Family fun:* An opportunity for the family to enjoy time together that isn't focused on specific learning or business topics. This includes games, activities, tournaments, talent shows, humor, meals, and celebrations.

SAMPLE FAMILY MEETING AGENDA IN THE ADOLESCENT STAGE

We are excited to meet again as a family next month. The agenda for the meeting is:

- Welcome
- Fun activity – Winter Survival Game – Individual versus Group Decision-making
- Adopting Summary Notes from June 2021 Meeting
- Updates
- Personal update question: What is an event in your life that has made you who you are today?
- Brief business update
- Brief ownership update
- Brief family foundation update
- Family values exercise: Using Values Edge Cards (Dennis Jaffe)
- Create personal values pyramid
- Create family values pyramid
- Presentation on Family Vision
- Review and discuss family vision with G4
- Refine family vision based on discussion
- Wrap-up and Summary

- *Promote financial responsibility*: Adolescence is a critical stage in which teens can gain a sense of financial responsibility. Learning at this stage includes understanding the connection between work and money and basic financial lingo, including budgets, cost-benefit analysis, principal, interest, credit, etc. Having teens prepare a monthly budget and fund it with proceeds from part-time work (or parents can fund this for younger adolescents) goes a long way toward promoting accountability and skills for future ownership decision-making. Such budgets can include everything from clothes to lunch money to school supplies or cell phones. Helping teens identify and follow through on a major goal like saving for a car or paying for their own cell phone plan also builds important financial awareness and skills. There are many fun apps for this purpose including those currently available: Allowance, Smarty Pig, Left To Spend, and others.
- *Build understanding of the meaning and purpose of your family's wealth*: It can be tricky to unveil the complete scale of the family enterprise and wealth. The leading generation rationalizes avoidance by saying, "They just were not ready to see that number of zeros!" or "We were afraid of them sharing with their friends." The most common refrain we have heard is, "I wanted them to work for a living—we don't want to raise entitled kids!" Finding the "right" time to broach these concepts is complicated and highly dependent on each family's unique dynamics and history. See the Box "When to Introduce a Family's Wealth Level" for ideas on approaching this complex topic.

WHEN TO INTRODUCE A FAMILY'S WEALTH LEVEL

The challenge of choosing the "right" time to teach about a family's wealth is real. The reasons behind this are multiple and complex.* But take heart in the fact that many in the rising generation are interested in more than money. In fact, iGen (born 1997-2012) and millennial (born 1981-1996) children of parents with a net worth estimated at over $1M say the most important thing they will inherit from their parents isn't their wealth but their values. More than 90 percent of these children reported that they don't regularly meet as a family to discuss family finances and 60 percent say such meetings would be valuable!

If the family enterprise goal is continuity, sharing knowledge early and consistently among the various nuclear branches (if you are multigenerational) in your family enterprise will yield the best results. We urge you to consider establishing an ongoing process with adolescents to build the complex skill set necessary to understand one's own wealth. Below are some additional tips:

1. *Context is important.* Start with your family enterprise context—teaching about your family values. You can also share societal context, sharing how your family has earned (or been endowed) more resources than many other families.

2. *Children rise to the level of expectations parents set for them.* By teaching children that they have a somewhat unique set of benefits—and associated responsibilities— you're modeling a belief that they're capable of handling the situation. Delaying the teaching tells the rising generation that you didn't believe they are qualified. And they often fulfill this belief.

3. *Involve your advisors in the process.* This has a dual benefit. First, these professionals have probably worked on wealth transition with other family enterprise clients, and therefore, have experience in laying out complex topics in an easy-to-understand way. Also, your advisors have a unique credibility in your adolescent's eyes. Often, children are willing to listen to these advisors when they can't hear the exact same message from you.

4. *Build knowledge, don't "reveal" it.* As with an owner's mindset, it's most effectively created over time. Share progressively more sophisticated concepts as the rising generation advance in age and maturity.

* Hughes Jr, J. E., Massenzio, S. E., & Whitaker, K. (2012). *The cycle of the gift: Family wealth and wisdom* (Vol. 168). Wiley; Grubman, J. (2013). Stranger in paradise. How families adapt to wealth across generations. *Family Wealth Consulting*

Sample Development Plan: Adolescent

Scenario: Zak, our family enterprise member from the opening, is now a 10th-grade student attending a private high school. He is driven, goal-oriented, and highly competitive. He is not particularly close with his siblings but has a strong connection with his parents and grandmother. Using the concepts from this chapter, he and his family outlined these development activities (Exhibit 3.4).

Exhibit 3.4 Owner's Mindset: Sample Development Plan for an Adolescent (Zak)

SAMPLE DEVELOPMENT PLAN FOR AN ADOLESCENT (ZAK)	
AREA	**DEVELOPMENTAL ACTIVITIES**
INDIVIDUAL	• Participate in a leadership program as a high achiever at his high school. • Continue to play team sports—current motto, "Don't WEAR your team colors, • BLEED them." • Get a driver's license after completing a driver's education course. • Lead the Alley Outreach for his school, a program that accumulates contributions of clothes and food from peers to put in backpacks to be distributed to the homeless and indiviuals with substance abuse issues. • Compete in provincial debate championships.

FAMILY	• Attend three family meetings: spring, fall, and winter. Topics include:
	    o Use of social media and cell phones
	    o Confidentiality
	    o Family conflicts
	    o Building financial literacy
	• Continue with family movie and game night. Friends invited.
	• Negotiate a new curfew and use of the car.
	• Bring girlfriend to a Sunday night family dinner.
	• Attend family holiday to Belize—each child chooses a friend to bring along.

OWNERSHIP	• Participate in two future ownership meetings to:
	    o Learn about being a beneficiary of a trust
	    o Review financials of the family trust
	    o Understand amendments to the family enterprise partnership agreement
	• Attend a financial literacy program for teens.
	• Participate in a financial investing club with a group of his friends led by Dad.

BUSINESS / INDUSTRY	• Work as painter or equipment operator during the summer at his family's enterprise. • Attend a two-day intrapreneurial program over the summer. • Attend an industry association meeting with his mother.

The sample development plan is offered as an example only and includes a variety of ideas—some of which you may already do in the normal course of development in your family. Our goal is to inspire you to take a more intentional approach to development by building a coordinated plan for your family appropriate to your specific circumstance and context.

Development Influencers

The "usual suspects" act as influencers in this stage—those who can help adolescents benefit from the proper development opportunities include:

- *Extended Family*: Parents remain primary sources of influence on adolescents. However, much of that influence will be indirect, given adolescents' focus on differentiating. Extended family members including grandparents, aunts, uncles, and cousins are also important influencers. Younger people are more likely to be influenced by their older, "cooler" cousins than their parents' generation. For instance, in a family meeting, a twenty-something cousin took aside a teen member when she saw the younger cousin rolling her eyes and focusing exclusively on her phone. "This stuff is dry but important," the older cousin said, motivating her younger peer to take such meetings more seriously. This type of role model behavior—whether direct or indirect—can be critical in ownership development.

  We'd like to draw special attention to the role of aunts and uncles who often share similar values and thus can be an invaluable resource within a family, especially during more challenging stages of life such as adolescence. Aunts and uncles don't have the parental control dynamic with their nieces and nephews and thus the relationship is more relaxed. They can share embarrassing stories about their parents which sets a tone of trust and camaraderie. They can also be great role models for family values and can serve as confidants when the child may not want to tell a parent something.[11]

- *Close family friends*: Many families have long-term friends who have known the children for a long period of time and have built strong bonds with them. Such friends can become great sources of guidance and support for adolescents. As with older cousins, such mentors can strongly influence a younger person in a way that parents might not be able to, making them powerful influencers during this stage.

- *Teachers, coaches, community, and spiritual leaders*: Adults, especially those in leadership roles, can also be strong influencers and mentors who spend significant time with adolescents at sports events, community service activities, etc. As in the young child stage, the influence here is more toward general development than ownership development, but it's strongly related to building better judgment and decision-making capacity. The objective is to seek those who will promote the most positive impact. See the Box

---

[11] Hughes Jr., J. E. (2004). *Family wealth: Keeping it in the family*. Bloomberg Publishing.

"When a Coach is Not a Great Influencer" for more on understanding a coach's impact.

WHEN A COACH IS NOT A GREAT INFLUENCER

Not all coaches, teachers, and community leaders are great influencers. Sometimes they represent poor examples of what we want our children to learn, such as emphasizing winning over growth or humiliating those who deliver poor performance. However, such individuals may hold power and control in your child's life in some way. When your adolescent raises concerns about an influencer, you have several ways to react. Here are three roads to consider:

Check in: Create the opportunity for the adolescent to express his feelings and emotions. Listen and provide a good sounding board. Use powerful questions and active listening techniques, work with the child to design respectful responses that align with his values (and hopefully your family values!), always remembering that taking a highly aggressive approach rarely results in positive outcomes for anyone.

Advocate: Where appropriate and with caution, offer to advocate for the adolescent with the relevant people.

Accept: In some cases, discuss it together and decide the right approach is to do nothing but use it as a learning tool for what *not* to do.

- *Advisors*: We think of family enterprise advisors as influencers by "design" who can promote ownership development. They are expected to approach advising work with impartiality and the family's best interests in mind so these professionals can help adolescent family members feel more "adult" and capable of moving toward more responsibility within the enterprise. Look for capable, thoughtful advisors able to connect with this age group and understand the complex dynamics of a family enterprise. It can be beneficial for these advisors to meet with the rising generation without the previous one present.

Where to Start?

This can be a time of overwhelming change for adolescents and their families. Stepping back to appreciate both the challenge and wonder of this stage is critical. Ask yourself what is already being done to promote general and ownership development, and what you want your adolescents to know and appreciate. What kind of space is being given for that? How well is it working? What could be better? For example, what could be done to engage adolescent family members in family meetings better—or at all? While performing this informal assessment, remember the idea of striking a balance between individual and collective development.

On the *individual* level, we have focused on understanding who your adolescent children naturally are and meeting them where they are, bringing the support and other resources they need. Some rising owners in this stage will already be highly engaged and wanting more. Others won't be. It's tempting to think their journey to adulthood is well underway or nearly complete, but it has really just begun. Help them explore who they are and what they want to be, without imposing enterprise-related obligations or ideas. Facilitating their development to a broad, healthy identity and sense of self will go farther in moving them toward becoming effective owners more than most *any* specific activity will.

At the *collective* level, it's about helping adolescents develop strong inter-personal skills and comfort in wide-ranging relationships. This happens more organically among siblings when adolescents appreciate different styles and temperaments and develop greater empathy. Family governance bodies and activities can support an intentional approach to the collective development of young people, but informal interactions, such as at family reunions, typi-cally form the foundation. Be proactive about including teens in business updates, summer jobs, internships, extended family reunions, and philan-thropic efforts. Provide structures for dialogue and interaction—like family meetings—while modeling good behavior in family relationships. Remember: it's not just about what you *say* but what you *do*.

Things to Look For

There are several potential hazards in fostering an owner's mindset in adoles-cents. Here are the most common:

- *Failure to engage*: This is "enemy number one" in business families. Failing to engage adolescents in some form of development or appreciation for the enterprise sets the stage for uninvolved, passive owners or could even result in the next generation's desire to relinquish the enterprise. Failure to engage can happen when there are no connections between younger family members and the enterprise, as well as when senior generations push too hard for engagement, ultimately making it feel like a chore or obligation. Instead, you should aim for the middle ground of exposure without expec-tation and opportunity without obligation. Engagement develops best in a fun, trust-rich context.

- *Hazardous adult-teen dynamics*: Some parents project their own issues onto the children or seek to live these out through the next generation, transferring anxiety, anger, ambition, and other emotions or aspirations to adolescents. Similarly, they may infantilize younger members and see them as incapable of making current or future contributions and engage in "helicopter" parenting by providing constant direction or control or "snowplow" parenting by clearing away all obstacles in their child's path. Still others fear setting strong boundaries will risk losing their child's affection. This will likely promote avoidance of ownership responsibilities among younger generations. Here, it is critical for parents to self-regulate and manage their own issues and anxieties, as well as to avoid transmitting these to the next generation and to increase adolescents' interest in ownership.

- *The slow life strategy*: Teens are growing up more slowly because families have fewer children and can spend more time and resources on each child.[12] And, over the last fifteen years and across socioeconomic backgrounds, American children have become more protected—experiencing driving, having a job, trying alcohol, dating, and sex later and less frequently than teens from prior generations. These trends have led to young adults having less life skills, such as not knowing how to manage a budget, meet deadlines, or even do their laundry. Dr. Jean Twenge in her book about iGens says, "*iGen'ers are scared, maybe even terrified. Growing up slowly, raised to value safety and frightened by the implications of income inequality, they have come to adolescence in a time when their devices have both extended their childhoods and isolated them from true human interaction. As a result, they are both the physically safest generation and the most mentally fragile.*" (p. 312). This phenomenon is more apparent in individualistic cultures in the U.S., Canada, and the U.K. Specific practices that can combat this society-wide challenge focus on encouraging teens to be more independent. For example, insist they get a driver's license. Encourage them to plan and take a trip with friends. Talk to them about the realities of college parties and how to avoid sexual assault. Consider a gap year between high school and college to provide dedicated time for them to gain adult skills.

- *Fear of entitlement*: Understandably, senior generations are often very afraid of raising entitled successors. Excessive fear can drive adolescents away from the business when there are overly restrictive policies about family employment or no opportunities to contribute to family governance. In fact, such fear often drives current owners to repeatedly postpone

---

[12] Twenge, Ph.D., J.M. (2017). *iGen: Why today's super-connected kids are growing up less rebellious, more tolerant, less happy-and completely unprepared for adulthood.* Simon & Schuster.

sharing family business knowledge and the magnitude of family business wealth. Delaying "the great reveal" and failing to grant the next generation agency until they're in their twenties or beyond usually results in losing a key opportunity to grow an owner's mindset and causes the next gen bitterness and regret. Recognize that entitlement isn't inherent in rising family members but emerges from how the senior generation models an approach to transparency, communication, responsibilities, and wealth. You need to be aware of the fears of potential entitlement *and* balance them by purposefully creating opportunities for development, growth, and responsibility.

On one hand, there remains plenty of time to develop owners in this stage. But on the other, the long-term effects of experience and influence in adolescence are significant and enduring. Adults often look back on what their parents did—and didn't do—to develop them as owners and people and realize that it's less about the number of efforts but *quality*. Therefore, aim to lay a strong but flexible foundation for development, recognizing that challenging dynamics and issues have a way of cascading down to future generations.

Exhibit 3.5: Adolescent Stage Summary Table

	WHY ADOLESCENT STAGE MATTERS	KEY MESSAGE	
WHY	• A critical time for identity development • Roles and responsibilities are being explored • An adolescent brain is still developing • Sensitivity in this stage is heightened	Consistently offer opportunities to learn and engage while being patient with adolescents' growing need for independence	

	DOMAIN	DEVELOPMENT GOALS	HOW- TOs	SAMPLE DEVELOPMENT PLAN FOR ZAK
WHAT	**Individual**	• Promote identity development including a well-formed sense of self related to interests, preferences, and passion. • Encourage an understanding of how the "real world" works — especially for those with few resources. This can help avoid a sense of entitlement.	• Expose them to the "real world" through travel, volunteer activities and other experiences • Create a rite of passage • Tell and discover stories • Establish clear personal boundaries	• Participate in a leadership program as a high achiever at his high school • Continue to play team sports —current motto— "Don't WEAR your team colors, BLEED them" • Get a driver's license after completing a driver's education course • Lead the Alley Outreach for his school, a program that accumulates contributions of clothes and food from peers to put in backpacks to be distributed to the homeless and individuals with substance abuse issues • Compete in provincial debate championships
	Family	• Promote development of strong interpersonal skills, including effective communication with family members. • Help youth appreciate the family's strength and bonds, while understanding the need for and value of boundaries.	• Foster friendship and good will among siblings and cousins by creating opportunities for next gen groups to play, work, give and make decisions together • Undertake family charitable activities • Develop a family code of conduct • Foster a constructive emotional environment by expecting and teaching self-awareness, communication and conflict management skills • Implement regular family governance	• Attend 3 family meetings: spring, fall and winter. Topics to include: - Use of social media and cell phones - Confidentiality - Family conflicts - Building financial literacy • Continue with family movie and game night. Friends invited • Negotiate a new curfew and use of the car • Bring girlfriend to a Sunday night family dinner • Attend Family holiday to Belize—each child chooses a friend to bring along

DOMAIN	DEVELOPMENT GOALS	HOW-TOs	SAMPLE DEVELOPMENT PLAN FOR ZAK
Ownership	• Promote building business fundamental knowledge. • Early in the stage, that might mean helping them understand what the business and industry do, along with fun visits to the office or facilities. Later, it may include summer work or internships, along with ensuring young people understand family employment policies and the rationale for these.	• Hold prospective owner meetings • Discuss family employment and other applicable policies • Choose a charity to donate money to	• Participate in two prospective owner meetings to: - Learn about being a beneficiary of a trust - Review financials of the family trust - Understand and sign amendments to the family enterprise partnership agreement • Attend a financial literacy program for teens • Participate in a financial investing club with a group of his friends led by Dad
Business/ Industry	• Promote an understanding of the basics of ownership, such as the difference between ownership and management, obligations and responsibilities of ownership, formal and informal roles owners take in the enterprise, and the beginnings of a working knowledge of ownership terms (see our Ownership Glossary). • Foster a healthy understanding and relationship to money.	• Learn business and industry basics • Encourage activities outside the family enterprise • Offer dynamic business updates • Provide family employment activities	• Work as painter or equipment operator during the summer at his family's enterprise • Attend a 2-day intrapreneurial program over the summer • Attend an industry association meeting with his mother

	SAMPLE STORIES, EXERCISES AND TOOLS DESCRIBED IN THE CHAPTER	KEY INFLUENCERS	KEY OWNERSHIP TERMS FOR THIS STAGE	THINGS TO WATCH OUT FOR
HOWTO	• A Founder's Mentality in Every Generation • Responding to the Visibility of Wealth • Building a Platform for Listening: Summers with Grammy • Teens Lead Charitable Giving Decisions • Top Eight Stressors for Teens • Create Meaningful Family Time • The Lee Family's Big Move • A Colombian Family's Right of Passage • Building Toilets in Laos-and Other Community-focused Efforts • Build a Strong Family Dynamic • Establishing Clear Boundaries • Prepare Non-family Employees for Youth Involvement • Build Basic Ownership Knowledge for Adolescent Stage • Four Cornerstones of Family Meetings • Sample Family Meeting Agenda for the Adolescent Stage • When to Introduce a Family's Wealth Level • When a Coach is Not a Great Influencer	• Family • Close family friends • Teachers, Coaches, Community and Spiritual leaders • Advisors (internal and external) • Implement regular family governance	• Advisory Board • Board of Directors • Family Governance • Legacy • Owners • Philanthropy • Stewardship	• Failure to engage • Hazardous adult-teen dynamics • The slow life strategy • Senior generation's fear of next gen entitlement

Suggested Additional Readings

10 Ways to Build and Preserve Better Boundaries. (2018, October 8). *Psych central*. https://psychcentral.com/lib/10-way-to-build-and-preserve-better-boundaries.

Aronoff, C., & Ward, J. (2011a). *Family Business Ownership: How to Be An Effective Shareholder (A family Business Publication)* (2nd ed.). Palgrave Macmillan.

Aronoff, C., & Ward, J. (2011b). *Family Meetings: How to Build a Stronger Family and a Stronger Business (A Family Business Publication)* (2nd ed.). Palgrave Macmillan.

Black, J., & Enns, G. (1998). *Better Boundaries: Owning and Treasuring Your Life*. New Harbinger Publications.

Bridges, W. (2004). *Transitions: Making Sense of Life's Changes*. Da Capo Press.

Cloud, H., & Townsend, J. (2017). *Boundaries, Updated and Expanded Edition: When to Say Yes, How to Say No to Take Control of Your Life*. Zondervan.

Damour Ph.D., L. (2016). *Untangled: Guiding Teenage Girls Through the Seven Transitions into Adulthood*. Ballantine Books.

Jensen, F. E., & Nutt, A. E. (2016). *The Teenage Brain: A Neuroscientist's Survival Guide to Raising Adolescents and Young Adults* (Reprint ed.). Harper Paperbacks.

Katherine, A. (2012). *Where to Draw the Line: How to Set Healthy Boundaries Every Day*. Simon and Schuster.

Levine Ph.D., M. (2006). *The Price of Privilege: How Parental Pressure and Material Advantage Are Creating a Generation of Disconnected and Unhappy kids* (1st ed.). Harper.

Linden, A. (2008). *Boundaries in Human Relationships: How to Be Separate and Connected*. Crown House Publishing.

Rothenburg, A. (2016). *Adolescence and creativity*. https://www.psychologytoday.com/us/blog/creative-explorations/201611/adolescence-and-creativity.

Stovall, J. (1999). *The Ultimate Gift* (Second printing). Executive Books.

Twenge Ph.D., J. M. (2017). iGen: *Why Today's Super-Connected Kids Are Growing Up Less Rebellious, More Tolerant, Less Happy and Completely Unprepared for Adulthood*. Simon & Schuster.

Williams, R., & Preisser, V. (2010). *Preparing Heirs: Five Steps to a Successful Transition of Family Wealth and Values* (1st ed.). Robert D. Reed Publishers.

4

Family Enterprise Participation Without Expectation: Emerging Adults (Ages 18 to 28)

W. Sage-Hayward et al., *Own It!*, A Family Business Publication,
https://doi.org/10.1007/978-3-030-20419-8_4

Zak and Zoe—Emerging Adult Stage

Zak and Zoe, our young, prospective family enterprise owners, are growing up. Both are in their early twenties now and attending college. Zak is studying engineering with a minor in business. Zoe is a finance major.

Their family businesses—both farming-related—are changing too. Zak's has doubled in size but is struggling to keep up with demand. Hiring capable employees has been especially difficult, and Zak's parents have been urging him to finish his studies quickly—or even drop out—so he can help with the business.

Zoe's family enterprise has also grown substantially. Some of her cousins are now employed in the business. Her family hasn't prepared for their entrance and there are no related policies. The challenges of understanding and managing the growing range of interests and abilities among the next generation has created tensions in the business and among family. Zoe heard from her cousins that their day-to-day roles in the business are stressful. This pressure, coupled with Zoe's passion for the environment, has fueled her intention to start her own business in sustainable small-scale organic farming. She has been inspired by the family enterprise but doesn't necessarily want to be part of it full-time.

"We Ride at Dawn": The Senft Family's Development Approach

"It's about making the *effort* roll, not the *honor* roll," Lauren Senft says.

Lauren, now 33, is a second-generation member of a Vancouver-based family that owns Tricor Pacific Capital. She explains her family's proactive approach to develop herself and her two siblings as owners from the time they reached young adulthood. The "effort-versus-honor roll" concept, which is a willingness to work hard is more important than the outcome, is an example of the values that founders Jeannie and Rod Senft sought to instill. Other values include the idea that the family is "stronger together than apart," and the family motto "We ride at dawn"—to emphasize that everyone has to show up ready to engage and participate, no matter how late they stayed up the night before.

Beyond passing on key values in this way, the Senfts engaged in multiple other ownership development activities. For example, they started holding family meetings when Lauren turned 21 to familiarize the next generation with governance processes and help them find their voice when it came to issues such as family employment. Similarly, the family attended multiple education programs together at Harvard University and other organizations focused on professional and personal development such as Landmark Forum. "It wasn't all easy and definitely involved some stress," Lauren says, "but we gained so much from taking part in those and became closer as a family." Derek, the Senft's middle son, suggests ownership development starting in the emerging adult stage offered several distinct advantages for their family, including increased engagement, greater attunement to family business concepts and strategies, and an elevated quality to their communication. Derek offers some sage advice for families: "Be proactive and also patient. You need to be intentional about ownership development—have a plan, look for opportunities to create exposure to the business, and practice through discussion and debate. But recognize that family business is a long game. Don't rush development. Finally, work on your communication as a team and make sure you have a way to understand each other."

The Senft family exemplifies a thoughtful, intentional approach to building an owner's mindset in family enterprise members during their emerging adult years. This chapter is about maximizing ownership development in this stage.

The Emerging Adult Stage (Ages 18 to 28) and Why It Matters

By "emerging adult," we mean current and future family enterprise owners about ages 18 to 28. Most will already be in college, have graduated, or may have begun their working life. This is a critical time for ownership development, as individuals, the family, and the whole enterprise can be affected by developmental changes typical in this stage, such as:

- *The window of focus on the nuclear family is closing.* Most young adults still feel a sense of belonging to their originating family, whether voiced or not. But unlike in earlier stages, that connection is likely waning as the individual prepares to leave the family home or has already been living independently. It's important to take advantage of this remaining closer connection to the nuclear family to further ownership development. Our view is primarily shaped by a Northern American/European perspective, where young adults become independent from their families earlier. Promoting independence in this stage is not the end goal, but more an intermediate objective. Ultimately, the goal is families with interdependent relationships where everyone's needs are considered. Making sure emerging adults become able to take care of themselves is, therefore, a required intermediary step.

- *Family roles and relationships are changing.* Shifts in family dynamics can be dramatic in this stage. For example, parents become empty nesters as their children transition into adulthood. Tensions may escalate as both parents and their offspring learn new roles, responsibilities, and boundaries.[1] Conflict often arises around issues of authority and independence, as those early in this stage can think and act as adults but usually remain economically dependent on their parents, who may want some say in the children's decisions ranging from education to housing to dating. Money can become a significant stressor, too, as grown children are expected to become more financially independent.

- *It's a time of self-discovery.* Most young adults embark on a journey of self-discovery to understand who they are across dimensions.[2] They say goodbye to the comforts and constraints of childhood and over time, take on adult responsibilities. This inevitably involves separating from the family to develop their individual identity. Many in this stage feel like they are "sort of" adults but not fully so. Some reject being an owner or employee in their family's business, as they want to make their own way in the world. This rejection can have a very negative and personal impact on the incumbent generation. However, many such reluctant young adults later return to the family business with greater confidence and skills that contribute to value creation for their enterprise. Gentle persistence, combined with invitations to participate in meaningful developmental experiences, can be an effective approach. At this stage, the founder's vision and personality can be sources of inspiration or become a "black hole," as discussed in the box "When the Founder's Vision Becomes a Black Hole." Later we'll discuss how these dynamics make it critical to involve individuals beyond the nuclear family in development, such as extended family members and non-family executives.

---

[1] For a contemporary take on parents and emerging adults, see Arnett. J. J., & Fishel, E. (2014). *Getting to 30: A parent's guide to the 20-something years* (Reprint ed.). Workman Publishing Company.

[2] Much of our thinking around developmental stages is shaped by the work of Erik Erikson, specifically his framework of age-related identity conflicts. Young adults tend to be dealing with two specific conflicts: identity vs. role confusion, and intimacy vs. isolation. Both are reflected heavily in the differentiation process, as young adults in family enterprise deal with anxiety about who they are and how they fit into different social systems including the family, enterprise, and others. See Erikson, E. H. (1993). *Childhood and Society* (Reissue ed.). W. W. Norton.

WHEN THE FOUNDER'S VISION BECOMES A BLACK HOLE

The dream and entrepreneurship of the founder generation can be a source of inspiration for rising generations—or a black hole that rules out other visions and career or lifestyle options.* Sometimes this black hole is obvious, such as when second-generation members are told they *must* join the family enterprise or risk losing future ownership. But it can also be more subtle. Sometimes the founder's powerful vision and energy simply inhibit the development of the rising generation as individuals and as a team. Then, when the time comes to function without the founder, the next generation lacks the skill or capacities to lead the business or make decisions together. Another subtle impact of the founder's vision is when well-meaning family and friends tell rising generation members they are just like their father. Family members who bask in this comparison as young people often question their connections later in life, asking, "Was this really the ideal place for me or am I here because I took on my family's dream and didn't explore other options?" The goal should be to create an open environment for rising members to make career and lifestyle decisions. That means being honest about expectations, providing opportunities for pressure-free exposure to the enterprise, and understanding that visions and goals often change dramatically in the emerging adult stage and beyond. Even the most basic conversations in this stage can shed much-needed light on a potential black hole represented by founders' visions or expectations.

*For more on this idea, see Hughes, J. E., Jr., Massenzio, S. E., & Whitaker, K. (2014). *The voice of the rising generation: Family wealth and wisdom* (Bloomberg) (1st ed.). Wiley.

- *Launching a career.* During this stage of life, most young adults are launching their careers. Some are doing this within their family enterprise, which can mean an extra level of intensity around performance expectations. Others are agonizing over whether to work in the family business or elsewhere. Still, others find work further afield to nurture their independence and interests. When designing development activities, keep in mind that anxiety and stress accompany starting a career. Where possible, make the activities relevant to young adults' work environment and role even if it is outside the family enterprise.
- *The neuroscience of young adulthood.* Research suggests our prefrontal cortex becomes complete around age 25.[3] That means our ability to inhibit ourselves and control impulses on multiple levels may not be completely developed until later in the emerging adult stage. That's a mixed bag for ownership development. For example, it can mean that young adults are more innovation-minded and less bound by conventional norms and can contribute inventive ideas. However, they also may have poor impulse control and be less able to put the brakes on their behavior.

---

[3] For more on brain development progression and consequences see Aamodt, S., & Wang, S. (2009). *Welcome to your brain: Why you lose your car keys but never forget how to drive and other puzzles of everyday life.* Bloomsbury.

The general idea is not to be discouraged by negative expressions from prospective future owners in this stage. This rejection is a normal part of human development. Instead, create space for connections and learning while enabling emerging adults to explore and express their independence. The goal is to help them understand that the door to involvement in the enterprise is open and that there are many paths through that door for eventual contribution.

Central Theme: The Challenges of Millennials and iGen

Given the social and cultural context in which this book is written, we need to point out particular challenges family enterprise members who fall into millennial (born 1981–1996) or iGen[4] cohorts (born 1997–2012) may face as emerging adults.

While any emerging adults face stress as they gain self-awareness and independence, millennials and iGens have to deal with additional dynamics, largely because they are the first generations to have grown up or experienced emerging adulthood in the Digital Age, including the influence of smart- phones and social media. Millennials, for example, are observed to prefer causes over cash, such as choosing a job that makes a difference instead of a large salary, or donating money to important causes even when on limited incomes.[5] They also face many of the same challenges as their later-born counterparts, iGen. This latter cohort has been associated with trends including rising rates of anxiety, depression and suicide, lower rates of dating and teen pregnancy, and less interest or movement toward independence—or what could be considered the responsibilities of adulthood, such as securing a driver's license or moving out of the house.[6]

Some see over-immersion in digital pursuits—online games, social media, popular sites like Reddit—as the source of these trends. Our goal is to highlight the anxiety, uncertainty, and stress these cohorts face. Anyone thinking about an emerging adult's development as owners needs to understand this

---

[4] Twenge, J. M. (2017). *The 10 trends shaping today's young people—And the nation*. Atria Books.

[5] See for example Gay, W. (2017, August 14). Millennials are effecting change with social responsibility. *Forbes*. https://www.forbes.com/sites/wesgay/2017/08/11/millennials-social-responsibility/#f71fc8d17d88.

[6] Many articles and books have been written about these and other trends in Gen Z (or what some call iGen). For more on the specific effects of smartphones and social media on this cohort, see Twenge, J. M. (2018, March 19). Have smartphones destroyed a generation? *The Atlantic*. https://www.theatlantic.com/magazine/archive/2017/09/has-the-smartphone-destroyed-a-generation/534198/.

greater context and approach it with empathy and thoughtfulness, while not enabling.

This context is especially true for older generations. The challenge we see repeatedly is that parents expect their children to be "like them," to have the same interests, aspirations, and goals. That approach fails to consider the broader context in which millennial and iGen family members must navigate the world and make choices. Seek to maintain sensitivity to these unique challenges as both ownership-development content and the process by which it is delivered is chosen. Don't sugarcoat, but communicate with care, empathy, and sensitivity.

Development Goals

We start, again, with "the end in mind" in any development stage. For this age range, consider these goals for developing an owner's mindset in emerging adults (Exhibit 4.1).

Exhibit 4.1 Owner's Mindset: Development Goals for Emerging Adults

OWNER'S MINDSET: DEVELOPMENT GOALS FOR EMERGING ADULTS	
AREA	**DEVELOPMENTAL GOALS**
INDIVIDUAL	• **Promote learning and education:** of an undergraduate degree, certification in a specific area or vocational training in an area of interest or passion • **Foster individuation:** ensure emerging adults develop a sense for who they are and what matters to them and how to put these into action within and outside the family • **Facilitate independence:** grow the ability to take care of one's own needs, finding solutions to challenges, and assuming responsibility for one's decisions while considering impacts on both people and their environment

FAMILY	• **Promote an understanding of the "I-We-It" trade-offs:** learning how decisions made within the family affect the individual (I), the family (We), and the enterprise (It)
	
	• **Advance teamwork capabilities:** As part of a rising team of owners, emerging adults need to advance their relational skills:
	    – Collaborative problem-solving
	    – Trust building
	    – Framing and reframing
	    – Reactivity management (how to contain and avoid disruptive emotional reactions)
	
	• **Redefine 'family':** The definition of 'who we are as a family' requires reflection and dialogue as they move into being a family of adults and away from the parent-child dynamic of the past

OWNERSHIP	• **Advance understanding of the "technical" aspects of ownership:** Including ownership and business structures, trusts, estate plans, prenuptial agreements, voting rights and business and family governance bodies and processes • **Foster responsibility and sense of stewardship:** Developing skills to care for and manage assets for future generations • **Promote financial literacy:** Furthering knowledge and understanding of reading and asking questions about business results including but not limited to financial performance

OWNER'S MINDSET: DEVELOPMENT GOALS FOR EMERGING ADULTS	
AREA	**DEVELOPMENTAL GOALS**
BUSINESS / INDUSTRY	• **Explore career interests and opportunities:** Post completion of education, promote a thorough exploration of goals, strengths and passion to find work interests that resonate and provide fulfillment • **Continue to build on knowledge of business and its industry:** Start at the appropriate level based on skill and education if working in the business; if not, then learning about the core functions of the business (e.g., operations, marketing, and the like) • **Foster personal leadership skills:** Set a direction and destination for your life and learning that good leadership consists first of learning to follow

How-Tos

The ideas here represent a strategic and intentional approach to developing an owner's mindset in emerging adults that will pay off in the short and long term.

- *Promote independence and accountability*: Steps to promote independence and accountability go a long way to helping young adults understand and move toward their personal and career goals (see the box, "Create a Culture of Accountability," for more on this idea).

CREATE A CULTURE OF ACCOUNTABILITY

Wealth brings great opportunity and high risk. Some first-generation wealthy families don't want their children to experience the pains they did, such as growing up poor or hungry. They also live in a world where generosity is often highly valued, which promotes giving generously to others including children without necessarily considering how accountability fits in. These two factors combine to create a parenting dilemma which frequently results in the thing parents fear most: entitlement. Instead, when parents foster a culture of accountability, it results in the following benefits for their young adult children:

- Greater self-confidence and the belief in their own capability
- Preparation for the demands of adulthood
- An ability to learn from their mistakes
- Increased personal satisfaction in life and with themselves
- Collaboration as part of a family of equals (i.e., rather than operating within a hierarchy based on power)

Without accountability, family members don't take responsibility for their actions, and instead blame others or find ways to justify their behavior when breaking the spoken or unspoken "rules." Accountability means every family member is responsible for their own actions and behaviors, including their reactions to stressful and difficult situations. Steps families take to build a sense of accountability in young adults include the following:

- Establishing agreed-upon expectations for interaction with one another (i.e., a code of conduct)
- Applying policies consistently to all family members
- Accessing wealth based upon completion of agreed-upon targets rather than age (e.g., taking an investment course, fully engaging in regular family governance, and so on)
- Handling their own bill payments, such as for cell phones and car insurance (rather than covering them through their company)
- Creating their own relationship with a financial advisor to build financial literacy
- Setting and measuring individual and collective goals (e.g., personal: saving to buy a car or finishing a real estate program; ownership: donating to a local charity of their choice)
- Acknowledging and celebrating achievements
- Adhering to a budget
- Giving a presentation on learning and takeaways gained from attending a family enterprise conference

---

Living on one's own, managing a budget (see "Zak's University Budget" in Exhibit 4.2 for a sample budget of a young adult enrolled in an out-of-state college), building relationships with professional service providers (e.g., financial planners, accountants, health professionals), and pursuing educational, career, and social opportunities will inevitably yield greater self- awareness.

Exhibit 4.2 Zak's University Budget

ZAK'S UNIVERSITY BUDGET		
LIVING EXPENSES	**MONTHLY COST**	**TOTAL ANNUAL COST**
Rent (12 months)	$720	$8,640
Telephone (12 months)	$65	$780
Groceries (8 months)	$800	$6,400
Clothing and Laundry (8 months)	$200	$1,600
Personal Spending (8 months)	$200	$1,600
Recreation/Entertainment (8 months)	$250	$2,000
Local Transportation (8 months)	$75	$600
Return Trips Home (3)		$3,600
TOTAL EXPENSES	**$2,310**	**$25,220**

In too many family enterprises, rising-generation members have never had to manage their own lives or finances—well into their thirties and forties—which stunts development and leads to ownership and succession challenges. Remember that future ownership could take the form of a beneficiary owner—someone who receives benefits from a trust that is administered by a trustee. The risk associated with this type of ownership is that it may inhibit the rising generation from managing their own finances. Teaching beneficiaries to have an owner's mindset can help them take a more active role in meaningfully contributing to the administration of the trust.

For an example of how one family enterprise promoted financial responsibility see the box, "How Zak Learned to Manage Money."

HOW ZAK LEARNED TO MANAGE MONEY
Zak remembers how his parents helped him appreciate the value of money when he did not stick to his budget during his first year of university. "Just before college, my parents gave me a credit card to use for necessities but made clear I couldn't spend above a certain limit. It was my first time with that kind of financial freedom, so I went a little overboard in the early months and passed the limit they'd set, buying clothes and college memorabilia, going out with my friends, and a bunch of frivolous stuff. My parents said they would pay the extra amount, but that I had to work it off by doing household chores in the summer. They created fees for different items such as cleaning the garage or walking our dogs — and they definitely didn't overpay! Those summer months of working hard around the house to pay for a bunch of things I didn't really need made me much more careful about spending. Even today, I still ask myself, 'Is this purchase worth the work?' for almost anything I want to buy but don't necessarily need."

- *Encourage travel*: Seeing how other people live helps to promote self-awareness, open-mindedness, and empathy. Domestic and foreign travel is an effective way to gain such perspective, whether as part of a formal program—such as a university foreign exchange opportunity—or a self-guided journey. Encourage young adults in the family enterprise to see a broad range of cultures, value systems, and socioeconomic levels, to experience and understand life situations very different from their own. For example, Zak's parents, through a connection with a close friend, set up an informal exchange program with a family in France with three sons. Zak visited Versailles for three weeks each summer, and the boys from the exchange family came to the United States for two weeks each summer over a three-year period. This exchange created a bond among the boys that still lasts today and impacted family dynamics. Zak came back the first summer, praising the value of cooking together as a family, which he did with his French counterparts for several hours every evening. Prior to that experience, Zak viewed eating more like a fuel intake process that occurred between activities than a valuable way to spend time with family.
- *Attend family enterprise education programs and conferences*: Many formal educational programs speak specifically to family enterprise needs related to governance, leadership, and rising generation issues. Some of these may be sponsored or offered by the family itself, but others take place at venues including universities, family business associations, and advisory firms. Many emerging adults benefit from these programs. We suggest approaching them strategically, such as setting criteria for participation (e.g., age, education level, interest in the family enterprise), and pairing senior and junior family members to attend together. Requiring attendees to present their learnings to family members can provide an opportunity to share lessons across the family and to cement the learnings in the presenter. Family business members often come back "guns blazing" from such programs, with enthusiasm for driving change on every level. One of the great benefits of attending these conferences over time is the possibility to join different organizing committees and foster leadership skills among peers while being exposed to more learning.
- *Establish clear family governance policies—including premarital agreements*: Having clear, logical family policies in place for everything from family employment (criteria for family members to work in the family business) to marriage agreements is critical for ownership development. Clarity on family policies communicates the importance of family involvement and helps to prevent feelings of unfairness, such as when one branch appears to get priority for involvement in the business or board. The *process of*

setting family policies can be a great way to promote greater learning and involvement among members of every generation and to ensure their voices are heard (see the box Family Governance for a sample list of family governance policy topics to consider).

SAMPLE LIST OF FAMILY GOVERNANCE POLICY TOPICS

- Code of Conduct
- Confidentiality/Privacy
- Conflict Resolution
- Decision-making
- Education Funding
- Expense Reimbursement
- Family Council Charter
- Family Discounts
- Family Heirlooms
- Family Law Agreements (e.g., prenuptial agreement)
- Family Vision, Mission, & Values
- Help in Crises
- Social Media

Premarital agreements are major topics for business families and potential sources of conflict and tension. Even raising the idea can be more challenging than the issue of confidentiality, as most family members will agree on the latter. The box "Pierre and the Prenuptial" provides an example of one family's experience when they didn't have a clear policy.

PIERRE AND THE PRENUPTIAL

When 28-year-old "Pierre," the oldest fifth-generation cousin in a 120-year-old U.S. manufacturing business, eloped with his longtime girlfriend, it set off an ownership crisis. Pierre's parents, and some other members of the generation with controlling interest, discovered the new marital status and mandated that all cousins in Pierre's generation commit to signing prenuptial agreements and completing estate plans. This command escalated tensions across the family, pitting generations against each other. While this example, based on a real-life incident, may be extreme, it highlights how important it is for emerging adults to take their participation in the family enterprise into account when making major life decisions. In addition, while each family arrives at their own policy decisions, fostering open dialogue about these matters, ideally well before they are actually needed, is best. Making uncomfortable subjects into taboo topics (as many families do) results in someone forcing the issue, as Pierre did.

Here is an example of how a family enterprise member could tactfully raise the idea of a prenuptial or similar agreement with a significant other to promote understanding and openness. Timing for this conversation is crucial;

ideally, it should happen before any members of the rising generation start dating in a serious way.

> "There is a sensitive topic I would like to talk about with you which can affect several people including us. One of the things that has brought us together is our devotion to family. As you know, our family business is likely going to be passed down to my siblings and me. Since it will be a shared asset, my family has implemented a policy that helps maintain those assets for future generations within our family. Therefore, we and other members of the family need to get a prenuptial agreement. This type of agreement is not only useful for me, but for you too. It's aimed at ensuring that everyone, including spouses, can be properly taken care of, without compromising the company or shared asset. This is a complex topic and also time-sensitive. But I'm confident that if we start talking about it openly, we can find an optimal way to develop an agreement that meets the family's expectations as well as our shared priorities for one another."

The above speaks to the importance of a proactive approach to expectations-setting, but also normalizes some of the challenges family enterprise owners face. Taking the time up front will help significant others understand how some decisions related to work, money, and children will likely be influenced by the family. It also clearly demonstrates that they are valued as new members of the family. This can go a long way to building stronger long-term bonds.

- *Manage Fiscal Inequality*: In 2016, Boston Consulting Group found that women held more than 31 percent of the private wealth in the world.[7] TD Ameritrade, in 2020, found that nearly a third of millennials believe that the more money you contribute to the relationship, the more say you should have over spending decisions.[8] The control of income and wealth are shifting among genders and generations. Also, gender identity norms impact marriage relationships. Some research suggest that when a wife earns more than the husband, a couple is less satisfied with their marriage and is more likely to divorce.[9] Like premarital agreements, dealing with these complex realities of differential income and wealth within relationships is tricky. However, families should discuss these topics that impact

[7] Zakrzewski, A. (2020, August 21). Managing the next decade of women's wealth. *BCG Global*. https://www.bcg.com/publications/2020/managing-next-decade-women-wealth.

[8] The Harris Poll on behalf of TD Ameritrade. (2020). Breadwinners Survey. https://s2.q4cdn.com/437609071/files/doc_news/research/2020/breadwinners-survey.pdf.

[9] Bertrand, M., Kamenica, E., & Pan, E. (2015). Gender identity and relative income within households. *The Quarterly Journal of Economics, 130*(2), 571–614.

family members. There are also some helpful practices to address these issues, including adding the topic of differential wealth to married-in onboarding programs and regularly making time during family meetings for discussions about money and decision-making rights around assets only one spouse inherits.[10]

- *Facilitate self-awareness and self-discovery*: Simple assessment tools are an effective way to increase self-awareness by highlighting strengths and areas of development. These tools can be used individually or with the ownership group as a whole. Typical tools include emotional intelligence and communication or conflict style inventories. Of course, some assessment tools are great, others are less reliable. Even with a very reputable tool, it's important to see this information as only one data point. We recommend avoiding use of these tools to over-categorize people or reduce them to an acronym. In general, we recommend working with an advisor certified in a given tool to insure the assessments are applied appropriately. (See the box, "A Sampling of Self-Awareness Tools," for tools used in family enterprise ownership development).

A SAMPLING OF SELF-AWARENESS TOOLS

- **Benchmarks:** Leadership skills assessment
- **DiSC Assessment:** Behavioral assessment
- **Emotional Intelligence Inventory** (EQ-i): Social and emotional intelligence assessment
- **Enneagram:** Personality type assessment
- Fundamental Interpersonal Relations Orientation-Behavior (FIRO-B): Interpersonal behaviors assessment
- **Hermann Brain Dominance Instrument** (HBDI): Thinking preferences assessment
- **Kolbe Index:** Assesses how people prefer to take action
- **Insights Discovery Styles:** Personality type assessment
- **Leadership Practices Inventory** (LPI): Leadership behaviors assessment
- **Myers-Briggs Type Indicator** (MBTI): Psychological preferences and tendencies assessment
- **Thomas-Kilmann Conflict Mode Instrument** (TKI): Conflict type assessment
- **Via:** Character strength assessment

- *Join industry or family business associations*: Getting involved in industry associations is a valuable way for young adults to "get their feet wet," secure important resources, network, and shape their future plans. Family business associations can also help young adult members learn about family

---

[10] Keffeler, K., Hughes, W., & Iglehart, A. (2020). When she has the money: Challenging ancient conventions and supporting the new normal. *Family Enterprise Xchange.* https://family-enterprise-xch ange.com/res/pub/docs/2017Symposium/FromFiscalUnequalsToFinancialDiversity.pdf.

enterprise dynamics, network with peers, and see examples of how current and future owners sought opportunities to contribute within and outside the enterprise. In one business family, the patriarch and founder died suddenly, and his son left his job to help run the family's retail business. One of the most helpful ways the son got up to speed about the new industry was by joining an industry association. He attended monthly events and interacted with a range of owners and operators, gaining knowledge and connections.

- *Join peer groups*: Meeting with peers from other family enterprises is helpful to young adult owners or prospective owners. It provides an opportunity to share stories and experiences that foster empathy, insights, and provide a better understanding of life in a family enterprise. Peer groups normalize the experience and reduce judgment associated with being part of a privileged family. They also provide leadership opportunities (such as leading peer group thinking or event-planning) outside the family for becoming more capable, confident leaders within and outside the enterprise. (For a discussion on how to get the most from peer groups read Chapter 6.)
- *Create a personal mission statement*: A personal mission statement can serve as a sort of North Star for emerging adults as they develop their passion, interests, and goals and helps other family members understand these better. The box "Create a Personal Mission Statement" provides pointers on how to create one.

CREATE A PERSONAL MISSION STATEMENT
Personal effectiveness expert Stephen Covey refers to developing a mission statement as "connecting with your own unique purpose and the profound satisfaction that comes from fulfilling it." A personal mission statement helps identify what is important to you and provides direction for your life. Here is a simple formula for starting a personal mission statement:
Step 1: Identify Past Successes. Identify four or five areas in which you have had personal success in recent years. These successes could be at school, work, in your community, within your nuclear or extended family, or elsewhere. Try to identify whether there is a common theme (or themes).
Step 2: Identify Core Values. Develop a list of attributes that you believe distinguish who you are and what your priorities are. The list can be as long as you need. If your family has already done a values identification exercise, you might start with that list and expand as needed. Once your list is complete, see if you can narrow your values down to five or six of the most important ones. Finally, see if you can choose the one value most significant to you. There are online aids that provide assessments and values lists that can provide a way to get this step started (e.g., Barrett Values Center https://www.valuescentre.com/tools-assessments/pva/).

Step 3: Identify Contributions.
Make a list of the ways you could make a difference. In an ideal situation, how could you contribute best to:
    • The world in general
    • Your nuclear and extended families
    • Your employer or future employers
    • Your friends
    • Your business, as an owner
    • The community

Step 4: Identify Goals. Spend some time thinking about your priorities in life and the goals you have for yourself. Make a list of your objectives, in the short term (up to three years) and the long term (beyond three years).
Step 5: Write Mission Statement. Based on the first four steps and a better understanding of yourself, begin writing your personal mission statement

- *Work within or outside the family business*: The family business can provide excellent professional development opportunities through internships, entry-level roles, or full-time positions, as long as they are actually needed in the organization and the next generation member is qualified. There is an inherent benefit in having family members work in the enterprise. They learn values and culture while building familiarity and, often, an emotional connection to the business. Middle management positions are an excellent way to observe and learn about the organization, including its market, customers, and dynamics within the company. Although these roles are often underestimated, they are valuable opportunities to build experience and relationships with employees while developing leadership skills and earning respect from colleagues. Aligning a position with an emerging adult's experience is very important. For example, giving well-qualified young adults a lower level of responsibilities would likely be demotivating, such as when someone with years of experience with outside companies is asked to start at the bottom rung of the corporate ladder to avoid the perception of nepotism. We recommend that structuring any opportunities with clear responsibilities and expected outcomes to maintain consistency and quality while promoting accountability. Some family enterprises have a long tradition of requiring rising members to work outside the family business before joining it. Such outside experience helps emerging adults "prove" themselves in an organization that doesn't bear their last name. This approach engenders confidence and credibility along with valuable skills and knowledge (industry, functional, and interpersonal). Working elsewhere also provides development time away from the shadow of strong personalities, which fosters greater independence and self-confidence. Whether someone should work outside or within the business first requires evaluating the needs of the younger family members, as well as the business.

- *Participate in enterprise governance*: Emerging adults can benefit from involvement in multiple aspects of governance, typically with a focus on *family* governance rather than the business board variety. This could involve serving on a family council or similar group, participating on a committee within that council (such as an education committee), or simply being included in shareholder meetings. Ideally, rising family members can help decide education topics to prioritize and deliver. Some families create board observer positions to expose members to the business board. The best approach is for families to develop guidelines on how members can become involved based on their age, education, or work experience.

- *Seek community service opportunities*: Community service can be an important part of development. It provides an opportunity to give back and see the problems of other people, which can promote greater self-awareness and empathy. Many family enterprises have private family foundations or participate in charitable activities, which are a good place to start. Becoming a coach or mentor within the community by working with younger kids through charitable activities or sports is another powerful opportunity to build leadership skills as well.

- *Seek mentorship*: Emerging adults learn from mentors, including those outside the family enterprise. A mentoring relationship is among the most important for human development, as it is meant to guide, through a dialogue and powerful questions, the mentees to "find those answers that will most enhance their self-awareness in their journey in pursuit of happiness." (Hughes, p. 166). A mentor differs from a coach, as the latter's mission is to develop skills and practices in the less experienced, while the mentor is engaged in a mutual learning process impacting both mentor and mentee self-awareness.[11] Young adults will benefit from hearing insights from those outside the system(s) who have undergone their own developmental journey, potentially including members of other family enterprises. Seek to promote such relationships without forcing them. Emerging adults are sometimes more willing to hear input from external mentors. Exhibit 4.3 highlights the benefits and challenges of using family members versus non-family members as mentors.

Exhibit 4.3 Benefits and Challenges of Different Mentor Types

BENEFITS AND CHALLENGES OF DIFFERENT MENTOR TYPES		
	FAMILY MEMBER MENTOR	NON-FAMILY MEMBER MENTOR
BENEFITS	• Able to provide guidance on ownership and leadership • Opportunity to learn from life experience in the business • Ability to pass on the family's value system and ethics	• Shares a different way to view the world than family • No family bias • Less emotional • Could have greater credibility
CHALLENGES	• A family member may lack skill to be a good mentor • Potential for unbalanced perspective • Disagreement between mentee and mentor could lead to family tension • Mentorship relationship can be affected negatively by political environment of family	• Pressure on non-family manager to report back to family • Difficulty giving tough feedback for fear of job security • May not be as strong on the core values of family

Sample Development Plan: Emerging Adult

Scenario: Zak is now a university student studying engineering and business administration. He has rented a house with six friends for this school year. His parents are providing him with a monthly budget he manages on his own and a first-time credit card (as presented earlier, in section "How-Tos"). Exhibit 4.4 illustrates a sample development plan based on the topics discussed in this chapter.

---

[11] For a deeper explanation about mentorship and the difference with other important guiding roles, see Hughes, J. E., Jr. (2010). *Family wealth: Keeping it in the family* (Vol. 34). Wiley.

Exhibit 4.4 Owner's Mindset: Sample Development Plan for an Emerging Adult (Zak)

SAMPLE DEVELOPMENT PLAN FOR AN EMERGING ADULT (ZAK)	
AREA	**DEVELOPMENTAL ACTIVITIES**
INDIVIDUAL	• Move into a house for the first time with friends. • Create budget for food, car, and general living expenses in addition to rent money. • Have a first credit card, with a limit of $500. He must pay the monthly balance off himself, within his budget. • Learn to balance food shopping, cooking, cleaning, and going to school for the first time. • Make time to for interests such as art and squash • Plan independent travel, with the goal of expanding perspectives by seeing new places and cultures; share details of the experience with the family, including lessons learned.
FAMILY	• Share a house with friends; have house meetings to sort out issues such as cleaning the house and sharing food. • Mom and Dad discuss with Zak his first serious girlfriend and the ground rules when they travel with the family for spring break. • Attend two family meetings during the year (July and December). • Plan an event with one senior generation member (e.g., concert or play) to create intergenerational bonds • Explain the value of spending time during breaks and holidays with siblings and cousins to stay in touch and stay updated on each other's lives. • Take on the responsibility to organize one of the family vacations, within a budget and in collaboration with a member of the previous generation.
OWNERSHIP	• Learn from parents' review of financial statements at annual general shareholders meeting. • Takes on the task, with cousins, of organizing a learning event over the summer for the annual general shareholder meeting. • Observes a foundation board meeting. • Selects the personal cause of Alzheimer's (because his grandmother suffers from it) to target for his annual donation; also attends Alzheimer organization's annual gala event and does the local Alzheimer's Walk with his family.
BUSINESS / INDUSTRY	• Complete a bachelor's degree in engineering with minor in business. • Secure a summer co-op position at a local firm and discuss learning objectives in advance with mentor. • Attend one or two Next Gen events run by a local advising firm or university-based center, with access to a national peer group. • Participate in quarterly calls with financial planner to review personal finances and build financial literacy. • Review or create a family bank policy.

The sample development plan is offered as an example only and includes a variety of ideas—some of which you may already do in the normal course of development in your family. Our goal is to inspire you to take a more intentional approach to development by building a coordinated plan for your family appropriate to your specific circumstance and context.

Development Influencers

Development opportunities can and should be shaped by a wide range of people within and outside the family and the enterprise. Think about people from the groups that follow as potential coaches, mentors, informal advisors, or general supporters for young adults.

- *Parents*. Parents are often the largest, most positive influences on development in this stage but also the most unwanted! Approaching the parent-child relationship with care, recognizing it is actively moving to an adult-to-adult dynamic, and giving space to grow are critical elements for getting parental influence right. Ideally, parents can serve as important providers of inspiration, influence, and information, while encouraging the next generation to pursue outside development opportunities.
- *Extended family members*. These can be the "secret weapons" of development at this stage, as young adults may be more willing to listen to extended family members than to parents, even if the messages delivered are similar. After all, as the joke goes, there's a reason grandparents and grandkids get along so well: they share a common enemy! Peers, especially older siblings or cousins, can be valuable partners on the development journey, as they have likely faced the same questions and decision points as those in young adulthood, including finding their potential role or contribution within the enterprise. Aunts, uncles, and in-laws may also be important influencers in this stage, so look for opportunities to promote communication between young adults and these relatives, such as through family reunions, shareholder meetings, or other events. Note that regardless of the influencer, it's especially important for family branches to communicate the same messages to young adults. For example, if one branch communicates that the family employment policy is unimportant, this can cause tension with other branches and across the system in general. See the box, "Alice's Unexpected Inspiration," for details on how a young family enterprise member was influenced by her grandfather.

ALICE'S UNEXPECTED INSPIRATION

"Alice," a third-generation member of a South America-based import business, faced a challenge. She had to secure approval for transportation of high-priced items into the country and struggled to get in touch with the officials responsible because of office closures, red tape, and other barriers. Thinking about the problem, Alice remembered stories she'd heard from her grandfather, the business founder, who'd died when she was still a teenager. Quick-thinking and resourceful, he had always found creative solutions to problems including how to deal with the country's challenging bureaucratic environment. Her grandfather told her with pride about the time he had booked a train ticket in the same car as a government official, to secure a much-needed permit. Inspired, Alice found a way to "accidentally" meet the official in charge of the approval she needed and won the much-needed authorization based on that personal contact. In this way, her departed grandfather indirectly served as a role model who helped accelerate Alice's development in young adulthood.

- *Non-family executives or directors.* Non-family leaders associated with the enterprise are high-potential sources of influence because they know the family intimately but are not formally part of the family. That can take the pressure off the family to provide tough development-related feedback, for example. Whether through formal mentorship programs, board observation, or casual interactions, look for ways to bring emerging adults into contact with these leaders for mutual benefit.
- *Outside advisors and community members.* In the family enterprise space, an increasing number of advisors are providing services related to succession, leadership, and other areas requiring personal development. Beyond family enterprise advisors, there is no shortage of mentors, coaches, teachers, therapists, and others fulfilling development-related roles in the broader community. Create opportunities to promote development through these relationships, as suggested by the box, "Zoe Finds a Money Mentor."

ZOE FINDS A MONEY MENTOR

While still in college, Zoe became interested in personal finance. Her parents were more than willing to help her think about saving, investment, and other financial strategies, but she realized she wanted someone outside the family who could provide a more impartial view. She approached one of her finance professors and offered to do some pro bono research for her in exchange for regular meetings to discuss money management. The arrangement worked very well. Zoe did research on the long-term effects of the Great Recession while hearing her professor's view on personal investing, including as related to stocks, bonds, real estate, and other asset classes. Zoe ended up advising her parents on investments with which they weren't familiar. This afforded her the opportunity to impress them while gaining their confidence about her money management skills.

- *Other entrepreneurs.* Having a network of businesspeople, including other family business owners, to mentor emerging adults can be quite powerful.

Where to Start?

We've offered a great deal of advice and strategies about developing an owner's mindset in emerging adults. But it's dangerous for a family to put too much on the plate of a rising generation family member given what is happening at this stage of their lives. So, where do you start? The general idea is to start where you are but within that context focus on promoting greater independence and resourcefulness.

Parents naturally focus on the collective element of development, wanting to ensure children appreciate the family system and continue being engaged. But this has to be balanced with creating opportunities for independence while communicating that independence and *inter*dependence are not mutually exclusive. It's important to be able to function independently of the family, but also to spend meaningful time together and interact to maintain cohesion in the family.

"Do I really want to be part of the enterprise, and if so, in what capacity?" is an ongoing question for family members in this stage. Helping the rising generation find an answer means not forcing a choice on them, and providing opportunities for greater independence, such as having them travel on their own, attend school away from home, or learn to manage their own money. Recognize also that the balance between independence and interdependence will shift and evolve over time. Emerging adults who state emphatically that at one stage they'd never join the enterprise in any form sometimes see the value of involvement once they experience the real world. It is also important for them to recognize that working with the business is far from the only way to be involved as an owner. Others, who seem committed to being part of the enterprise from an early age, may find the opportunity less lustrous in the face of other choices. Hopefully, by now, it is also clear that there are many ways to be part of an enterprising family and that working in the operating business is only one of many.

The idea is to be focused but flexible while promoting opportunities that foster independence and ensuring emerging adults see the value of remaining connected to the family and enterprise.

Things to Look For

Our discussion so far suggests that promoting an owner's mindset in emerging adults may not be easy. Here are several specific pitfalls to anticipate and avoid.

- *Overdoing it.* "I just want to go to school and hang out with friends, and you want to talk about the business 24–7," one young family enterprise member told his parents at a family meeting. It might be tempting, especially for do-it-all family enterprise owners, to bombard emerging adults with development opportunities, from internships to mentorship to service roles. Instead, you first try to understand your emerging adults' interests, capacity, and willingness to participate. It's perfectly natural for a 20-year-old not to want to observe a board meeting or plan a family reunion. Balance providing opportunities with giving room for independence. Let young adults have a say in what development goals and opportunities they prefer. Present content in an engaging way; strive to create appeal without forcing commitment. Also recognize that some later-generation owners provide too little exposure to the enterprise, making the rising generation wish they'd known more when they were younger. Aim for that tricky balance between too much and too little.
- *Failure to launch.* This is the name given to the collective issues facing emerging adults who fail to assume adult responsibilities such as financial self-sufficiency and independent decision-making. The causes vary and include untreated mental health issues, lack of motivation, and challenging family dynamics. The first step is to distinguish between failure-to-launch issues and more typical young adult challenges. If failure to launch is truly the concern, then setting and managing boundaries and expectations is a critical step. In addition, mental health professionals may also provide support to both the parents and the emerging adult.
- *Failure to appreciate natural developmental stages.* Families, as part of their life cycle, experience developmental stages that naturally either bring members together or take them apart, as shown in Exhibit 4.5.[12] Life stage forces that encourage closer bonds between family members include marriages, childbirth, child-rearing, and grandparenting. However, other stages of family development such as adolescence, mid-life crises, and retirement can cause families to move apart and become more dispersed.

---

[12] For more on this model of family development see Combrinck-Graham, L. E. E. (1985). A developmental model for family systems. *Family Process, 24*(2), 139–150.

Keep these dynamics in mind when considering development to balance fostering independence and interdependence.

Exhibit 4.5 The Family Development Life Cycle

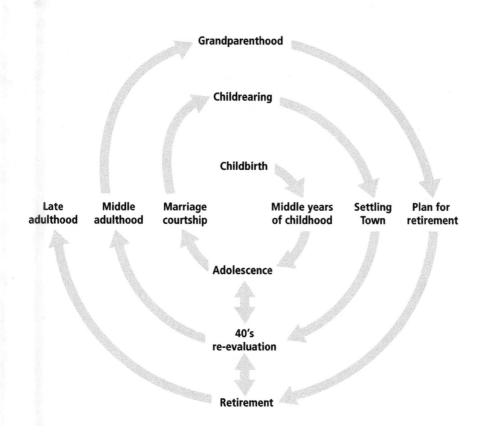

- *Stimulating excessive competition.* Competition is common in families, especially in business families who place a premium on success, including education and business results. While competition may stimulate increased performance, we discourage families from fostering internal competition by comparing children or pitting them against one another for specific roles. Development activities such as pursuing education, professional opportunities, and governance roles can breed the negative variety of competition. It's important that you provide development-related messages about the range of ways in which people with different styles, competences, and interests can participate in the business, governance, philanthropy, or other efforts. Align that message with stated family values of diversity and inclusiveness. Recognize there are multiple forms of intelligence and cele-brate them.[13] But also accept that some roles such as business leadership may be implicitly valued more highly by the family and broader society.

- *Unmanaged expectations.* When a family contemplates the sale of their enterprise, generation members who have been preparing for this role both emotionally and mentally as well as through education and development may be shocked and devasted. The loss of opportunity, shift in direction and goals, and perceived wasted time and energy for a nonexistent future can be traumatic (Hughes, 1999).[14] In these cases, ensuring healthy open dialogue about the sale before, during, and after it occurs is critical for mitigating a negative impact. In addition, helping the rising generation see their preparation for ownership as creating value for their future even though that future may differ from their expectations is paramount.

Strategies on developing an owner's mindset in emerging adults is provided in Exhibit 4.6, the Chapter Summary.

---

[13] See for example Armstrong, T. (1999). *7 kinds of smart: Identifying and developing your multiple intelligences* (Revised, Updated, Subsequent ed.). Plume.

[14] Hughes, J. E., Jr. (1999). A reflection of the sale of a family business as an event of trauma. *The Chase Journal, III*(2).

Exhibit 4.6 Emerging Adult Stage Summary

<table>
<tr><th colspan="2">WHY EMERGING ADULTS STAGE MATTERS</th><th>KEY MESSAGE</th></tr>
<tr><td rowspan="5" style="writing-mode:vertical-lr">WHY</td><td>

- The window of focus on the nuclear family is closing
- Family roles and relationships are changing
- It's a time of self-discovery
- Launching a career adds anxiety and stress
- Young adulthood is a stage that offers greater potential innovation but has lower impulse control
</td><td>The door to involvement in the enterprise is open and, there are many different paths through which next gens can contribute.</td></tr>
</table>

<table>
<tr><th></th><th>DOMAIN</th><th>DEVELOPMENT GOALS</th><th>HOW TOs</th><th>SAMPLE DEVELOPMENT PLAN FOR ZAK</th></tr>
<tr>
<td rowspan="2" style="writing-mode:vertical-lr">WHAT</td>
<td>Individual</td>
<td>

- **Promote learning and education:** of an undergraduate degree, certification in a specific area or vocational training in an area of interest or passion

- **Foster individuation:** ensure emerging adults develop a sense for who they are and what matters to them and how to put these into action within and outside the family

- **Facilitate independence:** grow the ability to take care of one's own needs, finding solutions to challenges, and assuming responsibility for one's decisions while considering impacts on both people and their environment
</td>
<td>

- Encourage travel
- Join peer groups
- Create a personal mission statement
- Seek community service opportunities
- Create accountability
- Facilitate self-awareness & self-discovery
</td>
<td>

- Move into a house for the first time with friends
- Create budget for food, car, and general living expenses in addition to rent money
- Get first credit card, with a limit of $500. Pay the monthly balance off himself, within his budget
- Learn to balance food shopping, cooking, cleaning and going to university for first time
- Make time to for interests such as art and squash
- Plan independent travel, with the goal of expanding perspectives by seeing new places and cultures; share details of the experience with the family including lessons learned
</td>
</tr>
<tr>
<td>Family</td>
<td>

- **Promote an understanding of the "I-We-It" tradeoffs:** learning how decisions made within the family affect the individual (I), the family (We), and the enterprise (It)

- **Advance teamwork capabilities:** As part of a rising team of owners, emerging adults need to advance their relational skills:
  - Collaborative problem-solving
  - Trust building
  - Framing and reframing
  - Reactivity management (how to contain and avoid disruptive emotional reactions)

- **Redefine 'family':** The definition of 'who we are as a family' requires reflection and dialogue as they move into being a family of adults and away from the parent-child dynamic of the past
</td>
<td>

- Attend family enterprise education programs and conferences
- Establish clear family governance policies—including premarital agreements
- Participate in family governance meetings
- Foster a constructive emotional environment by expecting and teaching self-awareness, communication and conflict management skills
</td>
<td>

- Share a house with friends; have house meetings to sort out issues such as cleaning the house and sharing food
- Mom and Dad discuss with Zak his first serious girlfriend and the ground rules when they travel with the family for spring break
- Attend two family meetings during the year (July and December)
- Plan an event with one senior generation member (e.g., concert or play) to create intergenerational bonds
- Plan to attend a family business conference with siblings and cousins to learn about family governance together
- Take on the responsibility to organize one family vacation within a budget and in collaboration with a member of the senior generation
</td>
</tr>
</table>

DOMAIN	DEVELOPMENT GOALS	HOW TOs	SAMPLE DEVELOPMENT PLAN FOR ZAK
Family			• Review and update family code of conduct. Build a policy on getting help during a crisis and sharing/maintaining your recreational property
Ownership	• **Advance understanding of the "technical" aspects of ownership:** Including ownership and business structures, trusts, estate plans, prenuptial agreements, voting rights and business and family governance bodies and processes • **Foster responsibility and sense of stewardship:** Developing skills to care for and manage assets for future generations • **Promote financial literacy:** Furthering knowledge and understanding of reading and asking questions about business results including but not limited to financial performance	• Seek mentorship • Meet and learn from key business and family advisors including attorneys, accountants and other professionals • Seek community service opportunities	• Review corporate structure and financial statements at annual general shareholders meeting • Start a cousin committee responsible for organizing a learning event over the summer for the annual general shareholder meeting (e.g., learn joint decision making) • Observe a foundation board meeting • Select the personal cause of Alzheimer's (because his grandmother suffers from it) to target for his annual donation; also attends Alzheimer organization's annual gala event and does the local Alzheimer's Walk with his family • Participate in quarterly calls with financial planner to review personal finances and build financial literacy • Review or create a family bank policy
Business/ Industry	• **Explore career interests and opportunities:** Post completion of education, promote a thorough exploration of goals, strengths and passion to find work interests that resonate and provide fulfillment • **Continue to build on knowledge of business and its industry:** Start at the appropriate level based on skill and education if working in the business; if not, then learning about the core functions of the business (e.g., operations, marketing, and the like) • **Foster personal leadership skills:** Set a direction and destination for your life and learning that good leadership consists first of learning to follow	• Join industry or family business associations • Work within or outside the family business • Join a peer group	• Complete a bachelor's degree in engineering with minor in business • Secure a summer co-op position at a local firm and discuss learning objectives in advance with mentor • Attend 1 or 2 Next Gen events run by a local advising firm or university-based family business center, with access to national peer group • Review & update (or create) family employment policies specifically compensation and reporting relationships as well as employment of family friends

SAMPLE STORIES, EXERCISES AND TOOLS DESCRIBED IN THE CHAPTER	KEY INFLUENCERS	KEY OWNERSHIP TERMS FOR THIS STAGE	THINGS TO WATCH OUT FOR
• "We Ride at Dawn": The Senft Family's Development Approach • When the Founder's Vision Becomes a Black Hole • Create a Culture of Accountability • Zak's University Budget and Budget to Money • Family Governance Policies • Pierre and the Prenuptial • How to Open Dialogue About Prenuptial and Similar Agreements • A Sampling of Self-Awareness Tools • Create a Personal Mission Statement • Benefits and Challenges of Different Mentor • Alice's Unexpected Inspiration • Zoe Finds a Money Mentor • The Family Development Lifecycle	• Parents • Extended family • Non-family executives or directors • Outside advisors and community members • Other entrepreneurs	• Articles of Incorporation • Beneficiary • Bylaws • Entity • Estate Planning • Family Foundation • Operating Agreement • Ownership Type • Shareholder Agreement • Succession • Sweat Equity • Trust, Trustee	• Overdoing it • Failure to launch • Failure to appreciate natural developmental stages • Stimulating excessive competition

HOW-TO

Suggested Additional Readings

Aronoff, C., Astrachan, J., & Ward, J. (2011). *Developing Family Business Policies: Your Guide to the Future.* A Family Business Publication. Palgrave Macmillan.

Burnett, B., & Evans, D. (2016). *Designing your life: How to build a well-lived, joyful life* (1st ed.). Knopf.

Grant, A. (2014). *Give and take: Why helping others drives our success* (Reprint ed.). Penguin Books.

Hibbs, J. B., & Rostain, A. (2019). *The stressed years of their lives: Helping your kid survive and thrive during their college years.* St. Martin's Press.

Hughes, J. E., Jr. (1997). *Family wealth: Keeping it in the family.* NetWrx.

Hughes, J. E., Jr., Massenzio, S. E., & Whitaker, K. (2014). *The voice of the rising generation: Family wealth and wisdom* (Bloomberg) (1st ed.). Hoboken, NJ: Wiley

Lermitte, P. W. (2018). *Decisions, dollars & sense: Helping you navigate your financial future (Family Finances: Dollars and Sense Book 3).* Family Finance Series. Independently Published.

Linden, A. (2008). *Boundaries in human relationships: How to be separate and connected.* Crown House Publishing.

Patterson, K., Grenny, J., McMillan, R., & Switzler, A. (2002). *Crucial conversations: Tools for talking when stakes are high* (1st ed.). McGraw-Hill Education.

5

Embracing Ownership Commitments: Early Adult (Ages 25 to 40)

W. Sage-Hayward et al., *Own It!*, A Family Business Publication,
https://doi.org/10.1007/978-3-030-20419-8_5

Zak and Zoe—Early Adult Stage

Zoe and Zak are now in their early thirties and have become more involved in their family enterprises in formal and informal ways.

Zoe has worked outside the family business since graduating from college. She attempted to launch an organic farming business but found too much competition in that space and pursued her interest in apparel instead. She took a job as a finance analyst with a clothing company, ultimately ascending to a position as VP of Sales and Marketing at a major company. Married to Tom, an investment banker, she is also an executive MBA student and new mom. She's now on extended maternity leave and is pondering her career future. She's enjoying her current role but has been asked by her cousins to consider returning to the family enterprise. With her new, expanded family, the potential to live closer to a support system and have more professional flexibility looks very appealing. She was gifted ownership about three years ago and has served on the board for a year.

Zak has taken a less linear career path since college. Initially working with an engineering consulting firm, he joined a group of college classmates working on an early-stage tech business, a new offering in the social media space. Zak has learned a great deal as an entrepreneur which has made him more interested in his family business, particularly in how technology could be used more effectively. Though he holds no formal role in the family business or its governance, Zak has hinted that he would like to help the business, potentially as a technology advisor. Meanwhile, Zak lives with his longtime girlfriend.

This chapter is about the development of an owner's mindset for family members like Zak and Zoe, individuals in their mid-twenties to late-thirties, who are typically juggling a range of professional and personal responsibilities. First, we start with a real-life family enterprise whose co-founder shares how the company started ownership development with their rising generation—early adult sons.

Developing the Next Generation at Danica Imports

For the two families that own Danica Imports, development of an owner's mindset is a constant work in progress.

In 1984, Rodney Benson and Jeremy Braude purchased Danica Imports, and in 2004 acquired Now Designs, creating a single home décor design company with a unique style. Their sons Gary and Jon joined the business while in their late twenties, and remain with the firm today, many years later. Jeremy shared with us some of what the families have learned on their ownership development journey.

"I really started thinking about ownership development only once our sons started in the business," Jeremy says. For example, he and Rod took Jon and Gary to Asia to have them meet their suppliers and learn about their operations and cultures. They also took great pains to ensure the next generation understood their values and guiding philosophy. "We want them to understand that our business is about advancing social good, not just about making money. We take an inverse-pyramid approach that puts the customer on top, sales reps and other employees next, and the owners at the bottom."

Ownership development also meant understanding what roles the sons were likely to take on in the future. For example, because of their age and interests, neither Jon nor Gary had contemplated taking on the CEO job until recently, so their fathers helped them understand how best to work with the non-family CEO who has been leading Danica since they retired. "We needed to make sure they would collaborate with the CEO and that the CEO became a good mentor for them," Jeremy says, recognizing this view required encouraging strong self-awareness in his son and Gary.

Rod and Jeremy also brought in outside advisors to help with developing an owner's mindset and other issues. "We wanted Jon and Gary to understand their roles and responsibilities especially as related to the financial side and to be able to interpret the numbers, so they understand how things are going," Jeremy says. "We also wanted them to admit it when they didn't understand something and when they made a mistake."

The first priority for both founders was promotion of collaboration and trust between their sons. "They need to support each other and try to take the emotion out of it," Jeremy says. "People build trust over time by being empathetic to one another." Jeremy and Rod believe a foundation of support, trust, and collaboration will help the next generation take on challenges such as creating a new shareholders agreement and working as directors to understand the business's strategy and direction. "In the end," Jeremy says, "both parties have to be satisfied with a decision. It doesn't work if only one person is satisfied."

On the family governance side, Jeremy explained, "The Braude family does not have structured family meetings as that is not how our family operates. What we do is have fairly constant discussions on this topic." This approach is a good illustration on not having a "one size fits all" approach to development. Each family needs to design its own development path based on its unique circumstances, requirements, and family culture. As our conversation with Jeremy highlighted, the families behind Danica have put into place the philosophies and processes that foster ownership development in early adulthood. This chapter focuses on helping early adults like Jon and Gary become effective owners.

The Early Adult Stage (Ages 25 to 40) and Why It Matters

This early adult stage is when many people will achieve major milestones such as finishing their education, building a career (or two or three), engaging in a longer-term romantic relationship, and having a family. It's a time of both stability and change as people settle into roles and relationships but also consider new ones that align with their interests, values, and capabilities.

Regarding family enterprise ownership, this stage is important for many reasons, including:

- *From becoming to being*: For some family enterprise members, this stage involves transition from a "rising" owner to a full-fledged owner with attendant rights and responsibilities. Therefore, one goes from a state of *becoming an* owner to actually *being* one, and must learn how best to *perform* as an owner. Of course, the timing of the transition will vary among families. In some enterprises, young children are already formal owners; others have members well into their forties, fifties, and even sixties who have very limited ownership. In this stage, people are also more likely to be involved formally in governance, as related to business, family, or philanthropy. This involvement can mean anything from just observing to serving as a director or chair. Gaining skills at the intersection of ownership and governance is critical.
- *Crystallized sense of stewardship and succession*: For early adults, the idea of succession is no longer abstract, as they often have an ownership role with full decision-making powers for the first time. Many people in this stage also may become parents and come to appreciate stewardship as a key principle. This gives them a stronger desire to take care of an enterprise they want to pass to the next generation and they begin to consider how to involve the next generation for their eventual ownership.
- *Multiple role demands*: Early adults face the challenge of managing and balancing multiple roles and responsibilities: spouse; parent; adult child; professional; family enterprise owner, employee, or both; volunteer; and others. Each role demands time and energy, which can make giving sufficient attention to any one role challenging and stressful.

- *Role transitions*: Siblings and cousins working together as owners for the first time often find that the new ownership role challenges their relationships, regardless of their familiarity as well as how they got along in the past. Clashes can erupt over roles and responsibilities. An owner's mindset, paired with strong ownership literacy, enables everyone to be more proactive and intentional, which leads to more effective and harmonious decision-making (see the box, "Smoothing Transition to the Next Generation").

SMOOTHING TRANSITION TO THE NEXT GENERATION

Zoe's father invited the whole family to attend a program called Road Map for Entrepreneurial Families, over a weekend. Eight members of the family, including two spouses, along with four other business families attended. The program provided an opportunity for Zoe's family to learn how families navigate the complex world of transitioning a business to the rising generation. In the process, they also learned so much from the other families in the room. One of the primary outcomes was that everyone felt relieved that they were not the only family experiencing the tension and conflict generalized by passing the baton to the next generation. Also, having everyone attend this weekend helped convey information and started the conversation among the cousins about being partners in the family enterprise, which Zoe's father felt was a giant step forward.

- *Need for collaboration and teamwork*: Strong relationships which are characterized by trust, communication, commitment, consistency, and empathy are generally associated with well-being across life domains.[1] In a family enterprise, strong relationships lead to better decision-making among owners and, ultimately, greater family harmony. Gibb Dyer calls this the "F Factor."[2] It is critical for owners in this stage to understand the power of these close bonds and have the capability to promote them, especially with cohort members such as siblings and cousins. An essential element of developing an owner's mindset is relationship-building and maintenance including repair skills among family members.[3]
- *"Already but not yet"*: "Already but Not Yet" is a challenging condition many early adults experience in family enterprise. They may already have

---

[1] See for example Feeney, B. & Collins, N. (2014). A New Look at Social Support: A Theoretical Perspective on Thriving Through Relationships. *Personality and Social Psychology Review*, Volume 19, Issue 2, 2015.

[2] Dyer, G. (2019). *The Family Edge*. Familius.

[3] Astrachan, C., Waldkirch, M., Michiels, A., Pieper, T., Bernhard, F., (2019). Professionalizing the Business Family. The Five Pillars of Competent, Committed and Sustainable Ownership. *Family Firm Institute Research Report*.

or soon will be an owner, but they don't yet have authority over the business or enterprise. They are often told, "This is your company," but they have little or no control. Decision-making and control typically remain the purview of the older generation. The best strategy is for the early adults to see this as an opportunity to continue learning and development (as it is a never-ending process). The young owners should be encouraged not to feel sidelined but to use the time and space they've been given to develop their capabilities on collective decision-making, problem-solving, conflict and boundary management, and other tasks. This process will help them boost their individual effectiveness while helping them develop strong relationships with fellow stakeholders including other owners in their generation, senior executives, and governance leaders. Such growth will accelerate early adults' timeline to making key decisions for the enterprise, stepping more quickly past the "not yet" part.

• *Transitioning from adult-to-child to adult-to-adult interactions*: As noted in the Emerging Adult chapter, but worth stressing here as well, one critical goal at this stage of life is for the interactions between parents and early adults to shift from being a parent-child relationship to where parents and their adult children are communicating more like peers on an adult-to-adult level (see Exhibit 5.1).[4]

---

[4] For more on how transactions between family members change over life see Berne, E. (1961). *Transactional Analysis in Psychotherapy*. Grove Press.

Exhibit 5.1 Evolution of Parent–Child Relationships

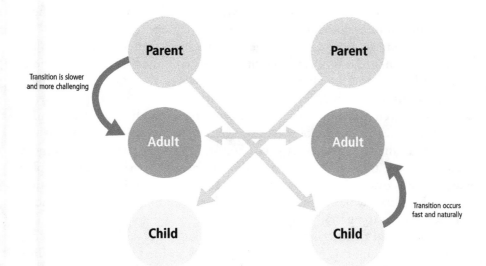

This transition is typically more challenging for the parents, given their role in the relationship. It is often less challenging for the "children" because growing into an adult can feel natural and fast to them. The box, "Please Don't Treat Me as a Child," provides an example of these often-challenging dynamics.

"PLEASE DON'T TREAT ME AS A CHILD!"

"Maya," the 37-year-old daughter and VP of a Mexico-based marketing agency, had struggled to gain credibility in the eyes of her father, the business's founder and CEO. "Please don't treat me like a child," she asked him when he opposed her attending key meetings and negotiations or taking on important initiatives earlier for the firm. Over time, he became better able to see her as the high-performing professional she was, and she rose to become one of his top executives. As her responsibilities grew, Maya sometimes talked down to her father, particularly about his inability to understand the value of new social media strategies, given his unfamiliarity with digital platforms. "Remember when you asked me not to speak to you as a child," he said to Maya. "Now, I ask you to do the same for me!" The two worked with an outside advisor who helped them recognize their relationship dynamics. The advisor taught them how to identify the ego state from which they were communicating (the "child" or the "adult") and, at the same time, to realize to which ego state they were sending their message. The advisor then facilitated monthly (and later quarterly) meetings where they discussed and assessed the success of their regular interactions and tried out alternative approaches. As they practiced and grew more proficient at treating one another as adults, they significantly reduced the tension between them and improved their relationship.

Central Theme: Adulting is Hard

"Adulting is hard." This is a popular saying and online meme among those approaching adulthood or recently arrived on the stage.

Many adults in this stage change jobs multiple times across domains. LinkedIn crunched numbers from its millions of users to find that job-hopping has become much more common than in the past, with younger adults leading the way, driven in part by the disappearance of "permanent" positions.[5] Even baby boomers (those born between the 1940s and mid-1960s) held nearly twelve jobs, on average, between the ages of 18 and 48, according to the U.S. Bureau of Labor Statistics.[6] People change *careers* more often now too, though this can be harder to measure. In addition, people's marital status often also changes, as reflected in the much broader definition of "family" today, which includes more single-parent households and blended families than in the past.

Another trend contributing to early adult challenges is the growing sense of loneliness among this cohort today, especially in the United States. While about 20 percent of American adults reported feeling lonely in 1980, the figure had more than doubled thirty years later.[7] Writer Brené Brown chalks up this increased loneliness to a growing feeling of social disconnection, powered largely by fear.[8] Fearfulness, she argues, has grown in the United States, especially since the terrorist acts of 9/11, but has been exacerbated by growing divides around race, gender, class, political affiliation, and other demographics.

Taken together, these trends suggest that early adults today struggle with both managing multiple roles and knowing exactly where they fit into society. When the role of *family enterprise owner is* added to this mix, it is not surprising that this feels overwhelming to many due to the sense of responsibility for one's family. That's a challenge many early adults face in this stage,

---

[5] Berger, G. (2016). Will This Year's College Grads Job-Hop More Than Previous Grads? *LinkedIn Blog*. Retrieved from https://blog.linkedin.com/2016/04/12/will-this-year_s-college-grads-job-hop-more-than-previous-grads.

[6] U.S. Department of Labor, Bureau of Labor Statistics Fact Sheet. Retrieved from https://www.bls.gov/nls/nlsfaqs.htm#anch41.

[7] The survey involved older adults (45 years +), but still captured a general sense of loneliness common among younger adults as well. See American Association of Retired Persons, "Loneliness Among Older Adults: A National Survey," (2010). Retrieved from https://assets.aarp.org/rgcenter/general/loneliness_2010.pdf.

[8] See for example Brown, B. (2017). America's Crisis of Disconnection Runs Deeper Than Politics. *Fast Company*. Retrieved from https://www.fastcompany.com/40465644/brene-brown-americas-crisis-of-disconnection-runs-deeper-than-politic.

as they work to develop knowledge, credibility, and capability as owners while managing many other roles and commitments.

You don't want to overwhelm owners or prospective owners in this already-challenging stage of life but it's essential that everyone understand these challenges so they can be effectively managed within the context of ownership development. The good news is that many of the skills required for effective ownership are the same ones needed for effective performance on most other major life dimensions, whether related to communication, collaboration, financial literacy, or other subjects covered in this book.

Development Goals

Here are the highest priority goals for early adults across our four key dimensions of ownership development (Exhibit 5.2).

Exhibit 5.2 Owner's Mindset: Development Goals For Early Adults

OWNER'S MINDSET: DEVELOPMENT GOALS FOR EARLY ADULTS	
AREA	**DEVELOPMENTAL GOALS**
INDIVIDUAL	Foster development on several interrelated dimensions at the individual level. • **Inner strength and fulfillment:** Strengthening competence, finding, and pursuing purpose and boosting intimacy and affiliation with others including partners and spouses, family, and friends. • **Emotional and social intelligence:** Gaining greater emotional intelligence, or EQ, smooths the way to better relationships and involves self-awareness, self-regulation, empathy, listening skills, conflict management, and many other people-focused capabilities. • **Engagement:** Early adults bring vital energy to family meetings, reunions, and other events, often because they are viewed as successors. So, maintaining or building positive experiences and feelings about the family and enterprise is an important goal in this stage.
FAMILY	With respect to family and relationships, promote and foster the following: • **Becoming interdependent:** This is about forming partnership relationships; leaving behind sibling rivalries and other issues by renegotiating family roles and relationships; accepting new members into the system (e.g., in-laws). • **Family Glue:** Relationships are critical as people come together around decision-making in the enterprise; such bonds are the glue holding the family together. Intentional focus on building close ties with family, board members, and executives is core to ownership development. • **Parenting/co-parenting skills:** Many early adults become parents. In family enterprise that means nurturing the next generation to become effective owners, such as preventing a sense of entitlement through having children help with household chores and understand family values. Previous chapters discuss fostering ownership skills in young children and adolescents. • **Emotional maturity:** We place even greater emphasis on healthy boundaries within the family in this stage, because early adults are finding their optimal roles within the family amidst complex dynamics including family employment and the arrival of grandchildren. Seemingly simple things such as managing how much time grandchildren and grandparents spend together can quickly illuminate boundary issues and should be handled proactively.
OWNERSHIP	Promote the goal of moving from becoming to being an owner, which requires: • **Vision and Goals:** Including defining one's own vision of how to create and participate in a more collective vision; communication and collaboration with other owners around the enterprise vision and its components including growth, risk, profits, and liquidity; how to create conditions (such as educational opportunities) that build effective owners in each generation. • **Ownership decision-making:** Develop a deeper understanding of ownership terms and decisions, with growing mastery in this area especially as it relates to making collective sibling and cousin decisions.

OWNER'S MINDSET: DEVELOPMENT GOALS FOR EARLY ADULTS	
AREA	**DEVELOPMENTAL GOALS**
OWNERSHIP	• **Contribute significantly to governance:** This might mean leading the charge to institute more formal governance (such as an ownership meeting, or a business board with independent directors). Knowledge related to governance goals (promoting oversight, commitment, communication transparency, development, and trust) and executing on these (through structure, process, and participation) is paramount.
BUSINESS / INDUSTRY	The development goals in this area are associated with different types of owners: • **Operating and governing owners:** This group should be gaining breadth and depth in areas ranging from strategy to finance to marketing, along with evolving leadership skills to be effective, rising managers. Early adults who will become operating owners should be advancing their functional expertise and planning, along with their coaching, decision-making, and problem-solving skills. • **Non-operating engaged owners:** Promote strengthening of their business and financial literacy so they understand financial and business reporting and can ask good questions of operating and governing leaders.

How-Tos

The ideas here describe multiple mutually reinforcing opportunities to promote the development of an owner's mindset in this stage. The core goal is to help early adults learn continuously and contribute broadly to positive dynamics and decision-making for the family and enterprise. This is especially important, given many rising generation members did not volunteer for the ownership role; rather, ownership is bestowed upon them. As Hughes et al. (2013) so aptly describe, when a meteoric gift (ownership) comes without spirit, education, and preparation it will rarely promote growth and enhancement. Frame ownership development activities in this stage as being important for early adults' growth and the family's legacy, but also design the activities to help them "earn" the responsibilities and benefits of ownership, by expressing their interest, capabilities, and enthusiasm for this role. Our suggested How-Tos for this stage include:

• *Include owner's meetings in your governance structures*: Often family firms focus on governance in the family and business systems but miss the ownership system. An owner's meeting (which at this stage may include prospective owners) could simply be an allocated time slot with specific agenda items or a separate meeting all together. Current and prospective owners benefit greatly from meeting to discuss topics related to the ownership system identified in the following list.

- Owners' vision and values
- Ownership Goals (profitability, growth, liquidity)
- Risk management
- Corporate Structure (legal)
- Shareholders' Agreements
- Election of Board of Directors
- Redemptions
- Trusts
- Distributions
- Policies (e.g., social media, dividends, family law agreements, etc.)
- Insurance Plans
- Estate Plans
- Ownership Succession
- Ownership Development
- Family enterprise governance
- Communication and Information Sharing

- *Clarify roles and responsibilities*: Role clarity facilitates effective working relationships. Families who delineate and specify roles early on—even well before the next generation reaches adulthood—reap rewards including engagement and interest in the enterprise and its governance. It's critical in this stage that everyone has a sense of who's responsible for what—whether as employees, governance leaders, or active owners—and how to address conflict around "border disputes."
- *Focus on boundary management*: Boundaries are fundamental to family enterprise, within the family itself and among other constituent groups like owners and managers. Poor boundaries can cause a lack of communication as well as clarity, disengagement, and relationship challenges at the person-to-person and collective family level. It is important for early adults in the enterprise to be mindful of boundaries and to identify and manage them. Often, breaking boundaries may be a symptom of failing to follow family values. For example, if one family member in a dispute with a cousin talks about the conflict with a third person (rather than the cousin with whom they have the conflict) they are triangulating.[9] This behavior

---

[9] Triangulation is a fundamental concept developed by Bowen. Triangulation occurs when a third person intervenes or is drawn into a conflicted relationship between two others in an attempt to ease tension and facilitate communication.

does not resolve the problem and likely violates the "direct communication" value that many families hold dear. Dealing with a porous or rigid boundary issue can strengthen both the value and the bond.[10]

- *Continually seek family enterprise education:* Family members are in an ideal position to benefit from learning in this stage, because (1) they have likely completed or will soon complete their formal general education and can now focus on knowledge areas in which they're most interested; (2) they have a growing base of experience to inform what they learn; and (3) they have specific opportunities to apply what they learn, such as to their family enterprise employment or governance roles. Key sources of continued family enterprise education are vast and include MBA and master's degrees, certificate programs through university-based or other family business centers, online courses relevant to family enterprise and other areas, and conferences or workshops.

- *Promote self-awareness:* Increased self-awareness, an essential element of emotional intelligence, helps people collaborate more effectively in any domain and reach higher levels of fulfillment. Understanding oneself on multiple dimensions is critical as part of development, including one's status needs, learning style, relational preferences, personality, triggers, and the like. All of this influences our interactions with others and approaches to decision-making. For example, understanding one's status needs tend to peak at this stage, due partly to the easy comparisons of status symbols (job title, real estate, cars, travel destinations, etc.) amplified by social media. According to neuroscience research, there are five key drivers of human motivation: status, certainty, autonomy, relatedness, and fairness (SCARF Model). Dr. David Rock, author of the book *Your Brain at Work*, calls these "guiding principles" for our brains.[11] Consider, for example, how the need for status impacts conflicts in family firms. Status is defined as our relative importance to others. In the family, status needs can work in two ways. First, it can motivate individual achievement, such as when siblings compete to be more "successful" or favored within the family, which can create tension over time. Second, the need for status can promote a quest for belonging, within and outside the family, or what can be thought of as a more communal sense of status that ultimately brings people together. Discussing how all five of these drivers impact both individuals and,

---

[10] For more on boundary issues and solutions see Cloud, H. (2013). *Boundaries for Leaders: Results, Relationships, and Being Ridiculously In Charge*. Harper Business.

[11] Rock, D. (2009). Your Brain at Work: Strategies for Overcoming Distraction, Regaining Focus, and Working Smarter All Day Long. Harper Business.

ultimately, the family system is one tangible way to explore the skill of self-awareness.

- *Strengthen self-management capabilities*: Self-management, another key element of emotional intelligence, has several key traits associated with it, including self-control, self-confidence, adaptability, transparency, initiative, and optimism.[12] Due to the complex nature of family enterprises, self-management is an essential skill to strengthen since it will help individuals navigate the multitude of challenges they'll face through succession and help them build stronger relationships and contribute more to the family enterprise. Learning to practice mindfulness—or being more conscious of what you're feeling, thinking, and doing—is an effective way to move toward better self-regulation. The goal of any mindfulness technique is to achieve a state of alert, focused relaxation by deliberately paying attention to thoughts and sensations without judgment.[13]

- *Handle the hard stuff*: Gaining greater self-awareness often means handling the hard stuff: understanding early influences on you that continue to affect who you are, how you react to people and experiences, and decisions you make. For example, early experiences have a tremendous bearing on who individuals grow up to be and how they handle various issues from money matters to sibling rivalry. It's not just about understanding and appreciating these influences; it's about dealing with their negative effects, including long-standing conflicts. While a full discussion of early and later family influence is beyond our scope, consider reading about helpful theories, tools, and analysis in this area, such as Murray Bowen's family systems theory, which illuminates the origins of emotional cutoff (estrangement) among family members and offers other helpful ideas.[14] This knowledge can help you promote better communication about sensitive issues and create a safe space to discuss and hopefully resolve them, utilizing outside advisors' help as needed. See the following box "Zak's Conflict with Uncle Pete" as an example.

---

[12] Goleman, D., McKee, A., & Boyatzis, R. (2002). *Primal Leadership: Realizing the Power of Emotional Intelligence*. Boston: Harvard Business Review Press.

[13] For more on mindfulness, see Benefits of Mindfulness - HelpGuide.org. (2019). Harvard Health. Retrieved from https://www.helpguide.org/harvard/benefits-of-mindfulness.htm. And Firestone, L. (2016). Benefits of Mindfulness. *Psychology Today*. Retrieved from https://www.psychologytoday.com/us/blog/compassion-matters/201303/benefits-mindfulness.

[14] For an overview of Bowen's work, see Kerr, M. E. (2000). One Family's Story: A Primer on Bowen Theory. The Bowen Center for the Study of the Family. Retrieved from http://www.thebowencenter.org.

ZAK'S CONFLICT WITH UNCLE PETE

Zak, our recurring family enterprise character, had always struggled in his relationship with his father's brother, Uncle Pete. From an early age, Pete tested Zak's limits, such as being hard on him when things didn't go well in Zak's high school hockey matches: "You took your eye off the puck and missed that goal!" Zak knew that Uncle Pete cared about him but felt put-off by Pete's explicit or thinly veiled criticism. Things came to a head when Zak was in his early twenties. Pete made a cutting remark about Zak's college grades at a family dinner, and Zak lost his temper: "You've always put me down!" he yelled, leaving the room. Neither made an effort to resolve the problem for the next two years. Finally, Zak's dad told Zak and Pete he "needed them to at least try to make up," for his sake, if nothing else. The two agreed to sit down with a family therapist and were able to talk about the problem between them for the first time, understanding that Uncle Pete actually respected Zak and felt he reminded him of himself: a smart young person who didn't try very hard. Pushing Zak was his way of trying to motivate his nephew. Zak forgave his uncle but asked him to be more sensitive while promising he would work hard to fulfill his potential.

- *Prepare for governance leadership*: Successful families take the preparation of governance leaders (for business boards, owner's council and family meetings) seriously, employing a full range of practices to develop owners who can oversee and lead the business, family, and philanthropic groups. Board shadowing and observation are typical early governance-related opportunities. Educational opportunities such as governance-related conferences and workshops—including those run by university-based family business centers—provide opportunities to learn key concepts from experts and fellow family enterprises. Service on family council committees before becoming a full family council member can also provide valuable experience. Some families develop customized governance leadership development programs that focus on general principles of governance and specific industry and market-related trends. Development programs like this can include a mix of formal and informal elements, such as skills gaps assessment, mentorship, and case studies. One family created a "mock board" to allow rising owners to develop their governance skills before joining the formal corporate board. They found this provided an excellent lower-pressure means of gaining critical capabilities. Finally, families offer specific on-the-job training and development opportunities for those interested in board or family council chair roles, as well, with an emphasis on leadership and communication.
- *Learn from peers*: Some of the best sources of knowledge and insights about ownership are peers from multiple domains. Within the family itself, same-age or older peers—such as cousins—who have held ownership or governance responsibilities can be excellent providers of wisdom and counsel as mentors or role models. Encouraging early adult family members to gather on their own—without senior family members present—to get

to know one another and start talking about ownership issues collectively can be highly valuable. In fact, it's critical for prospective owners to regularly gather to learn, discuss, and decide on their ownership team's guiding principles, practice joint decision-making, and build their relationships. Beyond the family, peer advisory groups comprising multiple family business members with ownership experience from diverse local family businesses can also foster development. (See more detail on how to get the most from peer groups in Chapter 6.)

• *Promote a collaborative approach and trust*: This one sounds like common sense, but many families fail to promote a basic sense of collaboration and attendant trust. Then they struggle to understand why they're not making progress on ownership.[15] Sometimes, the senior generation has clung excessively to control, failing to make room or opportunity for rising family members and creating a pervasive sense of distrust. Sometimes branches succumb to ongoing conflict and competition, thereby perpetuating the discord passed down through generations. Sibling rivalry or emphasis on competitiveness within a family, for example, develops strong individual performers but not good teammates. Sometimes there's no single issue that impedes collaboration or trust. But these qualities are needed for promoting communication around everything from the selection of board and family council members to making decisions about acquisitions and dividends. Whatever the exact situation, the idea is to promote collective progress by opening lines of communication wherever possible, recognizing and managing boundaries, and working through negative dynamics helped by family governance structures, outside advisors, and others. The following box, "Building Trust in the Family: Attune," highlights how one mother built stronger bonds within her family.

---

[15] Williams, R. & Preisser, V. (2010). *Preparing Heirs: Five Steps to a Successful Transition of Family Wealth and Values.* Robert Redd Publishers.

BUILDING TRUST IN THE FAMILY: ATTUNE

Zak's mother, Sue, understood the need for high trust in her family if they were to be successful in becoming a multigenerational family enterprise. She was always on the lookout for models about difficult subjects like trust that were not only simple to understand but also pragmatic. She did not like a lot of "nonsensical psychological mumbo-jumbo," as she put it. One Sunday evening she attended her regular monthly book club and one of the members was talking about Dr. John Gottman, one of the foremost experts on marriage and relationships. The member shared a model called ATTUNE, which Sue felt was worth sharing with her family. Ultimately the family adopted this approach as follows:

- **Awareness of the other's feelings/emotional state** – at the beginning of each meeting, family members very briefly stated how they were feeling that day and if they were excited to be at the meeting or not (for whatever reason).
- **Turning toward the emotion and person, rather than away from it** – when emotions escalated in the family, Sue ensured that the emotions did not get swept under the rug but rather she gently helped the family explore the feelings and underlying issues associated with it.
- **Tolerance for different viewpoints** – Sue would ensure that everyone had a chance to voice their perspective about the issue at hand and that no one felt judged for it.
- **Understanding, and taking the time to do so** – no one felt rushed through the process and if more time was needed, they would schedule another meeting or call as required. Emphasis was placed on the importance of sorting out issues before they became too entrenched. She had seen members of her parent's generation avoid conflict and then each other for years at a time.
- **Non-defensive responding** – everyone had an opportunity to respond to any feedback they received. Sue often reminded the family that they did not need to get into defensive or blaming mode but rather share the impact of the feedback and how they might go forward now that they are more informed about others' view.
- **Empathy expressed for and to others** – Sue was a role model for other family members in this regard. She would often listen carefully to each person and summarize in her own words what she understood them to mean and feel, helping everyone in the family to feel understood.

- *Develop leadership—and followership—skills*: Leadership is critical in a family enterprise, especially in less organized areas such as ownership. Research suggests that 70 percent of intergenerational wealth transfers fail, with a major contributing factor being limited development of the rising generation.[16] While some people are more natural leaders, everyone can improve such skills. There is also value in gaining "followership" skills or learning to be a strong contributing member of a team without leading it. Family members in this stage may take a narrow-minded approach to ownership, thinking they are the best-suited to lead the enterprise as owners. That view is unlikely to promote positive outcomes on any dimension. Before leading, people need to learn to follow by seeking experiences that will promote empathy and humility, within and outside the enterprise (such as volunteering in the community).

---

[16] Williams, R., & Preisser, V. (2010). *Philanthropy, Heirs & Values: How Successful Families Are Using Philanthropy To Prepare Their Heirs For Post-transition Responsibilities* (1st ed.). Robert Reed Publishers.

- *Understand the business*: Effective ownership requires an understanding of the family business, to help make well-informed decisions about issues such as growth, risk and liquidity. By this stage, many will have had some exposure to the business, even if they've never worked within it. But some may have had only limited exposure, especially those who live far from the business and have multiple pressing professional, family, and personal commitments. For this contingent, there can be frustration related to fulfilling expectations around the enterprise, along with a widening gap between them and siblings or cousins working more closely with the enterprise (and living closer to it too). Therefore, it's important for the family to recognize that potential tension and to help those far away maintain their connection, through family webinars, regular shareholder and family meetings, or quarterly email updates. These early adults who work in the business can benefit further from rotations among various business units or shadowing executives. The book *Human Resources in the Family Business* offers many tips for helping family members gain business knowledge and experience as part of their development as owners and professionals.[17]
- *Understand "technical" aspects of ownership*: Decisions related to growth, risk, liquidity, and profits (GRPL), the difference between a trustee and a beneficiary, buy-sell agreements, and shareholder agreements are among the many ownership structures and tools that owners need to understand (See Appendix A: Glossary of Terms). Having a strong base of ownership knowledge goes a long way. Of course, the type of ownership knowledge you need depends on the type of owner you are or hope to be. Operating and governing owners will need to understand issues at the intersection of business operations, governance, and ownership, for example, whereas non-operating but engaged owners may not need that depth of knowledge. In general, repetition is the best teacher; be patient as it will take multiple exposures for people to grasp some of these concepts. Besides repetition and patience, it takes hard work. Reread agreements or ask an advisor to explain them in order to understand the terms. Just signing them should not be an option. Working with fellow owners in small groups on such issues, led by a more experienced family member or an outside advisor, can also be effective and make it feel less like "work." Aim to advocate for the rising generation around gaining such knowledge, as others may not take up this important cause on their behalf.

---

[17] Ransburg, D., Sage-Hayward, W. & Schuman, A. M. (2015). *Human Resources in the Family Business: Maximizing the Power of Your People* (A Family Business Publication) (1st ed. 2016 ed.). Springer.

• *Strengthen financial literacy:* In many cases, ownership means not just ownership of an operating asset but ownership of inherited or newly created wealth. Many early adult owners must make decisions regarding the disposition of large amounts of money—whether for personal use or savings, engagement in philanthropy or other investments. Often, they must do this with little specific knowledge. The best approach involves gaining not only technical knowledge of money management (knowing where your money is coming from and going to, for example) but also understanding how individual and collective interests and values fit into the process (see the box, "The Family Foundation—A Pathway to Financial Literacy," for an example).

THE FAMILY FOUNDATION – A PATHWAY TO FINANCIAL LITERACY

Luke had been a successful entrepreneur all his adult life. His five children forged their own pathways outside his businesses. The siblings remained close over time and through the years, with some typical sibling rivalries and conflicts. When Luke was 70, he sold his company for over $50 million. He had a solid nest egg personally, so he decided to start a private foundation and involve his children. He quickly realized one of the core needs for being a good trustee was to understand the financial aspects of governing a private foundation. He also understood, wisely, that to give money away to charitable causes it was important for his children to not have significant financial issues of their own. Over a five-year period, Luke gave each of his children cash gifts to address any debt issues they might have and allow them to start building a nest egg. He also hired a financial coach who spent time monthly working with each of the adult children to build their financial capability as future trustees by first learning to better manage their personal financial matters.

In addition, enterprise owners with personal wealth need to understand finance at the personal and enterprise levels. As a discipline, finance can be daunting—it has its own specialized terminology—and isn't everyone's cup of tea. A one- to four-day course of "Finance for Non-Financial Managers" is often a place to build an understanding of the basics. Sometimes, this course is available with specifics for a particular industry. This can be followed up by short sessions introducing the family enterprise's own balance sheets and income statements. One family we know has a "board meeting before the board meeting" for family directors (and next gen board observers). In each quarterly session, the CFO spends extra time reviewing the financials and explaining a particular feature of the business, i.e., how management made a decision between repairing an asset and replacing it. It also offers time for family to ask what they might worry are "dumb" questions—ones they wouldn't raise in front of non-family directors during the board meeting. Over time, these sessions have raised the financial savvy of all family owners, contributing to the ownership team's alignment and decision-making speed.

- *Call on advisors*: This is the life stage when many owners or would-be owners work closely with family enterprise advisors. Advisors can provide helpful input on technical aspects of ownership, business knowledge, financial and legal advice, governance, leadership, and family dynamics. The challenge is recognizing where and how an advisor or team of advisors can be of most value and ensuring a *collaborative* approach within the broader family. Advisors do not always understand the context of the family enterprise environment, which can result in offering solutions that don't meet the client's needs in the long term or are too heavily focused on tax planning. An excellent resource for creating and managing advisory relationships is *How To Choose and Use Advisors* by Craig E. Aronoff and John L. Ward.[18]

- *Promote fun and engagement*: Structure and knowledge create discipline and understanding but aren't enough to engage people fully in an ongoing way. Positive attraction to the enterprise is a critical aspect of transition. Promoting a sense of cohesion and connection to the enterprise and the rest of the family, along with *fun*, is critical for generating passion, engagement, and alignment around a common vision for ownership. Engagement is paramount to foster as the family grows and people follow their own paths, often moving away from one another geographically or emotionally. Family reunions, fun retreats, and other outings, digital groups and newsletters, and other "softer" activities go a long way to build emotional bonds among and between people and the enterprise.

- *Travel or live abroad*: Self-exploration at this stage can mean global exploration, as people take time to travel or even live outside their home country. Such experience serves multiple purposes: appreciating and growing skills and capabilities, including self-reliance; understanding different cultural perspectives and becoming more open-minded; making independent decisions in unfamiliar circumstances; missing (and appreciating) your family of origin. We recommend seeking opportunities to experience the outside world directly in this way, whether through personal or professional travel or even relocation.

Here is an ideal development plan for an early adult.

---

[18] Aronoff, C., & Ward, J. (2011). *How to Choose and Use Advisors: Getting the Best Professional Family Business Advice* (A Family Business Publication). Palgrave Macmillan.

Sample Development Plan: Early Adult

Scenario: Zoe is 32 years old; she just had her first child and is on maternity leave. She had been working as a VP of Sales at a retail clothing giant outside the family enterprise, while operating as a Vice Chair and Director on the board of the family business. She is married to Tom, an investment banker. Zoe started an executive MBA program just before becoming pregnant and is taking a break from it until her child is about six months old. She has been given 5 percent ownership in her family enterprise. Her development included activities outlined in Exhibit 5.3 (to be completed over several years).

Exhibit 5.3 Owner's Mindset: Sample Development Plan for an Early Adult (Zoe)

SAMPLE DEVELOPMENT PLAN FOR AN EARLY ADULT (ZOE)	
AREA	**DEVELOPMENTAL ACTIVITIES**
INDIVIDUAL	• Attend Landmark Education Program (personal development) for understanding self and communication. • Work with a mentor and life coach twice per month. • Complete a weekend meditation retreat. • Take a cooking program at a local culinary school • Map out personal values
FAMILY	• Organize and participate in two family retreats per year. • Lead a family enterprise book club with her siblings (quarterly). • Onboard her husband Tom to family meetings. • Develop life goals and plan with Tom including a plan for how they want to co-parent. • Attend Family Governance Forum program at family enterprise consultancy with her mother. • Learn about parenthood as a new mother.
OWNERSHIP	• Serve as Vice Chair and Director on Family Enterprise Board. • Participate in sibling partnership meetings without the senior generation. • Serve as a Director on the Dress for Success Foundation which empowers women to achieve economic independence • Participate on a committee to develop a board evaluation process and tool. • Develop a shareholders agreement with siblings and key advisors.
BUSINESS / INDUSTRY	• Work toward an Executive MBA • Participate in a Peer Forum Group through the Family Enterprise Canada. • Completed a 360 Feedback Survey about her leadership at work • Secure key man insurance for the business

The sample development plan is offered as an example only and includes a variety of ideas—some of which you may already do in the normal course of development in your family. Our goal is to inspire you to take a more

intentional approach to development by building a coordinated plan for your family appropriate to your specific circumstance and context.

Development Influencers

A wide range of people can and should be involved developing an owner's mindset opportunities for early adults. The primary ones include:

- *Parents*: Parents continue to be strong sources of influence, even though the "children" are now adults. Ideally, the senior generation can offer a balance of active guidance and allow room to grow as early adults follow the life paths that make the most sense for them. Parents can be mentors, supporters, and even supervisors within the family enterprise, for example, but should also champion independent development and ensure they aren't promoting their own agendas, whether consciously or not.
- *Extended family*: While wide-ranging extended family members can serve as coaches, mentors, and role models, those about eight to ten years older than the early adults in the family may be especially valuable, as they are seen more as peers than authority figures. Parents and extended family members are valuable sources of information and guidance on how to handle relationships with the family, executives, board, and other stakeholders around ownership issues. They can also provide feedback across ownership dimensions as part of a supportive relationship that prioritizes the early adult owner's best interests without sacrificing the collective good. Those in this life stage will often serve as mentors for younger peers—adolescents and young adults—as discussed in previous chapters.
- *Instructors, coaches, family enterprise advisors, therapists*: Those who teach family enterprise courses and workshops provide important knowledge on the areas covered here and can be impartial influences on owners in this stage, especially if they get to know the enterprise well. Similarly, external coaches can work closely with early adults, with a focus on the continued development of all areas of ownership, especially if they understand the complex landscape of family enterprise. Advisors specialized in family enterprise can provide needed input on everything from legal issues to financial planning, leadership and family dynamics. Therapists provide one-on-one or group support and counseling around psychological and systems issues that affect the individual and family. These often prove the most challenging issues of all, but therapists without specific training in family enterprise advising should not be used to address enterprise issues.

- *Non-family executives and independent directors*: Business-owning families can sometimes encourage early adult owners to develop mentoring relationships with non-family executives and independent directors, ensuring the family members meet with them regularly to discuss their interests, goals, and pathways. In general, these seasoned professionals provide excellent perspectives and advice about ownership. Often, they've known their mentees for a long time and use what they know about them and the family as an important context for counsel.
- *Other family enterprises*: Peers and senior members of other family enterprises provide hard-to-find perspective, advice, and empathy to early adult owners. They've walked in the shoes of future owners and are often eager to share their thoughts and lessons learned. Educational opportunities and peer advisor groups are among the ways to connect with these valuable influences. Some families we know have simply contacted other family enterprises in their industry or community and have found them very willing to share what they've learned.

Where to Start?

Consider a multidimensional approach to developing early adults in your family enterprise.

- *Do a current state assessment*: Work among or with early adults to understand where they are on key dimensions such as governance, business and ownership knowledge, leadership and emotional intelligence, and relationships with other family members. Ask questions about the ownership areas that might matter most to each and being honest in your assessment. Is there enough capacity in a given area? Are there easily identifiable deficits or growth opportunities? If it becomes difficult to self-assess or to evaluate a family member, an outside professional may be a good choice to help in this process.
- *Develop a collective vision for the future*: Work with owners and prospective owners on a vision of the enterprise for the future, along with how they hope to contribute to it, using their interests, capabilities, and experience. What do members feel the purpose of the enterprise is or should be? How can they work to ensure it fulfills this purpose? What's their vision for their own future, regarding both professional and personal life? How does their individual vision align with that of the enterprise? These and other questions are especially important for early adults to answer, as they work toward their individual and collective goals.

- *Meet regularly*: It's ideal to have the rising generation meet regularly, with and without an outside facilitator. This strengthens their communication, camaraderie, and decision-making skills, while establishing their independence from more senior owners and family members. Meetings can be formal, with thoughtful agendas or looser and more informal, with a focus on sharing time and ideas. The important thing is to make such time together a priority. In general, while there's no "formula" for proceeding through ownership development for early adults, one thing we value most is a *collaborative element of the owner's mindset*[19] *and approach*. Owners have to work together to develop a collective vision for the enterprise's future—and how their own interests, experience, and preferences fit into this. If there's little collaboration among the early adults and others in the family, there will be little chance for meaningful progress. An explicit goal of the steps above is the development of a healthy sense of collaboration among current or future owners.

Things to Look for

Every life stage involves common pitfalls that may impede ownership development and related progress within the broader family enterprise system. Here are the main ones we've seen for early adults.

- *An "I'm done with development" mentality*: Many in early adulthood make the mistake of believing they're "done" with development across dimensions. The attitude is: "We know what we need to know, and no longer need to grow." That's especially harmful to ownership development as there's so much to learn and strive toward in every stage. Even if you know a great deal or have become an expert in certain areas, the system you inhabit will continue to evolve and you will have to grow to adapt to it. Take to heart our advice that to become a strong leader, you first need to be a capable follower. Learning to be a great No. 2 offers invaluable lessons.[20]
- *Unrealistic expectations*: These can originate within and without—we can expect too much of ourselves, or the broader system can. For example, early adults may expect that they will become top-level leaders within the business and its governance, along with spending quality time with family and on their own outside pursuits—all before age 35. Not surprisingly, unrealistic expectations lead to burnout from overcommitment and

---

[19] See Chapter 1 for the definition of the owner's mindset.
[20] Hughes Jr., J.E. (2007). *The compact among generations.* John Wiley & Sons.

a constant sense that "it's never enough." It's especially easy for ambitious rising owners to have "eyes bigger than their stomachs," given their appetite for ownership development across dimensions and to sometimes feel resentment or dismay that they haven't reached the title or level their parents did by a similar age (while forgetting the business was ten times smaller during the previous generation's rise, meaning a smaller scale of responsibilities!). The idea is to maintain more realistic expectations and to choose your "battles" (specific development areas). Be patient with yourself and others in expecting slow, steady progress while always monitoring for burnout and celebrating progress.

- *A deficit of external experience*: While many families emphasize the value of outside experience among owners, some neglect or devalue it. Many early adults gain highly valuable outside experience that not only builds their skills but also helps them appreciate what their family enterprise has to offer and how they can contribute to its advancement. One family enterprise member gained in-depth outside experience in sales and marketing before returning to her family's real estate business in her forties. Some members were skeptical of her potential impact because she "didn't know the industry," but she quickly proved them wrong, leading a rebranding and salesforce-enhancement effort resulting in dramatically higher sales within a year. Of course, external experience doesn't guarantee success, but it typically provides needed capability and perspective, so take seriously the idea of gaining some of this along the way (Exhibit 5.4).

Exhibit 5.4 Early Adult Stage Summary

	WHY EARLY ADULT STAGE MATTERS	KEY MESSAGE
WHY	• Moving from "becoming" to "being" an owner with rights and responsibilities • A crystallizing sense of stewardship and succession • Multiple role demands • Transition for siblings and cousins can challenge relationships • Need for collaboration and teamwork • Already have ownership but might not yet have authority • Transitioning from adult-to-child to adult-to-adult interactions	In the face of emerging authority and multiple roles, embrace the time commitment of ownership in its many forms and related responsibilities.

	DOMAIN	DEVELOPMENT GOALS	HOW TOs	SAMPLE DEVELOPMENT PLAN FOR ZOE
WHAT	Individual	• **Inner strength and fulfillment:** Strengthening competence, finding and pursuing purpose and boosting intimacy and affiliation with others including partners and spouses, family, and friends • **Emotional and social intelligence:** Gaining greater emotional intelligence, or EQ, smooths the way to better relationships and involves self-regulation, empathy, listening skills, conflict management and many other people-focused capabilities • **Engagement:** Early adults bring vital energy to family meetings, reunions, and other events, often because they are viewed as successors. So, maintaining or building positive experiences and feelings about the family and enterprise is an important goal in this stage	• Focus on boundary management • Promote self-awareness • Strengthen self-management capabilities • Provide skill building and opportunities to practice difficult conversations • Travel or live abroad	• Attend Landmark Education Program (personal development) for understanding self and communication • Work with a mentor and life coach 2x/month • Complete a weekend meditation retreat • Take a cooking program at a local culinary school • Map out personal values
	Family	• **Becoming interdependent:** This is about forming partnership relationships; leaving behind sibling rivalries and other issues by renegotiating family roles and relationships; accepting new members into the system (e.g., in-laws) • **Family glue:** Relationships are critical as people come together around decision-making in the enterprise; such bonds are the glue holding the family together. Intentional focus on building close ties with family, board members, and executives is core to ownership development • **Parenting and Co-Parenting skills:** Many early adults become parents. In family enterprise that means nurturing the next generation to become effective owners, such as preventing a sense of entitlement through having children help with household chores and understand family values. Previous chapters discuss fostering ownership skills in young children and adolescents	• Prepare for governance leadership • Clarify roles and responsibilities • Promote a collaborative mindset and trust • Engage in dialogue aimed at creating alignment on parenting approach • Foster family 'glue' • Review/create policies such as conflict of interest policy and personal loan policy	• Organize and participate in 2 family retreats per year • Lead a family enterprise book club with her siblings (4 times per year) • Onboard her husband Tom to family meetings • Develop life goals and plan with Tom including a plan for how they want to co-parent • Attend Family Governance Forum program at family enterprise consultancy with her mother • Learn about parenthood as a new mother

DOMAIN	DEVELOPMENT GOALS	HOW TOs	SAMPLE DEVELOPMENT PLAN FOR ZOE
	• **Emotional maturity:** We place even greater emphasis on healthy boundaries within the family in this stage, because early adults are finding their optimal roles within the family amidst complex dynamics including family employment and the arrival of grandchildren. Seemingly simple things such as managing how much time grandchildren and grandparents spend together can quickly illuminate boundary issues and should be handled proactively.		
Ownership	• **Vision and Goals:** Including defining one's own vision of how to create and participate in a more collective vision; communication and collaboration with other owners around the enterprise vision and its components including growth, risk, profits and liquidity; how to create conditions (such as educational opportunities) that build effective owners in each generation	• Develop leadership and follower-ship skills • Advance "technical" aspects of ownership • Build key ownership policies and agreements • Hold sibling meetings without senior generation involvement	• Serve as Vice-Chair and Director on Family Enterprise Board • Participate in sibling partnership meetings without senior generation • Serve as a Director on the Dress for Success Foundation, which empowers women to achieve economic independence • Participate on a committee to develop a board evaluation process and tool • Develop a shareholder's agreement with siblings and key advisors
	• **Ownership decision-making:** Develop a deeper understanding of ownership terms and decisions, with growing mastery in this area especially as it relates to making collective sibling and cousin decisions		
	• **Contribute significantly to governance:** This might mean leading the charge to institute more formal governance (such as an ownership meetings, or a business board with independent directors). Knowledge related to governance goals (promoting oversight, commitment, communication transparency, development, and trust) and executing on these (through structure, process, and participation) is paramount		
	The development goals in this area are associated with different types of owners:		
Business/ Industry	• **Operating and governing owners:** This group should be gaining breadth and depth in areas ranging from strategy to finance to marketing, along with evolving leadership skills to be effective, rising managers. Early adults who will become operating owners should be advancing their functional expertise and planning, along with their coaching, decision-making and problem-solving skills	• Strengthen financial literacy • Obtain feedback on leadership capability • Develop key business policies such as media relations and promotions or in-law employment	• Work toward an Executive MBA • Participate in a Peer Forum Group through the Family Enterprise Canada • Completed a 360 Feedback Survey about her leadership at work • Secure key man insurance for the business
	• **Non-operating engaged owners:** Promote strengthening of their business and financial literacy so they understand financial and business reporting and can ask good questions of operating and governing leaders		

WHAT

SAMPLE STORIES, EXERCISES AND TOOLS DESCRIBED IN THE CHAPTER	KEY INFLUENCERS	KEY OWNERSHIP TERMS FOR THIS STAGE	THINGS TO WATCH OUT FOR
• Developing the Next Generation at Danica Imports • Smoothing Transition to the Next Generation • Evolution of Parent-Child Relationships • "Please Don't Treat Me as a Child!" • Nurture the Golden Goose • Five Things Our Brains Need • Zak's Conflict with Uncle Pete • Choose the Right Peer Group • Building Trust in the Family: ATTUNE • The Family Foundation—A Pathway to Financial Literacy	• Parents • Extended family • Instructors, coaches, family enterprise advisors, therapists • Non-family executive and independent directors • Other family enterprises	• Advisory Board • Board of Directors • Buy-Sell Agreement • Dividend and Distribution • Estate Tax • Family • Family Council • Independent Director • Ownership Form • Valuation	• "I'm done with development" mentality • Unrealistic expectations • A deficit of external experience

(HOW TO)

Suggested Additional Readings

Aronoff, C., & Ward, J. (2011a). *Family business governance: Maximizing family and business potential (A Family Business Publication)*. Palgrave Macmillan.

Aronoff, C., & Ward, J. (2011b). *From siblings to cousins: Prospering in the third generation and beyond (A Family Business Publication)*. Palgrave Macmillan.

Covey Jr., S. (2008). *The speed of trust: The one thing that changes everything* (Reprint ed.). Free Press.

Coyle, D. (2018). *The culture code: The secrets of highly successful groups*. Bantam.

Klein, M. A. (2012). *Trapped in the family business: A practical guide to uncovering and managing this hidden dilemma*. MK Insights LLC.

Rezac, D., Thomson, J., Hallgren, G., & Donohue, T. (2003). *The frog and prince: Secrets of positive networking to change your life*. Frog & Prince Networking Corp.

Richo, D. (2002). *How to be an adult in relationships: The five keys to mindful loving* (1st ed.). Shambhala.

Schuman, A. M., Sage-Hayward, W., & Ransburg, D. (2015). *Human resources in the family business: Maximizing the power of your people (A Family Business Publication)* (1st ed.). Palgrave Macmillan.

Stone, D., Patton, B., & Heen, S. (2010). *Difficult conversations: How to discuss what matters most* (Anniversary, Updated ed.). Penguin Books.

6

Advancing Leadership Capabilities: Middle Adult (Ages 35 to 65)

W. Sage-Hayward et al., *Own It!*, A Family Business Publication,
https://doi.org/10.1007/978-3-030-20419-8_6

Zak and Zoe—Middle Adult Stage

Zoe and Zak have matured a great deal since the last chapter. Both are well into their adult years now, with a range of responsibilities and goals in and outside the family enterprise.

Zoe is now age 50. She decided not to return to the family business as an employee. However, she and her husband moved closer to the family enterprise headquarters, which helped her engage more as a director on the board and with her six co-owning cousins. Zoe took a part-time position as General Manager for a small boutique retail business in her neighborhood, which gave her the time and energy to devote to both directorship and motherhood—as she and Tom have four children. At 48, Zoe assumed the role of board chair and poured her energy into formalizing the business and engaging more of the family in leadership roles—there is now a well-functioning family council that leads regular, engaging, and well-attended family meetings that afford a critical role in educating eighteen G4s from 3 to 28 years old.

Zak is also 50, a milestone he himself finds hard to acknowledge. For many years, he pursued an entrepreneurial path outside the family enterprise, helping to launch and run a start-up in the social media space. After many ups and downs, including gaining significant venture capital funding, Zak and the other leaders of the business opted to close it, having found it too difficult to scale and compete with the major players in that tech subsector.

He then worked as a tech consultant for several years, finding he enjoyed creating technology solutions focused on HR within growing businesses. In his mid-thirties, Zak married his longtime girlfriend, a nurse practitioner, and they now have three children: two teens and a tween.

Zak's non-linear path ultimately led him back to the family firm. He had always discussed opportunities to use technology in the company, and teased his dad about being stuck in an "old-world" business that was unwilling to "change with the times." Zak's father invited him to join the business as a technology manager, and Zak grew the role steadily over the years to rise to VP of People and Technology, creating tech solutions for HR, operations, and other areas, earning his father's and his team's respect while motivating Zak to think about leading the business someday as CEO.

Zak's father's health has been an issue, as has the behavior of Zak's cousin, who works as VP of finance for the business. The "Sample Development Plan" section of this chapter provides more details on these challenges.

This chapter further explores the ownership development of family members like Zak and Zoe, who—at this point—are in "middle adulthood," from age 35 to 65. In these thirty years, people typically have a very wide range of roles, within professional and personal domains. The chapter outlines the considerations and challenges of this life stage as well as development goals and identifies where to start or continue your development efforts.

Passing Along the Right Values at Danica Imports

"Values are as or more important than development goals," says Rodney Benson, co-founder of Danica Imports. Business partners Rodney Benson and Jeremy Braude purchased Danica Imports decades ago, as mentioned in the previous chapter (Early Adult). Their sons Gary and Jon (respectively) joined the business in their late twenties and still work with the company today, many years later. The last chapter presented several lessons Jeremy shared about developing the next generation as owners and employees when they were in their late twenties. Here, his co-founder Rod discusses development practices they've continued to use as their sons have ascended into middle adulthood.

Rod has been especially focused on ensuring Gary and Jon learn and practice the values on which Danica was founded, particularly on how to treat people—which applies to both business and ownership issues. To do that, they use several practices for working with the rising generation including:

- *Weekly Development Meetings*: Rodney meets with his son, Gary, weekly to further his skills around leadership, business acumen, and governance.
- *Corporate Culture Meetings*: Prior to Rod and Jeremy's retirement, they held weekly discussions on key topics such as how to treat customers, suppliers, and employees.
- *Future Director Meetings*: Post-retirement, Rod and Jeremy meet with G2 to strengthen and hone their board governance capabilities as future board members and then invited to participate on the board as directors.
- *Family Meetings*: The Benson family (founder, rising generation, and spouses) hold structured meetings on a quarterly basis with a rotating chairperson and formal agendas to discuss family-related matters with a casual discussion of business progress and other ownership topics.

Rod has found the Corporate Culture Meetings particularly valuable for the owners who are active in the operations of the company. "Early on, we created an ongoing list of topics for the meetings to which anyone could contribute," he says. "At the end of the year, when we got to the bottom of the list, we'd start over, to layer the understanding with deeper knowledge about how to deal with people and situations." Even today, he continues to use the list and lessons learned for Gary's ongoing development, including in their weekly development meetings. Here are some of the topics covered in the meetings:

- Understanding and executing human resource policies
- Building loyalty with external and internal people
- Respecting customer needs
- Handling challenging or unreasonable customer requests
- Handling setbacks or problems (using real-life case studies)

Along the way, Rod brought in outside advisors to help the next generation with both their evaluation and development as owners and employees. "Get more independent advice even if you don't think you need it," he says. "It helps you think through planning in an unemotional way."

Rodney has been very happy with the results of these proactive development efforts. "When I look back to ten years ago, I see how far Gary and Jon have come with respect to understanding the human side of things," he says. The results are also evident in the company's ongoing strong performance.

Danica's approach to development in middle adulthood reflects many of the themes discussed in this chapter, which focuses on fostering ownership development in this family enterprise cohort.

The Middle Adult Stage (Ages 35 to 65) and Why It Matters

This is the stage in which many adults will experience prime performance and, hopefully, fulfillment in multiple dimensions, including family, career, and community. This is also a time of significant changes and is often marked by transitions. In many ways, middle adulthood is a "bridge" stage or a transition between youth and later adulthood. Adults in this phase of life are no longer considered young in most settings, but they are also not "old" by most standards, especially since today's life span in many developed nations stretches past eighty years. Chronological age is even less important in this stage since people in this age group be at very different stations of life depending on their status regarding career, marriage, family, health, etc. Some 40-year-olds run major companies while others have struggled to move out of their parents' home.

In this context, some of the key factors that make middle adulthood an especially important time for developing an owner's mindset include:

- *Family dynamics and transitions*: Many adults in this stage will have families of their own, often with children of various ages. This exposes families to more potential dynamics across generations. Some are positive, such as when generations bond over the emergence and development of grandchildren. Other shared experiences can be more challenging, such as the pursuit of controversial career paths or rising tension with new in-laws. Emotional cutoffs such as the estrangement of family members may occur and endure into middle adulthood. How middle adults engage with their children also changes markedly over this stage, usually moving from an **adult-to-child** to **adult-to-adult** relationship. That requires adjustment for all parties, especially related to succession and other ownership issues. Sometimes the later part of this stage may be marked by the end of a long period of family members working side-by-side in the family enterprise, implying a shift in major responsibilities, such as when the middle adult becomes the family's new leader. Adults at this time may look around and ask, "Who's the grown-up here?" and realize it's now *them*. Or, maybe middle adults will face tough ownership decisions for the first time. The bottom line: those in this stage require key ownership and communication skills to navigate its uncertain waters, paired with self-awareness and the capacity to recognize and accept new responsibilities.
- *The evolving self*: Many in middle adulthood continue to have questions around identity and life goals. They ask: What fits me best in terms of career, family, romantic relationships, geography, and involvement in the family enterprise? Sometimes the answers can be surprising. A large proportion of marriages end in this stage, and many new career paths are begun. Thus, it's important for middle adults to think about what roles they prefer as owners and to develop or refine the capabilities to take on such roles.
- *Aging parents*: In this stage, middle adults typically have to deal with the aging process of their parents. One of the most common mistakes is to consider their parents simply an "older version of the people they had always been." Accepting and attending the geriatric development[1] of parents—those once very passionate, active, and successful individuals—is a difficult and potentially scary process. Understanding and being patient with parents' physical and mental decline, and becoming increasingly set in their ways or stuck in the past, can bring a shadow of both sadness and concern. Traversing this pathway is involved, to say the least, and often requires middle adults to rise to the challenge.

---

[1] Solie, D. (2004). *How to say it to seniors: Closing the communication gap with our elders*. Penguin.

- *A time of stepping up—amidst high expectations*: Middle adulthood is a time when people "come into their own," including individuals who may have been lagging or languishing in previous stages. Those who have assumed a role in the enterprise often feel more comfortable sharing their ideas and wielding their influence. This tendency to *step up* carries with it a responsibility to focus more intently on their own development to ensure they have the most positive impact. The box "Sara Steps Up" provides an example of a middle adult's progression to greater involvement and trust in the family. Whether or not middle adults step up to greater maturity and responsibility, the senior generation tends to express high expectations of individuals in this stage. They will ask questions such as "Why aren't you advancing faster?" or "When will we have grandchildren?" and "Will you be a good owner?" These expectations can create stress between and within generations, because of mismatched expectations, rivalry, and other factors. Having a deeper understanding of the ownership role and responsibility, along with a stronger ownership skillset, can help to manage expectations and create a more collaborative environment

---

SARA STEPS UP

Sara has been frustrating to her family throughout her twenties. A second-generation member of a successful family-owned retail enterprise, she had spent most of that decade flitting among career interests (screenwriting, fashion journalism, and others), traveling the world (on her parents' dime), and making professional and other plans that never came to fruition. When her parents asked her to focus her career or rein in her spending, she called them "unfair." Not surprisingly, Sara's family didn't see her as a successor or owner of influence. But in her early thirties, Sara displayed greater maturity. She worked in social media for a high-profile fashion brand, was rewarded with a fast promotion based on a highly successful campaign she developed, and soon led a small marketing team. She also expressed to her family she had been "young and immature" before, and took much greater interest in family meetings, serving as notetaker and suggesting creative ideas for family engagement. As Sara stepped up in these ways, the family – including her siblings and cousins, also prospective future owners – saw her as a likely future governance leader, a role in which she expressed great interest. "I guess it was just a matter of growing up," Sara said. "It was like the seeds my parents planted as a kid finally bloomed in me." She was excited to continue to prove herself within the enterprise, quickly dispelling her early reputation as less serious. In this example, the family was flexible and recognized Sara's development, and adjusted to her new behaviors, rather than being stuck in the past.

- *A time of renewal*: Middle age, for many, is a time of renewal—of energy, dreams, and goals. People may find they haven't accomplished what they wanted so they may redouble efforts, recognizing that the time left to fulfill key goals is not infinite. Or they may discover surprising answers to the "Who do I want to be?" question and think about how to attain this vision. Understanding where ownership-related roles and responsibility fit into this time of renewal is critical.

- *Greater acceptance and confidence*: While some middle adults will struggle with identity and personal vision, many others will find growing acceptance of who they have become and greater confidence about what they do or want to do in life. Most will be more fully individuated from their original families at this stage, without a sense of rebellion or embarrassment typical of the earlier stages. Many will have families of their own, as mentioned earlier. Middle adults often undertake much greater responsibility and capacity for risk, related to ownership, now that they have the experience, self-acceptance, and wherewithal to drive greater impact. But they need to channel their will, intention, and energy effectively, requiring care with the development of the owner's mindset and skills—see the box "High Stakes in Relationship, Career, and Finances" for an example.

HIGH STAKES IN RELATIONSHIP, CAREER, AND FINANCES

A father and his son spent some time trying to work together in the business founded by the father. It was complicated and hurt their personal relationship. The son decided to leave the business, move to another city, and start working on his career elsewhere. Both father and son then invested time and energy to improve their relationship and had positive results.

One day, the father called his son and said, "Son, I'm of a certain age now, and I'd like for you to come back home, and I'd like for you to join the business as my partner." The son, surprised by the offer, said, "Dad, come on, we just got our relationship back on track; we know working together was a recipe for disaster, and it won't work now. Do you really want to do this?"

Very calmly, the father responded, "Well, son, I thought about it a lot. And I really think this is the right thing for me, for you, and for the company. Will you please come home and see me?" The son, now intrigued by the offer, replied, "Well, OK, you are my father. I will come. By the way, I will have a return ticket for a flight the same day. I want you to know in advance that my return ticket will be in my back pocket."

The son flew home, and during lunch together, the father laid down why he thought his plan was indeed in everyone's best interest. The son was amazed. By the end of the lunch, he said to his father, "You are right, Dad, I don't know how you came to all this, but I think this is what I should do and what I would like to do."

The father said, "I am very relieved. And there are going to be two rules." At this point, the son, concerned about the possible conditions, reached for his back pocket to find the return ticket. Dad continued, "The first rule is because we are father and son, we need no written agreement." The son said, "Fine, I agree." At that point, the son was very curious and a bit anxious, wondering what the second rule could be. And the father immediately added, "Here is the second rule: I would like an understanding that, as my partner, we have an absolute agreement that either one of us can veto any deal."

The son was very surprised at that point, and said, "Really? Why Dad? I hear you, but what are you telling me"? The father explained further, "Well, my son, this is what I am telling you: if you come and work with me, I know so much more about this venture than you know now. And I am pretty sure that I will want to take risks that you will be uncomfortable with. Therefore, I agree that if you say no at this early stage, there is no need for further discussion. Now comes the hard part. I know that when you learn this business and I get old, I won't be able to take as much risk as you will in the future. And then it will be my turn to trust you and let go."

By agreeing ahead of time how they would decide and acknowledging the future challenges of letting go, this father and son team embodied the owner's mindset belief of being "better together." At that point, the son didn't need further explanation, offered his hand to his father, and they never looked back.*

* Hughes Jr., J.E., Personal Communication.

- *High stakes*: As the points above imply, there are high stakes for ownership development in this stage, at both individual and collective levels. For the individual, there are the looming questions of generativity[2] (how to guide and nurture others) and legacy, as fueled by the growing recognition of time's limited nature: What will you leave behind for future

---

[2] Erickson, E. (1993) (reissue). *Childhood and Society*. W.W. Norton & Company.

generations, in terms of the business, shares, lessons, and stories? What do you want for next generation family members (including your children, if any) as far as ownership? What lies ahead for you? These and other critical questions must be faced directly and thoughtfully to inform key decisions. Those with a more developed owner's mindset are better able to do that. Put bluntly, at the collective level, families that haven't yet done the work of development for current or future owners by late in this stage will face many challenges, including confusion and ambiguity around decision-making and potential large-scale conflicts. The "A Tale of Two Families" box illustrates this reality starkly.

A TALE OF TWO FAMILIES

The Wilson and Ramirez families, both owners of third-generation businesses, took very different approaches to ownership development. The Wilsons, owners of a large real estate development business, paid little attention to development, believing members would "figure it out" as they grew older. As a result, childhood conflicts among siblings and cousins were not only maintained but amplified in adulthood so the siblings, now the main owners of the business, only communicate through lawyers. Many of the cousins (third generation) have never met and there is an ongoing battle over ownership stakes. In contrast, the Ramirez family, which owns a Latin American beverage distributor, took a deliberate, comprehensive approach to ownership, helping siblings understand important ownership-related values from an early age and creating thoughtful policies and practices for ownership development and conflict resolution. Today, the four siblings in the second Ramirez generation work together with a high degree of trust. Any conflicts can be worked through given their well-developed communication capabilities and using the family's long-standing values. The third-generation cousins know each other well and are already learning to appreciate the family's emphasis on healthy ownership – a strong foundation for their own future ownership decision-making.

The development of greater ownership capabilities and perspective in middle adulthood is most effective when built on a foundation of development in prior stages. An organized, deliberate, and cohesive approach will help the family take on a wide range of enterprise-related challenges while serving individual and collective needs.

Central Theme: The Transitions and Trade-offs of Middle Adulthood

In this time of significant transition—from younger to older, from contributor to professional, from prospective owner to owner with full power—people must often choose among competing priorities. As the finite nature of life and available resources (including health and money) becomes clear, some early visions for oneself may no longer seem feasible, and trade-offs become necessary. That's the challenge most middle adults face, especially as this stage marches on.

One situation many middle adults grapple with has earned them the label "The Sandwich Generation."[3] Specifically, according to the Pew Research Center, nearly half (47 percent) of Americans in their forties have at least one parent 65 or older and are raising young children or supporting a child over age 18. Being sandwiched in this way between generations may place a significant financial and support burden on some, especially if there has been no exit planning from the family business by the senior generation. An increasing portion of that pressure stems from the need to provide support to a grown child. Again, nearly half (48 percent) of adults in this age range have had to provide some financial help to their grown children and 27 percent have provided primary support (a significant increase from earlier in the millennium). As people have children at later ages, their odds of facing these Sandwich Generation burdens have increased.[4] Consequently, much of the mental, financial, and other resources of those in middle adulthood will go toward the generations on either side, influencing the trade-offs they make, including those related to roles as owners.

Similarly, expectations run high in this life stage—those held by oneself and others. For example, often, both men and women expect to juggle career, family, civic responsibilities, social life, and personal pursuits. But for most, careers hit their peaks in middle adulthood, requiring devotion of a large amount of time, energy, and other resources. This comes at the same time when family obligations loom large as well, whether going to children's sports events or spending time with an aging parent, with consequent trade-offs. Leaving work early for a daughter's softball game, for example, may be seen as a lack of commitment to a demanding job. Many middle adults, today's Gen-X, have seen their baby boomer parents give up too much of their family life for work and wish to strike a different path for themselves. Inevitably they still run up against different expectations regarding work-life balance. One notion getting greater traction is career-family flexibility. Given that work can now be completed almost anywhere, the hope is that people can find a greater compromise regarding work-life expectations. However, that particular challenge may be especially daunting for *women*. On the one hand,

[3] Parker, K. & Patten, E. (2013). The Sandwich Generation: Rising Financial Burdens for Middle-Aged Americans. Pew Research Center Social and Demographic Trends. Retrieved from http://www.pewsocialtrends.org/2013/01/30/the-sandwich-generation/.
[4] See for example Lamagna, M. (2018). American Women Are Having Babies Later—and in 2017 Are Still Conflicted about It. Marketwatch. Retrieved from https://www.marketwatch.com/story/american-women-are-having-babies-later-and-are-still-conflicted-about-it-2017-05-19.

women are in the workforce in unprecedented numbers, contributing significantly to household incomes.[5] On the other, they still face very real glass ceilings and are doing more of the housework and child-rearing. Some studies show that women do as much as 60 percent more housework than men in the house.[6]

In family enterprise, many women have more means to pay for childcare and other home help, given the family's resources, but this raises its own set of issues, including a potential judgment by others or guilt about "outsourcing" such work. One prominent founding-generation couple in Canada built their family enterprise on the foundation of what they call the "Power of Together." They recognized early on that if they worked together at all levels—as parents and business owners—their combined energy and accomplishments were much greater than that of just two people.

Because middle adulthood is a time of great expectations and fulfillment of potential, and also one of significant challenges related to transitions and trade-offs, understandably, many decisions feel like "either/or" ones versus "both/and" options. Adding ownership-related development and responsibilities to the mix may seem understandably overwhelming. However, it can also be a means of focusing on priorities and understanding what matters most. If having a voice in ownership decisions is important, for example, then you must find the time and energy for this priority. In this way, taking on responsibilities in the ownership circle of family enterprise will help sharpen your focus and field of vision, for your benefit and that of the broader enterprise. If the family as a collective can agree to move toward being a learning family to foster a collective owner's mindset, the enterprise and everyone within it will benefit.

Development Goals

Many middle adults will have grown significantly regarding ownership development, but most have plenty more to gain and grow across dimensions to

---

[5] Glynn, S. J. (2019, May 10). Breadwinning Mothers Continue To Be the U.S. Norm. Center for American Progress. https://www.americanprogress.org/issues/women/reports/2019/05/10/469739/breadwinning-mothers-continue-u-s-norm/.

[6] See for example Burkeman, O. (2018). Dirty Secret: Why Is There Still a Housework Gap? The Guardian. https://www.theguardian.com/inequality/2018/feb/17/dirty-secret-why-housework-gender-gap.

maximize their impact. We recommend prioritizing the areas in Exhibit 6.1 in the ongoing journey of building an owner's mindset.

Exhibit 6.1 Owner's Mindset: Development Goals for Middle Adults

OWNER'S MINDSET: DEVELOPMENT GOALS FOR MIDDLE ADULTS	
AREA	**DEVELOPMENTAL GOALS**
INDIVIDUAL	• **Deepen a sense of identity, role and values:** A core goal at this stage is to deepen your understanding of where you derive the most meaning in life – why do you do the things you do, what kind of impact do you want to have and how do you continue to advance your capacity as an owner? Boosting the ability of those in this stage to understand the context of decisions, challenges, and opportunities of ownership benefits all owners and the broader system. • **Strengthen ability to self-manage:** Self-management can be one of the more challenging capabilities to master, especially during a life stage involving multiple demands and roles. Our physical, mental, and emotional resources can become low or tapped out. Being steady in the whirlwind is a critically important skill as the ownership system becomes more complex. Too often, challenges within a family enterprise stem from individuals who don't have the maturity or self-awareness to function effectively, so look to gain greater self-management skills.
FAMILY	• **Collaboration and teamwork:** Building skills that focus on finding common ground or shared interests and resolving – or preventing – disputes go a long way to creating trust and credibility. • **Building and maintaining family culture:** Another important goal for this stage is to be intentional about the type of family culture you want to build. This includes fostering traditions, creating a safe space for family members to share their hopes, dreams, and challenges (along with creating a family vision), and welcoming new members into the family as the rising generation finds partners and has children. • **Co-parenting:** Many middle adults are parents, obliging them to take an intentional, proactive approach to raising the next generation of the family as well-adjusted people and well-prepared future owners. Effective co-parenting where both parents are truly involved is a critical dynamic even when a couple is divorced. This involves appreciating that the "power of together" yields greater results.
OWNERSHIP	• **Navigating the tools for continuity:** Middle-adult owners should be "fully in the pool" with regard to key structures, policies, and processes that aid the succession of leadership and ownership in a family enterprise. Documents such as shareholders' agreements, trust documents, wills, insurance, and others must be more fully understood at this stage because middle adults have greater involvement in designing and modifying them to suit the broader family's interests. • **Leading governance:** Those in this stage will likely take on governance responsibilities and roles such as corporate director, family council member, or trustee for a foundation. Having the business, governance, and interpersonal skills to take on these roles effectively and help develop others for future such roles is critical.

OWNER'S MINDSET: DEVELOPMENT GOALS FOR MIDDLE ADULTS	
AREA	DEVELOPMENTAL GOALS
OWNERSHIP	• **Involvement or leadership of ownership direction and goals:** At this stage, owners will be increasing their knowledge around the financial side of running a business and how that relates to the family's preferences for growth, risk, profitability, and liquidity ("GRPL") – as discussed earlier in the book. Along with this territory goes an understanding and appreciation for management, especially the burden operating owners bear for the family and the importance of maintaining strong boundaries between management and ownership.
BUSINESS / INDUSTRY	• **Honing leadership skills and capabilities:** For operating owners, middle adulthood is a time to sharpen skills in management and leadership realms such as management, delegation, communication, relationship-building, time management, strategic thinking, and the like. In addition, taking on profit center responsibility builds a deeper understanding of building and managing a business. • **Expanding knowledge beyond the business:** During this stage, especially in larger multigenerational family enterprises, the assets owned include more than just the business. Owners and prospective owners need to expand their knowledge to better understand how the family manages their financial assets • (e.g., investment strategy), deferred assets (i.e., insurance and annuities), philanthropic assets (approaches to charitable giving), and heirloom assets (e.g., vacation property).

How-Tos

In middle adulthood, complexity rises as owners are "playing on two fields" simultaneously: thinking about their own development and that of the next generation—their children and nieces and nephews. Our how-tos here focus on development in both areas.

- *Build family culture through traditions*: Building a strong family culture happens through intention and with clear purpose, and an early start. When families are young is the time to design a family culture. There is no better way to do this than by initiating or continuing great family traditions—anything from a fun singing contest over the holidays to an annual trip for grandparents and grandchildren. Traditions are often a core component of family life and provide a sense of belonging. Such rituals are a core part of a family's identity and foster cohesion and connection.
- *Grow _with_ your children*: In middle adulthood, as our offspring grow and evolve, it is easy to recognize that as parents, we learn as much from our children as they do from us. This dynamic cross-generational process makes us better human beings if we are open to learning what it has to offer. Admittedly, it is helpful to recognize this counterintuitive notion early on

and to embrace it to gain maximum benefit rather than to fight or dismiss it. This philosophy greatly assists with the transition from an adult-to-child relationship to an adult-to-adult connection.

- *Promote transition of roles and responsibilities*: Ownership development is not an "individual sport." The senior generation has to willingly transition key ownership roles and responsibilities to rising generation members. Mentoring or making promises of future transition is not enough. Do whatever is possible to help the senior generation understand the importance of providing middle adults a view of decision-making processes and actual decision-making roles in the enterprise, for the good of the enterprise and family. See the box "What If the Senior Generation Doesn't Want to Transition?" for more insights and about this critical development priority.

<table>
<tr><td colspan="1">

WHAT IF THE SENIOR GENERATION DOESN'T WANT TO TRANSITION?

Many business families face the challenge of the senior generation wanting to retain control over key ownership decisions in perpetuity. What can "rising owners" and "would-be owners" do in this challenging situation? While there's no magic bullet for next-generation owners, we believe it's about being respectful and proactive in seeking a greater role and responsibility.

"If you don't ask, you don't get," a business family member said, and we agree. In some cases, it's simply a misunderstanding, where both sides try to avoid placing pressure on the other around the transition. First promote open communication and probe topics that aren't clear. If it's not a misunderstanding, you're facing a more complex challenge. In this case, investigate why the senior generation is retaining control. Typical explanations fall into these categories:

- **Personal:** Incumbents may not be ready to let go because of their passion, sense of identity, a sense of "unfinished life mission," or fears related to the enterprise. The Senior Adult chapter discusses these challenges in detail.
- **Concern about next gen:** In this case, the senior generation perceives the next generation (individuals or the team) as ill-prepared to succeed them, whether related to abilities, knowledge, maturity, experience, engagement, or other factors.
- **Concern about the business:** The business may be facing a particular crisis or time of change, such that the family doesn't want to add the challenge of succession to the picture.
- **Suggested actions:** More often than not, more than one of the factors above is in play. Gaining clarity around the source of any reluctance enables you to address issues that are often unspoken. Some specific suggestions on managing these issues include:
  - **Anchor the conversation in vision:** Often we know what we don't want but don't always know what we do want. Too frequently, we jump to solution mode before we truly understand the problem and concerns. Stephen Covey's principle of "begin with the end in mind" is an important imperative to start with when the incumbent generation is reluctant to let go. Take the time to listen closely to each person's vision of what they want and need in the future. Then seek alignment on an endgame you collectively hope to achieve that also meets individual goals.
  - **Work with a facilitator:** Seek the services of an experienced, well-trained facilitator who can ask the right questions to get at the heart of the concerns. A facilitator is a neutral resource who can deftly illuminate the various perspectives, identify points of contention (as well as agreement!), keep the conversation on track, and guide your family towards potential actions and quick wins. Almost everyone's behavior changes when an independent person is involved in the conversation. A facilitator allows everyone to participate rather than leaving one family member with the responsibility of moderating.
  - **Take some chips off the table:** If the incumbent generation feels their lifestyle or stability is potentially exposed to variations in business performance post-transition, the senior generation may transfer assets or shares over time rather than all at once or put debt on the balance sheet. Offering this partial or time-related transition allows the senior generation some comfort that they will be taken care of in their golden years.

</td></tr>
</table>

- *Learn to share control*: As ownership transitions to the rising generation, incumbent owner(s) certainly have the final decision around how both value and control will be distributed. And, senior generation owners often find that sharing the value of the assets among a next generation is easier than sharing control. Unhooking these aspects of ownership, that is, sharing **value** among all of the next generations while concentrating **control** in the hands of one or a few, can lead to uncomfortable and damaging conflict. As middle adults prepare to receive ownership-value, control, or both—they sometimes don't feel they have the right to "look a gift horse in the mouth." And yet, the mix of value and control they receive is likely to affect the very essence of their ownership. First, voicing how they might prefer value and control to be distributed is valuable. And they must recognize that the senior generation holds the final say and may ignore their requests. Next, taking the time to learn how to share control and power is one of the key capabilities of an owner's skillset. Having built upon the belief system described in Chapter 1 will support this skill development. Mutual respect, boundaries, and reciprocity are prerequisites for sharing power. All parties need to be willing to take responsibility for themselves, for the joint decisions, and the resulting outcomes without pointing fingers and laying blame.

- *Welcoming new members*: Middle adulthood is a time when the family expands most as family members find partners and start their own families. The challenge for spouses and step- or adopted children to join a business-owning family is often underestimated, especially where the business and reputation of the family are highly visible to the public. Consider developing an onboarding process to foster a welcoming atmosphere to help new members feel comfortable and knowledgeable about the purpose and operation of family meetings and other important family enterprise structures with which they may be involved, such as philanthropy.

- *Find the right peer group*: Once again we highlight the value of peer groups for gaining perspective, mentorship, and inspiration from those at similar or slightly more advanced positions within family enterprises, such as individuals who recently became more active owners of their family businesses. We continue to advocate this development route but also caution you to aim for peer groups with family enterprise participants so they will understand the specific dynamics and challenges rising owners face. Filter any advice through your own judgment about what's best for you and your family in your specific context. Read the box "It's All or Nothing: The Risks of Peer Group Advice" for more on the need to proceed cautiously with peer groups.

"It's All or Nothing": The Risks of Peer Group Advice

Paola, a second-generation member of a family business, had eagerly taken on greater leadership responsibilities as the CEO when she agreed to be a co-owner with her three brothers. She had already proven herself as a capable leader but felt that her siblings were reluctant to allow her the full decision authority she felt she needed to move the company forward and foster growth. When she brought up the issue with her peer group, they suggested, "You need to issue an ultimatum to your brothers. They'll respect your courage and won't want to lose your leadership. You're too valuable." When Paola followed their advice – "It's either all or nothing," she wrote to her siblings in a strongly worded email – she created a great divide. Her mother, still an owner in several of their businesses, felt especially hurt that Paola had taken such an aggressive approach and hadn't included her in the communication. It took several months and the help of an outside advisor for the family to repair their relationship. Paola's example drives home the importance of being cautious with peer groups as sources of mentorship and advice. It's critical that you select one composed of other family business owners that are run by facilitators with a deep understanding of family firms. That's because groups including mostly executives running non-family businesses tend to dismiss the huge role that the family, its history, and dynamics have on the business. Many groups, for example, emphasize leadership and making your mark, striving to reach maximum decision-making power in your organization by climbing up the ladder of succession as quickly as possible. That's not necessarily the best approach for rising owners, as Paola's example suggests. Look for groups where people are experienced with family business issues, more open to understanding situations beyond their own, and more likely to advocate a slower, more collaborative approach to change.

- *Take on leading roles in philanthropy*: In each stage-focused chapter, we've emphasized the value of getting involved in the family's philanthropic efforts to take on decision-making roles and gain important skills and experience along with understanding the positive link between family enterprise and the broader community. In middle adulthood, this could mean serving on the board of the family's foundation, managing relationships with charitable organizations to which the family donates, and/or potentially sitting on the board of one, or representing the family in the community, such as by attending or hosting fundraising events.
- *Build governance and the respective policies in the family*: In the middle stages of adulthood, the extended family includes significant others and offspring. Greater numbers bring greater complexity. Spend time at this stage collectively discussing potential consequences—even unintended—and from there collaborate to develop key policies that create greater clarity, consistency, perceived fairness, and transparency. For example, grandparents may be paying the tuition fees for their grandchildren's education but nothing is written down, and no one is clear about what percentage is covered or what exactly is covered (i.e., tuition, housing, books, etc.), for how long (i.e., elementary, secondary, university, or postgraduate), and whether there are any performance expectations (e.g., good grades). The middle adult group is grateful for the help and hesitant to ask questions for fear of sounding entitled, so the confusion proliferates. Using family governance meetings to map out the guidelines and expectations

creates understanding for all. Writing it down in a *simple* policy cements the family's understanding and provides a record for future reference. An education policy is only one of many policies of families that can be created during this stage (see sample list of policies in Appendix B). However, this endeavor should not be a "race" to complete all policies. Taking the time to hear diverse perspectives and ensure the resulting policies fairly represent those voices builds alignment and commitment. It takes patience, a willingness to reflect deeply on what matters, and an openness for integrating divergent perspectives on each topic.

- *Work on continuity structures for the future*: Middle adulthood is a time to gain deeper, more actionable ownership knowledge. This means that family members are ideally *working together on* building or modifying ownership structures such as shareholders' agreements, trusts, and distribution policies to suit evolving family needs. Aiming for educational opportunities early in this stage (i.e., when people are in their thirties and forties) together as a family is an effective way to dramatically improve ownership capability. This is how long-standing, multigenerational families have embedded being a learning family as part of their culture.

- *Navigate the intersection of family and money*: Money can be a volatile topic in a family enterprise. Issues from who gets what when, fiscal imbalance, varying values around spending, and more abound. Gender issues may also add to this volatility for some families. For example, women are now inheriting, generating, and managing significantly more wealth than in previous generations. Building an owner's mindset includes helping family members develop skills to navigate things like fiscal inequality in their relationships.[7]

- *Address compensation transparently*: The box "Four Types of Compensation in a Family Enterprise"[8] has important information about financial rewards associated with divergent roles in the enterprise. For ownership development specifically, it can be tricky for families to understand whether and how much to pay those who have undertaken more formal development activities that have potentially led to roles with greater responsibility. Compensation, in this case, can also be a way to create a clearer sense of accountability among future owners—it's not just about showing up but *earning* the rights and rewards of ownership.

---

[7] Hughes Jr., J.E., Bronfman, J. & Merrill, J. (2000). Reflections on Fiscal Unequals. The Chase Journal, Vol. IV, Issue 4.

[8] From Schneider F. S. & Schneider Malek, K. Four Ways of Differentiating Compensation in a Family Business.

FOUR TYPES OF COMPENSATION IN A FAMILY ENTERPRISE
Even many family enterprise members don't recognize that there are four distinct types of compensation or financial benefit in this setting: • **Compensation for what you do:** This includes salary, stipend, hourly rates or fees for employment in the family enterprise (full-time or part-time position, internship, special projects, consulting, governance role), or, potentially, for undergoing ownership development • **Compensation for how well you do what you do:** Bonuses and long-term incentives associated with any official employment in the enterprise • **Compensation for what you own:** This includes dividends, distributions, rent for property owned by the family, and others • **Compensation for who you are (family member):** Gifts of money, a car, a down payment for a house, and similar benefits It's important to treat each type of compensation distincly. For example, work in the enterprise is typically compensated by salary and bonus, meaning an owner who works in the business would earn that compensation in addition to dividends (if dividends were declared and paid to owners), whereas owners who do not work in the business would receive dividends only. In addition, we advocate for market-rate-based compensation for family employees performing different roles and at different levels in the family enterprise. Market-rate compensation, determined through a fair and open process, is a way to build alignment and trust among operating and non-operating owners alike. Some families compensate family members working in the business with additional shares which is often considered sweat equity (an increased interest earned from effort) due to the additional responsibility of taking care of the "family" business. We recommend an open, fair process for the calculation of this type of additional compensation, as well as for base compensation.

- *Engage in experiential learning*: Many families provide experiential learning opportunities for those early in this stage to gain practice with ownership and governance before having to make high-impact decisions. Sometimes rising owners may be given a small but meaningful amount of money to invest or manage to gain skills with this critical activity of ownership. Board observer or more "ceremonial" early board roles may also serve this purpose regarding governance experience, ideally with outside conversations to ensure people are learning. Rising owners may be asked to present on specific, focused ownership or philanthropic issues—such as their recommendations for charities to support. Of course, many in this age range will be in full ownership or leadership roles already, some having gone through a trial-by-fire period due to the unexpected passing of a senior generation member and the need to fill those shoes quickly. But usually, it's ideal to have some practice before assuming full responsibilities of ownership, governance, and leadership. Such experiences provide valuable skills and insights while helping soon-to-be owners gain credibility, confidence, and comfort with likely future roles.

- *Collaborate with peers in the family*: In families with the best outcomes, owners work well with their siblings and cousins to create a shared vision, strategy, and plan for the family. The best way to learn how to work with peers is by actually doing it. An example of this is the "partnership exploration meetings" created by one family for the three siblings in the second generation (all of whom worked outside the business), to discuss: how they saw themselves working together as owners, what decision-making practices suited them best as a group, and what values mattered most to them. It's important for some of these interactions to take place without parents or other senior-generation members present, to enable middle adults to develop a sense of direction and confidence with collaborative decision-making.

- *Create feedback loops*: Growth and learning rarely happen without some kind of feedback. During this stage, feedback will likely occur from within *and* outside of the family enterprise system, such as from family governance leaders, managers (whether working at or outside the family business), mentors, and others. The feedback may be formal through performance evaluation in the business or informal through channels such as peer coaching or mentoring. Asking for feedback is one of the most important attributes of great leaders.[9] Search for and cultivate feedback loops in the various roles you play. Then earnestly make changes to be the best you can be.

- *Work on the tough relational issues*: We talk a lot about *doing* in family enterprise—what to do to enhance the development of ownership literacy and capability. But often *undoing* is also critical: undoing negative patterns and habits in the family that can serve as barriers to ownership development. Families naturally accumulate baggage and struggle to address it proactively: difficult relationships, emotional cutoffs, poor communication, and other resource-depleting issues. If they are not resolved by the people who experience the relational struggle directly, the risk is to pass the same tussles to future generations, who will most likely continue struggling even harder. To clear a path for positive ownership development and action, be willing to work on undoing these patterns through more open communication, being willing to change, and employing forgiveness. This process may require working through issues with an outside therapist or other advisor.

---

[9] For more on feedback and leadership see Kouzes. J. M., & Posner, B. Z. (2003) *The Leadership Challenge*. Jossey-Bass.

Sample Development Plan: Middle Adult

Scenario: Zak is now age 50 and has been married for sixteen years. He has three children (two older boys and a daughter) ages 15, 13, and 10. His wife is a nurse practitioner and does shift work in the geriatric unit at the local hospital. After many years working outside the family business, Zak is now Vice President of People and Technology for the family's agricultural firm and is doing well in his job.

Recently, Zak's father's health has declined, which has left Zak with quickly mounting governance responsibilities. His father wishes to implement a more formal board with independent directors, but Zak thinks this is a waste of time and money and does not see value in having outside people "interfering" in their business. Compounding Zak's leadership challenges is that his cousin, VP of Finance for the business, often works secretively, not sharing information openly about key financials or "pet projects" he has taken on—an ongoing source of stress for Zak. His development plan includes the activities outlined in Exhibit 6.2, which Zak will tackle over several years.

Exhibit 6.2 Owner's Mindset: Sample Development Plan for a Middle Adult (Zak)

SAMPLE DEVELOPMENT PLAN FOR A MIDDLE ADULT (ZAK)	
AREA	DEVELOPMENTAL ACTIVITIES
INDIVIDUAL	• Complete a triathlon • Attend a three-day mindfulness retreat • Set out his five-year personal goals and review with spouse and family • Read articles and books on the art of delegation and time management • Create a shareholders' agreement with cousins • Attend Directors Education program to improve governance knowledge and competence
FAMILY	• Initiate a conversation with his family on an important question for all of them to consider together: "Why, what for, and for whom they are building our family enterprise over the next twenty years?" • Schedule a dinner with each family member to check in, catch up, and share stories on a regular basis • Develop an onboarding policy for newcomers to family meetings
OWNERSHIP	• Create a network map of key relationships in personal, operational, and strategic domains (see below for more details) • Hire a financial planner for personal family finances • Review and adjust personal wills with spouse and children • Create a practice investment fund with his children • Step into a family leadership role (such as head of family council) • Create a shareholders' agreement with cousins • Attend Directors Education program to improve governance knowledge and competence
BUSINESS / INDUSTRY	• Put together a case study on how to read financial statements for family's enterprise • Attend Strategic Coach program to build leadership and entrepreneurial skills • Work with his father on all aspects of a deal to purchase a five-acre parcel of industrial real estate • Take an even higher senior management role with P/L responsibility and five direct reports • Develop family employment policies • Work on influencing cousin (VP of finance) to be more open, possibly working with outside facilitators

The sample development plan is offered as an example only and includes a variety of ideas—some of which you may already do in the normal course of development in your family. Our goal is to inspire you to take a more intentional approach to development by building a coordinated plan for your family appropriate to your specific circumstance and context.

Development Influencers and Network Management

The middle adulthood stage is an important time to intentionally identify and map out key influencers for you and your family enterprise in a strategic manner. Cultivating this network of relationships is one of the most important aspects of being a leader and business owner. These networks can fall into three overlapping areas: operational, personal, and strategic.[10]

- *Operational networks* include those people who are important for getting things done under your responsibility—people to whom you can delegate or who can support or impede the tasks you need to accomplish.
- *Personal networks* are those people with whom you can exchange referrals or get mentoring and coaching from (or give it to). In personal networks, people help each other develop skill, make connections, and advance professionally.
- *Strategic networks* include relationships among those who help each other attain future goals and aspirations, as well as to address potential challenges to achieving those goals. Consider creating a network map with people from the following groups. In some families, the wealth creator or wealth-creating couple or group may be able to play a key role in development as "wisdom-keepers," helping to guide, mentor, or influence middle adults. Note, however, that not all senior-generation members can play that role well. In general, extended family members will exert a strong influence, especially siblings and cousins, as part of peer-to-peer development—such as an older cousin and current senior executive mentoring a middle adult in a middle-management role. Spouses may also be sources of influence. Regardless of the mix of influencers, it is important for those in the same cohort to spend quality time together. For middle adults, that can mean merely getting together regularly or brainstorming, planning and making decisions, and working to understand ownership roles, dynamics, and the collaborative process, such as by attending conferences and other learning events together. In this way, the group will grow closer and be more able to have positive, collective impact. See the box "The Benefits of Learning Together as a Family" and Chapter 8 for more on this idea.[11]

---

[10] Ibarra, H., & Hunter, M. L. (2007). How Leaders Create and Use Networks. Harvard Business Review.

[11] See Chapter 8 for more information about the learning family.

THE BENEFITS OF LEARNING TOGETHER AS A FAMILY

We believe strongly in current or prospective owners taking the time to learn and grow together. This can be especially important in middle adulthood as future owners move toward formal ownership. Collaborative education includes both formal modes such as conferences and workshops or less formal activities such as reading family enterprise books together. Among the many benefits of learning together are:

- **A common language and perspective:** By learning the same family enterprise frameworks – three-circle mode, the family enterprise model, four types of compensation, family development life cycle, among others – members begin to speak the same language and connect it to their situation, with similar core perspectives.
- **A foundation for decision-making:** Speaking the same language and sharing perspective serves as a strong foundation for decision-making and a way to understand the often-complex issues within family enterprise.
- **Better ideas:** Family members who learn together may be able to generate better ideas, in part because learning together breeds creativity and collaboration, both important elements of ownership-related decision-making.
- **Stronger bonds:** Going through any kind of activity together will generate deeper emotional connections and relationships. Many families who travel to conferences together or work with an advisor on ownership issues report becoming closer through the process and better able to work together, with greater shared understanding and goodwill.

- *Authentic friendships*: Authentic friendship has major benefits for adults navigating this stage. First, it provides a space for exchanging personal thoughts and feelings, encouragement, and empathy outside the family system. Second, friends share activities of mutual interest, being business or leisure-related. Finally, they can be a source of fun and recreation. The combination of these dimensions has multiple positive effects, such as boosting happiness and self-esteem.[12] Another positive element related to friendship is that the act of *choosing* one another brings feelings of being admired and liked over others, which enhances emotional well-being. Differently from some family members, who may remain stuck in past family roles,[13] friends can, in fact, see you as competent and capable, legitimizing positive self-perceptions. By providing emotional support and companionship across a life span, they can be a safe space for brainstorming important business, ownership, and family decisions, and receiving authentic feedback on interpersonal strengths and weaknesses.
- *Executives and independent directors*: Here, we are referring not only to senior executives and independent board members in the family enterprise but also to those with similar roles at customer firms, suppliers, partner businesses, and industry associations. Such individuals often have deep knowledge and experience related to a family business and thus can serve as

[12] De Vries, B. (1996). The understanding of friendship: An adult life course perspective. In *Handbook of emotion, adult development, and aging* (pp. 249–268). Academic Press.

[13] Siebert, D. C., Mutran, E. J., & Reitzes, D. C. (1999). Friendship and social support: The importance of role identity to aging adults. *Social work, 44*(6), 522–533.

mentors and influencers on a range of ownership issues. Be aware of such people in your universe and don't be afraid to seek development guidance from them.

- *Other family enterprises*: Among the most important and effective influencers in this life stage are middle adults and older members of outside family enterprises—especially fellow future or formal owners. We have seen firsthand the power of families guiding families over the tricky terrain of ownership, business, and family. There are many formal routes through which to meet peer families, including industry associations, conferences, and networks like local Family Business Centers or more international groups such as the Family Business Network (www.fbn-i.org). Of course, you can also contact other families informally through your network, community, or even online sources like LinkedIn. Once you've done your due diligence around their ability to keep information confidential, their support will be among the most precious.

- *Advisors, mentors, coaches*: As in other stages, advisors and other outside professionals can serve valuable purposes for developing middle adults as owners. During middle adulthood, it is critical to have someone outside the storm in your camp. These individuals help owners or owners-to-be learn how to resolve conflict and gain important business and ownership knowledge, ideally serving as a neutral, objective, but supportive voice across issues especially for navigating family and other relationships. It's natural for advisors to align themselves with those who retained them. Take care to find optimal advisors who fit your family's culture and values well and represent the full complement of family enterprise members—not just one generation or perspective. For more, see the box "How to Choose Your Advisors."

How to Choose Your Advisors

Step 1: Identify Your Needs
• What do we want to accomplish?
  o individuals?
  o as a family?
  o as a family enterprise?
• What are our goals and priorities?
• What type of expert advice do we need?
• What style works best with our family?
• How much time, energy, and resources are we willing to invest?
• How do we best source our options?
Step 2: Source Potential Advisors from your network, referrals, and the internet
Step 3: Interview Advisors to find the Best Fit
• Design your interview process. Here are a few questions to consider:
  o Tell me about your designations and what kind of work you specialize in.
  o How long have you been doing this work?
  o Have you received special training in working with family businesses? If so, where and what? (e.g., do you hold a FEA designation or a Certificate in Family Business Advising?)
  o Can you give us some examples of other family businesses with whom you have worked?
  o What issues do you see in the family, business, and ownership systems?
  o Where do you typically start with a family?
  o Who do you see as the client? The goal of this question is to understand whether they work with the family as a whole or with single individuals, and how they include the enterprise in their work.
  o What is the scope of the work? What will it cost?
  o Do you belong to a professional society or group that delivers continuing education focused on the special challenges of family businesses? Do you participate in these?
  o Do you have a network of professionals who you can call on to help you with complexities as they arise?
  o Are you willing to work with my advisors? How will you help my team of advisors overcome challenges that arise?
  o How do you get paid?
  o How long is a typical engagement?
  o Beyond making money, why do you do this work?
  o Beyond your technical expertise, what do you bring to the table?

• *Community leaders:* Religious, political, nonprofit, and other leaders within the community may be able to offer valuable advice and insight to middle adult owners. This is in part because family enterprise is tied closely to the community in which it operates, including employment, philanthropy, and other dimensions. But it is also because community leaders have perspective on pursuing missions aligned with their own values and purpose—thus, they can help those in this stage answer the critical question, "Who am I and how do I want to express that in the world?" Think about leaders in your community who may have such insights and consider connecting with them for guidance or inspiration.

Where to Start?

This can be a challenging life stage in which to start ownership development in earnest because: (1) ideally, such development would already be well underway; (2) there is potentially significant *undoing* work if the family is in a difficult place or has been for some time; and (3) there are so many dimensions to consider—governance, communication, and business knowledge, to name just a few—and those in middle adulthood are already managing many obligations beyond those related to ownership.

There is only one right place from which to start, which is from *where you are*. Consider where you are on each of the four main dimensions in our model: individual, family, ownership, and business (see earlier *Development Goals section*). Then start with whichever category needs the most work— and is feasible to address. Sometimes, that will mean focusing on difficult individual and/or family issues that have been in place for a long time, such as emotional cutoffs or substance-use issues. The goal is not to deny such challenges but to address them directly, often helped by outside parties and to set reasonable expectations for yourself and others.

A common issue for middle adult owners or rising owners is that the senior (theoretically outgoing) generation hasn't created the right environment for development, whether because of destructive conflict in that generation, an unwillingness to share or cede decision-making, or lack of awareness around these possibilities, or some combination of these factors. Consider carefully whether progress can be made in such situations. Sometimes it's not possible to overcome senior generation issues. But that doesn't have to stifle development. Instead, it is important for the next generation to take a proactive approach, thinking about where the family is and where they collectively wish to take ownership. Middle adults will likely lead that process, one aimed at creating trust, cohesion, and a forward-looking mindset. In many families, an individual or small group leads this charge, acting as a "Family Champion." See the box "What Makes a Family Champion"[14] for more on this important role.

---

[14] Greenleaf, G., & Nacht, J. (2018). *Family Champions and Champion Families: Developing Family Leaders to Sustain the Family Enterprise* (1st ed.). The Family Business Consulting Group, Inc.

WHAT MAKES A FAMILY CHAMPION

Family business consultants Josh Nacht and Greg Greenleaf define a "family champion" as a family owner or leader who serves as a catalyst – inspiring family members to fulfill their individual and collective potential as owners. The champion's efforts lead to widespread benefits for the family and its enterprise, including clearer vision, better relationships, and better communication with management. The typical characteristics of family champions include:

- Commitment to family development
- High awareness of family needs and dynamics
- Willingness to work as part of a team
- Ability to speak and act on what the family needs
- Ability and willingness to wear many hats
- Wide-ranging skills from business capabilities to interpersonal abilities

Think about what family member, including yourself, may be able to play the role of a family champion.

The implication of the discussion above is to start the development process for middle adults by assessing whether people can work together within their generation or, ideally, across generations. If the group does not have strong bonds, then work on tackling difficult issues such as communication and conflict resolution and advance the collective's emotional intelligence. Then work to gain key ownership and governance knowledge and capabilities, to position yourself and the group for more effective decision-making. Again, focus on what is most pressing for members and the broader family. If the family has strong business knowledge, for example, then ownership knowledge and capability would be the priority. Building, maintaining, and repairing family relationships should be a priority for almost any family to create a strong platform for building an owner's mindset at any stage.

Things to Look for

Middle adulthood is an especially critical time for ownership development, as people in this age range are often moving from aspiration to action on a range of ownership dimensions. The most common pitfalls for middle adult development include:

- *Being stuck in historic conflicts*: What needs to be *undone* is often as important or more important than what needs to be done in a family. It is human nature to want to sweep difficult issues like family conflicts under the proverbial rug. People deny there are any major problems and artificially dissociate family and business issues ("We just won't bring family issues into business and ownership decisions"). You are unlikely to make progress with ownership development if this is the case. Assess the need for undoing, then take steps to achieve it.

- *Too busy to engage*: Most middle adults have busy lives and will likely struggle to make time for ownership development amidst professional, family, and other obligations. Often, many family business members are too busy working *in* the business to work *on* business and ownership issues. This is likely to occur early in a family business's evolution, when many family members have both employee and owner roles, making it hard to recognize the distinction. Even finding time to get members within and across generations together can feel like a herculean task. This challenge is compounded for those in middle adulthood, who are often striving to "take back their lives" from highly demanding professional obligations—to spend more quality time with family and on personal pursuits. Strive to be proactive about understanding these very real forces pushing you or a middle adult in your enterprise away from development and determine how to make ownership development a fulfilling priority rather than just another burden.
- *Spousal expectations*: It's no surprise that spousal and other life partners play an important role in family and ownership dynamics. In this stage, when adults step up to larger roles in the business and ownership circles, spousal expectations, values, and preferences may conflict with what their partner has committed to. Spouses may be frustrated, for example, that their partner has given up a highly lucrative corporate position to work in the family enterprise, relocate to a small city, and be a more involved owner. Managing these dynamics with highly influential married-ins is an important priority and a challenge not to be overlooked.
- *Getting caught between the needs of children and parents*: This requires recognition and management of the double role middle adults play. One as a parent who appreciates the growing need for independence and responsibility in the rising generation. At the same time, they are still a "child" of their parents—and could be waiting for him/her to relinquish control of the business to them. This time can be a very delicate dynamic to navigate with awareness, patience, and ongoing support.

Given the volume and weight of potential challenges in middle adulthood, be strategic about the starting point and dedicate at least some time toward development. Start where you have the energy to do so.

Exhibit 6.3 Middle Adult Stage Summary Table

	WHY MIDDLE ADULT STAGE MATTERS	KEY MESSAGE	
WHY	• Family dynamics and multiple transitions • The evolving sense of self • Aging parents require increasing attention and understanding • A time of stepping up—amidst high expectations • A time of renewal • Greater acceptance and confidence • High stakes	Building on years of preparation, emerge as a knowledgeable, committed, wise family enterprise leader.	

	DOMAIN	DEVELOPMENT GOALS	HOW TOs	SAMPLE DEVELOPMENT PLAN FOR ZAK
WHAT	Individual	• **Deepen a sense of identity, role and values:** A core goal at this stage is to deepen your understanding of where you derive the most meaning in life—why do you do the things you do, what kind of impact do you want to have and how do you continue to advance your capacity as an owner? Boosting the ability of those in this stage to understand the context of decisions, challenges, and opportunities of ownership benefits all owners and the broader system. • **Strengthen ability to self-manage:** Self-management can be one of the more challenging capabilities to master, especially during a life stage involving multiple demands and roles Our physical, mental, and emotional resources can become low or tapped out. Being steady in the whirlwind is a critically important skill as the ownership system becomes more complex. Too often, challenges within a family enterprise stem from individuals who don't have the maturity or self-awareness to function effectively, so look to gain greater self-management skills.	• Take on leading roles in philanthropy • Engage in experiential learning • Collaborate with peers in the family • Create feedback loops • Work on the tough relational issues	• Complete a triathlon • Attend a 3-day mindfulness retreat • Set out his 5-year personal goals and review with spouse and family • Read articles and books on the art of delegation and time management
	Family	• **Collaboration and teamwork:** Building skills that focus on finding common ground or shared interests, and resolving—or preventing—disputes go a long way to creating the trust and credibility • **Building and maintaining family culture:** Another important goal for this stage is to be intentional about the type of family culture you want to build. This includes fostering traditions, creating a safe space for family members to share their hopes, dreams and challenges (along with creating a family vision), and welcoming new members into the family as the rising generation finds partners and has children.	• Build family culture through tradition • Grow with your children • Welcome new members • Build governance and other policies in the family • Work on continuity structures for the future	• Initiate a conversation with his family on an important question for all of them to consider together:"Why, what for, and for whom they are building our family enterprise over the next 20 years?" • Schedule a dinner with each family member to check-in, catch up, and share stories on a regular basis • Develop an onboarding policy for newcomers to family meetings

DOMAIN	DEVELOPMENT GOALS	HOWTOs	SAMPLE DEVELOPMENT PLAN FOR ZAK
	• **Co-parenting:** Many middle adults are parents, obliging them to take an intentional, proactive approach to raising the next generation of the family as well-adjusted people and well-prepared future owners. Effective co-parenting where both parents are truly involved is a critical dynamic even when a couple is divorced. This involves appreciating that the "power of two" yields greater results.		
Ownership	• **Navigating the tools for continuity:** Middle-adult owners should be "fully in the pool" with regard to key structures, policies and processes that aid the succession of leadership and ownership in a family enterprise. Documents such as shareholders' agreements, trust documents, wills, insurance and others must be more fully understood at this stage because middle adults have greater involvement in designing and modifying them to suit the broader family's interests. • **Leading governance:** Those in this stage will likely take on governance responsibilities and roles including leadership roles such as corporate director, family council and trustees for a foundation Having the business, governance, and interpersonal skills to take on these roles effectively and help develop others for future such roles is critical. • **Involvement or leadership of ownership direction and goals:** At this stage, owners will be increasing their knowledge around the financial side of running a business and how that relates to the family's preferences for growth, risk, profitability and liquidity ("GRPL")—as discussed earlier in the book. Along with this territory goes an understanding and appreciation for management, especially the burden operating owners bear for the family and the importance of maintaining strong boundaries between management and ownership.	• Find the right peer group • Thoroughly understand shareholders' agreements, trust documents, wills, insurance, and others technical ownership aspects • Navigate the intersection of family and money	• Create a network map of key relationships in personal, operational, and strategic domains (see below for more details) • Hire a financial planner for personal family finances • Review and adjust personal wills with spouse and children • Create a practice investment fund with his children • Step up to ownership leader role for family enterprise (such as head of family council) • Create a shareholders' agreement with cousins • Attend Directors Education program to improve governance knowledge and competence

DOMAIN	DEVELOPMENT GOALS	HOWTOs	SAMPLE DEVELOPMENT PLAN FOR ZAK
WHAT — Business/Industry	• **Honing leadership skills and capabilities:** For operating owners, middle adulthood is a time to sharpen skills in management and leadership realms such as management, delegation, communication,relationship-building, time management,strategic thinking and the like. In addition,taking on profit center responsibility builds a deeper understanding of building and managing a business • **Expanding knowledge beyond the business:** During this stage, especially in larger multi-generational family enterprises, the assets owned include more than just the business Owners and prospective owners need to expand their knowledge to better understand how the family manages their financial assets (e.g., investment strategy), deferred assets (i.e, insurance and annuities), philanthropic assets (approaches to charitable giving), and heirloom assets (e.g., vacation property).	• Promote transition of roles and responsibilities • Learn about the wider family enterprise assets or create plan for diversification	• Put together a case study on how to read financial statements for family's enterprise • Attend Strategic Coach program to build leadership and entrepreneurial skills • Work with his father on all aspects of a deal to purchase a 5-acre parcel of industrial real estate • Take an even higher senior management role with P/L responsibility and 5 direct reports • Develop family employment policies • Work on influencing cousin (VP of finance) to be more open, possibly working with outside facilitators

	SAMPLE STORIES, EXERCISES AND TOOLS DESCRIBED IN THE CHAPTER	KEY INFLUENCERS	THINGS TO WATCH OUT FOR
HOWTO	• Passing Along the Right Values at Danica Imports • Sara Steps Up • High Stakes in Relationship, Career and Finances • A Tale of Two Families • What If the Senior Generation Doesn't Want toTransition • "It's All or Nothing":The Risks of Peer Group Advice • Four Types of Compensation in Family Enterprise • The Benefits of Learning Together – Becoming a Learning Family • How to Choose YourAdvisors • What Makes a Family Champion?	• Immediate and extended family • Executives and independent directors • Other family enterprises • Advisors, mentors, coaches • Community leaders	• Being stuck in historicconflicts • Too busy to engage • Spousal expectations • Getting caught between the needs of children and parents

Suggested Additional Readings

Arnett, J. J., & Fishel, E. (2014). *Getting to 30: A parent's guide to the 20-something years* (Reprint ed.). Workman Publishing Company.

Aronoff, C. E., Mendoza, D. S., Ward, J. L., & Astrachan, J. H. (1997). *Making sibling teams work: The next generation (Family Business Leadership Series Volume 10).* Business Owner Resources.

Bottke, A. (2010). *Setting boundaries with your aging parents: Finding balance between burnout and respect*. Harvest House Publishers.

Craig, J. B., & Moores, K. (2017). *Leading a family business: Best practices for long-term stewardship*. Praeger.

Eckrick, C., & McClure, S. (2012). The family council handbook: How to create, run, and maintain a successful family business council (A Family Business Publication). Palgrave Macmillan.

Ghadiri, A., Habermacher, A., & Peters, T. (2013). *Neuroleadership: A journey through the brain for business leaders (Management for Professionals)*. Springer Publishing.

Grubman, J. (2013). *Strangers in paradise: How families adapt to wealth across generations*. Family Wealth Consulting.

Sinek, S., Mead, D., & Docker, P. (2017). *Find your why: A practical guide for discovering purpose for you and your team*. Portfolio.

Spring, J. A. (2004). *How can i forgive you?: The courage to forgive, the freedom not to* (1st ed.). Harper.

7

Mentoring While Letting Go: Later Adult (Ages 60 to 100+)

W. Sage-Hayward et al., *Own It!*, A Family Business Publication,
https://doi.org/10.1007/978-3-030-20419-8_7

Zak and Zoe—Later Adult Stage

Zak and Zoe are older now—both in their mid-seventies. It has been a long and often winding road of ownership development for each.

Zak and his wife have three adult children, ages 41, 39, and 36. After serving in ascending executive roles with the family business, including CEO, Zak helped hire a non-family top executive but stayed on as board chair. He leads a board that includes three independent directors and plays a vital role in ensuring the voice of ownership in strategic decisions.

Zak's children all completed their education at reputable universities and have shown interest and aptitude for the business, but ultimately pursued career paths outside the family enterprise—landing two of them far from their hometown. All have reached executive levels in their employing firms. They each became owners when the oldest turned 35. Today Zak is frustrated with their lack of engagement as owners. He offered them director roles on the board; but they do not participate actively, due in part to their busy life stage with professional careers and young families.

The family recently hired a family enterprise advisor to help them think about ownership-related challenges. After interviewing the family and observing family meetings, the advisor shared with Zak that the meetings mostly consisted of a "download of information" about the business that did not actively foster interaction with G3. Zak was advised to pose relevant ownership issues and decisions to the next generation, to facilitate discussion and provide members an opportunity to share their views and discuss potential best options. The advisor also suggested that Zak hire a facilitator to foster this dialogue in the family and business.

While Zak agreed with the suggestions and is eager to retire to a life of travel and other hobbies, he lacks the confidence that his children will rise to the challenge of active ownership, despite demonstrated capabilities in their chosen fields.

Zoe is now 70, with four adult children, ages 38, 35, 33, and 30. She has been the board chair of her family enterprise for twenty-five years, which has grown tremendously with newly acquired farmland, as well as an expanded tasting room, retail space, restaurant, and other commercial real estate. The business is now valued at $108 million.

Ownership complexity over this time has grown too—from three siblings to seven cousins—and will continue to expand as the next generation already consists of twenty family members.

Zoe is proud of the growth and professionalism she helped to establish. However, the family experienced some significant challenges when transitioning from Generation 2 to 3 due to a lack of structure and planning. She is eager to involve the next generation as owners but worries it may be too soon. Only four members of the rising generation work in the business and are performing well in their roles and as a family team.

Zoe struggles to put her finger on her reluctance about passing on ownership, but it has to do with feeling the next generation is not quite ready. While they are eager to be involved as owners, they have made little progress on related tasks, such as creating a family constitution and shareholders' agreement—items Zoe asked them to do with an attorney and family enterprise advisor. When she asks about it, the rising generation says they are "working on it," but she is skeptical about their ability to complete these key tasks, and increasingly concerned she will have to do everything herself. Zoe remains unsure of the best approach to transition ownership to the rising generation.

Zoe and Zak face challenges typical of family enterprise members in the later adult stage, or those ages 60 to about 100.

The Wandon Family: Building a Strong Family for the Long Run

Russ Wandon wants to build a family that will remain cohesive and connected after he is gone.

The 80-year-old founder of the Wandon Family Enterprise doesn't want an omnipotent monarchy-like power structure, but rather a system set up to transfer wealth, ownership responsibility, and values systematically to the next generation while attending to broader stakeholder needs. In his case, that means transitioning to his three children ranging in age from their early thirties to early fifties. "It's the opposite of a 'capitalist' approach to family wealth," Wandon says. "That's where you spend a lot more money outside the family, in pursuit of a lavish lifestyle with fancy clothes, fast cars, and frivolous things." He was inspired by a conversation with leaders of the Porsche family, observing, "They had a desire to succeed not just in business but also in the family. That meant having a strong set of values and being good to others, not just making a buck."

Wandon shares the principles he applied when building his own family dynasty:

- *Maintain family interaction, promote broad participation.* It is largely about communication—of goals, ideas, and visions. Families that talk openly about issues, including sensitive ones like wealth, are more likely to develop a working system to transition assets of every kind, with broad participation across the family.
- *Invest in education.* The next generation can and should benefit from a variety of educational opportunities, including undergraduate courses in business and related fields, governance programs to build director skills, and others. Wandon himself took advantage of structured learning opportunities and informal conversations with leaders of other family enterprises over many years to shape his priorities and plans.
- *Respect passions, personalities, and differences.* People will naturally have divergent interests within and across generations. Working with family members will mean respecting others' interests and seeking common ground without forcing one's own perspective and preferences. Being mindful of and receptive to diversity will mean getting the most from the family system while building strong bonds to support ownership transition and other issues. For example, both of Wandon's sons pursued career paths in business, while his daughter followed a career in the nonprofit mental health world. "Kids need to follow their passion," Wandon says.
- *Think beyond the family.* Building a dynasty also means thinking about stakeholders beyond the family, as Wandon notes: "I want to set the right example not just for my family but for the 400 people who work here and look up to us. I want to share our values with them too. That means communicating a sense of caring, warmth, and support." On the philanthropic front, Wandon started a private family foundation focused on health care.
- *Find the right consultants.* Wandon looked for consultants who "understood the importance of a family structure and dynamic and would include everyone in any process and offer prudent advice." He found a trusted advisor who worked with his family for more than a decade.

Adhering to these and other principles has helped Wandon think about what he wants for the future of his family and take steps to achieve it. "Continuing with a multigenerational family enterprise may not be the course our next generations choose to follow," he says, "due to different personalities, needs, and goals, such as those related to work-life balance." The statement clarifies that he's living by the principle of respecting differences, even those that may emerge among future family members long after his time.

Russ Wandon's perspective and priorities exemplify those held by many later-stage adults or family enterprise owners in our focal stage for this chapter.

The Later Adult Stage (Ages 60 to 100+) and Why It Matters

It is significant that we're including the age group of 100 and older. This group represents the fastest-growing age segment worldwide, and there will be an estimated 3.7 million centenarians—or those 100 years or older—in the world by 2050.[1]

This stage can last a long time, given large-scale improvements in life expectancy in recent decades.[2] That's one reason this stage warrants careful attention to ownership development: owners can contribute meaningfully for decades in their later years, whether they've worked for the enterprise or not.

Many feel they are "complete" by the time this stage rolls around, and therefore no development is required; however, learning happens at *every* stage of life, including this one, although with key differences. Below are additional reasons why it is important to continue ownership development well into the "golden years" of life.

- *Letting go.* Dr. Hawkins defines letting go as "an actual mechanism of the mind which looks like the sudden cessation of an inner pressure or the dropping of a weight. It is accompanied by a sudden feeling of relief and lightness, with increased happiness and freedom."[3] The theme of "letting go" will repeatedly arise in this chapter, with good reason. Owners in this life stage have often filled valuable roles within the enterprise: executive, chair/director of the board, family council leader, and others. While it is important to share their experience with rising generations, as noted above, it is also about giving the next generation space to grow their capacity in becoming the confident and capable "new guard." This is another tricky balance to strike: some outgoing leaders cling to the steering wheel, refusing to give up control; others take their hands off altogether, no

---

[1] Stepler, R. (2020, May 30). World population ages 100 and up to grow eightfold by 2050, UN projects. http://www.pewresearch.org/fact-tank/2016/04/21/worlds-centenarian-population-projected-to-grow-eightfold-by-2050/.

[2] Falkingham Dean of the Faculty of Social, J. (2019, November 11). Rising life expectancy and why we need to rethink the meaning of old age. http://theconversation.com/rising-life-expectancy-and-why-we-need-to-rethink-the-meaning-of-old-age-64990.

[3] Hawkins, D. R. (2014). *Letting Go: The Pathway of Surrender* (p. 8). Hay House, Inc.

longer providing critical guidance or advice to younger generations. Grand-parents can have a significant and positive influence on grandchildren. The oldest generation can set an example for the youngest one and help new family members appreciate the value of ownership in a way that the middle generation might not be able to, given their busy life stage.

- *Wisdom keepers.* The senior years can be considered a time of integrity which involves integrating and reconciling roles, knowledge, and experience. In their attempt to define their legacy, individuals in this stage often want to pass along what they have learned. At the same time, the senior generation may not be naturally gifted at mentoring. The later adult may need to develop new skills to better share their wisdom and legacy. Making sure the contributions and guidance of the senior generation are captured and shared is the job of the entire family of owners, not just the senior generation. We all know families where challenging dynamics prevent this from occurring, resulting in losing valuable interactions between generations.
- *Co-creation.* The aforementioned points suggest that benefiting from the eldest generation's knowledge is a two-way street: both older and younger family members have to be willing to carry the ball together and "allow" sharing wisdom while creating space to learn from each generation's successes and mistakes. Divergent values may get in the way here. For example, the outgoing baby boomer patriarch is all about action, but his millennial grandkids want a more balanced work life. This can lead to some trust issues related to the transition of ownership. We have also observed the rising generation complain that the older generation set up "playdates" for them to meet cousins and interact but gave them no real decision-making authority. This ultimately created an "illusion of involvement" that failed to promote ownership-related growth in the younger cohort. In general, all generations need to be open to co-creating the future and working through the inevitable tensions and missteps. The "Involvement Without Disempowerment" box provides an example of a tricky situation in this arena.

INVOLVEMENT WITHOUT DISEMPOWERMENT

The Hesmith family, owners of a growing automotive-parts manufacturing business, faced the challenge of transitioning from the first to second generation once the elder cohort reached his mid-seventies. The industry was changing rapidly—including the advent of self-driving cars—and the older generation had critical sector and strategic knowledge, including key risk management factors, supply chain relationships, and a history of value creation. However, they struggled with the right level of sharing and involvement, particularly how to transfer their depth of knowledge without disempowering the younger generation and effectively making decisions for them. The concern was that the rising generation would struggle to gain the knowledge and perspective necessary to occupy the metaphorical driver's seat as leaders and owners because of a lack of capability or interest. Both sides felt tension and anxiety about creating the level of interaction. Fortunately, the family had made progress by taking a structured approach to the challenge with weekly meetings to discuss business and governance issues, having younger-generation members take on observer director roles and other steps. While the challenge of finding the right level of involvement remained a key issue, the senior generation's sensitivity to this issue and interactive approach paved the way to a more positive future situation.

- *Owning shares and sharing decisions.* Sometimes *how* to transition the value of ownership can be clear but shifting the related decision-making responsibility is more complicated. The family may be accustomed to being led or influenced by a given individual or group for decades; therefore, shifting that role to others is challenging, no matter how capable the successor(s) may be. Similarly, the outgoing leaders or decision-makers (typically later adults) have to trust the younger cohort with decisions, even though their values may be different. The best antidote to these challenges is always a strong, ongoing focus on multidimensional ownership development, including that of the oldest family members. The box "Both Hands on the Baton" presents a valuable perspective on this issue.

BOTH HANDS ON THE BATON

To outsiders, ownership and leadership succession in a family enterprise can appear to be clean, quick transitions where one generation seamlessly passes the proverbial baton to the other. That is how Zoe, our ongoing family enterprise character (now 70 years old), has been viewing succession, leading to reluctance because she felt her children were not ready. In reality, this is far from true for many families, where there is a period when *both* generations will have their hands on the baton, especially when the rising generation is in the middle adult stage. The "passing the baton" metaphor obscures the reality that succession is more often a nonlinear, ongoing process that requires a "co-leading" between generations before the incumbent generation moves completely out. More and more frequently, succession involves this prolonged interaction.* Members of both cohorts may have formal and informal roles as leaders, governors, and influencers of the enterprise, making collective decisions. Here, the best outcomes happen when there is a strong sense of trust and mutuality among the generations, with all members focused on stewardship and the longer term. But it is not easy. Families, upon recommendations of advisors, often spend a great deal of energy planning succession; they usually don't spend enough time exploring the challenges of co-leading. Ownership generally means control, and there will inevitably be tensions around who gets to decide what. A strategic, thoughtful approach will go a long way to ensure members carry the baton well together, setting the stage for a positive eventual handoff. Helped by an outside consultant, Zoe slowly took this perspective to heart and trusted her children with more governance (board observer roles) and decision-making responsibilities (input into family liquidity needs), enabling them to grip the baton of ownership succession more firmly with her for a period of time.

* Marchisio, G. (2018). When a three-legged relay race replaces passing the Baton. FFI Weekly Edition.

- *Newcomers and challenging family dynamics.* Complex dynamics can be more prominent and amplified in this stage of adulthood, especially as formal ownership transition becomes imminent. For example, the involvement and influence of partners and adult children may grow. Spouses, for instance, may become especially vocal about the sacrifices they and the sibling owner or to-be owner may have made for the enterprise, such as moving to a new city or giving up higher-paying jobs for family business roles. Such sentiments may be linked specifically to ownership stakes, as in "Which family members deserve more and why?" In such scenarios, later adult owners can easily be caught "in-between," struggling to appease both sides while serving their own interests as well. These issues speak to the general challenge of creating a perception of fairness across the family. Fairness is a more intense issue in a family enterprise because members compare themselves on status related to both family and work.[4] Ownership development can help individuals and the broader group reach more trust-based mutual decisions about ownership and other critical issues.

---

[4] For more on fairness in family enterprise see Rosenblatt, P. C., De Mik, L., Anderson, R. M., & Johnson, P. A. (1985). *The Family in Business* (Jossey Bass Business & Management Series) (1st ed.). Jossey-Bass.

- *Narrowing window of time.* In a truly collective process, progress will be limited by those with the least knowledge, experience, or willingness. This can be especially difficult if owners in this stage have not been involved much in decision-making until *after* the incumbent generation has passed on. Sometimes, members think the outgoing generation has put needed structure in place. It is a rude awakening when they discover this is not the case. The stakes around transition are remarkably high—in terms of relationships, emotional well-being, money, and other key areas—so it is important to gain related ownership knowledge long before that time comes. Ideally, this should happen well before later adulthood, but in the earliest years of this stage, if nothing else.

- *Physical and mental changes.* No one is surprised to hear people's functioning declines in the last stage of life, but people are often caught off-guard by how *quickly* this happens, in domains ranging from eyesight to memory to mobility. It is important to appreciate the impact of physical and cognitive changes and constraints, especially on ownership-related issues, as these represent challenges for the entire family in most cases. Indeed, brain weight and volume declines by about 5 percent for every ten years, and neurotransmitters associated with cognitive performance, such as dopamine, also diminish with time.[5] What looks like a diminished capacity can sometimes be a change that allows individuals to complete the natural, end-of-life task of reflecting and pondering on life experiences.[6] The good news is that it's not all bad: research suggests that despite the increase in physical and mental challenges, most older people are well-adjusted emotionally in their later years. Together, these suggest that owners or prospective owners in later adulthood (especially its later years) should anticipate some decline in function but remain optimistic about their ability to contribute meaningfully to the enterprise. Ownership development can ensure they do.

---

[5] Scahill, R. I., Frost, C., Jenkins, R., Whitwell, J. L., Rossor, M. N., & Fox, N. C. (2003). A longitudinal study of brain volume changes in normal aging using serial registered magnetic resonance imaging. *Archives of Neurology, 60* (7), 989–994.

[6] Solie, D. (2004). *How to Say It to Seniors: Closing the Communication Gap With Our Elders* (Fourth Printing ed.). Prentice Hall Press.

Central Theme: Challenge of Letting Go and Shaping Legacy

Earlier we mentioned that later adulthood is largely about the challenge of letting go while creating a legacy: moving out of ownership and leadership roles and into a family elder or advisor role; transitioning from decision-maker to influencer and mentor; moving, ultimately, toward a new purpose, ideally with a sense of fulfillment and acceptance. Making these shifts proactively, with intentionality and grace, is the goal, and a challenging one.

Letting go of roles and control involves multiple, often contradictory feelings. For example, the excitement for continuing your life's work beyond your own direct role often accompanies the sadness of not being in control anymore and the fear of an unknown future. Letting go, therefore, is not a one-time event but a *process* that occurs over time and can take ten to twenty years or even longer. It is a process of transition that starts with letting natural feelings emerge and accepting that they are normal. This acknowledgment allows a subtler give-and-take that must occur for people to get the most out of the transition. As I have suggested, the outgoing and incoming generations must be made to feel valued and involved and given space for independent growth and transition.

Letting go works in conjunction with building a meaningful legacy, either consciously or unconsciously. In this process, individuals look back at people, events, and relationships and assign them new importance, which becomes part of their legacy. This powerful act is called recontextualizing life, and helps rediscover blessings buried in difficult moments.[7] Allowing time and space for this crucial discovery is important not only for the senior generation, but for the whole family and the enterprise. At the same time, this prioritization of legacy and how others perceive their life's work can lead to decisions that seem out of character. A later adult who, for the bulk of his or her life, was focused on how to secure the future of the family and enterprise seems to suddenly shift their priority to defining what they will leave behind. For example, we have observed a patriarch who created his estate plan in his fifties, transferring ownership of the operating company to the two (of four) siblings who work in the business. At that time, the patriarch prioritized business continuity and acknowledgment of the hard work and sacrifice of the operating siblings. Once in his mid-seventies, the same patriarch changed his estate plan to gift the operating company to all four siblings. At this stage in

---

[7] Schachter-Shalomi, Z., & Miller, R. S. (1998). *From Age-ing to Sage-ing. A Revolutionary Approach to Growing Older*. Grand Central Publishing.

his life, it was more important that his heirs view him as allocating wealth equally rather than to ensure business continuity. The purpose of sharing this example is to illustrate normal shifts in priorities for individuals as they grow older. It is important to continuously monitor the changing needs of individuals, the family, and the enterprise so that alterations to the estate plan can be made if necessary. Creating regular and effective communication channels will help avoid shocking surprises later. The process of examining and sharing legacy is a key part of ownership development for later adults. And can come with some unexpected consequences. We present practical tips for making this transition successfully later in this chapter. Here, we want to call out some of the key transition-related themes to remember for those in this latest stage of ownership development.

- *Contributing in a different way.* Later adulthood, handled optimally, means a shift in the role you will play in the enterprise, whether moving from CEO to board chair, or decision-maker to coach. Regardless of the exact transition, the goal is to transfer as much knowledge, skill, and capacity as you can to the family on various dimensions including ownership, business, governance, and leadership. While their presence in the enterprise may be reduced, the elder's relevance in the family remains hugely important. Hughes et al. (2017), in particular, suggest a few important roles that allow the family to crystallize and store their identity through telling stories, reminding of agreed-upon rules, and leading rituals. Additionally, elders can encourage the importance of togetherness by effectively mediating internal disputes.[8] For example, a European family creates videos of older generation members sharing their lessons learned, resulting in a "library of life experience" from which next generation members can learn—directly from the source, even after these family members are gone.
- *Managing loneliness and incapacitation.* As we alluded to earlier, this stage can involve large-scale changes in physical, cognitive, and social functioning. Most families, regardless of location and financial status, are underprepared for this. A spouse may die, for example, and leave their partner feeling lost and disconnected from the family and the broader world. A later-stage adult eager to share their knowledge and experience may face an unexpectedly chilly reception from the family. It's often assumed, particularly in some cultures, that senior members will handle the challenges of this stage on their own, especially the psychosocial changes it involves, but that's a shortsighted viewpoint that can create tension

---

[8] Hughes Jr., J. E., Massenzio, S. E., & Whitaker, K. (2017). *Complete Family Wealth.* John Wiley & Sons.

and problems family-wide. The senior member should take a proactive approach, but the family needs to be involved, with a full discussion of needs and expectations before declines in health force the issue. Indeed, the hardest situation can be when a family member's capacity for contribution has declined, but he or she remains interested in having some involvement. We have seen many such situations devolve quickly, with the outgoing generation clinging to control (ownership, voting rights, etc.) while the next generation tries to wrest it from them. We recommend a proactive approach that considers all possible future scenarios and surfaces everyone's hopes, fears, and ideas, helped by outside advisors as needed.

- *Managing the interface of generations.* As people live longer, there will be more generations represented in the family enterprise. A family today, for example, could easily have members from the boomer, Gen X, millennial, and iGen cohorts. Recognizing these groups will have different values and lived experience (boomers and iGens may clash about social and environmental values, for example), it is critical to create an environment where ownership issues can be discussed comfortably and effectively. Families who do this well often display these behaviors:

1. Make the time and space for *family* (not just business-related) communication to occur regularly.
2. Ask the tough questions (respectfully!) and listen carefully to the answers,
3. Focus on interests (needs) not positions (demands); look for many possible ways to meet the needs collaboratively, instead of getting stuck on one solution to meet individual demands.[9]
4. Respect differences (which does not mean you have to agree with them).
5. Put in as much effort as possible to create consensus but choose another decision model when this becomes destructive rather than constructive.
6. Utilize a facilitator when there are too many undiscussables or conflicts to manage yourselves.

- *Finding meaning.* Much of the discussion about the later life stage is about what is given up: mobility, energy, and car keys. But it should also be about what is *gained.* Schachter-Shalomi describes the process as "*consciously transforming the downward arc of aging into the upward arc of expanded consciousness that crowns an elder's life with meaning and purpose*" and calls

---

[9] Raines, S. S. (2019). *Conflict Management For Managers: Resolving Workplace, Client, and Policy Disputes.* Rowman & Littlefield.

this model of late life development sage-ing, instead of age-ing.[10] This is so powerful because those who find meaning in their later years not only live more fulfilling lives but longer, healthier ones.[11] This meaning should apply to their roles and contributions as owners, as well, as these may be enriched by the pursuit of everything from philanthropy to political office. In contrast, if you feel you have nothing left to learn or gain, your contributions—and likely your life— will be much more limited in every arena. As we will discuss later in the chapter, taking an intentional, proactive approach to the challenge of finding meaning, rather than just hoping it happens naturally, is a critical part of navigating later adulthood. Sage-ing enables older people to become spiritually radiant, physically vital, and socially responsible "elders of the tribe" for the benefit of the family and the enterprise too. To this, Schachter-Shalomi asserts: "*Sages can help redirect us from selfish, short-term thinking to broader, inspired approaches that take into account the welfare of our endangered planet, with its limited resources and environmental challenges. By their presence in the family and the community, they also can show us how to grow beyond our overreliance on materialism by cultivating an inner-directed lifestyle. Elders model to others how to put quality of being before standard of living. With joy and compassion, they embody the fruits of having explored the deep psychological and spiritual dimensions of life.*"[12]

- *Being effective trustees and growing capable beneficiaries.* The role of trustee and beneficiary is critically important as most family enterprises, by the third generation, have much of their assets transitioning to the rising generations through a trust. Yet, very little attention is paid to developing beneficiaries. Being the recipient of wealth often without decision-making power is a confusing role. Advancing success in the transition process involves being a great trustee who sees one of their key responsibilities as growing great beneficiaries. This significant endeavor deserves a whole book on its own! We direct those who wish to go deeper to resources in our footnote.[13]

- *Promoting contribution.* Finally, it is important for the entire family to embrace promoting ongoing contributions from later adult members.

---

[10] Schachter-Shalomi, Z., & Miller, R. S. (1998). *From Age-ing to Sage-ing. A Revolutionary Approach to Growing Older*. Grand Central Publishing.

[11] See for example, MacMillan, A. (2017, August 16). *People age better if they have a purpose in life*. http://time.com/4903166/purpose-in-life-aging/.

[12] Schachter-Shalomi (1998, p. XV).

[13] For further reading on the roles of trustee and beneficiary please see Goldstone, H., & Wiseman, K. (2012). *Trustworthy: New angles on trusts from beneficiaries and trustees*; Goldstone, H., Hughes, Jr., J. E., & Whitaker, K. (2016). *Family Trusts*. John Wiley & Sons.

Early in this stage, that may be ongoing leadership of the business, board, family, or philanthropy. In later stages it may mean serving as an advisor, mentor, and/or storyteller. Sometimes, just the senior generation's "being" (rather than doing) can result in a contribution to the family. The presence of the founder of the business or the matriarch of the family is a vital reminder for the whole family of their identity and legacy.

It is essential for everyone to keep in mind that the "soul never gets old." How one grows and contributes within the enterprise will certainly change over time, and may be more limited in later years, but an emphasis on fostering meaningful contribution is important across the life span. For example, two uncles in their later years, who had recently retired from their roles as board directors, wrote letters to the extended family (over 155 family members), sharing funny stories about the founding generation's quirky personality traits; the anecdotes were later included in the family enterprise's history book.

Development Goals

In later adulthood, the objectives are both individual and collective, given the large focus on creating and leaving a legacy—or sharing wisdom and transitioning assets and responsibilities to the next generation. Here are the primary goals to consider for ownership development in the later adulthood stage (Exhibit 7.1).

Exhibit 7.1 Owner's Mindset: Development Goals for Later Adults

OWNER'S MINDSET: DEVELOPMENT GOALS FOR LATER ADULTS	
AREA	DEVELOPMENTAL GOALS
INDIVIDUAL	• **Letting go and finding new purpose:** Later adults will benefit by exploring what they truly want to spend their time on in this stage of life. Often a new purpose emerges around philanthropy and giving back, or mentoring, or finding joy in relaxation and travel, or stepping more fully into the grandparent role. Regardless of which path is taken, it is useful to take time to reflect and examine what is most meaningful to you as an individual. • **Managing the aging process:** As we've already suggested, this stage is marked by physiological change. These changes can be emotionally challenging for some to accept and manage, even if the changes are primarily appearance related. Accepting these changes is important, while taking care to attend to any health matters and putting in place good health management routines around exercise, diet, and sleep. • **Dealing with loss and being frail:** Later in this stage, later adults need coping skills to deal with the loss of family, friends, colleagues, and independence. This process naturally also involves learning to lean on others for support and care. • **Cultivating friendship:** Because of physical changes, loss, and retirement, friendship is very important for older people. In many cases, friends are as important as families. Friends are able to know you holistically (beyond the family or the business role), are someone through whom you can see yourself, and are someone with whom to share experiences. They can represent a link to your authentic self, and your life history. Cultivating long life relationships, or exploring new ones in new circles, might become a more intentional activity.
FAMILY	• **Strengthening and evolving family culture and tradition:** Spending time to advance and embed a strong family culture, especially as the family continues to grow and evolve, is a valuable aspect of legacy. During this stage more than others, recognition of the importance of family is often more visible. Keeping the concept of building family culture and traditions at the forefront is an important role for later adults, but the goal is to do this through influence, rather than by coercion or guilt. • **Designing the grandparenting role:** Some later adults and/or family cultures are child-centric, while others are more adult-centric. Exploring who you are and want to be as a grandparent is an important step in this stage of life. Being intentional about designing this role with your children and grandchildren is important. There can be significant tension around this role in some families due to unmet hopes and desires. Spending time reflecting on and talking about expectations can maximize the benefit of this role in your family. • **Fostering family leadership in rising generation:** We tend to focus on transitioning leadership in the business and ownership systems and forget about the importance of leadership in the family system. Strong continuity in a family enterprise demands that someone in the family system is providing the glue that holds the family together. Later adults may recognize this more than others in the family, so their role in cultivating this is crucial.

OWNER'S MINDSET: DEVELOPMENT GOALS FOR LATER ADULTS	
AREA	**DEVELOPMENTAL GOALS**
OWNERSHIP	• **Advancing continuity planning:** Although hopefully some estate planning has been completed by this stage, it needs to continually evolve to fit the family's changing needs. As a later-stage adult, keep an eye on how to advance your estate plan through ongoing, regular conversations with the rising generations. They can't make these changes, so you must. However, they have to live with the plan once you are gone, so ensuring they are aligned around it and that there are no surprises is critical • **Legacy:** By this stage it's ideal to have a strong sense of what you want to leave behind: not just financially such as wealth or shares, but what you'd want future generations to know about your life story and the values it reflects. We believe it's important to humbly but deliberately paint a picture of what you want for your grandchildren and great-grandchildren, including those you'll never meet. What do you want to be the most prized, sustained elements of your legacy? Identify and work toward those.
BUSINESS / INDUSTRY	• **Executive development:** Early later adults who have not yet had an opportunity to develop skills and capability in the executive leadership functions may find an opportunity to step into this role at this stage of life. Typically, executive leadership involves overseeing business activities such as fulfilling organizational goals, strategic planning development, and overall direction. • **Fertilizing family talent:** At this stage, the talents in the rising generations are often more apparent, so later-stage adults' time is well-spent on coaching and mentoring those family members who have the interest, commitment, and capability to be future leaders. Developmental goals here involve learning to listen, influence, and coach rather than tell and direct • **Formalizing and professionalizing:** As a business's size expands so does the need for process and structure, which can sometimes go against the "entrepreneurial grain." Recognizing the need for creating consistent and well-understood approaches to how you do business as a family enterprise is often a vital role for the incumbent generation to fulfill. Younger generations may be hesitant to take this on for fear of changing the traditional way of doing things, so senior adults may need to lead.

How-Tos

No one has all the answers. For many, that becomes clear by this later stage of life. A central theme of this chapter is exploring the willingness to let go and transition control and decision-making gracefully to rising family members. This section presents practical tips for developing as an owner in later adulthood—while helping younger family members do the same.

• *Accept, plan, reflect, repeat.* This stage is ideally about a mix of acceptance, proactive planning, reflection, and a willingness to bring others into your process and ideas. Some later adults understand that truth more easily and embrace it more readily. Others may not. But the idea is for later adults to ask important questions of themselves: Where have I been? What have I learned from it—as an owner, employee, family member? What do I want the next stage to look like? For many, the "next stage," after retirement, may appear blank, or even bleak, as they have never thought about life beyond working years. Get ahead of that by actively envisioning the future and what you want it to be. Remember: our brains do not like uncertainty,[14] so painting a picture of your future will feel satisfying on the most primal level. There is lots of outside help for planning your transition: seminars, workshops, advisors, and peer groups. And there are many people facing the same challenge, especially as baby boomers in the United States and other later-stage adults worldwide face retirement.

- *Take a proactive approach.* Find people in the same situation, and learn and grow together, for everyone's benefit. The box, "From Somebody to Somebody," provides examples and additional ideas, and the "What's Next" box walks you through key questions to ask yourself as you consider the path ahead once the involvement in the enterprise diminishes.

FROM SOMEBODY TO SOMEBODY

An executive of a Fortune 500 company dreads his impending retirement, especially going from "somebody to nobody"—relinquishing an important, well-recognized role in the world to descending into obscurity and anonymity. But he pushes past that fear to envision a different future for himself, one where he learns to counsel others facing similar transitions. He follows through by earning a counseling degree and becoming a sought-after executive coach for post-career transitions. This is not a hypothetical example but a real-life one of a senior tech executive who did exactly that. He is not alone. Many people have found there's a "third act" to life after all, from U.S. presidents (Carter led humanitarian efforts, the Clintons started their Global Initiatives organization, and George W. Bush became a painter of some renown) to ordinary people engaged in fulfilling governance, service, and leisure activities in their later years. The idea is to go from "somebody to somebody"—not the somebody you were before, but somebody with a purpose and passion, who finds fulfillment in multiple aspects of life. Think about your somebody-to-somebody path, then start down it.

---

[14] DiSalvo, D. (2016, March 30). *This is how uncertainty makes you lose your mind.* https://www.for bes.com/sites/daviddisalvo/2016/03/30/this-is-how-uncertainty-makes-you-lose-your-mind/.

WHAT'S NEXT EXERCISE
As you consider what's next for you, rank the items below to understand your order of priorities.
With those rankings in mind, think about how you'd answer these questions, to get to the activities you'd most enjoy over the next five years (assuming you will decrease your focus on work responsibilities): 1. What might you like to do with your "extra" time? (Second career, volunteering, hobbies, learning, relaxing?) 2. Who do you want to spend time with? (Spouse, family, friends, new friends?) 3. What travel plans appeal most? (Number of trips, destinations, mode of travel, companions?) 4. How do you intend to stay healthy and active? (Physically, mentally, spiritually?) 5. How do you want to make a difference? (With regard to family, friends, community, others?) 6. What legacy do you want to leave? (Family, friend, school, spiritual, others?)

- *Fertilizing the talent.* Anything you want to grow in life requires tender loving care (i.e., TLC). Family talent is no exception. There are numerous ways that later-stage adults in a family enterprise can fertilize the abilities in the rising generation, such as creating a "think tank" environment for the siblings or cousins in which to discuss important ideas about business, politics, philanthropy, and other social issues. One family, for example, creates learning expeditions for a group of interested next generation members to travel abroad and source new materials and products for their retail distribution business. Another family took members to Asia to learn their customs and traditions while building business connections with suppliers. Then they expanded their luxury goods business into one of the countries of focus the following year. Consider what think tanks—or "act tanks"— might fit your family best. It is also about transmitting values to the rising generation. A patriarch in Canada made it a point to get to know his twenty-plus grandchildren on a personal level, to understand their interests but also to exert some influence on them, especially around family values and culture—the idea, for example, that as family enterprise members they were part of something bigger than any one of them. One way some families nurture talent and entrepreneurship is to set up a family bank. At their best, a family bank provides two key opportunities. First, it allows family capital to fund start-ups, risky or small ventures that couldn't get capital elsewhere. Second, it creates a space to practice policy development, joint decision-making, accountability, and sometimes, difficult discussions. Often, though, what seems like a slam-dunk idea doesn't foster engagement among the next generation. Sometimes the concept creates family division. In our experience, the limited success of family banks is usually because the bank's purpose isn't clear and policies are not in place to manage expectations. One of the first choices to make about any "family bank" is: Is it about family capital that will be decided upon by the whole family or is it about the senior generation's capital over which they will retain final decision rights? A well-executed family bank creates a shared experience, supporting the family's growth of all capitals (financial, spiritual, intellectual, social, and human). The key is to have clear rules and expectations around accountability especially. See the box "Key Rules for a Family Bank."

KEY RULES FOR A FAMILY BANK

A family bank is a process and structure whereby family members can access funds to start or support business ventures within the family. The bank is governed by a set of rules designed by the family that set the process for securing a family start-up loan as well as how family members are expected to pay back monies owed. One family began a family bank to support their family values of entrepreneurism and innovation—they decided to follow philosophy with action. They created the following expectations for family loans from their bank.

1. Family will invest no more than $100,000 in the first round.
2. Family will invest no more than the family member undertaking the new venture is investing.
3. Family will invest no more than 25 percent of total capital required for the investment in the first round of raising capital.
4. The family member starting the business must be the full-time CEO, not just an investor in the new venture.
5. The new business venture must set up a small board of directors with a non-executive chairperson; board must meet at least every six weeks.
6. The business or family member must start paying back the loan the year after the first year of profitability in an agreed upon amount which does not put the new venture at risk.

- *Thoughtfully decide on how to transition value AND control*. When designing ownership structures for the rising generation, it is important to reflect on how value and control will be shared by future owners. We often see a bias in families and their advisors toward equally sharing value among siblings or cousins but putting control in the hands of one or a few. We advocate for taking time to reflect on and discuss each of these critical elements of transitioning ownership separately. Questions to consider include: How do we want the rising generation to share in the value of our assets? How do we want the rising generation to share control and authority over decisions? In answering these questions, start by considering the potential repercussions on the relationships in the family—especially over time. First, identify your family's enterprise needs from a leadership and governance perspective including any legal and tax implications. Own the process and be inclusive in consulting others. Big decisions like these have a significant impact on individuals' lives. Therefore, it is essential for the rising generation to be exposed to and consulted with on these matters. However, the final decision of how to pass ownership on remains in the hands of the current owners.

- *Form a cousin club.* Beyond grandparent camp, the senior generation can provide funding for the group of cousins to build connections and get to know one another better over time and through their ages and stages of life. Senior generation family members can help the cousins select a leader, and work with them (or pay for an outside advisor) to build structure and clarity around what they want to learn or do together as a group of prospective owners. When the time is right, step away and let them run with it while providing mentoring and check-ins.

- *Address old wounds in the family.* Many families have historical wounds that have been swept under the rug rather than truly resolved. The senior generation, in their process or reviewing life, with wisdom and experience, may be able to lead the way (partly by role modeling) for these hurts to be properly discussed, addressed, and forgiven. Of course, this takes emotional maturity and willingness by all parties to come to the table for what might be emotionally charged discussions. A highly skilled and trusted facilitator may be helpful in navigating this sensitive and challenging process. The bottom line: the senior generation can and should play a vital role in ensuring relationship issues that exist within or between generations do not cascade into the next.

- *Relearn the art of listening.* Later adults, especially founding generation members, have often mastered the "directing and getting things done" mode of being an owner. So, during this later stage of life, sometimes it is useful to *relearn* the art of listening versus telling. Rising generation family members are frequently full of energy, ideas, and enthusiasm about how they can contribute in a meaningful way. This is a time when later stage adults utilize their wisdom by listening and influencing rather than directing and usurping.

- *Plan as a managing owner.* How managing and non-managing owners plan for transition will likely differ on key points. Here, consider how an operating owner may plan (we consider non-operating owners next); such owners typically start with transition of management responsibilities, followed by ownership-related ones. Moving on from a leadership role should involve reflection and thinking about the best potential successor, including conversations with the rising generation to understand what they want and how well set up they are for a transition. Are there strong successor candidates among them? Are next generation relationships—among siblings or cousins—sufficiently strong to handle the transition? Such planning usually involves the business board (ideally one with independent and family directors) and, sometimes, non-family executives. Together with the departing operating owners, these people can help formulate and carry out a plan, including addressing key development needs in the rising generation. As we have emphasized, the best such process will be truly collective and collaborative, rather than marked by battles over control and decision-making. Managing owners, ideally, will provide a depth of guidance on the business and ownership, without disempowering the next generation, as the box, "Stay or Get Out of the Way?" suggests.

STAY OR GET OUT OF THE WAY?

Should I stay or get out of the way? That becomes a critical question for later-stage adult owners in family enterprises, as they face the transition from greater to lesser involvement. As we've noted, those in this life stage often err on one side of that decision or the other: they cling to control or decision-making at the expense of the rising generation's growth, or they take an overly hands-off approach, letting the next generation fend for itself. Indeed, our ongoing family enterprise characters Zak and Zoe are both dealing with this challenge of later adulthood, as they struggle to understand how much to be involved in the business. What senior adults do is based on their individual personalities and interests as well as the family dynamic. We encourage later-stage adult owners to look for the right balance of staying to provide key guidance and getting out of the way to promote opportunities for growth. Use your wisdom and experience to help rising family members find their own footing and create a vision for what they want while still upholding the family's values, culture, and legacy. Like most things in life, there is a lot of gray area here, and no single right answer. Use that reality to take a balanced and collective approach while staying true to your values and needs. In both and Zoe's and Zak's cases, this will mean continuing to be involved while passing along key ownership responsibilities to the next generation, including making decisions about liquidity, risk, and other areas.

- *Plan as a non-operating owner.* Non-operating owners may face less of an identity transition than those helping to operate the family business, but relinquishing ownership or governance responsibilities still requires significant adjustment. If you're in this category, plan ahead for formal changes such as the legal transition of shares or governance roles, but also for less formal, "softer" things such as seeing people less often because you may not be attending ownership, board, or family council meetings. That can feel like a loss, and indeed it is one. Ideally, exit planning is something the family will think about collectively, so there is a clear set of policies and protocols in place by the time later adults transition as owners and/or from other roles; by the early phase of this stage, work toward creating those if they're not already in place. Just like prenuptial agreements, such discussions and formal policies are critical, but nobody wants to talk about them.

Be the one willing to raise the issues, for the collective and individual good. Look for outside help, such as that of advisors, to facilitate related conversations. Be aware of sensitive issues such conversations will raise, like status differences between owners and non-owners, including those transitioning from one status to the other. As always, think about how best to maintain family relationships as an overarching goal, while not overlooking individual voices and needs. Better to try to strike that tricky balance than to ignore its importance or to figuratively throw up your hands about getting it right.

- *Groom a family leader.* Family leaders are sometimes called Chief Emotional Officer (CEmO), or "the glue that keeps the family together," because they intentionally provide emotional support, ensure communication, welcome and educate in-laws, protect the culture, foster the owner's mindset, and promote fun interactions.[15] This role is sometimes coupled with the role of CEO, although as generations go by, and the family grows, the grooming and appointment of a different family member as CEmO becomes critically important. Very charismatic founders sometimes play both roles unconsciously. Being aware of it, and intentionally filling this profound role, is a very delicate task. It requires time to decide whether to leave the role as implied or a more formalized one; and identify the right candidate, who needs to be trained around major competencies: facilitation skills for collaborative decision-making, conflict management, emotional intelligence, and emotional maturity, to name a few.

- *Create an adequate "development system."* As we mentioned earlier in the chapter, families with formal development systems for governance leadership and other areas feel much more confident about continuity than those who do not have such systems. They need not be large, formal programs, but some structure and standardization can be important to create an effective means to prepare people for important responsibilities. System components include evaluation of next generation members' strengths and development needs, coaching relationships, protocols regarding education and other development aids, and ongoing monitoring of progress. Families with particularly large cohorts of next generation members can benefit from outside advice on such systems, as some advisors specialize in creating these systems for maximum effect.

- *Do an impact analysis on yourself.* Family enterprise advisor Stephanie Brun de Pontet points out that many of those transitioning from influential

---

[15] Lowe, C., & Evansb, J. (2015). Harmony, productivity, and informed decision making: The fundamental competencies of the chief emotional officer. *Sociology Study,* 5 (1), 60–73.

positions in family enterprise fail to understand how deeply their departure affects multiple systems within which they operate, including the family and business systems.[16] Don't make that mistake. Take a comprehensive approach to recognizing the impact of your transition (or that of another family member), including on the family (spouse, siblings, and children), ownership group, and business. A simple example is the large number of spouses who are surprised to find how difficult it is to adjust to their partner's being home full-time after decades in a professional role, reflecting a disruption in the family system. Think about such adjustments, communicate your needs related to them, solicit others' hopes and concerns, and take a generally proactive approach to transition within the systems you inhabit.

- *Repurpose your purpose.* This is much easier said than done. As you transition out of decades-long roles, work hard to identify the things that will give you meaning—ideally, activities that involve ongoing learning and growth—and work hard to create opportunities for yourself in these areas. That might mean roles similar to those you once occupied (such as serving on business or nonprofit boards) or entirely new pursuits (such as community service or learning an art). Experiment to find the right fit.

- *Share your desires for the latest stage.* Finally, think hard about what you want your latest life stage to look like—from where you would like to live to what activities give you joy. In his bestselling book *Being Mortal*, Atul Gawande discusses how critical it is to identify what's most meaningful with the reality that your health—and life—won't last forever.[17] Too many people don't think about or communicate what's most meaningful to them and how that affects medical and other key decisions until it's too late. Interestingly, research shows that people seriously ill don't want to be a burden on others. Not discussing, or documenting these end-of-life care wishes, and leaving them to family members who will be grieving, puts an incredible emotional load on loved ones. An additional risk to consider is the fact that when grieving, decision-making capacity is significantly diminished. Finding support to discuss alternatives when still in good health, pondering the consequences of your choices, and communicating your finalized care plan with your family will protect them from feeling bereaved, guilty, or uncertain, and allow you to fulfill your preferences.[18]

---

[16] For more see De Pontet, S. B. (2017). *Transitioning from the top: Personal continuity planning for the retiring family business leader.* Springer.

[17] Gawande, A. (2014). *Being mortal: Medicine and what matters in the end.* Metropolitan Books.

[18] Healey, J. (2017). *End of life issues.* Spinney Press.

Sample Development Plan: Later Adult

Scenario: As noted at the start of this chapter, Zoe is now 70, with four grown children. She is board chair of the family enterprise, which is valued at $200 million and growing, with substantial new investments in real estate, a retail store, and other areas. Two of Zoe's children work in the business, and while Zoe sees the next generation as capable, she's not ready to transition ownership responsibilities in a large way, in part because the rising generation has made little progress on tasks such as creating a new shareholders' agreement. Zoe's development plan includes these priorities (Exhibit 7.2).

Exhibit 7.2 Owner's Mindset: Sample Development Plan for a Later Adult (Zoe)

SAMPLE DEVELOPMENT PLAN FOR A LATER ADULT (ZOE)	
AREA	**DEVELOPMENTAL ACTIVITIES**
INDIVIDUAL	• Working with a coach to revisit life purpose • Hiring a personal trainer to maintain strength and flexibility • Golfing once per week with friends and colleagues • Sitting on the board of breast cancer nonprofit
FAMILY	• Running grandparents camp in the summer for her six grandchildren and their cousins • Mentoring her nephew George to take on the role of family leader • Setting aside needed time to have a special one-on-one weekend trip with each grandchild
OWNERSHIP	• Working with others to select and mentor a new board chair • Leading recruitment of two new independent directors • Working with G4 to help them build a robust shareholders' agreement for their cousin partnership • Completing an estate freeze in preparation for transferring shares to G4 • Establishing an education trust for future generations, secured with an income-producing asset • Developing family bank and incubator policy (see the box Rules For a Family Bank for an example of one family's approach)
BUSINESS / INDUSTRY	• Serving as president of the national wine association • Doing an internal weekly blog on leadership, culture, and teamwork to all employees • Participating in a chairperson peer group

The sample development plan is offered as an example only and includes a variety of ideas—some of which you may already do in the normal course of development in your family. Our goal is to inspire you to take a more

intentional approach to development by weaving a coordinated plan for your family appropriate to your specific circumstance and context.

In previous chapters, we highlighted the importance and role of key influencers in the process of building an owner's mindset. The later adult stage is no exception. Key influencers are as critically important at this stage as they are in others. In Chapter 6, we highlighted executives, independent directors, close friendships, other family enterprises, advisors, mentors, and community leaders as key influencers. Similarly, these individuals provide advice, insights, and assistance in ownership development for later-stage adults. Please see Chapter 6 for more information on how these people provide support for building an owner's mindset.

Where to Start?

Preparing to transition ownership control and other responsibilities in a family enterprise is not for the faint of heart. It may well be one of the more difficult adjustments a person can face.

So, rather than pointing to one specific starting point or practical step, we would like to emphasize here a healthy *mentality* to have as a later-stage adult moving toward an ownership transition. It includes the components below:

- *Aim for self-awareness and honesty.* Self-awareness requires profound honesty with oneself. As we noted earlier in this chapter, strive to be aware of what matters at this stage of your life, and what you want to leave behind. What will be of greatest meaning to you on both of those counts? If you can get some clarity around that, it will help you make related decisions and communicate your needs to others.
- *Focus on acceptance as a process.* Sonnenfeld suggests we recognize and embrace the multiple steps of this adjustment, where acceptance comes at the end of a few stages.[19] The process begins with a period of denial that the career is going to end. It is potentially followed by anger toward the opportunities the next generation have before them. Bargaining is the next, and often manifests in negotiating for staying to deal with special projects. Depression may follow as second last: it is normal to feel defeated with unfinished business and wonder where the time went. Working through it, finally a feeling of contentment emerges and creates space for feeling pride and accomplishment. It is crucial to consider that this process is not

---

[19] Sonnenfeld, J. (1991). *The hero's farewell: What happens when CEOs retire.* Oxford University Press.

easy—for yourself and those around you. Individuals experience loss associated with leadership, power, status, and routine. Empathy, self-awareness, and honesty foster a sense of acceptance of self and others. Engaging in difficult conversations more openly is much better than choosing the path of silence or superficiality.

- *Embrace paradoxes.* Family enterprise is a large set of paradoxes: tradition and change, constraint and freedom, and many others. But the tension around paradoxes flows from people thinking of the choices these represent as "either-or" rather than "both-and" options. Family enterprise can respect traditional values while striving for needed market-related changes, for example.[20] In the same way, ownership of the family business is yours until it isn't; most later-stage owners don't wish to be the last owners. So, embrace the paradox of yours-but-not-yours and help others in your cohort do the same. Feeling the difficulty of this paradox-rich transition is not only to be expected but normal, so help to normalize for others to the extent that you can.

- *Exist in the in-between.* According to William Bridges, every transition has three phases: an ending, an in-between, and a new beginning.[21] He uses the metaphor of a jump from one trapeze to another. We focus only on the trapeze parts, or the ending of one thing and the start of another. That is largely because the in-between space, the mid-air part in the metaphor, feels uncomfortable for people, as it is marked by uncertainty and the anticipation of a potentially uncomfortable change. As Bridges and others suggest, try to think of the in-between less as a threat and more as an opportunity: to take stock, to celebrate, to breathe, and to prepare. Do your best to exist in the in-between, as it will help you accept and even embrace what comes next.

Things to Look For

Among the most common challenges or pitfalls to consider regarding ownership development in this life stage align again around the theme of transition.

- *Letting the family's expectations become your own.* Unlike the issue above, this is where the family's needs might exert a disproportionate influence on your own. For example, a later-stage owner may be ready to move into

---

[20] For more on paradox in family enterprise see Schuman, A. M., Stutz, S., & Ward, J. L. (2010). *Family business as paradox.* Palgrave Macmillan.

[21] For more see Bridges, W. (2004). *Transitions: Making sense of life's changes.* Cambridge.

retirement, but the family feels they will be lost without this influential person. The result might be a reluctantly continuing owner, which is not good for the system. To avoid that, be as aware of and honest about your motivations as possible, with yourself and others. Promote healthy involvement of others in the system by providing space to grow and establishing ownership development programs. In this way, what is best for both you and the family will likely be the same.

- *Ignoring signs indicating it is time to move on.* This is a large challenge for many family enterprises: managing owners who deny they should make room for others. That can mean failing to support next generation members' development as owners or leaders, or assuming your influence is needed. In fact, owners with this mindset often create situations where they *are* needed because other members in the system have not been helped to gain the capacity to make ownership decisions. This is often a collective problem, but it typically starts with the individual owner who is unwilling to give up control. Strive for self-awareness and objectivity to understand whether you fall into this category before tensions and conflict rise because of an unwillingness to move on.

- *Get past the first two years of retirement.* It is not uncommon that the first two years of retirement are exciting as individuals have the time and the means to indulge in all the things they always wanted to do. After an initial period of new adventures, the power of distraction may lessen and a retiree could increasingly miss the sense of gratification and meaning of their work.[22] In some severe cases, senior family members go back to business or ownership responsibilities, becoming a "boomerang owner." Stepping back in and expecting to replace the CEO or board chair usually causes major relational consequences. When planning for the time after retirement, don't forget to include meaningful, not just recreational, activities to fulfill your need for deeper gratification. As mentioned earlier, preparing for the uncertainty ahead and accepting the natural sense of loss accompanying any transition are critical to avoiding this boomerang trajectory. Think about factors—beyond a sense of boredom or a lack of personal satisfaction—that may prompt a relapse, such as failure to trust those left behind with key responsibilities. Take steps to address these factors in advance. It can also help to establish clear criteria for when it may be appropriate to step back in, or when the family can ask you to do so, such as in an extraordinarily difficult ownership decision.

---

[22] Sonnenefeld (1991).

- *Underestimating the impact on the couple.* Retirement is one of the most relationship-altering events in a couple's life, mainly because the time spent typically increases significantly, making such relationship central.[23] For many this may be a great relief and coping mechanism, for others, a major source of stress. This is because spouses had long awaited the day when the daily routine was not driven by enterprise priorities. The outcome of this prolonged waiting varies considerably between extremes: from spouse's excited presence to complete absence. This manifests with the case of a patient and devoted spouse, who is now ready to travel the world together or engage in delayed hobbies; or a more independent one with a full life, as a response to prior neglect of family life; or the death of a spouse. While planning for this time, know that aging well is correlated to being in a positive and nurturing relationship, in particular, marital ones. Creating close companionship, mutual support, and little conflict requires intentional effort, which pays back incredibly well. In doing so, also don't underestimate that although children are grown up and live independently, couples don't stop worrying about them. Different perspectives on whom to involve in ownership and leadership positions may strain marital relationships. Therefore, initiating these conversations in advance and with the appropriate support may help tremendously.

Don't forget that as humans, we are a work in progress, even at the later stage of life. We can always improve and learn. A critical question to ask at this juncture is: What are you most motivated to learn at this stage of life? The Later Adult Stage Summary (Exhibit 7.3) provides key highlights of developing an owner's mindset for later adults in a family enterprise.

---

[23] Fishel, A. K. (2018). *A life-cycle approach to treating couples: From dating to death.* Momentum Press.

Exhibit 7.3 Later Adult Stage Summary Table

	WHY LATER ADULT STAGE MATTERS	KEY MESSAGE	
WHY	• Wisdom keepers for family and enterprise • Letting go requires patience and practice • Opportunity to co-create with following generations • Owning shares and transitioning final authority • Newcomers and challenging family dynamics • The transition stakes are very high if no structure is in place • Physical and mental changes	Letting go must be accomplished to achieve enterprise goals and it may involve the setting aside of an individual's identity, ego and personal goals.	

	DOMAIN	DEVELOPMENT GOALS	HOW TOs	SAMPLE DEVELOPMENT PLAN FOR ZOE
WHAT	Individual	• **Letting go and finding new purpose:** Senior adults will benefit by exploring what they truly want to spend their time on in this stage of life. Often a new purpose emerges around philanthropy and giving back, or mentoring, or finding joy in relaxation and travel, or stepping more fully into the grandparent role. Regardless of which path is taken, it is useful to take time to reflect and examine what is most meaningful to you as an individual. • **Managing the aging process:** As we've already suggested, this stage is marked by physiological change. These changes can be emotionally challenging for some to accept and manage, even if the changes are primarily appearance-related. Accepting these changes is important, while taking care to attend to any health matters and putting in place good health management routines around exercise, diet, and sleep. • **Dealing with loss and being frail:** Later in this stage, senior adults need coping skills to deal with the loss of family, friends, colleagues, and independence. This process naturally also involves learning to lean on others for support and care. • **Cultivating friendship:** Because of physical changes, loss and retirement, friendship is very important for older people. In many cases, friends are as important as families. Friends are able to know you holistically (beyond the family or the business role), are someone through whom you can see yourself and are someone with whom to share experiences. They can represent a link to your authentic self, and your life history. Cultivating long life relationships, or exploring new ones in new circles might become a more intentional activity.	• Accept, plan, reflect, repeat • Address old wounds in the family • Relearn the art of listening • Repurpose your purpose	• Working with a coach to revisit life purpose • Hiring a personal trainer to maintain strength and flexibility • Golfing once per week with friends and colleagues • Sitting on the board of breast cancer nonprofit

	DOMAIN	DEVELOPMENT GOALS	HOW TOs	SAMPLE DEVELOPMENT PLAN FOR ZOE
WHAT	Family	• **Strengthening and evolving family culture and tradition:** Spending time to advance and embed a strong family culture, especially as the family continues to grow and evolve, is a valuable aspect of legacy. During this stage more than others, the recognition of the importance of family is often more visible. Keeping the concept of building family culture and traditions at the forefront is an important role for senior adults, but the goal is to do this through influence, rather than by coercion or guilt. • **Designing the grandparenting role:** Some senior adults and/or family cultures are child-centric, while others are more adult-centric. Exploring who you are and want to be as a grandparent is an important step in this stage of life. Being intentional about designing this role with your children and grandchildren is important. There can be signifi cant tension around this role in some families due to unmet hopes and desires. Spending time reflecting on and talking about expectations can maximize the benefit of this role in your family. • **Fostering family leadership in rising generation:** We tend to focus on transitioning leadership in the business and ownership systems, and forget about the importance of leadership in the family system. Strong continuity in a family enterprise demands that someone in the family system is providing the glue that holds the family together. Senior adults may recognize this more than others in the family, so their role in cultiv ating this is crucial.	• Form a cousin club • Onboard grandchildren into family governance	• Running grandparents camp in the summer for her 6 grandchildren and their cousins • Mentoring her nephew George to take on the role of family leader • Setting aside needed time to have a special one-on-one week end trip with each grandchild
	Ownership	• **Advancing continuity planning:** Although hopefully some estate planning has been completed by this stage, it needs to continually evolve to fit the family's changing needs. As a later-stage adult, keep an eye on how to advance your estate plan through ongoing, regular conversations with the rising generations. They can't mak e these changes, so you must. However, they have to live with the plan once you are gone, so ensuring they are aligned around it and that there are no surprises is critical. • **Legacy:** By this stage it's ideal to have a strong sense of what you want to leave behind: not just financially such as wealth or shares, but what you'd want future generations to know about your life story and the values it reflects. We believe it's important to humbly	• Lead ownership development process for rising generation • Do an impact analysis on yourself	• Working with others to select and mentor a new Board Chair • Leading recruitment of two new independent directors • Working with G4 to help them build a robust shareholders' agreement for their cousin partnership • Completing an estate freeze in preparation for transferring shares to G4 • Establishing an education trust for future generations, secured with an income-producing asset • Developing family bank and incubator policy (see Box titled Rules for a Family Bank for an example of one family's approach)

but deliberately paint a picture of what you want for your grandchildren and great-grandchildren, including those you'll never meet. What do you want to be the most prized, sustained elements of your legacy? Identify and work toward those.

DOMAIN	DEVELOPMENT GOALS	HOW TOs	SAMPLE DEVELOPMENT PLAN FOR ZOE
Business/ Industry	• **Executive development:** Early senior adults who have not yet had an opportunity to develop skills and capability in the executive leadership functions may find an opportunity to step into this role at this stage of life. Typically, executive leadership involves overseeing business activities such as fulfilling organizational goals, strategic planning development, and overall direction. • **Fertilizing family talent:** At this stage, the talents in the rising generations are often more apparent, so later-stage adults' time is well-spent on coaching and mentoring those family members who have the interest, commitment, and capability to be future leaders. Developmental goals here involve learning to listen, influence, and coach rather than tell and direct. • **Formalizing and professionalizing:** As a business's size expands so does the need for process and structure, which can sometimes go against the "entrepreneurial grain." Recognizing the need for creating consistent and well-understood approaches to how you do business as a family enterprise is often a vital role for the incumbent generation to fulfill. Younger generations may be hesitant to take this on for fear of changing the traditional way of doing things so senior adults may need to lead.	• As an operating owner, develop a process for leadership succession	• Serve as President of the national wine association • Doing an internal weekly blog on leadership, culture and teamwork to all employees • Participate in a board chair peer group

HOW TO	SAMPLE STORIES, EXERCISES AND TOOLS DESCRIBED IN THE CHAPTER	KEY INFLUENCERS	THINGS TO WATCH OUT FOR	
	• The Wandon Family: Building a Strong Family for the Long Run • Involvement Without Disempowerment • Both Hands on the Baton • From Somebody to Somebody • What's Next Exercise • Key Rules for a Family Bank • Stay or Get Out of the Way?	• Parents • Adult children • Grandchildren • Non-family management • Independent directors • Trusted Advisors	• Becoming a "boomerang owner" • Letting the family's expectations become your own • Ignoring signs indicating it's time to move on • Get past the first two years of retirement • Underestimating the impact on the couple • Dying with your boots on	

Suggested Additional Readings

Brun de Pontet, S. B. (2017). *Transitioning From the Top: Personal Continuity Planning for the Retiring Family Business Leader (A Family Business Publication)* (1st ed.). Palgrave Macmillan.

Gawande, A. (2014). *Being Mortal: Medicine and What Matters in the End* (1st ed.). Metropolitan Books.

Hughes Jr., J. E., Massenzio, S. E., & Whitaker, K. (2012). *The Cycle of the Gift: Family Wealth and Wisdom* (1st ed.). Bloomberg Press.

Nichols, M. P. (2009). *The Lost Art of Listening: How Learning to Listen Can Improve Relationships* (2nd ed.). The Guilford Press.

Raines, S. S. (2019). *Conflict Management for Managers: Resolving Workplace, Client, and Policy Disputes*. Rowman & Littlefield.

Schachter-Shalomi, Z., & Miller, R. S. (1998). *From Age-ing to Sage-ing. A Revolutionary Approach to Growing Older*. Grand Central Publishing.

Solie, D. (2004). *How to Say It to Seniors: Closing the Communication Gap with Our Elders* (Fourth Printing ed.). Prentice Hall Press.

Sonnenfeld, J. (1988). *The Hero's Farewell: What Happens When CEOs Retire*. Oxford University Press.

8

Becoming a Learning Family

W. Sage-Hayward et al., *Own It!*, A Family Business Publication,
https://doi.org/10.1007/978-3-030-20419-8_8

Learning Family

As we've explained, an owner's mindset is developed simultaneously at the individual and collective levels. In this chapter we're focusing solely on development at the *collective* level. Specifically, we're highlighting learning for a "team" of current and prospective owners across stages of life which is first initiated in the family system, and it is where an owner's mindset germinates. We advocate starting early at the collective level for this specific reason.

With that in mind, we present material with a similar structure to that of the stage-focused chapters: a sense of why family development matters; definition of a learning family; goals for collective development; how-tos; where to start; and things to watch out for. We start off hearing about a real family's journey of ownership learning: The Burtons.

The Burton Family's Journey Toward Becoming a Learning Family

Jim Burton recently experienced a liquidity event through the sale of his longtime business—PPI Management Inc. He decided to take a significant portion of the proceeds from this sale to invest in building a multigenerational family legacy with his six next generation family members and their respective families. He set up a large private family foundation called the James A. Burton and Family Foundation and invited his adult children to participate as members and co-creators. Their shared family dream is to create "an empowered society inspired to foster enduring growth and betterment in their communities."

Although Jim has been philanthropic his whole life, this was an opportunity to build a family legacy *with* his children, and as a family. For the past few years, the Burton family has been building their collective knowledge and capability around philanthropy, good governance, and family communication. Their development activities include a mixture of regular family meetings, conferences and program attendance, monthly financial coaching, personal development sessions, bimonthly family webinars, and having access to information resources such as books, articles, and podcasts. In addition, each rising generation member is advancing their individual knowledge and learning in their personal areas of interest.

One of the first goals for Jim has been to provide a basic financial base for each of the rising generation family members, thus allowing them the freedom to create a personal vision and to dream bigger for themselves. By providing a financial base (but not so much that they don't have to work!), it has enabled the rising generation to open up their thinking about the future beyond just survival. Jim states, "They have not really had a chance to think about this before without concern around financial stability." This process has also helped the next generation build personal financial literacy, which will translate well into their need to understand financial matters related to their family foundation.

Jim indicates the experience has been incredibly rewarding. "It has allowed us to build a new vision, including roles and dreams for each other and our collective family legacy. This process has not been about just *giving* them something but rather *working side-by-side* with them, which is a very different picture. It is a shift in learning—and more stimulating for me. Having the chance to participate in this process *with* my kids has been a huge gift. It is a great privilege and a progressive step toward building a true multigenerational family legacy."

The Burton Family's approach to collective development highlights a thoughtful and deliberate approach to advancing their shared knowledge and skill, which is the focus of this chapter.

Why Collective Ownership Development Matters

Combined with individual development, collective ownership development is critical for many reasons. First, preserving family wealth (both qualitative and quantitative) is a dynamic process.[1] Simply maintaining what exists, rather than growing it, puts the family capital (human, social, intellectual, spiritual, and financial) in danger of decay. Creating collective family development is among the most effective ways to build family capitals and achieve that necessary growth. (See Exhibit 8.1—Individual and Collective Ownership development.)

---

[1] Hughes Jr., J. E., Massenzio, S. E., & Whitaker, K. (2017). *Complete family wealth*. Wiley.

Exhibit 8.1 Individual and Collective Ownership Development

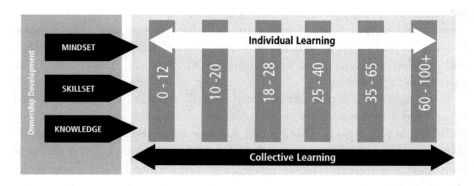

This is also supported by Jaffe's recent research,[2] where he shows that as family enterprises grow in size and complexity, it's critical to move beyond individual development and advance the entire family. As Jaffe found, this investment in the next generation is fundamental to the continuity of the family enterprise itself.

Beyond that core motivation, here are two other reasons to make collective learning a priority:

- *It increases owner team alignment.* One key objective of collective development is to create alignment within and across the family. The goal of trying to reach consensus by hearing all perspectives does not negate a family's need to make decisions by majority at times which everyone may not agree on, such as those related to business risk, dividends, and fairness. Collective development helps build alignment on multiple levels. First, the family enterprise membership is dispersed and diverse in multiple dimensions, including age, gender, geography, knowledge, abilities, values, interests, and family roles. Collective ownership development promotes cohesion,[3] connection, and trust among family members who may "look," think, and behave differently, enabling the group to come to consensus decisions. Second, any team working on complex issues requires a common set of frameworks and vocabulary for effective dialogue. A family enterprise is no different. Collective family enterprise education yields a shared language across members, including as related to business terms (growth,

---

[2] Jaffe, D. (2020). *Borrowed from your grandchildren.* Wiley.

[3] "Family cohesion is defined as the emotional bonding that family members have toward one another," Olson, D. H., Russell, C. S., & Sprenkle, D. H. (1983). Circumplex model of marital and family systems: VI. Theoretical update. *Family Process, 22* (1), 69–83.

risk, profits, and liquidity), ownership terms (trust, shareholders agreement, and dividends), communication terms (empathy, consensus, and active listening), and psychology (enmeshment, triangulation, psychological safety), for a more level playing field and efficient, effective decision-making processes. Finally, joint learning creates a collective memory that helps reinforce and build on individual learnings.[4]

- *It builds the skills of the group.* Specifically, we are referring to skills that a specific group possesses—not the skills of individuals applied in a group setting. An owner team is called on to make infrequent and high-stakes decisions, e.g., sell or buy a portion of a business, elect a director, etc. Without the "playing field" on which owners can practice discussing and deciding, they will be ill-equipped to effectively make these challenging decisions. Collective learning creates the space for a current or prospective owner team to "flex their group muscles" and learn to work together. In addition, the process of learning together normalizes differences, and gives people permission to talk about difficult subjects, including those related to money, conflict, and continuity, among others. Development isn't only about tangible, "agenda-driven" knowledge people gain, but the ability to trust one another and communicate and collaborate for the long term. The right approach to collective development breaks negative patterns and fosters healthier ones at the family and individual levels.

Become a Learning Family

A helpful concept in pursuing collective development is that of the learning family, based on the broader idea of a learning organization. We encourage you to think of development as moving your family toward becoming a learning community of family owners, based on the ideas here.

A learning organization, as defined by Peter Senge, is a group of people working together to transform and enhance their collective capacity to create results they really care about.[5] We define a Learning Family as a group of family members who are passionate about their jointly held (current or future) assets, and collaborate to actively build an owner's mindset and skillset to enhance their family's capitals (spiritual, financial, human, social and intellectual). It is an aspirational state and the outcome of a continuous process

---

[4] Easterby-Smith, M., Araujo, L., & Burgoyne, J. (Eds.). (1999). *Organizational learning and the learning organization: Developments in theory and practice.* Sage.

[5] Senge, P. M. (2014). *The fifth discipline fieldbook: Strategies and tools for building a learning organization.* Crown Business.

of learning and growing. Therefore, it is the journey of becoming a learning family rather than the destination of being a learning family that generates the benefits of collective development.

In this context, learning families display:

- *Proactivity*: A learning family proactively designs learning opportunities to advance both individual talent and the collective brain trust. They also establish uninterrupted times and places to build capacity, working toward this goal as individuals and as a group.
- *Deliberateness*: The family jointly creates the vision for and expectations of development opportunities, including a budget and a set of action steps. When the family doesn't know for sure what the outcome can or will be, they say so.
- *Responsiveness*: Learning and development activities are designed in response to family members' needs and interests in addition to the business needs.
- *Smart risk-taking*: In a learning family, members experiment, take risks and try new ways of doing things without fear of reprisal or getting it wrong. Mistakes are considered part of the learning process.
- *Psychological Safety*: Family discussions are viewed as safe places to challenge assumptions, biases, and sacred cows, without being punished for mistakes or risk-taking.[6] Every topic is up for discussion. Family members give and receive feedback openly and constructively, as feedback is viewed as critical for growth and progress. Feedback loops are encouraged and expected.[7]
- *Inculsiveness*: The vision of the family enterprise emerges from a creative process involving the broad perspectives contributed by family members and other key stakeholders. In addition, a learning family invites members to learn about *all* aspects of the family enterprise, so they understand their role and potential opportunities within it.
- *Fiduciary approach*: Time and effort are expended to foster actions and relationships centered on duty of care and loyalty. The family is committed to managing their biases. All of the above are learned behaviors that can be improved over time.

---

[6] "The term (psychological safety) is meant to suggest neither a careless sense of permissiveness, nor an unrelentingly positive affect but, rather, a sense of confidence that the team will not embarrass, reject, or punish someone for speaking up. This confidence stems from mutual respect and trust among team members." (p. 354). Edmondson, A. (1999). Psychological safety and learning behavior in work teams. *Administrative Science Quarterly, 44*(2), 350–383.

[7] To learn more about psychological safety, see Edmondson, A. C. (2018). *The fearless organization: Creating psychological safety in the workplace for learning, innovation, and growth.* Wiley; Delizonna, L. (2017). High-performing teams need psychological safety. Here's how to create it. *Harvard Business Review, 8,* 1–5.

Collective Development Goals

In conjunction with individual development goals, the objectives of collective development are focused mainly on skills and knowledge that enhance cohesion and collaboration. In particular:

- *Build trust and respect.* Even the best-informed family enterprise members will fail to make much progress and will likely end up in the wrong place without a collective sense of trust and respect. Trust, in particular, is not a monolithic elusive quality; rather, it is a very tangible and actionable asset, which includes character, competence, and reliability along with specific behaviors.[8] Although perhaps considered unconventional wisdom, trust can be regenerated once it is broken. Collective development processes should be aimed at generating greater trust among the ownership group.
- *Strengthen communication capabilities.* Owners of all ages, stages, skills, and roles need to be able to express their opinions and ideas in a respectful way while making space for those of others. Each family member will have a unique and personal style for how they interact and communicate in the family. *Everyone* who is committed can improve skills related to empathy, listening, reflection, synthesis of ideas, and many others. This is especially critical for having difficult conversations, as family enterprise owners often must.
- *Advance capacity to collaborate effectively.* Family members must be able to agree and manage disagreement productively and peacefully on everything from a shared vision to family employment to establishing effective governance policies. Collaboration is at the heart of family enterprise continuity, and among the key beliefs of an owner's mindset. Thus, one of the most central priorities of collective development is promoting collaboration skills and a sense of partnership among family members, which can be passed down through the generations.
- *Develop collective decision-making capacity.* A key capability to develop in a family and future shareholder group is collective decision-making which is the ability for the group to analyze alternatives and decide on a path forward in a participatory fashion. In this process, all voices are heard and opinions are honestly shared. When agreement is important and consensus can't be reached, revisiting the issue again later may be the appropriate action depending on the urgency and significance of the decision. Establishing a "fair process" is crucial here, as it can reduce the occurrence of

---

[8] Covey, S. R., & Merrill, R. R. (2006). *The speed of trust: The one thing that changes everything.* Simon and Schuster.

conflicts and minimize its strength. In particular, pay attention to three key elements: first, being consistent in the procedure, across time and persons; second, assuring representativeness in all the phases; and, finally, providing accurate information, in time and allowing for correctability.[9]

- *Create shared language and understanding.* Even groups that have a foundation of communication and collaboration require shared language and understanding of key concepts, structures, and processes to maximize their effectiveness. Given the unique and complex nature of the family enterprise landscape, collective development should aim to educate family members on the "language of family enterprise" which includes topics related to leadership, governance, philanthropy, ownership, personal development, relationships, wealth, and family enterprise strategy.

The items just explained serve as both goals for development *and* the foundation on which to promote and reap the rewards of development. It is ideal to have basic levels of communication, collaboration, shared understanding, and decision-making in place when you take on individual and collective ownership development. If the family is struggling in this regard, such as experiencing long-standing conflicts or rifts, then working through such blocks needs to be the priority before more specific ownership-focused development can proceed. In such cases, an attempt at collective healing should be the first step to determine what's even possible for more specific development.

How-Tos

The most important choice to make here is to commit to collective development and becoming a learning family. Subsequently, you have many options to pursue in execution. Here are collective development options, guidelines, and strategies that we have found most effective for families across a range of areas. You should remember the importance of creating some balance among knowledge, skills, beliefs, and recognizing the ongoing maturing and evolving of people.

- *Create buy-in.* Learning is one of those activities where efforts and benefits are often diluted over time. Most often individuals experience present sacrifice for future rewards, which requires capacity for delayed gratification. Delaying gratification typically presents a trade-off between an

---

[9] Van der Heyden, L., Blondel, C., & Carlock, R. S. (2005). Fair process: Striving for justice in family business. *Family Business Review, 18*(1), 1–21.

immediately available reward and a larger reward available later.[10] Don't underestimate that delayed gratification is less common and more complex than it might appear. Depending on the age and stage of family members, it is recommended to create fun rituals and habits around learning for the youngest, so it becomes second nature for them through modeling and repetition. In the case of more adult members, focus on single behavior change to begin with, which can relieve some current struggles too, easy to implement, and finally provide some support.[11]

- *Conduct a learning needs assessment.* Given most families are heavily focused on working in the business, it may be hard to pin down exactly what educational needs the family may have as a collective. A needs assessment is a good first step to help a family determine where they are today in terms of their knowledge, skills, and capability and where they want to be based on their vision, passion, and interests, ideally in each of the three circles.[12] See Appendix C for a sample.

- *Hold in-house learning sessions.* It is ideal to include a learning activity or event at each family or ownership governance meeting, where feasible. An example could be to have one of the executive partners put together a few sessions. A family in New Mexico chose this option and their trusted advisor organized a mini-workshop on finance for non-financial managers almost every month for two years, for more than twenty sessions. It was a huge hit, especially with the rising generation family members and others who needed to build greater financial literacy. Other families hire experts to come in-house to build capacity in having difficult conversations and similar interpersonal topics, strengthening their ability to be assertive and communicate effectively.

- *Be open-minded to new topics.* To promote participation, inclusion, and intergenerational learning, families often have success when they invite next generation members to educate the whole family on latest technologies, social media, or general trends. While they may be topics not immediately related to the enterprise, they can be very effective in promoting intergenerational understanding and closeness.

---

[10] The famous "marshmallow test" developed by the Stanford psychologist Walter Mischel in the 1960s introduced the concept of delayed gratification. A researcher was offering kids a choice between an immediate treat (marshmallow) or a larger amount of the same treat upon the return of the researcher at a later time (unspecified and usually 15–30 min). The kids were left alone in the room, in front of the treat and with a hidden camera, which was recording the challenge of smaller sooner, versus larger-later. Mischel, W., & Ebbesen, E. B. (1970). Attention in delay of gratification. *Journal of Personality and Social Psychology, 16*(2), 329.

[11] Somers, M. (2018). *Advice that sticks: How to give financial advice that people will follow.* Practical Inspiration Publishing.

[12] Family, Business, and Ownership.

- *Run multifamily workshops.* A valuable resource for business families is other business families. We strongly suggest you find opportunities to learn with other families, either locally or otherwise. One family enterprise matriarch, for example, said that attending a two-day workshop on family governance halfway across the country was invaluable for her family because they "didn't know anyone" and that anonymity enabled them to explore multiple issues more freely. Not all families need such privacy, but all families benefit from learning with others who walk or have walked in their shoes. Conferences and public programs in family business matters like those offered at family enterprise centers are also great forums that create a strong multifamily platform for learning. A family in the Pacific Northwest held a one-day conference on family enterprise dynamics and invited five other local families to attend. "Build it and they will come" was their philosophy, and it worked. The program led to a series of shorter learning sessions all the families continued to attend. If a multifamily workshop is not easy to organize, another family can be invited to present and share at your family retreat. Inviting multiple members of different generations and creating peer groups between and among different generations can originate fun and fruitful exchanges of ideas and perspectives.
- *Engage in policy development.* As enterprising families evolve and professionalize over time, creating meaningful structures like policies is important to help clarify "how things work around here." Working together to design policies and processes helps to align family members on the most effective way for them to navigate the complex landscape in which business and family are intertwined. Appendix B includes a list of common policies for each of the three family enterprise systems: family, business, and ownership. Policy development is a tool, not the panacea, to resolve all the past, present, and future issues families may experience. It is a very helpful process that doesn't substitute the need to foster interpersonal relationships and to continuously consider how needs evolve.
- *Start a family book club.* Some families love to read, others, not so much. If your family is inspired by book-based learning, then having a family book club is an excellent way to create a common base of knowledge and to learn about key topics related to your business and your family. Keep it simple by following the ideas in the box Family Book Club Guidelines.

FAMILY BOOK CLUB GUIDELINES
Follow these tips to start and enjoy a learning-focused family book club. • **Number of books:** Choose no more than four books per year • **Choice of books:** Rotate choice of book among family members • **Structure:** Schedule a two-hour discussion around the book and send out three to five questions in advance to prompt thinking ahead of time • **Moderator:** Choose a moderator for each meeting, ideally one with the skill to keep the conversation on topic (at least for the first hour!)

- *Strengthen and extend your social network.* Families have social capital in addition to financial capital. When considering family learning and development, strategically building your network is an important part of the process, as suggested by earlier points about learning alongside other families. We recommend actively developing inspiring relationships and ensuring that younger family members have opportunities to build connections with key stakeholders—from trusted long-time family advisors to key non-family leaders in the business, to reap the large rewards of mentoring, development roles, and other activities.

- *Go on learning expeditions.* Learning families recognize that true innovation and change means leaving your own backyard, expanding your horizons, and getting out of your comfort zone. Learning expeditions involve going to new regions and territories to stimulate thinking and foster insight. This may mean traveling together to a conference or to hear an industry speaker or going as a group to a country (or region) where you hope to expand your business to learn about the regional customs, build relationships, challenge assumptions, and gather market intelligence, among other activities. It is a process that involves the cycle of observing, doing, reflecting, and integrating new knowledge and information into your way of doing business. See the box "Retail Expedition in Asia" about one family's effort to help the rising generation understand the market into which they planned to expand their business.

RETAIL EXPEDITION IN ASIA

The Terrot family, which owned a large retail business in the Midwest, designed a five-day learning expedition in Singapore and Shanghai for a group of third-generation family members working in the business.

Primary objectives for the expedition were:
- To develop a better understanding of Asia as their next potential market of growth
- To get inspired by best practices in retail
- To identify potential partners
- To solve a specific challenge around how to leverage data analytics to best position the company's locations and brand within their target countries

The Family hired an advisor with good relationships and connections in the region to set up and manage the process for them. The advisor also facilitated integration sessions after each meeting with a retailer or potential supplier to help family members reflect on what they learned and how they might incorporate this knowledge into their strategic planning for expansion. The shared experiences and learnings brought the next generation family members closer together and gave them confidence in the company's strategy and their role within that strategy.

- *Strengthen communication skills.* Owners and prospective owners in your family must be able to communicate about a range of topics, from vision to values to risk. That includes formulating and presenting ideas and opinions and engaging in thoughtful, respectful, productive discussion and debate. There is a wide range of resources to boost individual and group communication skills, including university-based programs, online materials, and outside advisors. The critical thing is to *commit* to improving communication skills through formal and informal resources, followed by a willingness to practice what is learned. The box "The Wilsons Commit to Communication" provides an example of how one family made communication a priority.

THE WILSONS COMMIT TO COMMUNICATION

The Wilsons are a third-generation auto-parts family enterprise in the Pacific Northwest. From early on, the family made communication a top priority. That included family meetings, a separate owners' council, and informal meetups such as family dinners and reunions. Each generation was expected to contribute to meetings. All three generations had an opportunity to contribute to the agenda, and members across all age groups presented ideas and insights. Even the middle-school-age grandchildren presented on topics ranging from what they were learning in school to philanthropic causes such as hunger and the environment. The Wilsons also regularly attended local university workshops on communication and brought in experts for sessions on improving communication about vision, conflicts, and other areas—again with an emphasis on the participation of all age groups. The family's focus on communication has promoted a culture of empathy, openness, and sharing, and facilitated highly effective decision-making while preparing the next generation of owners to care and succeed.

- *Promote collective ownership, business, and financial literacy.* It's no surprise that collective ownership development requires a shared vocabulary and understanding around ownership, business, and financial concepts and terms such as shareholders agreements, family employment policies, dividends, risk, liquidity, and many other areas. Owners need this knowledge to both discuss and make prudent, well-informed decisions about an operating business or a portfolio of business holdings or stock. Some families have pre- or post-board meeting meetings. One family in the Midwest gathers all shareholders two days before the board meeting to jointly review the board packet and discuss the high priority matters that will be covered during the board meeting. Most importantly, they have a chance to ask questions and dive deep in a lower pressure environment—with just family owners and a facilitator and none of the independent directors. Other families hold post-board meeting meetings, where important different perspectives are explored more in depth.

- *Enhance philanthropy knowledge and skill.* Many enterprising families who have succeeded financially prioritize giving back to their communities and the broader world. Therefore, learning about causes, need, and impact as well as how to assess nonprofit organizations, among others, is a different and important set of capabilities to develop. An approach to consider here is shared service-learning activities. Instead of having only lectures or conversations about environmental crises, social needs, or sharing resources, family members engage in service-learning activities[13] together. In doing so they are active in creating and retaining the knowledge and the emotional experience associated with it. The benefits of these experiential forms of collective learning are multiple. Through engaging in meaningful projects that require understanding of the specific needs, crafting solutions, and helping with the implementation, family members have an important opportunity to put in practice and test multiple skills (leadership, communication, project management, etc.) and knowledge (financial, marketing, strategic, etc.). In addition, service-learning activities create a deeper mindset shift: from charity to solidarity. Charity implies that individuals are somehow above the people they are assisting, and don't capture the benefits they receive in exchange. When the shift to solidarity happens, family members appreciate both a sense of the shared human condition with those who are in need, and the betterment that comes from helping.

---

[13] Cress, C. M., Collier, P. J., & Reitenauer, V. L. (2013). *Learning through serving: A student guidebook for service-learning and civic engagement across academic disciplines and cultural communities.* Stylus Publishing, LLC.

This manifests itself among the owners by increasing their capacity to collaborate and support each other.

- *Aim for authenticity.* Entrepreneurs, including those in family enterprise, are often overly focused on practical solutions and processes. However, it is also important to foster honest, authentic behavior and interactions. For example, in one enterprise's family meeting, a senior owner took responsibility for not sharing more with the family about his personal challenges while running their enterprise. It was a very emotional moment that resulted in a new understanding and greater intimacy among family members, thereby galvanizing them. Sharing, authenticity, and vulnerability go a long way to bringing people together around ownership. But, of course, one can't force it. Instead, aim to create a culture of openness where people feel comfortable being honest and "real." Lead by example in this dimension, wherever possible.

- *Have fun.* It has been proven how positive emotions improve learning.[14] Amidst the push to gain, consolidate, and apply ownership knowledge, don't forget to have fun. Fun in the process of ownership development isn't frivolous; it is a critical way of fostering engagement and interest, especially among younger family members. Effective owners place significant emphasis on doing fun activities as part of their learning and together time. That includes playing games at meetings or engaging in a cooking class at the end of a meeting or asking members to put on humorous skits at the start or end of a family event. Customizing fun activities so the content to be learned—such as a *Jeopardy!* game based on ownership terms—is a great way to boost engagement and knowledge retention.

- *Engage in sporting events and other team-building experiences.* Sport is an immediate metaphor and an excellent tool for team-building opportunities and development. The choice of games is critical. Be careful not to fan the flames of unhealthy competition. Pick sports that offer lessons in different skills. For example, sailing teaches collaboration and coordination, quick decision-making, and responding to changes in the external environment. Assign roles to allow members to leverage their differences and learn the crucial lesson that as a family, you need the synergy of a diverse set of skills to accomplish your goals. Setting up sports events for a family reunion strengthens budgeting, contingency planning, prioritizing, organizing and accountability skills. The box "From a Game to a Spontaneous Life Lesson" shares an example of how a children's game evolved into

---

[14] Tying, C. M., Amin, H. U., Saad, M. N., & Malik, A. S. (2017). The influences of emotion on learning and Memory. *Frontiers in Psychology, 8,* 1454.

a powerful and long-lasting learning moment for the rising generation in a European learning family.

FROM A GAME TO A SPONTANEOUS LIFE LESSON

Giada, a fourth-generation owner now in her late forties, still remembers vividly the joy of visiting her grandmother, who was the founder, at their family business when she was a child. She loved her Granny's office; it appeared serious and at the same time very familiar, full of family pictures. Among her favorite moments was going to the office supplies cabinet, which was twice her size and filled with the most incredible items, including pens and highlighters of every color. She was used to playing with them for hours, pretending that she was selling them to imaginary customers. One day, she and her cousin were playing together. Their grandmother joined them to go home together, to have a family dinner. She saw the girls keeping one of the highlighters and an eraser. Granny softly asked what they were doing. "Can we bring it home?" they asked their Granny, in sync. Gently, she explained that it belonged to the company and was for the people working there to use. "I don't understand," Giada replied, "Isn't the company ours?" Her cousin nodded, indicating the same confusion. It became a great opportunity to explain the difference between the resources of the company and those of the family and owners. Forty years later, these now owners still recall how it was the first time they understood the concept of boundaries, and how important these were and still are in their family and enterprise.

Sample Development Plan: A Learning Family

Scenario: When she was in middle adulthood, Zoe's family sat down just before the holidays to map out their family learning plan for the next year. Although there were some moans and groans about the time commitment, everyone ultimately embraced the value of collective learning. Their plan included the components in Exhibit 8.2. They budgeted nearly $40,000 to cover conference fees and travel and expedition costs, not including facilitator fees for the quarterly meetings.

Exhibit 8.2 Owner's Mindset: Sample Development Plan for a Learning Family (Zoe's Family)

ACTIVITY	DETAILS

Meeting activities	• Include a development activity at each quarterly family meeting. Topics to include:
	  o Exploring individual purpose
	  o Learning to manage boundaries in a family enterprise

Financial literacy program	• Understanding our relationship to money and wealth • Reading a financial statement case study • Complete a financial literacy program with the family's private banker for G4 group of cousins

Webinars	• Offer six family enterprise webinars with subject matter experts using Zoom:
	  o Building consensus in a family enterprise
	  o Starting a family foundation
	  o Preparing for year-end tax planning
	  o Choosing a financial advisor
	  o The value of mentoring and coaching
	  o Designing your purpose

Conference	• Attend and present at a Family Business Conference: • Three family members attend and participate on a panel regarding next-generation development; attendees develop a few bullet points on what they learned and recommended action items to present at a family meeting
Learning expedition	• Conduct a learning expedition with all rising generation family members to Napa Valley to tour three to five family wineries
External speaker	• Schedule Pioneer Seed Company to present at annual general shareholder meeting on how plants and seeds are being genetically modified for drought and insect resistance

Family Book Club	• Participate in a family book club (adults) which includes the following books:
	  o *The Culture Code* by Daniel Coyle
	  o *Being Mortal* by Atul Gwande
	  o *Innovation in the Family Business* by Joe Schmieder

The sample development plan is offered as an example only and includes a variety of ideas—some of which you may already do in the normal course of development in your family. Our goal is to inspire you to take a more intentional approach to development by weaving a coordinated plan for your family appropriate to your specific circumstance and context.

Where to Start?

The ideal place to start ownership development and movement toward learning-family status is with communication.

Begin a conversation about the need for collective development, about the benefits of being a learning family, and about other family members' passion and appetite for the same. The level of interest in the topic should quickly become clear, as will red flags such as trust issues. See the box "If We Were a Learning Family Exercise" for how one family began the process.

"IF WE WERE A LEARNING FAMILY" EXERCISE

Over the years, Zak kept hearing from Zoe about how she was fostering a learning environment in her family and was eager to get something like this going in his family. So, he decided to put discussion of the learning family concept on the agenda for the next family meeting.

At the meeting, Zak shared what Zoe and her family had accomplished and led his family through an exercise using the introduction and questions below:

Imagine it is five years from now and we have created a family that is passionate about being the best multigenerational family enterprise we can be. Let's describe what we think we would see and experience at that future time.

1. What policies, events, and activities help us to thrive?
2. How do family members behave with each other in good times? In bad times?
3. How do we interact with our key stakeholders?
4. How do family members feel about the family and our enterprise?
5. What do we care most about?
6. What are we able to do that we can't or don't do today?
7. What value are we creating for our family, our customers, and our community?
8. How do we define and measure our success?
9. How is all of the above different from how we operate today?
10. What are the roadblocks we face to becoming a learning family?

We recommend making the development process simple, fun, and personal to your family members. Consider starting with the aforementioned exercise above, then pick one or two of the suggestions from earlier in this chapter—such as a learning trip, developing a key policy, or building financial literacy—and start by relating it to family members' personal situations. For example, one family had third-generation family members just entering grade school. The founding generation wanted to help support their grandchildren's education and suggested that at the next family meeting, they work on building an education-funding policy. Reading material was sent out in advance, as well as some key questions to stimulate everyone's thinking. This example illustrates how learning can be both intake of new information (i.e., reading articles and asking thought-provoking questions) and experiential (i.e., developing a policy together).

It can also be helpful to target development at specific types of owners within your broader pool, such as new or prospective owners, operating owners, non-operating owners, and the like. Some development approaches will apply to all the groups, but some should be customized to that cohort's specific needs.

Finally, start with patience and a long-term view. Be intentional in creating a positive experience around learning encounters. The investment of time in any kind of ownership development is critical. The value of development is rarely visible after each meeting or activity but builds over time and becomes more evident when tested—such as when a young family member contributes their first idea or insight at a family meeting. Keep at it but be patient about results and trust they will emerge organically over time.

Things to Look For

As in previous chapters, here we call out the most common pitfalls on the pathway to collective development:

- *Too much too soon.* Becoming a learning family is a long-life process. Introducing too many activities too soon may cause a reaction of overwhelm. Systems need time to change and adjust. Clarity and buy-in are paramount to transformation.
- *Giving up too soon.* It can be tempting to give up on family learning, especially during the stages of life when everyone is busy with building the business and managing young families. One patriarch threw around the phrase "You clearly haven't prioritized this" whenever family members didn't attend one of his learning events. This just made the next generation feel misunderstood and frustrated. Engaging family members in learning is more of an art than science. It requires patiently exploring areas of individual interest and passion and marrying that with business needs and priorities, ideally in creative ways. One family involved in the pet products industry set up a cooking class with a specialist to develop dog and cat food recipes. Several members of the rising generation loved cooking and so this was a way to introduce them to the business and incorporate their expertise and interests simultaneously.
- *A failure to prioritize trust and communication.* Development simply isn't possible without trust and communication. It can be tempting to move into collective development without first assessing levels of trust and communication capability in the family. Don't make that mistake: low trust will not only impede development but might result in further erosion of family dynamics if people try to force development on a system that can't

handle it. Make assessment and improvement of trust and communication the first priority as a foundation for more specific ownership development.

- *Sacrificing the needs of the many for the issues of the few.* Every family faces the dilemma of whose needs to put first: the group's or the individual's? Ideally, both types of needs can be satisfied with relationships, policies, practices, and values related to ownership and other areas. But sometimes, families' ownership development efforts can be derailed by the issues surrounding one individual or a small subset of people—such as an unwillingness to buy into a collective vision or to abide by long-standing policies. Many families will try to engage *everyone* around all things, especially something as important as ownership development. But sometimes that's simply not feasible, and it makes sense to move ahead on ownership development with those who are willing to learn and grow rather than to let one person exert a disproportionate influence on the enterprise's future. Skillful moderation is critical in such circumstances, whether by the family or outside advisors.

- *Being too rigid and disconnecting from the family.* With the best intention of creating structure to support the learning efforts, there might be cases in which the requirements are perceived to be too rigid as opposed to the associated rewards for attending (i.e., paid attendance) which creates a more transactional approach toward learning. This attitude can produce less than desirable effects, including disengaged family members. We recommend involving family members when designing collective learning practices. Be flexible around learning methodology or experiences and begin with the challenges they presently experience.

- *Individual learning fails to become collective learning.* In a learning family, individual growth influences collective growth and vice versa. A great reward for individual efforts is to create engaging opportunities to share the learning with a larger group. When an individual attends a conference, or reads a great book, or meets an inspiring individual, create time and space for such learning to be shared in a fun and effective way, according to the talents of every family member. Not everything needs to be in a written document; today, easy access to HD technology allows for fun videos, engaging conversations, visual arts, and the like.

- *Not facing hard choices: I-We Tension.* Sometimes, ownership development means being realistic about the possibility that the current or prospective ownership group just can't perform well together. Perhaps there is simply too much historic conflict. Maybe there are significant values or vision differences among owners. Or owners might have very different risk tolerance or financial needs or goals. Regardless, sometimes "stepping up" means observing that not owning together may be best for family relationships. Sometimes called "pruning the family tree," or more delicately, "ownership consolidation," this process often requires the leadership and diplomacy we've outlined already. Families can navigate this difficult process effectively, ultimately supporting the repair and growth of family relationships once ownership no longer gets in the way (see Exhibit 8.3).

Exhibit 8.3 Becoming a Learning Family Summary Table

	WHY BECOMING A LEARNING FAMILY MATTERS	INSPIRING WORDS OR KEY MESSAGE	
WHY	• A group of owners won't become an effective team simply because they must make joint decisions • There is a need to create alignment within and across generations due to different perspectives,interests and goals • Any group working on complex issues requires a common set of frameworks and vocabulary for effective dialogue • Cohesion and connection are imperatives for continuity	A learning family is a team that works together to transform and enhance their collective capacity with the aim of creating results they all really care about	

	COLLECTIVE DEVELOPMENT GOALS	HOWTOs	SAMPLE DEVELOPMENT PLAN FOR ZOE'S LEARNING FAMILY

WHAT	• Build trust and respect
	• Strengthen communication capabilities
	• Advance capacity to collaborate effectively
	• Develop collective decision-making capability
	• Create shared language and understanding
		• Conduct a learning needs assessment
		
		• Hold in-house learning sessions during family meetings
		
		• Run multi-family workshops with a local expert advisor
		
		• Engage in policy development
		
		• Start a family book club
		
		• Strengthen and extend your social networks to other family members
		
		• Go on learning expeditions
		
		• Learn new ways of communication with one another
		
		• Promote ownership, business, and financial literacy
		
		• Enhance philanthropy and related knowledge and skills
		
		• Learn how to have frank, honest and transparent conversation with respect and sensitivity
		
		• Design fun activities and events
			• Meeting Activities
			  - Include a development activity at each quarterly family meeting. Sample topics include:
			    - Exploring individual purpose
			    - Learning to manage boundaries in a family enterprise
			    - Understanding our relationship to money and wealth
			    - Reading a financial statement - case study
			• Financial Literacy
			  - Complete a financial literacy program with the family's private banker for G3 group of cousins
			  - Hire a personal CFO coach for family members
			• Webinars – Offer 6 family enterprise webinars with field experts (sample topics include):
			  - Building consensus in a family enterprise
			  - Starting a family foundation
			  - Preparing for year-end tax planning
			  - Choosing a financial advisor
			  - The value of mentoring and coaching
			  - Managing difficult conversations
			• Collectively attend and present at a Family Business Conference (e.g., 3 family members attend and participate on a panel regarding next-generation development)
			• Conduct a learning expedition with all rising generation family members to Napa Valley to tour 3-5 family wineries
			• Schedule an external speaker to present at annual general shareholder meeting relevant to your family enterprise business and industry
			• Family Book Club – Participate in a family book club (adults) which includes the following books:
			    - **The Culture Code** by Daniel Coyle
			    - **Being Mortal** by Atul Gwande
			    - **Innovation in the Family Business** by Joe Schmieder

	SAMPLE STORIES, EXERCISES AND TOOLS DESCRIBED IN THE CHAPTER	THINGS TO WATCH OUT FOR		
HOW TO	• Family Book Club Guidelines • Retail Expedition in Asia • The Wilsons Commit to Communication • From a Game to a Spontaneous Life Lesson • "If We Were a Learning Family" Exercise	• Giving up too soon • A failure to prioritize trust and communication • Sacrificing the needs of the many for the issues of the few • Too much too soon		

Suggested Additional Readings

Carlock, R., & Ward, J. (2010). *When Family Businesses Are Best: The Parallel Planning Process for Family Harmony and Business Success (A Family Business Publication)*. Palgrave Macmillan.

Leach, P. (2009). *Family Businesses: The Essentials*. Profile Books.

Nacht, J., & Greenleaf, G. (2018). *Family Champions and Champion Families: Developing Family Leaders to Sustain the Family Enterprise* (1st ed.). Family Business Consulting Group, Inc.

Schuman, A. M., & Ward, J. L. (2009). *Family Education for Business-Owning Families: Strengthening Bonds by Learning Together*. Family Business Consulting Group, Inc.

Schwarz, R. M. (2002). *The Skilled Facilitator: A Comprehensive Resource for Consultants, Facilitators, Managers, Trainers, and Coaches*. Wiley.

Senge, P. M. (2014). *The Fifth Discipline Fieldbook: Strategies and Tools for Building a Learning Organization*. Crown Business.

Ward, J. L. (2004). *Perpetuating the Family Business: 50 Lessons Learned From Long-Lasting, Successful Families in Business (A Family Business Publication)* (1st ed.). Palgrave Macmillan.

9

Where and How to Start

© The Author(s), under exclusive license to Springer Nature
Switzerland AG 2022
W. Sage-Hayward et al., *Own It!*, A Family Business Publication,
https://doi.org/10.1007/978-3-030-20419-8_9

Zak and Zoe—Where to Start

Our primary goal, to this point, has been to help you gain perspective on ownership development. We've explored how to build an owner's mindset including building knowledge and skill for all ages. We laid out why development matters and shared tools to apply in your family enterprise development process. We hope you feel more confident and capable regarding ownership than ever before.

However, a critical question remains: Where to start? That's what this chapter is about: taking a practical approach to launching the process of ownership development in your family, or continuing it in a more systematic manner, using the ideas in this book.

The 4 A's: Assess, Acknowledge, Act, Adjust

There is simply no one-size-fits-all solution. In the case of family enterprise, *one-size* development plan fits *one*. Every family has its own structure, learning styles, and other unique dynamics. Even families that "look" similar in demographics, culture, or other features, often have different development needs based on the configuration of their family.

We suggest a simple and flexible framework to help develop your own set of strategies and practical steps with your family. We call it the 4 A's (see Exhibit 9.1) which stands for:

Exhibit 9.1 The 4 A's

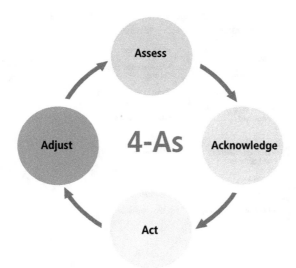

- *Assess*: Gauge where your family and individual members are in owner-ship stage, beliefs, capabilities, needs, and potential challenges, including concerns and level of motivation.
- *Acknowledge*: Take to heart that operating, owning, and transitioning a family enterprise to the rising generation is a complex endeavor, and should be thought of as a continuous process. Help your family understand the truth of this assertion as a context for going down the road of development together
- *Act*: Identify and undertake a set of ownership development strategies based on the ideas in this book that work for your family enterprise. Execute on those activities to build new skills and capabilities. In doing so, be sensitive to ranking abilities and skills among family members as these comparisons can yield a range of reactions in the family.
- *Adjust*: Evaluate the progress you have made after a period of time and then consider the requirements and changes of new life stages, including additional players (in-laws), availability, commitment, and so on to adjust for continuous changes in your family, enterprise, and industry. Create clarity and buy-in among family members around criteria to measure improvement.

Exhibit 9.2 Fixed and Growth Mindsets

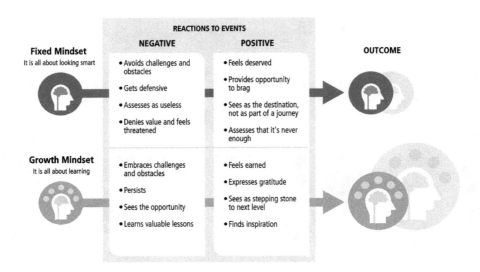

We recommend periodically completing an assessment of the current state of ownership development and then acknowledging, acting, and adjusting as required. Each of these steps is discussed in greater detail.

Assess Where You Are

Our definition of an owner's mindset lists "development as a continuous process" as its first characteristic. This principle leverages Carol Dwek's "growth mindset" concept. Dr. Dweck is a Professor of Psychology at Stanford University and a leading researcher on motivation and mindsets. She focuses her work on why people succeed. Her research identifies two types of mindsets[1] as depicted in Exhibit 9.2. A fixed mindset is defined as an individual who believes their personal qualities are static. A growth mindset consists of a person who continuously cultivates and improves their abilities through effort and training. People with a growth mindset still experience failure, but they see mistakes as an opportunity to learn. Acquiring a growth mindset unleashes unimaginable potential and thus is a crucial concept for family members to understand.

Once improvement is understood as a possibility for everyone, you need a starting point. With ownership development, that means assessing where

---

[1] Dweck, C. S. (2008). *Mindset: The new psychology of success*. Random House Digital, Inc.

your family is within the different dimensions of development discussed in this book.

With this in mind, the first step is to gauge family members' current mindset, through an inventory of beliefs in action. The goal of such exercise is to create more awareness around how everyone's mind automatically makes assumptions and interpretations, drawing conclusions that influence decisions and interactions among owners.

Once you have a better understanding of the current belief system in operation among the family and the owners, it is important to avoid judging them as "good" or "bad." This judgment may generate reactivity among individuals and potentially become a roadblock to positive change. The goal is to share a constructive desire to "update and upgrade" to a shared set of beliefs. This is similar to upgrading to a newer iOs system in your family as current events, people, and circumstances cause an evolution of your enterprise.

Another important question to consider is the level of motivation of self and others. For example, how interested are family members in ownership development, especially for themselves? You, the person reading this book, likely care a great deal about development—or you probably wouldn't be reading it! But for others, maybe not so much. The young children in your family are busy (hopefully) having fun and growing up. Adolescents are, well, adolescents! Emerging and early adults are navigating career, relationships, and starting and raising their own families. Middle adults are in the thick of their careers and navigating issues such as empty nesting and mid-life transitions and anxiety. Later-stage adults often feel "done" with learning and developing, and may want to take on less, rather than more.

What this suggests is everyone has potential reasons to take it easy on ownership development or avoid it altogether. As noted in other chapters, very little development will take place if people aren't motivated or if the family has challenging dynamics that may act as barriers to the development process, such as emotional cutoffs or other painful interactions. Some families can't gather without an altercation of some kind. So, try to get a sense of individual and collective motivation for development as a first step. But other than in seemingly extreme situations, do not make assumptions about people's motivation levels. It is better to ask, "I have been reading about ownership development and it seems like we could really benefit from thinking about it more strategically. What do you think?" than to assume a lack of interest. You may be pleasantly surprised.

To assess people's motivation more fully, consider using the "Assessment of Commitment to the Family Enterprise" in Exhibit 9.3.[2]

Exhibit 9.3 Assessment of Commitment to Family Enterprise

> This brief evaluation can help you understand family members' commitment to the enterprise—and thus to developing an owner's mindset.
> Ask members to rate each statement on a scale from 5 (Strongly Agree) to 1 (Strongly Disagree), then total their score to understand their commitment level. Looking at individual and collective scores can give you a sense of commitment level across members, generations, and branches and inform your efforts toward developing an owner's mindset. As with any survey, be very clear at the outset about what level of anonymity you'll offer respondents (e.g., their name won't be associated with the score, but their generation will). Sometimes survey results can inadvertently be used to place blame and divide a family. Also work hard to use the results as a way to build understanding and unite the family.
>
> 1. I am willing to put in a great deal of effort to help our family enterprise be successful.
> 2. I support our family enterprise in discussions with employees and other family members.
> 3. I feel loyal to our family and our enterprise.
> 4. I find that my personal values are compatible with my family's values.
> 5. I am proud to tell others that I am part of our family enterprise.
> 6. There is much to be gained by contributing to our family enterprise on a long-term basis.
> 7. I feel a responsibility for our family enterprise's success.
> 8. I really care about the fate of my family.
> 9. Being involved with our family enterprise has a positive influence on me.
> 10. I support our family's vision for the family and enterprise.
>
> **Scoring:** Total up the scores and see the scoring grid below to understand your level of motivation.
> **38 to 50** – This score indicates a higher level of motivation and willingness to engage in ownership development activities.
> **25 to 37** – This score indicates an average level of motivation and interest in engaging in ownership development activities.
> **25 or Below** – This score indicates a low level of motivation to engage in ownership development activities.

Acknowledge the Importance and Challenge of Development

Even if the family seems ready for more proactive, systematic ownership development, it is important to collectively acknowledge why development is important, along with the challenge ahead. The reality is many families and their members do not even think of ownership development at all—whether they are simply too busy working or tending to family and personal matters or may not believe that such development is critical.

---

[2] Adapted from Carlock, R. S., & Ward, J. L. (2002). *Strategic planning for the family business.* Palgrave.

So here too, do not assume everyone is ready to dive into development. As a first step, create a broader sense of awareness and acknowledgment of development among family members. Talk about why you think development is important—see the first chapter and early "why this matters" sections of each of the stage-focused chapters for guidance—and why you hope they will agree. As part of these early conversations, help the family understand that development is not about checking off some list or reaching some visible or invisible finish line. As much as possible, create small wins, some impact in family members' lives, attributable to the development. The clearer the connection between learning and improvements in life, around some common struggles, the stronger the intrinsic motivation. Rather, it is an ongoing process of continuous learning and growth—something people will need to make time for starting now and throughout their tenure as owners.

It may help to remind people, including yourself, that families who take ownership development seriously and try to make it happen are more likely to reap rewards of every type: business success and family success, in positive financial, psychological, social, and relational returns. They feel they have taken control of their individual and collective destinies and are better equipped to handle whatever lies ahead, making the most of new opportunities and weathering whatever challenges they may face, including seemingly catastrophic ones. Work to understand the importance of development and the related challenges ahead, and help others do the same.

Act on Building an Owner's Mindset

Now the most challenging A: act. This means taking practical steps toward ownership development.

We can't prescribe what you should do to promote ownership development in your specific family enterprise because it depends on where your family is regarding motivation and other dimensions. However, we can still offer these guidelines, tips, and principles to help you move down the development path:

- *Nurture motivation and engagement first.* Even an initial conversation with family leaders about whether and how to discuss *ownership development* would be a good starting point. Remember that inertia works both ways. A body at rest stays at rest (hello, procrastination!), but a body in motion stays in motion. That means that once you take even just the first step, it can become self-perpetuating, leading to more, bigger steps and even leaps forward. Help your family take that idea to heart.

- *Next, employ structure.* The concept that "structure will set you free" sounds paradoxical, yet effective in enterprising families. Even the most minimal structure (such as assigning a moderator for your meetings, or defining deadlines, goals, and budgets) can build momentum and give a sense of forward movement. For ownership development, this can mean something as basic as getting time on the calendar to discuss priorities, or something more involved such as putting a development committee together to complete a gap analysis and build a learning plan. However, it is important that whatever you do results in measurable action; otherwise, family members get cynical and lose interest. Think about what types of structures might help you get moving on ownership development, and work to put them in place. For example, some families include ownership development planning in their annual strategic retreat. Others ensure there is a budget for learning and development so the financial component is not a roadblock for getting it done. Do just as the Goldilocks Principle[3] implies: don't underdo or overkill but try to do development in *just the right* amount.
- *Shift beliefs.* Changing beliefs is neither straightforward nor simple. As we suggested above, a Beliefs Inventory self-assessment will demonstrate that this shift requires an ability to deeply reflect on who you are and who you want to be. Therefore, a good place to begin is shifting smaller beliefs through open-mindedness and then working on bigger beliefs once your confidence is built. Support from a skilled facilitator may be helpful in this endeavor.
- *Be flexible, expect change.* The only constant in most families and businesses is change. It is expected and normal for people's interests and commitment levels to ebb and flow over time. A family leader suddenly decides to retire. New children. New business opportunities. Divorce. Death. When you embark on an ownership development plan, you have to approach it with flexibility and the assumption that things will change across the enterprise. This can be especially true with commitment about ownership development among family members. The good news is that while some family members' interest may wane, other's interests may rise. Hopefully, you'll have some support across membership as you go down this path. The even better news is that ownership development is human development, and some of the perspectives and capabilities people gain will help your family manage unexpected changes with foresight, strategy, and calmness.

---

[3] The Goldilocks principle is named by analogy to the children's story, where a little girl named Goldilocks tastes three different bowls of porridge and finds that she prefers porridge that is neither too hot nor too cold, but has just the right temperature. The concept of "just the right amount" is easily understood and applied. Retrieved from https://en.wikipedia.org/wiki/Goldilocks_principle.

- *Try individual planning.* If rallying collective interests proves challenging, work with individuals to create *personal development plans.* An individual plan can help build engagement one family member at a time. Personal development planning involves helping each family member discover their life purpose and passions and identify learning and development opportunities to help them move toward achieving their goals.

As far as more practical steps for development, the six stage-focused chapters provide guidance for family members of all ages. Review those chapters material—especially the How-Tos and sample development plans—for your family members across ages (ideally with them beside you, especially for those beyond the young child and adolescent ages) and see what makes sense for them to pursue. Where are the gaps? What are they most interested in? What will create the most value for themselves and the enterprise?

Get people at similar ages/stages together to work toward development. The more of a group activity you can make it, the more commitment and continuity you are likely to promote, with benefits for all.

Adjust as Required

Due to the constant evolution and change in enterprising families, it is necessary to periodically take stock of the dynamic and emerging needs to adjust course as required. A highly successful learning and development process requires structure to create clarity, keep things organized and efficient, and provide a road map for how things will work. However, this also demands flexibility to adapt and adjust to situations and needs that surface during the process. A powerful example was offered by a family who set out a development plan around strengthening family communication, trust, and cohesion. The program involved coaching, conferences, and mini workshops over an eighteen-month period. During the first six months, everything went smoothly, but progress slowed down considerably when the family realized a mental health issue had gone untreated. The program leader immediately altered course by bringing in the appropriate resources and establishing a mechanism for family members to learn to manage the issue better, and the individual of concern entered treatment to address the problem.

There may be one final "**A**" not yet mentioned, which is *Accept.* Some family situations may make ongoing collective progress on ownership development challenging, if not near impossible, at some points. If that's the reality in your family, see the aforementioned tips about starting small and with structure, but be willing to accept there might not be enough motivation or capability for the family to move forward with these efforts together. Work on your own ownership development, and on that of other willing family members, with some hope that larger-scale development may be a possibility in the future, even if it means waiting for the rising generation to be more involved. Always remember that growth and development are rarely a straightforward and fast journey. Most often, they take unexpected turns.

Things to Look for

In each stage-focused chapter, we offered pitfalls or potential challenges on the road to ownership development for that age group or maturity level. In addition to the previous points, here are some of the most common ones to think about in this general process.

- *Forgetting the heart*. Everyone is aware of the existence and importance of the emotional dimension in our lives. Some individuals may be inclined to disregard it and somehow expect it will take care of itself. While this is understandable, please, don't forget that learning and growth don't only happen in "the head," but also involve the "heart."[4] Above all, remember that a shift in mindset impacts behaviors, thinking, and feelings. Honoring it is very important and will likely avoid a burst of reactivity. That is why having a designated Chief Emotional Officer (CEmO)[5] in the family is so important, as they are well equipped to deal with emotional needs.
- *Low readiness*. Jumping the gun on ownership development is a common and understandable issue, given that once certain family members recognize the value of development, they may be eager to push everyone to move forward. This can be off-putting for some, resulting in family members saying, "We do not want to do this."
- *Failure to educate*. People do not know what they do not know. Even if family members like or love the idea of ownership development, they may not have the basic understanding to move toward it on multiple dimensions. Many families start with ownership-focused educational programs at university-based or other family enterprise centers. Others bring advisors in to promote awareness and education. Even simple tools like our Glossary of Ownership terms (see Appendix A) can be helpful. Think about

---

[4] Kegan, R., Kegan, L. L. L. R., & Lahey, L. L. (2009). *Immunity to change: How to overcome it and unlock potential in yourself and your organization.* Harvard Business Press.
[5] See Chapter 7 for Chief Emotional Officer.

what your family needs to set the right stage for ownership development while building key knowledge, perspective, and interest.

- *Off the corner of your desk syndrome.* As we mentioned earlier, if the process kicks off well but no actions follow, it will create cynicism, which is hard to recover from the next time someone embarks on this journey. If possible, do not add the responsibility of ownership development to the busiest person in the family simply because those are the people who usually get things done. Rather, ensure that whoever's responsibility it becomes has the time, interest, and energy to make the process stimulating, fun, and valuable for the family. Create ad-hoc committees which create more capacity for planning and execution and provide opportunities to experience collaboration, getting to know family members in a working environment, and practice communication skills.

- *Failing to include owner's meetings in the governance system.* As we identified several times in previous chapters, many families and the advisors who serve them focus primarily on family and business governance. Given the significance of the owner's role in the continuity of a family enterprise, we advocate for including ownership meetings in your governance structures. Failure to do so, in our opinion, leaves a gaping hole in the communication and decision-making process of your family enterprise ecosystem. We know one G1-G2 family enterprise who addresses all three systems of governance in one day. The morning consists of a family meeting with all family members including spouses. Then everyone has lunch together and the spouses, who are not owners, take their young children home. The early afternoon agenda focuses on ownership topics. Then Mom leaves for home and the family members who work in the business (Dad and three adult children) finish the day with topics related to the business system. This example illustrates that covering the governance of three systems can be relatively simple.

- *Hiring the wrong advisors.* There is a growing contingent of advisors focused broadly on family enterprises: investment advisors, accountants, attorneys, psychologists, and others. Many will profess to help with ownership development. But some simply won't be effective, especially if they have historically been focused on specific areas like wealth and financial planning or have typically advised only one generation. Look for advisors with broad-ranging experience with ownership development, ideally across families of different shapes, sizes, and needs. Talk to families you know who have had success with ownership development and ask them how they approached it, including regarding retaining the right advisors. Also remember that being knowledgeable about something does not equal being able to transfer that knowledge to others. Those who advise need to be aware of the complex science of learning to be effective and engaging. Verify that people supporting you in your journey have enough education, experience, and wisdom to advise well.

- *Too top-down.* Successful development processes are very often the result of collaboration and inclusion of different perspectives. "Too much, too soon, too required" are enemies of long-term sustainable transformation. Finding and managing the right balance between being "effective and efficient" is a crucial art to cultivate among owners.

Final Words

If you think about ownership development as we have presented it, it can feel like having to figure out how to eat the proverbial elephant—a vast amount of information to digest, areas to assess, and action plans to create. We know that can be overwhelming. But remember the advice on how best to eat the "elephant": one bite at a time.

As emphasized in this chapter, approach ownership development by starting small and slow, but with a big vision for change. That will help you take early steps and gain momentum. Below is specific advice for different types of readers of this book.

- *To the family members trying to lead ownership development.* Congrats on being the one or part of a small group willing to take the family on this critical journey. All the advice in this chapter applies, in terms of starting small and with structure, expecting change, and others. But don't try to do it all yourself. Enlist the help of other willing family members, including younger ones who may not have much experience but can contribute enthusiasm and energy. Work with non-family executives and advisors with experience, advice, and insights to offer. Think for the long term but give yourself a break when needed. This is hard stuff, but ultimately rewarding.
- *To the younger family members engaged in the early stages of development who have been given this book by a sage generation member!* It is great you may be embarking on the journey of ownership development, which will have many rewards for you and your family. We believe it is critical to understand what people are asking you to do and to make development-related choices for yourself based on your capacity, interests, and time. Try to work with older family members on a development plan that makes sense for *you*. If you feel you do not have much choice in the matter, try to speak

up and find a family member who can help you be heard. Advisors can play this role too, but it has to start with *you*. Self-awareness and self-advocacy are critical parts of ownership development, so develop and use these however you can. It sets the right precedent.

- *To family enterprise advisors working with families on ownership development.* You know as well as we do that each family member you work with will have different priorities, abilities, perspectives, knowledge, and needs. You may well have your own approach to ownership development work, we hope the ideas in this book can offer guidance and structure. We want to emphasize that working on ownership development is more than a plan or program—it is working on people's *lives*. Every choice the family has to make has profound repercussions on multiple systems, both in the short and long term, sometimes way after you are no longer in the picture. Be equipped to take on the work, including the ideas here such as starting small, using structure, building momentum, and aiming for quick wins. It is also critical to ensure family members understand the time commitment required and that they are ready to be held accountable for doing their part. Overall, strive to make development a fun, safe, and unifying process that everyone can benefit from.

- *To non-family executives working in a family enterprise or a family office, and to independent directors.* For this group ownership development may seem like an add-on to an already long list of services and objectives. However, family members who think and act with an owner's mindset actually make your job easier as there may be better communication from owners to the board and management around purpose, vision, financial goals, as well as other critical areas. Support the general concept of development and specific areas such as mentoring rising-generation members on business and leadership skills within it as best you can. And remember: involve them, don't just act for them.

For everyone interested in or engaged in ownership development, we encourage you to maintain an open mind and growth mindset, to be patient and think for the long term and to use the ideas presented to find the development path that works best for your family and its individual members, taking thoughtful steps and celebrating all wins along the way.

We wish you the best on your journey toward developing an owner's mindset! We hope you can now OWN IT!

Suggested Additional Readings

Aronoff, C., & Ward, J. (2011). *How to choose and use advisors: Getting the best professional family business advice (A Family Business Publication)*. Palgrave Macmillan.

Gabrielson, E., & Petit, M. (2019). *Our fear never sleeps: Let go to fight for what is possible*. Indie Books International.

Appendix A: Glossary of Terms

Glossary of Terms

Acquisition:
The transaction of a company purchasing 50% or more of another company's stock to gain control of that company. This allows the acquirer to make decisions regarding the newly acquired company's without the consultation of its shareholders.

Annual Shareholders Meeting:
The annual mandatory meeting of owners to review company performance elect officers and directors, amend bylaws, and conduct other business.

Articles of Incorporation:
The formal documents filed with a government body to legally document the creation of a corporation outlining basic information including name owners, directors, and stock issued.

Asset:
Any resource with an economic value owned by a person or business. Assets can be classified as capital/fixed current, tangible or intangible, and expressed in terms of their cash value on financial statements.

Beliefs:
Ideas individuals hold as true. They are assumptions, conscious or unconscious, that

W. Sage-Hayward et al., *Own It!*, A Family Business Publication, https://doi.org/10.1007/978-3-030-20419-8

	individuals about themselves, others in the world, and how they expect things to be. They are very powerful as they are at the base of how individuals interpret the world and act within it.
Board of Directors:	A group of individuals selected by owners of a company to represent their best interests and oversee company strategy. A fiduciary board has a legal fiduciary duty to shareholders and has voting authority on key items usually defined in company bylaws. A Board of Directors may include family members, family owners, and non-family members with expertise in specific business or industry domains.
Boomer:	See Generations definition.
Buy-sell Agreement:	A document that defines how an owner may sell their portion of the business, who is eligible to buy it, under what circumstances it can or must be sold, how the shares will be valued, and how the company would fund the purchase.
Bylaws:	The set of rules defining how a company will be run, the duties and decisions of owners and managers, and how internal disputes will be resolved. Bylaws are required, whereas shareholder and operating agreements are optional.
Charter:	A written document outlining the purpose rights, and responsibilities of a business. Boards of Directors and Family Councils function most effectively over time when they are governed by a jointly developed charter. Charters typically address the following topics: purpose, membership, terms, officers and their duties, member removal, committee structure, compensation, decision-making, communication structure, and interaction with other governing bodies.

Consensus: A process where members of a group *generally* agree on the direction, solution, or decision after a comprehensive discussion. Members may not be fully on board with a decision but agree to go along with it or abstain from the vote. Consensus is sometimes confused with unanimity which is where members of a group *fully* agree with a decision, action, or solution.

Distribution: A payout to a company's shareholders from its mutual funds or stock and bonds in the form of cash. Distributions are made before-tax income which can lower the company's tax burden since payouts will figure into an investor's cost basis.

Dividend: A share of income from a portion of a company's profits that is paid to its shareholders as opposed to an equity stake in the company. Dividends are decided and managed by the company's Board of Directors, though they must be approved by shareholders through their voting rights. Dividends can be received in the form of cash, shares, or other types of property.

Emotional Intelligence: The ability to recognize, understand, and manage our own emotions as well as understand the emotions of others and its influence on the relationship.

Empathy: The ability to sense another's emotions and the ability to imagine what another person might be feeling or thinking.

Enmeshment: A relationship between two or more people in which personal boundaries are permeable and unclear.

Enterprising Family: A family who deploys its capital across a variety of asset classes to preserve and grow its wealth.

Entitlement: A belief that one has a claim to something due to who they are or circumstances in which they exist. Sometimes a family member may not have legitimate grounds for feeling entitled such as when they do not earn something. However there are also circumstances under which family members may have legitimate grounds for feeling entitled to something.

Equity: Refers to the value of an ownership interest in a business such as shares of stock held. Equity is defined as retained earnings plus the sum of inventory and other assets, and minus liabilities on a balance sheet.

Estate: All money and assets owned by an individual which are sold, given away, or transitioned to the rising generation upon death.

Estate Planning: The process of creating a plan outlining how to dispose of an individual's assets including transfer to designated heirs in compliance with the settlement of estate taxes, upon the owner's death or incapacitation.

Estate Tax: A tax calculated on the net value of an individual's estate at the time of their passing. Typically, the amount is calculated using the value that exceeds an exclusion limit set by law.

Fair Process: A decision-making process that actively engages family members in how decisions will be made (such as consensus voting, etc.) and determines what criteria will be used for the decision ahead of time. There are three elements that define fair process: engagement, explanation, and clarity of expectation. If a family believes a process is fair, often they can accept a decision even though they may not personally agree.

Family: A major subsystem within a family enterprise that delineates lineal descendants and clear governance roles of a family. Different types of family members can be classified for various roles within the family system such as in-laws, partners, stepchildren, lineal descendants, and ex-spouses. An enterprise needs to setup a clear family structure to give definition of governance roles and define who may have access to certain information, attend family events, and own the family business.

Family Assembly: A gathering of the full set of family members in an enterprise in order to share information, build closer relationships, plan, make decisions, discuss topics relevant to family enterprise owners and the board, and have fun.

Family Association: Typically a subset of the full family usually defined by age, who make decisions on election of family council members, family business policies, updates to family guiding principles, and allocation of resources to family owner development.

Family Bank: A wealth preservation strategy whereby a family designates a portion of its wealth for loans such as starting a new business venture within the family or supporting family member education. The bank is governed by a set of formal rules designed by the family for receiving a start-up loan, as well as how family members are expected to pay back monies owed.

Family Business: The operating business(es) owned by an enterprising family. Early in the evolution of a family business it often represents the majority of an enterprising family's wealth.

Family Constitution: A set of documents that includes the family's jointly defined guiding principles philosophies, policies, values, and rules—some moral, some prescriptive, and some legally binding.

Family Council: A selected or elected body that represents the full family. They usually play the leading role in planning and implementing family meetings especially the portions that address

Family Enterprise:

family owner development. Family councils are most effective when governed by a jointly defined charter.

Consists of a variety of assets beyond the commonly pictured operating business. It may include *financial assets* such as stock and bond portfolios or cash; *real estate assets* of any kind; *philanthropic assets* such as a family foundation, *heirloom assets* such as jewelry, art collections, cars, or a family cabin; *deferred assets* such as insurance, annuities, and specific types of trusts that monetize after passing; and *non-financial, human assets* consisting of intellectual knowledge, strong relationships, leadership capability, and the like. Not all family enterprises own every asset class, and the enterprise includes all people, structures, and other components required for operation and governance.

Family Foundation:

A type of foundation set-up, funded, and governed by a single family who serve as trustees or directors of its board. The foundation's guiding principles a typically driven by the family's vision, values and history.

Family Office:

Serves as an interface between family members and the family's assets providing services that enable responsible and comprehensive management of the family's wealth while concurrently providing for the development of family members in their roles as wealth owners and beneficiaries.

Generations:

For the purposes of this book, we have defined the generations as:

- *Boomer (born 1946–1964)*
- *GenX (born 1965–1979)*
- *Millennial (born 1980–1994); and*
- *iGen (born 1995–2012).*

Generativity:	A concern for establishing and guiding the next generation. From Erik Erikson's theory of psychosocial development.
Genogram:	A family tree that illustrates relationships among family members and often identifies additional details such as age, gender, education, role as owners or employees in the family business, and the like.
GenX:	See Generations definition.
Gross Income:	The total amount of money a business or individual earns before taxes and deductions.
Governance:	The formal structures and processes by which enterprising families communicate, share information, and make decisions. Each system (family, business, and ownership) has unique and distinct governance structures that foster dialogue and decision-making around issues and matters unique to that system.
GRPL (Growth, Risk, Profit, and Liquidity):	Key decisions made by ownership including the following: (1) *Growth*—How you want business to grow? (e.g., fast/moderate/slow, geographically, acquisitions, markets, products, customers); (2) *Risk*—What is level of risk you choose to take for the business? (e.g., Loss of capital, volatility, decrease in value, damage to relationships); (3) *Profitability*—What level of profitability is sought? (*e.g.,* rate of return expected for capital at risk); (4) *Liquidity*—How will profits be used and how do owners sell their shares? (e.g., access to capital of ownership via dividends and/or redemptions).
iGen:	See Generations definition.
Independent Director:	A member of a board of directors who does not have a material relationship with the company or family. Typically independent directors are not employed by the business, are not family members, friends of family

members, or current advisors or consultants to the business.

Individuation:
The process of an individual discerning their own identity as separate and apart from that of their own nuclear and extended family members.

Legacy:
A set of beliefs, values, and attitudes that are passed down from generation to generation that creates an honorable effect and memory around the family enterprise.

Liability:
Legal financial debts and obligations such as money owed on a loan or mortgage, of the business. The value of a business is the difference between its assets and liabilities.

Liquidity:
The degree to which an asset can be easily converted into cash. Available cash indicates that a business can pay off debt easily when due dates occur.

Merger:
An agreement that combines two companies into a single legal entity.

Millennial:
See Generations definition.

Mindset:
A set of beliefs which drive and shape what we do, how we engage with others, and how we behave in every moment and situation.

Net Income:
The residual amount of earnings after all expenses including cost of goods sold, depreciation, interest, and taxes have been deducted. It is used to determine the profitability of a venture.

Owners:
Individuals or entities that have a stake in one or more classes of assets which ultimately gives them rights and control over property, along with responsibilities. Owners can own operating businesses, real estate, physical assets, financial assets (bank deposits, bonds, and stocks), and other types (or classes) of assets. In addition to control, ownership offers economic benefits delivered either through distribution of the

profits or through the increased value of the property owned.

Owner's Mindset: A set of beliefs that drive how owners engage with one another, with others in the family, and in the enterprise. An owner's mindset includes the following beliefs:

- *Development is a continuous individual and collective process;*
- *Ownership requires deep commitment and responsibility;*
- *Proactivity is paramount;*
- *Abundance over scarcity;*
- *Win-win solutions;*
- *Diversity and inclusion matter; and*
- *Owners are stronger together than apart.*

Ownership Council (or Owners Council): A permanent forum for representation of the owners which regularly discusses and decides ownership-related issues and communicates those decisions to the board.

Ownership Form: Partial ownership in an entity can be represented by shares stock, percentage, or units, depending on what kind of entity (e.g., corporation, limited liability company, partnership, etc.) the entity is owned within. Descriptions below refer to "share" ownership. Some of the concepts can be applied to stocks, percentage ownership, or unit ownership.

Common Share: The customary type of share, in which every share is treated equally. If an individual owns common stock, their shares carry all the voting and other rights inherent in them.

Preferred Share: These shares offer their bearers a higher claim to dividends or asset distribution than those of common stockholders. In case of liquidation of the company, the preferential shareholders will be paid out first, once all debts of the business are settled. Only once this is done will common stockholders be paid out. Sometimes preferred shares do not carry voting rights.

Equity Shares with Differential Voting Rights: These shares are often issued to founders or CEOs so that they may have greater control over the day-to-day affairs of the company.

Ownership Type:

There are seven types of ownership. Understanding the type of owners within an enterprise allows for owners start having calm discussions about what ownership means for them, making compromise possible.

Operating Owner: An owner who is employed by the family business, typically in the day-to-day operations.

Governing Owner: An owner who provides formal oversight of the enterprise, but is not involved in day-to-day operations.

Active Owner: An owner who is not employed by the enterprise but is genuinely interested in its affairs and is actively involved in activities such as the family council or special ownership-related projects.

Investor Owner: An owner who is satisfied with the return on investment made by the enterprise (both financial and non-financial) and makes an active decision to remain an owner.

Passive Owner: An owner who collects dividends, does not make any attempt to be engaged in the business, and may not make a conscious decision to remain an owner.

Proud Owner: An owner who is not significantly engaged in the business—or very knowledgeable about it—but is proud of the family's legacy and heritage. *Emotional (or Psychological) Ownership*: Held by a family member with no legal ownership but who acts with the same commitment and thus extends time and energy to supporting it.

Philanthropy: The act of giving back, creating a lasting impact in society through values and legacy. Philanthropy can include giving of time, talent, and treasure.

Profit: The financial benefit or net income generated from business activities after accounting for all expenses, costs, and taxes.

Psychological Safety: An environment among a group or team where it is safe to be open, honest, and candid without fear of judgment, criticism, or retribution from other members.

Redemption: When a shareholder sells a portion of their stock back to the business. Typically, the shareholder agreement will stipulate the conditions for how the buyback will occur.

Revenue: The total amount of income generated, value of all sales of goods, or services recognized by a company's primary operations.

Shareholder Agreements: Legally binding arrangements among shareholders describing shareholders' rights and obligations, along with specific privileges and protections as needed, to ensure fair treatment.

Socioemotional Wealth: Certain types of non-financial value created in the family enterprise including having influence on the business (such as through family values); relationships with and responsibility to non-family employees, suppliers, distributors, and the community at large; bonding and affection among family members; and the opportunity to transfer the family values and the enterprise to future generations.

Stewardship:

The supervision and careful management of assets. Stewardship is an attitude that one's legacy (both financial and non-financial assets) should be preserved and passed on through generations.

Succession:

The planning process for transitioning ownership and leadership of a family enterprise to the next generation.

Sweat Equity:

The investment of labor or voluntary unpaid work that individuals contribute to a business venture. Its value can be determined by comparing the salary that the individual working within the business would have been paid for similar work elsewhere. In a family enterprise, sweat equity is sometimes how equity in the business gets transferred to the rising generation.

Tax planning:

The set of related activities carried out to analyze an individual's potential income and estate tax liability and develop an approach that both mitigates that liability and fulfills the individual's other planning goals (e.g., passing enterprise ownership to specific members of the next generation).

Triangulation:

Occurs when a third person intervenes or is drawn into a conflicted relationship between two others in an attempt to ease tension and facilitate communication. Sometimes the third person can become more aligned with one individual over another. Or, the third person can play a constructive role by active listening, asking powerful questions, or helping frame how one might speak about their issues directly to the other in the conflicted relationship.

Trust:

A fiduciary agreement created by a party (the Grantor) through which a second party (the Trustee) holds rights of assets for a third party (the Beneficiary) of both: (1) control; and (2) economic benefit. The control rights (fiduciary duty and administration) are appointed to trustees to provide legal protection of the trustor's assets. Economic benefits are appointed to beneficiaries through access to income generated from the assets that are owned within the trust—they cannot be separated from the control rights.

> *Beneficiary*: The person or the entity appointed to receive the benefits of the trust arrangements, such as cash distributions. Beneficiaries' rights may vary depending on the type of trust that has been put in place. In some cases, beneficiaries are given the right to change the designated trustee.
>
> *Grantor (or Trustor or Settlor)*: The individual who sets up the trust and provides the terms and conditions.
>
> *Trust Agreement*: The legal document containing instructions on how assets held in the trust are to be managed for the trust's beneficiaries.
>
> *Trustee*: An individual or a group appointed by the grantor, who have been given control or powers of administration over the assets in trust with a legal obligation to administer it solely for the purposes specified. Trustees have a fiduciary duty to manage the asset in the best interest of the beneficiaries.

Unanimity:

A process where members of a group fully agree on the direction, solution, or decision after a thorough discussion. Unanimity is sometimes confused with consensus, which is where members of a group generally agree to go along with a decision, action, or solution or will abstain from the vote.

Valuation: An analytical process to estimate the current or projected total worth of a company. There are various methods and approaches when placing a value on a company, such as the business's management, the composition of its capital structure, the prospect of future earnings, and the market value of its assets, among other things.

Working Capital: A financial metric that represents a company's ability to pay its current liabilities with its current assets—both tangible and intangible—to measure its financial health. If the current assets are less than current liabilities, a business would be described as having a working capital deficit.

Appendix B: Sample List of Policies for Family Enterprise Development

This appendix provides a list of policies that family enterprises create over time to align family members around how they will operate together. Policy creation is an excellent tool to use for collective development in a family enterprise.

Policy development is a process whereby the family collectively defines and agrees upon how they wish to operate their enterprise together. Developing policies collectively provides an opportunity for a family to create alignment about a variety of matters including the more challenging ones such as compensation and share transfer. The process of *discussing* these issues is as important as the final *written* outcome. The benefits of collective policy development include:

- Helps prevent problems before they occur
- Reduces family tension
- Strengthens family cohesion by reaching agreement
- Clarifies the family's position on key issue which reduces misunderstandings
- Improves future decisions by ensuring that policy formation is informed and objective rather than made in the heat of the moment
- Increases the likelihood of long-term business and family success, survival, and prosperity

© The Editor(s) (if applicable) and The Author(s) under, exclusive licence to Springer Nature Switzerland AG 2022
W. Sage-Hayward et al., *Own It!*, A Family Business Publication,
https://doi.org/10.1007/978-3-030-20419-8

Family System Policies	
Code of conduct	An agreement of how the family agrees to interact with one another. These standards may include how family members resolve conflicts, communicate, make decisions, and generally interact with one another, customers, suppliers, and others
Confidentiality/Privacy	This policy provides guidelines to safeguard sensitive information and prevent unauthorized disclosure
Conflict resolution	This policy outlines an escalation process with regard to how family conflicts are handled and resolved
Decision-making	This policy defines what decisions are made and by whom within each component of the family enterprise system (i.e., family, business, and ownership)
Education funding	This policy clarifies who, when, what, and how funds are going to be used for education and/or training for family members
Expense reimbursement	This policy describes how family credit cards are managed and what type of expenses the family business will reimburse
Fair process	This policy defines how the family will implement fair process in how they work and make decisions together
Family council charter	This policy provides guidelines for how the family council will serve as an advisory body to the family, what decisions they will make, and how they will operate to foster the well-being of the family
Family discounts	This policy defines what discounts or incentives are available with regard to the family business products and services. It safeguards the family business and its members from potential misuse or abuse in acquiring products or services from the enterprise
Family heirlooms	This policy sets forth the rules for how heirlooms and other legacy items may be borrowed and exchanged between members, as well as how they will be maintained and transferred to the next generation

(continued)

(continued)

Family System Policies	
Family vision, mission, and values	These statements are an expression of the family's desired future and belief system. They provide direction and focus that guides behavior and decision-making
Help in crises	This policy outlines how a family firm will help a family member in the event of a crisis
Housing grant	This policy defines the "why and how" of a grant given to each rising generation family member for developing a unique and personal home environment in which to grow and flourish with their own families
Media relations/Social media	This policy identifies guidelines for how family members will interact with the media and what private family information can and cannot be disclosed to the public, including social media sites
Personal loans	This policy addresses the availability of loans between family members or other entities in the family enterprise system. It outlines who can receive a loan for how much, under what circumstances, and with what terms
Philanthropic vision, values, and charter	This policy helps align the family around its giving purpose, values, and decision-making processes. Philanthropic initiatives provide an excellent opportunity for establishing legacy, providing leadership roles outside of the business, and strengthening cohesion and connection within the family
Shared recreational property	This policy helps define successful joint ownership regarding the use and care of shared land and property. It defines how to protect and respect each other's rights, privacy, and long-term interests in the property

Ownership System Policies	
Advisory council	This policy outlines the roles and responsibilities of an advisory council to the family business or board of directors by outlining how it represents the interests of the family in the overall governance system

(continued)

(continued)

Ownership System Policies	
Airplane use	This policy governs the usage of the family aircraft (excluding commercial airlines) around how and when company personnel and family may use it for official business or otherwise
Board observer role	This policy defines the process and structure of providing rising generation family members an opportunity to observe board of directors meetings to gain exposure to the operation of this governance structure
Co-investment/Venture	This policy outlines the procedures and guidelines for how family members may co-fund and potentially co-operate a new venture with the family enterprise
Conflict of interest	This policy outlines a process for protecting the interest of the family enterprise when entering into a transaction or arrangement that might benefit the private interest of one or more family member over others
Dispute resolution	This process outlines a responsible escalation process for addressing how family conflicts are handled and resolved with regard to the family enterprise
Dividends/Distribution	This policy refers to the proportion of the firm's earnings to be paid out to the shareholders on an annual basis. Typically, dividends are issued as cash payments but can be shares of stock or other property. Distributions are always paid out in the form of cash and come with different tax implications than dividends
Exit or buy-sell agreement	This policy stipulates how an owner's stock may be transferred or sold if that partner dies or otherwise leaves the business
Family bank	This policy outlines the process for how family members may access capital to start a business venture that is either peripheral or not to the existing family business
Family board of director membership	This policy addresses the circumstances and conditions under which a family member participates as a member of the family board of directors
Family Law agreements	This policy sets out how prenuptials or marriage contracts will be utilized as a means of preserving ownership of the enterprise for future generations of the family

(continued)

Ownership System Policies	
Insurance planning	This policy outlines how the family utilizes insurance to cover the taxes payable by their successors, equalize the inheritance across heirs, and potentially increase the legacy they leave
Openness and transparency	This policy is designed to foster openness and collaboration by defining how the family will promote fairness and equity in their business interactions and decisions as well as share information about potential business/investment opportunities
Redemptions	This policy outlines how family members can sell or transfer all or a portion of their stock to others in the family or otherwise
Responsible ownership	This policy defines what "responsible ownership" means to the family and what responsibilities contribute to the interests of the collective group of owners
Shared ownership and transfer	This agreement covers a variety of issues including who can own stock, who has voting rights, how and when stock is transferred, and the terms and conditions under which it may be bought and sold
Sharing and storing information	This policy defines guidelines for how the family will store and share information and protect the privacy of the family and the enterprise
Valuation	This policy defines an agreed upon valuation process and method for buy-sell purposes or otherwise. This is often part of a shareholders or buy-sell agreement

Business System Policies	
Board evaluation	This policy defines how the board will evaluate its performance and what course of action to take in the event the results are less than desired. It brings a consistent method of accountability to the board and its members
Family member compensation	This policy defines the family's principles regarding compensation for family members working in the enterprise, including bonuses and pay raises
Employment of family friends	This policy outlines the conditions under which family friends can participate as employees in the family enterprise

(continued)

(continued)

Business System Policies	
Employment of significant others/spouses	This policy describes the rules by which significant others can participate as employees in the family enterprise
Entry requirements for family members	This component of family employment policies defines the qualifications, education, and experience needed to work in the family enterprise
Hiring family members	This policy defines the process by which family members may get hired in the enterprise to ensure equity and fair process
Performance reviews for family members	This policy sets forth the process for how family employees receive performance reviews and outlines the performance expectations for family members so that there are no surprises about how family members are evaluated within the enterprise
Promotions	This policy defines the conditions for how family members receive promotions and advancements in the family enterprise
Reporting relationships	This policy pertains to family reporting relationships inside the family enterprise. The goal is to prevent issues that may lead to power struggles or other challenges that affect family members' ability to function successfully
Retirement	This policy outlines retirement guidelines that define benefits or continued salary for family members when retiring from the family enterprise
Sub-contracting	This policy serves to help ensure fair process and accountability for sub-contracting work to family or friends the family business
Summer employment	This policy defines opportunities for youth to become engaged in the family business during summers and holiday breaks
Termination/Re-entry	This policy defines the rules and processes for terminating employment of family members and the circumstances under which they may be rehired
Travel expense policy	This policy defines what travel expenses will be reimbursed by the enterprise for business-related events and activities

(continued)

(continued)

Business System Policies	
Vendors and supplier policy	This policy helps manage potential conflicts of interest in inter-family business opportunities by ensuring healthy competition among vendors, resulting in quality vendor relations and long-term profits for the family
General Policy Amendment	This policy specifies guidelines for reviewing and amending family enterprise policies on a regular basis to ensure they evolve with the family's needs and dynamics

Appendix C: Family Enterprise Learning Needs Assessment

This appendix provides a tool for families to assess their strengths and areas of learning for building an owner's mindset in the family. Please review the instructions and complete the form. A scoring sheet is included at the end of the questions.

Instructions: Rate the extent to which you agree with each of the following statements. 1 = no or very low agreement with the statement; 5 = high agreement with the statement.

Family and individual motivation	Rating scale				
1. Our family has a philosophy of life-long learning and continuous improvement	1	2	3	4	5
2. Our family believes learning and development is vital to successful continuity of our family enterprise	1	2	3	4	5
3. Our family creates an annual budget for learning and development related to building an owner's mindset	1	2	3	4	5
4. We have a family member or advisor who champions learning for our family	1	2	3	4	5
5. Family members pursue education, training, and development in areas that they are passionate about including ownership	1	2	3	4	5
Family enterprise strategy	Rating scale				
6. Our family has a well-defined and commonly understood strategic vision, values statement, and goals for our family enterprise	1	2	3	4	5
7. Our family has a clearly articulated strategic plan which outlines how we are going to achieve our family enterprise vision and goals	1	2	3	4	5
8. Our family actively manages the human resource aspect of family employment and family participation in our enterprise well	1	2	3	4	5

(continued)

© The Editor(s) (if applicable) and The Author(s) under, exclusive licence to Springer Nature Switzerland AG 2022
W. Sage-Hayward et al., *Own It!*, A Family Business Publication,
https://doi.org/10.1007/978-3-030-20419-8

(continued)

	Rating scale				
9. Our family intentionally builds a strong culture within our family enterprise focused on honoring our family values	1	2	3	4	5
10. Our family cultivates its unique abilities and resources and uses them as a competitive advantage for our family enterprise	1	2	3	4	5
Family enterprise governance	**Rating scale**				
11. Our family has strong family governance in place such as regular family meetings, a family council, and well-defined family governance policies	1	2	3	4	5
12. Our owners have regular meetings focused on ownership topics and have put in place good quality ownership policies such as shareholders agreements, corporate structures, estate plans, etc.dividend policies	1	2	3	4	5
13. The operating businesses have functioning boards of directors with independent members which adds value and contributes meaningfully to the success of our family enterprise	1	2	3	4	5
14. Family members understand the importance and value of governance for our family enterprise and are actively engaged in governance meetings where appropriate	1	2	3	4	5
15. Our governance structures (family council, board of directors/advisors, and ownership meetings) communicate regularly and are apprised of key outputs and decisions of one another	1	2	3	4	5
Family enterprise leadership	**Rating scale**				
16. Our family respects the need for strong leadership and has structures in place to develop family leadership at all levels	1	2	3	4	5
17. Our family fosters the development of entrepreneurial skills and capabilities	1	2	3	4	5
18. Our family appreciates different styles of leadership and helps individuals assess and build their personal leadership style and approach	1	2	3	4	5
19. Our family promotes chair and moderator role development	1	2	3	4	5
20. Our family manages transitions effectively	1	2	3	4	5
Family enterprise ownership	**Rating scale**				
21. family understands the stages and types of ownership in a family enterprise	1	2	3	4	5
22. Our family fosters clarity around ownership roles and responsibilities	1	2	3	4	5
23. Our family openly discusses risk appetite and risk management strategies at our ownership meetings	1	2	3	4	5
24. Members of our family have strong financial literacy and are able to ask good questions when discussing financial matters in our family enterprise	1	2	3	4	5
25. Our family has a multigenerational view of ownership and builds an owner's mindset in the rising generation	1	2	3	4	5
Family philanthropy	**Rating scale**				
26. Our family believes in charitable giving and contributes significantly to charities and organizations consistent with our values and beliefs	1	2	3	4	5
27. Our family has a structured approach to its charitable giving with strong governance policies and practices	1	2	3	4	5
28. Information about our charitable giving is widely shared and understood within our family	1	2	3	4	5
29. Our family's charitable giving is guided by a collective vision and values and we have a strategy to support how we will achieve our philanthropic vision	1	2	3	4	5
30. We celebrate our ability to give back within the communities in which we live	1	2	3	4	5

(continued)

(continued)

Family relationships	Rating scale				
31. Our family understands and recognizes the complexity of relationships within a family enterprise and actively works on improving them within our family	1	2	3	4	5
32. Our family values, appreciates, and honors different communication styles and preferences	1	2	3	4	5
33. Our family invests time in hearing diverse opinions and perspectives and seeks consensus whenever possible	1	2	3	4	5
34. Our family navigates difficult conversations and conflict well	1	2	3	4	5
35. Our family actively cultivates its networks and relationships	1	2	3	4	5
Wealth and money	**Rating scale**				
36. Our family comfortably talks about money and we have a collective understanding of the purpose of wealth in our family	1	2	3	4	5
37. Our family promotes wealth preservation in a healthy manner	1	2	3	4	5
38. Our family understands the challenges related to inheriting wealth and fosters a positive relationship to money including accountability and money management	1	2	3	4	5
39. Our family focuses on building social, intellectual, human, and spiritual capital in addition to financial capital	1	2	3	4	5
40. Our family has a robust process for choosing and working with financial advisors	1	2	3	4	5
Personal development	**Rating scale**				
41. Family members have a good self-understanding including their personality type, learning style, role in the family, and other self-defining features	1	2	3	4	5
42. Family members are confident, able to assert their views and feelings without shutting others down, listen well, and collaborate effectively with others	1	2	3	4	5
43. Family members are accountable and responsive to others	1	2	3	4	5
44. Family members manage themselves appropriately especially during conflicts and stress	1	2	3	4	5
45. Family members are personally motivated to learn and grow as owners	1	2	3	4	5

When you have completed the assessment, turn to the scoring sheet below.

Scoring Sheet

Instructions: Transfer the number you circled for each statement on the assessment form to the scoring grid below, and add the columns. Evaluate your scores in each separate skill area as follows:

19–25 points: Your family has high capability in this category of skill.

12–18 points: Your family has some skill in this area but could use more learning and practice.

5–11 points: Your family would likely benefit from learning and development in this area.

Motivation	Strategy	Governance
1.	6.	11.
2.	7.	12.
3.	8.	13.
4.	9.	14.
Total out of 25	Total out of 25	Total out of 25
Leadership	**Ownership**	**Philanthropy**
16.	21.	26.
17.	22.	27.
18.	23.	28.
19.	24.	29.
20.	25.	30.
Total out of 25	Total out of 25	Total out of 25
Relationships	**Wealth and Money**	**Personal Development**
31.	36.	41.
32.	37.	42.
33.	38.	43.
34.	39.	44.
35.	40.	45.
Total out of 25	Total out of 25	Total out of 25

If possible, have each family member complete this assessment individually. In addition, ask close family enterprise advisors or executives to assess your skills as a family. Use this data as a comparative to the family data which will provide a reality check on your self-assessment scores.

References

Chapter 1

Anderson, R. C., & Reeb, D. M. (2003). Founding-family ownership and firm performance: Evidence from the S&P 500. *The Journal of Finance, 58*(3), 1301–1328.

Angus, P. (2015). *The trustee primer.* A Guide for Personal Trustees.

Arbinger Institute. (2016). *The outward mindset: Seeing beyond ourselves.* Berrett-Koehler Publishers.

Aronoff, C. E., & Ward, J. L. (2011). *Family business ownership: How to be an effective shareholder.* Palgrave Macmillan, Springer.

Aronoff, C., & Ward, J. (2016). *Family business ownership: How to be an effective shareholder.* Springer.

Astrachan, C., Waldkirch, M., Michiels, A., Pieper, T., Bernhard, F., (2019). Professionalizing the business family. The five pillars of competent, committed and sustainable ownership. *Family Firm Institute Research Report.*

Berrone, P., Cruz, C., & Gomez-Mejia, L. R. (2012). Socioemotional wealth in family firms: Theoretical dimensions, assessment approaches, and agenda for future research. *Family Business Review, 25*(3), 258–279.

Björnberg, Å., & Nicholson, N. (2012). Emotional ownership: The next generation's relationship with the family firm. *Family Business Review, 25*(4), 374–390.

Bloch, A., Kachaner, N., & Stalk, G. (2012). *What you can learn from family business.* Harvard Business Review.

Boaz, N., & Fox, E. A. (2014). Change leader, change thyself. *McKinsey Quarterly,* 11.

Bruner, J. S. (1960). *The process of education.* Harvard University Press.

© The Editor(s) (if applicable) and The Author(s) under, exclusive licence to Springer Nature Switzerland AG 2022
W. Sage-Hayward et al., *Own It!,* A Family Business Publication,
https://doi.org/10.1007/978-3-030-20419-8

Cunningham, Judi. (2011). Family enterprise asset model [PowerPoint Presentation].

Eckrich, Christopher J., & McClure, S. L. (2012). *The family council handbook: How to create, run, and maintain a successful family business council* (A Family Business Publication) (Kindle Locations 146–150). Palgrave Macmillan. Kindle Edition.

EY and University of St. Gallen Global Family Business Index. (n.d.). http://family businessindex.com/.

Field, J. (2000). *Lifelong learning and the new educational order*. Trentham Books, Ltd., Westview House, 734 London Road, Stoke on Trent, ST4 5NP.

Freebairn-Smith, L. (2010). *Abundance and scarcity mental models in leaders* (Doctoral dissertation, Saybrook University).

Gardner, H. (1983). *Frames of mind: The theory of multiple intelligences*. Basic Books.

Gersick, K., Davis, J. A., Hampton, M. M., & Lansberg, I. (1997). *Generation to generation: Life cycles of the family business*. Harvard Business Review Press.

Goldstone, H., & Wiseman, K. (2012). *Trustworthy: New angles on trusts from beneficiaries and trustees*. CreateSpace Independent Publishing Platform.

Gompers, P., & Kovvali, S. (July-August 2018). *The other diversity dividend*. Harvard Business Review.

Grant, A. M. (2013). *Give and take: A revolutionary approach to success*. Penguin.

Hughes Jr., J. E. (2007a). *A reflection of the path of the stakeholder owner: Organizational and management science*. http://www.jamesehughes.com/articles/PathOfSta keholder.pdf.

Hughes Jr, J. E. (2007b). *Family: The compact among generations* (Vol. 31). John Wiley & Sons.

Hughes Jr, J. E. (2010). *Family wealth: Keeping it in the family* (Vol. 34). John Wiley & Sons.

Hughes, J. E., Jr., Massenzio, S. E., & Whitaker, K. (2017). *Complete family wealth*. John Wiley & Sons.

Jaffe, D. T., & Grubman, J. (2016). *Cross cultures: How global families negotiate change across generations*. Create Space Independent Publishing Platform.

Lansberg, I. (1999). *Succeeding generations: Realizing the dream of families in business*. Harvard Business School Press.

Martínez, J. I., Stöhr, B. S., & Quiroga, B. F. (2007). Family ownership and firm performance: Evidence from public companies in Chile. *Family Business Review, 20*(2), 83–94.

Massenzio, S. E., Whitaker, K. & Hughes, J. E., (2012). *The cycle of the gift: family wealth and wisdom* (1st ed.). Bloomberg Press.

Olson, D. H. (2000). Circumplex model of marital and family systems. *Journal of Family Therapy, 22*(2), 144–167.

Patterson, J. M. (1988). Families experiencing stress: I. The family adjustment and adaptation response model: II. Applying the FAAR model to health-related issues for intervention and research. *Family Systems Medicine, 6*(2), 202.

Renkert-Thomas, A. (2016). *Engaged ownership: A guide for owners of family businesses.* Wiley & Sons.

Schwarz, R. M. (2002). *The skilled facilitator: A comprehensive resource for consultants, facilitators, managers, trainers, and coaches.* John Wiley & Sons.

Sciascia, S., & Mazzola, P. (2008). Family involvement in ownership and management: Exploring nonlinear effects on performance. *Family Business Review, 21*(4), 331–345.

Shickler, S., & Waller, J. (2011). *The 7 mindsets to live your ultimate life.* Dweck, C. S. (2008).

Siegel, D. J. (2010). *Mindsight: The new science of personal transformation.* Bantam.

Southwick, S. M., Bonanno, G. A., Masten, A. S., Panter-Brick, C., & Yehuda, R. (2014). Resilience definitions, theory, and challenges: Interdisciplinary perspectives. *European Journal of Psychotraumatology, 5,* Article 25338.

Sraer, D., & Thesmar, D. (2007). Performance and behavior of family firms: Evidence from the French stock market. *Journal of the European Economic Association, 5*(4), 709–751.

Villalonga, B., & Amit, R. (2006). How do family ownership, control and management affect firm value? *Journal of Financial Economics, 80*(2), 385–417.

Ward, J. L. (2016). *Keeping the family business healthy: How to plan for continuing growth, profitability, and family leadership.* Springer.

Chapter 2

Boll, T., Ferring, D., & Filipp, S.-H. (2003). Perceived parental differential treatment in middle adulthood: Curvilinear relations with individuals' experienced relationship quality to sibling and parents. *Journal of Family Psychology, 17*(4), 472–487.

Cohen, A. R., & Sharma, P. (2016). *Entrepreneurs in every generation: how successful family businesses develop their next leaders.* Berrett-Koehler Publishers.

Covey, S. R. (2013). *The 7 habits of highly effective people: Powerful lessons in personal change (Anniversary).* Simon & Schuster.

Duke, M. P., Lazarus, A., & Fivush, R. (2008*).* Knowledge of family history as a clinically useful index of psychological well-being and prognosis: A brief report. *Psychotherapy: Theory, Research, Practice, Training, 45*(2), 268–272.

Godfrey, J. (2013). *Raising financially fit kids.* Ten Speed Press.

Gurian, M. (2017a). *Saving our sons: A new path for raising healthy and resilient boys: With special sections on motivating boys and managing their technology use.* Gurian Institute.

Gurian, M. (2017b). *The minds of girls: A new path for raising healthy, resilient, and successful women.* Gurian Institute.

Hughes Jr., J. E., Massenzio, S. E., & Whitaker, K. (2014). *The voice of the rising generation: Family wealth and wisdom.* Wiley & Sons.

Jaffe, D. (2019, January 28). *The 'shirtsleeves-to-shirtsleeves' curse: How family wealth can survive it.* https://www.forbes.com/sites/dennisjaffe/2019/01/28/the-shirtslee ves-to-shirtsleeves-curse-how-family-wealth-can-survive-it/#2a4994e46c8d.

Lieber, R. (2015). *The opposite of spoiled: Raising kids who are grounded, generous, and smart about money.* HarperCollins.

Peck, S. J. (2007). *Money and meaning: New ways to have conversations about money with your clients: A guide for therapists, coaches, and other professionals* (1st ed.). Wiley.

Perry, N. B., Dollar, J. M., Calkins, S. D., Keane, S. P., & Shanahan, L. (2018). Childhood self-regulation as a mechanism through which early over control-ling parenting is associated with adjustment in preadolescence. *Developmental Psychology, 54*(8), 1542–1554.

Pew Research Center. (2020, May 30). 1. *The American family today.* Pew Research Center's Social & Demographic Trends Project. https://www.pewsocialtrends.org/2015/12/17/1-the-american-family-today/.

Phillips, K. (2014, October 1). *How diversity makes us smarter.* https://www.scient ificamerican.com/article/how-diversity-makes-us-smarter/.

Purdue, M. (2017). *How to communicate values to children: Templates, activities, and resources for embedding a positive family business culture* (How to make your family business last) (2nd ed., Vol. 2). CreateSpace.

Siegel, D. J. (2015). *The developing mind: How relationships and the brain interact to shape who we are.* Guilford Press.

Williams, R. O., & Preisser, V. (2010). *Preparing heirs: Five steps to a successful transition of family wealth and values.* Robert D. Reed Publishers.

Chapter 3

American Psychological Association Survey. (2014). Shows that teen stress rivals that of Adults. http://www.apa.org/news/press/releases/2014/02/teen-stress.aspx.

Benson, P. L., Hawkins, J. D., Hill, K. G., Oesterle, S., Pashak, T. J., & Scales, P. C. (2016). The dimensions of successful young adult development: A conceptual and measurement framework. *Applied Developmental Science, 20*(3), 150–174.

Blum, M. E. (2009). Self-defined leadership: Exploring family history to enhance future leadership. *Global Leadership,* 9–19.

Eckrich, C. J., & McClure, S. L. (2012). *The family council handbook: How to create, run and maintain a successful family business council.* Palgrave Macmillan.

Fivush, R. (2016). *The "do you know?" 20 questions About family stories.* https://www.psychologytoday.com/us/blog/the-stories-our-lives/201611/the-do-you-know-20-questions-about-family-stories.

Grubman, J. (2013). *Stranger in paradise. How families adapt to wealth across generations.* Family Wealth Consulting.

Hughes Jr., J. E. (2004). *Family wealth: Keeping it in the family.* Bloomberg Publishing.

Hughes Jr., J. E., Massenzio, S. E., & Whitaker, K. (201 2). The cycle of the gift: Family wealth and wisdom (Vol. 168). Wiley.

McVeigh, T. (2016, September 24). *It's never been easy being a teenager. But is this now a generation in crisis?* https://www.theguardian.com/society/2016/sep/24/tee nagers-generation-in-crisis.

Morin, A. (2018). *Top 10 social issues teens struggle with today.* https://www.verywe llfamily.com/startling-facts-about-todays-teenagers-2608914.

Sage-Hayward, W. (2014). *Four cornerstones of family meetings.*

Shellenbarger, S. (2017). *Step away from your over-scheduled high school student.* https://www.wsj.com/articles/step-away-from-your-over-scheduled-teen-1511282108.

The Power of Stories. (n.d.). https://www.psychologytoday.com/us/collections/201 106/the-power-stories.

Twenge Ph.D., J. M. (2017). *iGen: Why today's super-connected kids are growing up less rebellious, more tolerant, less happy-and completely unprepared for adulthood.* Simon & Schuster.

Chapter 4

Aamodt, S., & Wang, S. (2009). *Welcome to your brain: Why you lose your car keys but never forget how to drive and other puzzles of everyday life.* Bloomsbury.

Armstrong, T. (1999). *7 kinds of smart: Identifying and developing your multiple intelligences.* Plume.

Arnett, J. J., & Fishel, E. (2014). *Getting to 30: A parent's guide to the 20-something years.* Workman Publishing Company.

Bertrand, M., Kamenica, E., & Pan, E. (2015). Gender identity and relative income within households. *The Quarterly Journal of Economics, 130*(2), 571–614.

Combrinck-Graham, L. E. E. (1985). A developmental model for family systems. *Family Process, 24*(2), 139–150.

Covey, S. R., Merrill, A. R., & Merrill, R. R. (1996). *First things first* (Reprinted ed.). Free Press.

Erikson, E. H. (1950). *Childhood and society.* W. W. Norton.

Gay, W. (2017, August 11). *Millennials are effecting change with social responsibility.* https://www.forbes.com/sites/wesgay/2017/08/11/millennials-social-responsib ility/#4a97f07717d8.

Hughes, J. E., Jr. (1999). A reflection of the sale of a family business as an event of trauma. *The Chase Journal, III*(2).

Hughes, J. E., Jr. (2010). *Family wealth: Keeping it in the family* (Vol. 34). Wiley.

Hughes, J. E., Jr., Massenzio, S. E., & Whitaker, K. (2014). *The voice of the rising generation: Family wealth and wisdom.* Wiley.

Keffeler, K., Hughes, W., & Iglehart, A. (2020). When she has the money: Challenging ancient conventions and supporting the new normal. *Family*

Enterprise Xchange. https://family-enterprise-xchange.com/res/pub/docs/2017Symposium/FromFiscalUnequalsToFinancialDiversity.pdf.

The Harris Poll on behalf of TD Ameritrade. (2020). Breadwinners Survey. https://s2.q4cdn.com/437609071/files/doc_news/research/2020/breadwinners-survey.pdf.

Twenge, J. M. (2017a). *Have smartphones destroyed a generation?* https://www.theatlantic.com/magazine/archive/2017/09/has-the-smartphone-destroyed-a-generation/534198.

Twenge, J. M. (2017b). *The 10 trends shaping today's young people—And the Nation.* Atria Books.

Zakrzewski, A. (2020). Managing the next decade of women's wealth. *BCG Global.* https://www.bcg.com/publications/2020/managing-next-decade-women-wealth.

Chapter 5

Aronoff, C. E., & Ward, J. L. (2011c). *How to choose and use advisors: Getting the best professional family business advice.* Palgrave Macmillan.

Astrachan, C., Waldkirch, M., Michiels, A., Pieper, T., Bernhard, F. (2019). Professionalizing the business family. The five pillars of competent, committed and sustainable ownership. *Family Firm Institute Research Report.*Benefits of Mindfulness. (2019, August 19). https://www.helpguide.org/harvard/benefits-of-mindfulness.htm.

Berger, G. (2016, April 12). *Will this year's college grads job-hop more than previous grads?* https://blog.linkedin.com/2016/04/12/will-this-year_s-college-grads-job-hop-more-than-previous-grads.

Berne, E. (1961). *Transactional analysis in psychotherapy.* Grove Press, Inc.

Brown, B. (2017, September 12). *Brené Brown: America's crisis of disconnection runs deeper than politics.* https://www.fastcompany.com/40465644/brene-brown-americas-crisis-of-disconnection-runs-deeper-than-politics.

Cloud, H. (2013). *Boundaries for leaders: Results, relationships, and being ridiculously in charge.* HarperBusiness.

Dyer, G. (2019). *The family edge: How your biggest competitive advantage in business isn't what you've been taught...it's your family.* Familius LLC.

Feeney, B. C., & Collins, N. L. (2014). A new look at social support: A theoretical perspective on thriving through relationships. *Personality and Social Psychology Review, 19*(2), 113–147. https://doi.org/10.1177/1088868314544222

Firestone, L. (2013, March 6). *Benefits of mindfulness.* https://www.psychologytoday.com/us/blog/compassion-matters/201303/benefits-mindfulness.

Goleman, D., Boyatzis, R. E., & McKee, A. (2002). P*rimal leadership: Realizing the Power of Emotional.*

Hughes, J. E., Jr. (2007). *The compact among generations.* John Wiley & Sons.

Hughes Jr., J. E., Massenzio, S. E., & Whitaker, K. (2012). *The cycle of the gift: Family wealth and wisdom (Vol. 168).* John Wiley & Sons.

Kerr, Michael E. (2000). *One family's story: A primer on Bowen theory. The Bowen center for the study of the family*. http://www.thebowencenter.org.

Landmark Worldwide. (n.d.). https://www.landmarkworldwide.com/#landmarkf orum.

Preisser, V. & Williams, R. O. (2005). Philanthropy, heirs & values: How successful families are using philanthropy to prepare their heirs for post-transition responsibilities. Robert D. Reed Publishers.

Preisser, V. & Williams, R. O. (2010). *Preparing heirs: Five steps to a successful transition of family wealth and values*. Robert D. Reed Publishers.

Ransburg, D., Sage-Hayward, W., & Schuman, A. M. (2015). *Human resources in the family business: Maximizing the power of your people*. Palgrave Macmillan.

Rock, D. (2009). *Your brain at work: Strategies for overcoming distraction, regaining focus, and working smarter all day long*. HarperBusiness.

Whiteside, M. F., Mendoza, D., Ward, J. L. (2010) How families work together. Palgrave MacMillan.

Chapter 6

Burkeman, O. (2018). Dirty secret: Why is there still a housework gender gap? https://www.theguardian.com/inequality/2018/feb/17/dirty-secret-why-hou sework-gender-gap.

De Vries, B. (1996). The understanding of friendship: An adult life course perspective. In *Handbook of emotion, adult development, and aging* (pp. 249–268). Academic Press.

Erickson, E. H. (1993). Childhood and society (Reissue). W.W. Norton & Company.

Schneider, F. S., & Schneider Malek, K. Four ways of differentiating compensation in a family business.

Greenleaf, G., & Nacht, J. (2018). *Family champions and champion families: Developing family leaders to sustain the family enterprise* (1st ed.). The Family Business Consulting Group, Inc.

Hughes Jr., J. E., Bronfman, J. & Merrill, J. (2000). Reflections on fiscal unequals. *The Chase Journal*, Vol IV, Issue 4.

Ibarra, H., & Hunter, M. (2007). How leaders create and use networks. *Harvard Business Review, 85*(40–7), 124.

Kouzes, J. M., & Posner, B. Z. (2003). *The Leadership Challenge*. Jossey-Bass.

LaMagna, M. (2018). More American women are having babies in their 30s than their 20s. https://www.marketwatch.com/story/american-women-are-having-bab ies-later-and-are-still-conflicted-about-it-2017-05-19.

Parker, K., & Patten, E. (2013). The sandwich generation. http://www.pewsocialtre nds.org/2013/01/30/the-sandwich-generation/.

Siebert, D. C., Mutran, E. J., & Reitzes, D. C. (1999). Friendship and social support: The importance of role identity to aging adults. *Social work, 44*(6), 522–533.

Smeeding, T. (n.d.). The changing fortunes of American and Wisconsin families, An introduction to the issues. https://dcf.wisconsin.gov/files/fotf/pdf/01-27-16-speaker-presentation.pdf.

Solie, D. (2004). *How to say it to seniors: Closing the communication gap with our elders.* Penguin.

Chapter 7

Bridges, W. (2004). *Transitions: Making sense of life's changes.* Cambridge.

DiSalvo, D. (2016, March 30). *This is how uncertainty makes you lose your mind.* https://www.forbes.com/sites/daviddisalvo/2016/03/30/this-is-how-uncertainty-makes-you-lose-your-mind/.

Falkingham Dean of the Faculty of Social, J. (2019, November 11). *Rising life expectancy and why we need to rethink the meaning of old age.* http://theconversation.com/rising-life-expectancy-and-why-we-need-to-rethink-the-meaning-of-old-age-64990.

Fishel, A. K. (2018). *A life-cycle approach to treating couples: From dating to death.* Momentum Press.

Gawande, A. (2014). *Being mortal: Medicine and what matters in the end* (1st ed.). Metropolitan Books.

Hawkins, D. R. (2014). *Letting go: The pathway of surrender.* Hay House, Inc.

Healey, J. (2017). *End of life issues.* Spinney Press.

Hughes Jr., J. E., Massenzio, S. E., & Whitaker, K. (2017). *Complete family wealth.* John Wiley & Sons.

Lowe, C., & Evansb, J. (2015). Harmony, productivity, and informed decision making: The fundamental competencies of the chief emotional officer. *Sociology Study, 5*(1), 60–73.

MacMillan, A. (2017, August 16). *People age better if they have a purpose in life.* http://time.com/4903166/purpose-in-life-aging/.

Marchisio, G. (2018). *When a three-legged relay race replaces passing the baton.* FFI Weekly Edition.

Pontet, S. B. de. (2017). *Transitioning from the top: Personal continuity planning for the retiring family business leader.* Palgrave Macmillan.

Raines, S. S. (2019). *Conflict management for managers: Resolving workplace, client, and policy disputes.* Rowman & Littlefield.

Rosenblatt, P. C., De Mik, L., Anderson, R. M., & Johnson, P. A., & (1985). *The family in business* (Jossey Bass Business & Management Series) (1st ed.). Jossey-Bass.

Schachter-Shalomi, Z., & Miller, R. S. (1998). *From age-ing to sage-ing. A revolutionary approach to growing older.* Grand Central Publishing.

Scahill, R. I., Frost, C., Jenkins, R., Whitwell, J. L., Rossor, M. N., & Fox, N. C. (2003). A longitudinal study of brain volume changes in normal aging using serial registered magnetic resonance imaging. *Archives of Neurology, 60*(7), 989–994.

Schuman, A. M., Stutz, S., & Ward, J. L. (2010). *Family business as paradox.* Palgrave Macmillan.

Solie, D. (2004). *How to say it to seniors: Closing the communication gap with our elders* (Fourth Printing ed.). Prentice Hall Press.

Sonnenfeld, J. (1988). *The hero's farewell: What happens when CEOs retire.* Oxford University Press.

Stepler, R. (2020, May 30). *World population ages 100 and up to grow eightfold by 2050, UN projects.* http://www.pewresearch.org/fact-tank/2016/04/21/worlds-centenarian-population-projected-to-grow-eightfold-by-2050/.

Chapter 8

Covey, S. R., & Merrill, R. R. (2006). *The speed of trust: The one thing that changes everything.* Simon and Schuster.

Cress, C. M., Collier, P. J., & Reitenauer, V. L. (2013). *Learning through serving: A student guidebook for service-learning and civic engagement across academic disciplines and cultural communities.* Stylus Publishing, LLC.

Delizonna, L. (2017). High-performing teams need psychological safety. Here's how to create It. *Harvard Business Review, 8,* 1–5.

Easterby-Smith, M., Araujo, L., & Burgoyne, J. (Eds.). (1999). *Organizational learning and the learning organization: Developments in theory and practice.* Sage.

Edmondson, A. (1999). Psychological safety and learning behavior in work teams. *Administrative Science Quarterly, 44*(2), 350–383.

Edmondson, A. C. (2018). *The fearless organization: Creating psychological safety in the workplace for learning, innovation, and growth.* Wiley.

Hughes Jr, J. E., Massenzio, S. E., & Whitaker, K. (2017). *Complete family wealth.* Wiley.

Jaffe, D. (2020). *Borrowed from your grandchildren.* Wiley.

Mischel, W., & Ebbesen, E. B. (1970). Attention in delay of gratification. *Journal of Personality and Social Psychology, 16*(2), 329.

Olson, D. H., Russell, C. S., & Sprenkle, D. H. (1983). Circumplex model of marital and family systems: VI. *Theoretical Update. Family Process, 22*(1), 69–83.

Örtenblad, A. (2001). On differences between organizational learning and learning organization. *The learning organization.*

Senge, P. M. (2014). *The fifth discipline fieldbook: Strategies and tools for building a learning organization.* Crown Business.

Somers, M. (2018). *Advice that Sticks: How to give financial advice that people will follow.* Practical Inspiration Publishing.

Tying, C. M., Amin, H. U., Saad, M. N., & Malik, A. S. (2017). The influences of emotion on learning and memory. *Frontiers in Psychology, 8,* 1454.

Van der Heyden, L., Blondel, C., & Carlock, R. S. (2005). Fair process: Striving for justice in family business. *Family Business Review, 18*(1), 1–21.

Chapter 9

Carlock, R. S., & Ward, J. L. (2002). *Strategic planning for the family business.* Palgrave.

Dana, L. Ph.D. – Family Business Specialist Adviser in Australia.

Dweck, C. S. (2008). *Mindset: The new psychology of success.* Random House Digital, Inc.

Kegan, R., Kegan, L. L. L. R., & Lahey, L. L. (2009). *Immunity to change: How to overcome it and unlock potential in yourself and your organization.* Harvard Business Press.

Index

© The Editor(s) (if applicable) and The Author(s) under, exclusive licence to Springer
Nature Switzerland AG 2022
W. Sage-Hayward et al., *Own It!*, A Family Business Publication,
https://doi.org/10.1007/978-3-030-20419-8

BACKYARD BIRDS OF
Florida

Bill Fenimore

Gibbs Smith, Publisher
TO ENRICH AND INSPIRE HUMANKIND
Salt Lake City | Charleston | Santa Fe | Santa Barbara

To my brothers, Leonard and Larry,
intrepid outdoorsmen and nature lovers

First Edition
12 11 10 09 08   5 4 3 2 1

Text © 2008 Bill Fenimore
Maps © Cornell Lab of Ornithology
Photo Credits: Gary Aspenall: page 28; Randy Chatelain: page 52; Brian L. Currie: page 30; Lee Duer: page 44; Keith Evans: page 26; George Jett: pages 34, 36 (inset), 44 (inset), 60; Jerry Liguori: pages 20, 24, 32, 46, 56, 66; Judd Patterson: pages 2, 36, 40, 48 (inset), 50, 64; Tom Pawlesh: page 18; Robert R. Ruszala: page 26 (inset); Kelly Thurgood: pages 22, 28 (inset), 48, 54, 58; VIREO: cover, pages 38, 42, 62

Published by
Gibbs Smith, Publisher
P.O. Box 667
Layton, Utah 84041

Orders: 1.800.835.4993
www.gibbs-smith.com

Designed by Rudy Ramos
Printed and bound in Hong Kong

Library of Congress Cataloging-in-Publication Data

Fenimore, Bill.
  Backyard birds of Florida : how to identify and attract the top 25 birds / Bill Fenimore. — 1st ed.
      p. cm.
  ISBN-13: 978-1-4236-0352-8
  ISBN-10: 1-4236-0352-4
  1. Birds—Florida--Identification. 2. Birds—Florida—Pictorial works. I. Title.

QL684.F6F46 2008
598.09759—dc22
                          2007052702

Contents

Foreword

When I first met Bill Fenimore in 2001, I knew a lifelong friendship was underway. We were about the same age, had grandchildren, and traveled many of the same paths around the world—but that's not what I mean exactly. What struck me most deeply was Bill's infectious enthusiasm for wild birds and his keen desire to share that excitement with others. In many ways, this guide is an inevitable extension of Bill's personality, a natural outlet for his deep appreciation for the satisfactions that come with learning more about wild birds. In this book, Bill has identified those wild birds you will likely see in your own backyard because he knows that your life will never be the same.

In my own work, I often say that the closer we live to each other, the greater we need to live closer to nature. These days, many of us feel the daily pressures of urban or suburban living and yearn for a simpler time when we lived more in tune with natural rhythms and seasonal cycles. We may also feel a tug of desire to live within a smaller framework where we can make a positive contribution to the natural world around us.

In that sense, this guide makes an enormous contribution by revealing new ways to bring more peace and tranquility into our lives by watching and feeding wild birds around our homes.

GEORGE H. PETRIDES SR.
Founder and Chairman
Wild Bird Centers of America, Inc.

Introduction

This guide will enable you to identify and properly name the top twenty-five birds using your backyard bird sanctuary. You will also learn which bird species visit as spring and fall migrants, which are nesting birds, which are winter residents, and which are permanent year-round residents. This guide will educate you about the cover (vegetation), food, and water needs for these birds. It will also show you a variety of ways that you can improve your backyard habitat for birds and the enjoyment you can have watching and caring for them.

Hook Birds
Most birders who develop the enthusiasm that I have can tell you which bird it was that got them hooked. These "hook birds" have been responsible for providing me and others with many years of enjoyment. Some people, like me, get hooked early in life. Others don't feel the hook until much later. I have included here two hook bird stories: mine, which happened when I was a young lad, and that of my brother, who got hooked after retiring from a successful career in the United States Air Force.

Bill's Story
When I was ten years old, I saw a strange-looking bird along the Chester River where I was fishing in southeastern Pennsylvania. I had no idea what it was. At that age, I could have told you what a house sparrow, starling, pigeon, or a robin was, but that was about it. This bird was like none of those familiar birds. It was perched on a log overlooking the river, close to the water surface. Its bill was long and pointed. The bird was motionless, like a statue, poised over the water on its perch. It was watching small minnows swimming ever closer to its position. I noticed it was a slender bird, with blue and green feathers on its back. It had a

dark cap with shaggy feathers on the back of its neck. The head and neck were a chestnut color.

Suddenly the bird struck. Its bill pierced the water and it came up with a minnow, neatly held at the tip of its bill. The bird quickly swallowed its catch and with a bold abrasive *kyowk* flew off, soon out of sight, around a bend in the river. I stood there watching in amazement as the bird disappeared. *What was that?* I asked myself.

Later that day I was telling a neighbor who was a local schoolteacher about the strange bird. He went into his house and brought out a book about birds. He instructed me to look through the book and see if I could identify the bird that I had seen along the river. Turning the pages of his field guide, I was impressed with the many beautiful birds that were illustrated on each page. Most of the birds were new to me. They had names that I had never heard before: crossbill, sapsucker, oriole, and so forth. Suddenly, turning the next page, I saw the exact bird I had seen catch the minnow. Excitedly, I pointed it out. "There it is, look," I said. "Why, that's a green heron," the teacher told me. I borrowed the book and studied the green heron's picture the rest of that day. What an amazing bird, I thought. And what an amazing book with all manner of strange birds illustrated in it. That night at the dinner table, I announced to my family that I had seen a green heron while fishing down at the river that day. "What's a green heron?" my father asked me. I pulled out my book and showed him the bird's picture. He stared at it and said, "I've seen this bird before. We always called them mud hens. I never knew their proper name."

I was dumbstruck! As a young fellow, I thought that Dad knew everything. To think that there was something that he didn't know, and that I knew, was a very amazing circumstance. The following day I showed my friends the bird's picture. None of them knew what it was. Well, now I was on to something. I could study this book and learn about birds. Then I could tell my family and friends about them. This was the beginning of my birding hobby, which I have carried on for some fifty-odd years. It has been a very rewarding pastime. It has helped me better identify with nature and appreciate the outdoors.

Brother Len's Story

When I was a kid growing up in Pennsylvania, I only had a mild interest in birds, and that was probably due to my brother's "serious" interest. In those days I remember my brother, Bill, as being the "go-to guy" if you had a question about birds. But my passive interest changed in 1996. Shortly after I retired from the Air Force I joined Bill on a weeklong field trip to Yellowstone National Park. Bill told me in advance to bring along binoculars so that I could better enjoy the wildlife. I expected to see a lot of wildlife. What I didn't expect was to come home with a passion for birding.

On the five-hour drive from Utah to Yellowstone, I noticed that Bill spent more time looking up in the sky than he did looking at the road. "Red-tailed hawk," he would say, spotting a bird soaring high in the sky. Sometimes he would point to a hawk sitting on a telephone pole as we were driving by and say, "Swainson's hawk." His knowledge and skill at being able to identify birds without binoculars (while going sixty miles an hour) impressed me. It wasn't long before he had me doing it. Looking up in the clouds at a bird, I would say, "Red-tailed hawk." Looking at the same bird, Bill would correct me and say, "uh, turkey vulture." *Hmmm,* I would say to myself. *This isn't as easy as it looks.*

We stayed in cabins in Yellowstone's Lamar Valley. Bill quickly befriended another birder. Together they would stop and look at every passing bird and identify it. The excitement and enthusiasm they shared was contagious and I got caught up in the excitement. I would quickly point at a bird flying by that Bill seemed to be ignoring and ask, "What's that?" "Brewer's blackbird," Bill would nonchalantly reply.

After dinner each night we would go out on the porch to watch the wildlife. Under the eaves of the cabin a barn swallow had built a nest. In it were four nestlings. Suddenly an adult flew in, fed each of the begging mouths, and then flew off. Moments later another adult appeared. This went on until dark. To me, it was a magical sight. The next day I saw a mountain bluebird, a beautiful male flying over the field next to our cabin. The bird was the color of the clear blue sky above. I was mesmerized, watching the beauty of the bird as it crisscrossed the field catching insects. At that moment I knew that birding was something I could enjoy.

Since my Yellowstone adventure, my interest in birds has continued to grow. I have traveled extensively across North America and to other countries, learning about birds. I have become an officer in my Audubon chapter, and I even took a Cornell University course on bird biology.

It seems I have found the perfect hobby for my retirement: birding. Thanks, Bill.

Why Feed Backyard Birds?

When I was a toddler, I would watch my mother throw bread crumbs onto the snow of our Pennsylvania yard for the birds. She felt that the birds needed her help weathering cold winter days. It is still a fond memory of mine, some fifty years later. I became fascinated with those birds as I watched them enjoy Mom's treat.

Birds provide a terrific keyhole into the natural world. Once there, you can wade in as deep as you feel comfortable. Some will be content, like Mom, to simply put food out for the birds in winter. Others will want to learn more about the birds, especially about identifying them correctly. Still more will desire to learn how they can help birds, as they enjoy watching them. There are others who enjoy birding so much that they continue the knowledge quest by enrolling in citizen science programs, available through the Audubon Society and the Cornell Lab of Ornithology. Whichever category you fall into, birds are wonderful creatures to enjoy.

What Is Backyard Bird Habitat?

When I was a college student, I read a statement in an American history book that I have never forgotten. It created a powerful and lasting image in my mind. The statement was this: "The forest in northeastern America was so dense when the pilgrims landed at Plymouth Rock that a squirrel could travel from the East Coast to the beginning of the Great Plains without ever touching the ground." Imagine that wonderful expanse of natural habitat for the birds that dwelled there.

Today that expansive and contiguous forest does not exist; such has been the impact of development and spread of our rural, urban, and suburban communities. However, it occurred to me as I began to study birds and their habitat needs that there are many "contiguous backyards" throughout America today. Imagine the positive impact we may have on birds by creating a bird-friendly backyard habitat.

What is habitat? Simply put, habitat is cover, food, and water within a reasonable distance from one another. As birds go about their daily activities, the presence of these three elements is essential. Cover refers to the vegetation that exists in a given area. It provides nesting, roosting, loafing, perching, and shelter areas as well as natural foods. Birds will eat nectar, seed, nuts, acorns, berries, and fruits produced by native and cultivated plantings.

Bird Identification

One of the first things you want to do when determining the identity of a bird is to remember the key physical features of the bird that you observed. You can then consult your backyard bird guide to identify the specific bird you have seen, using those physical features noted as clues. Writing down key physical features always helps me remember them more accurately when later reviewing my guide. The advent of digital cameras makes it easier to take a photograph for later study. Making a simple sketch is also helpful. You can make marks and notes on your sketch that will later help you whittle down the possible suspect list.

Think of yourself as a detective solving a crime. The witness is being asked key questions to help identify the prime suspect. "Was the suspect tall?" you, the detective, ask. "No," the witness answers, "he was short, about five feet." "What was he wearing?" The witness describes his straw hat, red shirt, and brown slacks. "Did he have any scars or tattoos?" And so it goes, until there are sufficient key clues for you, the detective, to positively identify the suspect that you observed.

These questioning techniques will be helpful as you use your backyard bird guide. A helpful first step in bird identification is to note the relative size of the bird you observe. Compare it to the profiled bird scale on the bottom of the page. Move forward or backward in the guide until you are in the correct size range of the bird that you have observed. Profiled birds are the hummingbird (3 3/4 inches), wren (4 3/4 inches), sparrow (6 inches), starling (8 1/2 inches), robin (10 inches), dove (12 inches),

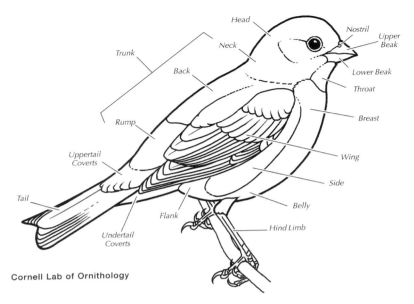

Head

Nostril

Upper Beak

Neck

Trunk

Back

Lower Beak

Throat

Rump

Breast

Uppertail Coverts

Wing

Tail

Side

Flank

Belly

Undertail Coverts

Hind Limb

Cornell Lab of Ornithology

and crow (18 inches). Become familiar with these relative sizes so that you know whether to move forward or backward in the guide.

After noting the relative size of your suspect bird, ask yourself other helpful identification questions. What is the hue of the bird's feathers? Are there any significant identification marks, like the black-and-white-striped crown of a white-crowned sparrow? What is the shape of the bird's mandible (bill or beak)? Is it conical shaped, like that of a house finch? A conical-shaped bill is used for crushing seed and denotes a seed-eating bird. These subtle hints displayed by the bird's physical features will help you narrow the list of suspect birds.

What was the bird doing? Behaviors such as fly catching, drilling into a tree, or eating fruit or nectar are all helpful clues that can separate one bird from another. For example, a robin-size bird eating fruit could be one of the jays, a bluebird, a mockingbird, a waxwing, or a robin. Taking note that this particular bird's feathers were mostly blue eliminates the mockingbird, waxwing, and robin but leaves the jays and bluebirds. The suspect list is getting smaller.

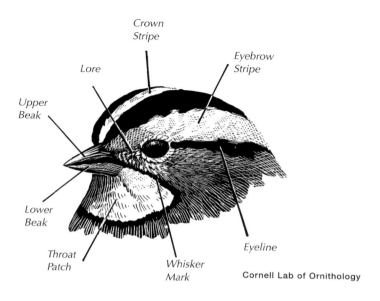

Crown
Stripe

Lore

Eyebrow
Stripe

Upper
Beak

Lower
Beak

Throat
Patch

Whisker
Mark

Eyeline

Cornell Lab of Ornithology

Now check the range distribution map in your bird guide for those remaining suspect birds. The area of the range distribution map where the depicted bird occurs in the nonbreeding season (fall/winter) is colored orange. Summer resident map range distribution areas are colored blue. Green-colored map areas denote permanent year-round residents. This range distribution map will help confirm the presence or absence of the remaining suspect birds: jays and bluebirds. We will use a cold day in February in my native Pennsylvania for our example. The range distribution map for blue jays shows the entire Pennsylvania map colored in green. Aha! Blue jays are permanent residents. The eastern bluebird range distribution range map shows a blue-colored area for the summer. My suspect bird is not likely an eastern bluebird, I begin to think.

Continuing the investigation in our example, I see that the bird at my feeder is eating black oil sunflower seed and it has a crest of feathers raised on its head. Reading the behavior description for the eastern bluebird, I note that it is an insectivore, not a seed eater.

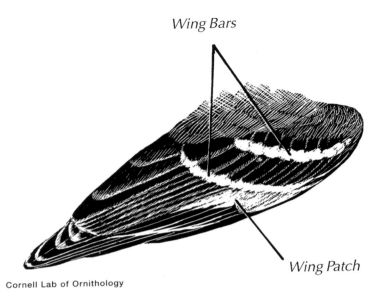

Wing Bars

Wing Patch

Cornell Lab of Ornithology

Last but not least, I look at the photographs of both remaining suspect birds, eastern bluebird and blue jay. I can see that the blue jay has a crest of feathers on its head. The eastern bluebird does not show a crest. Now I can confidently see that the bird eating black oil sunflower at my feeder is a blue jay. Its plumage matches the photograph. The crest on my bird is there too. His size is larger than the 7-inch eastern bluebird and the time-of-year range distribution map confirms the blue jay's presence, with the absence of the eastern bluebird in winter.

You will be very pleased to note your progress in being able to sort through the possible suspects until you have determined which visiting bird you are enjoying in your backyard bird sanctuary.

Ruby-throated Hummingbird

Archilochus colubris

DESCRIPTION: The ruby-throated hummingbird is a flying jewel. The male has an iridescent ruby throat called a gorget when it is flashed. The throat looks black when not lit up, contrasting with a white chest and green sides. The tail is black. The bill is long, straight, and black. It has a green crown with green upperparts. The female has green upperparts and white underparts. She has white outer tips on her tail feathers.

BEHAVIOR: The ruby-throated hummingbird feeds on the nectar from wildflowers, which it helps pollinate. It will also take insects and spiders, particularly when feeding young, as a source of protein. It will rob insects from spiderwebs and hawk insects in flight. It will also take sap from sapsucker wells and insects trapped in the sap. Males fly a pendulum display flight that forms a 180-degree arc.

SONG: Rapid chatter; twitter notes.

HABITAT: Suburban landscapes, parks, and gardens; fields with wildflowers.

NESTING: The female builds a small cup nest from soft plant material, thistle down, and lichen, bound together with spider webbing. The nest is just large enough to contain the jellybean-size eggs. Two white eggs are incubated for 11 to 16 days by the female. Altricial young (born naked, eyes closed, and helpless) fledge within 22 days.

RANGE: Throughout the eastern United States and west to the Mississippi River.

SIZE: $3^{3}/_{4}$ inches with a wingspan of $4^{1}/_{4}$ to $4^{1}/_{2}$ inches.

 To Attract: Offer nectar made from water and sugar (4:1 ratio of water to sugar). Do not use red food dye. Boil water 2 minutes at a rolling boil. Turn off heat. Slowly pour sugar into the hot water while stirring until sugar dissolves and goes into solution. Cool. Make more than you need and store extra in refrigerator. Change nectar every 3 to 4 days so that it remains fresh. Specialty nature stores offer a convenient liquid nectar or quick-dissolving powder. Plant flowers and vines with tube- or bell-shaped blossoms.

Hummingbird	Wren	Sparrow	Starling	Robin	Dove	Crow
$3^{3}/_{4}$''	$4^{3}/_{4}$''	6''	$8^{1}/_{2}$''	10''	12''	18''

Carolina Chickadee

Poecile carolinensis

■ **Year-round**

DESCRIPTION: The Carolina chickadee has a black cap and bib with white cheeks. The upperparts are gray with gray edging on the forward part of the wing. Underparts are white with buffy gray on flanks. It has a short, dartlike, pointed black bill. The tail is short and shows a slight notch in it. Both sexes are similarly plumaged.

BEHAVIOR: The Carolina chickadee is a regular visitor to backyard habitats with trees and woody shrubs. It is found in pairs during the breeding season. It will form mixed flocks with downy woodpeckers, juncos, kinglets, nuthatches, titmice, and other small songbirds in winter.

Suet and sunflower seed feeders are good attractors. Chickadees will also glean insects, spiders, moths, and caterpillars from foliage. They will eat small berries when available.

SONG: Four-note *see-bee-see-bay* whistled quickly with the first and third notes high pitched. The *chick-a-dee-dee-dee* call is used as a warning signal, with the increased number of *dees* at the end indicating the presence and type of danger.

HABITAT: Deciduous forests with clearings; edges and backyard suburban areas.

NESTING: The chickadee is a cavity nester that will readily use a nest box. Make the entrance hole opening $1^1/_8$ to $1^1/_2$ inches in size. Place 1 to 2 inches of wood chips on the bottom of the nest box.

RANGE: South of an irregular boundary that slices through southern New Jersey and Pennsylvania, and bisects Ohio, Indiana, Illinois, Missouri, and southern Kansas.

SIZE: $4^3/_4$ inches with a wingspan of $7^1/_2$ inches.

To Attract: Erect a convertible nest box that chickadees can use for nesting. The nest box, which can be found in specialty nature stores, includes a viewing panel and, later, a winter roost. Mount it on a tree trunk at Grandpa's hoisting height (the height that you can hold up a grandchild to look into it).

Hummingbird	Wren	Sparrow	Starling	Robin	Dove	Crow
$3^3/_4$''	$4^3/_4$''	6''	$8^1/_2$''	10''	12''	18''

American Goldfinch

Carduelis tristis

DESCRIPTION: The American goldfinch is the beautiful yellow "canary" of backyard habitats. Adult male breeding plumage is a bright yellow, set off by black wings with white wing bars and a black cap. The female is grayish brown with an all-yellow head.

Many backyard observers do not recognize the winter goldfinch when it loses its bright yellow breeding plumage. It molts into a rather drab grayish or brownish plumage so that its energy can go into maintaining its body rather than its bright feathers during winter.

BEHAVIOR: The goldfinch is a flocking bird in winter that gathers around backyard feeders and habitats. It feeds on seed-producing flowers, like dandelion and weed seeds. A shallow water feature where it can bathe and drink is a welcome mat for the goldfinch.

SONG: The goldfinch is very vocal, especially in flight where its call note is likened to the mnemonic "po-tato-chip" or "per-chick-oree, perchickoree."

HABITAT: Open areas with trees and shrubs. Backyards provide ideal habitats. Easily attracted to feeders and water features.

NESTING: The nest is woven plant material with plant down, especially from the thistle. The goldfinch incorporates spider silk and caterpillar webbing in its nest construction. Four to six bluish-white eggs are incubated by the female for 10 to 12 days. Fledging takes place within 11 to 17 days. It has one or two broods per year. Both parents feed the young.

RANGE: Throughout the continental United States.

SIZE: 5 inches with a wingspan of 8 to 9 inches.

 **To Attract:** Use Nyjer and black oil sunflower seed. Nyjer seed in a sock or tube feeder is an ideal way to attract these colorful songbirds.

Hummingbird	Wren	Sparrow	Starling	Robin	Dove	Crow
3¾"	4¾"	6"	8½"	10"	12"	18"

Carolina Wren

Thryothorus ludovicianus

■ **Year-round**

DESCRIPTION: The Carolina wren features a bold white stripe above its eye, set off by the reddish brown of its head feathers. The back and upperparts are a rich rusty brown. The wings and tail show bars of darker brown. The mandible is long and has a slight downward curve. The chin, throat, and breast are white. The lower underparts are tawny brown.

BEHAVIOR: Carolina wrens remain in pair groups throughout the year and mate for life. They frequent thickets and are more often heard than seen. However, making squeaky "pishing" sounds will often bring out these curious birds. The tail is held up over the back as the bird probes and digs for insects, caterpillars, larvae, vertebrates, and berries.

SONG: The mnemonic for the song of the Carolina wren is "tea kettle, tea kettle, tea kettle." Only the male sings, and he is very vocal, singing from an exposed perch. Neighboring males may often have singing duels from the large repertoire of more than thirty songs.

HABITAT: Woodlots, farms, and suburban yards in and around deciduous trees and woody shrubs.

NESTING: The wren is a cavity nester that will use a nest box. The female incubates four to eight white to light pink eggs. Altricial young (born naked, eyes closed, and helpless) fledge within 14 days. Both parents will feed the young.

RANGE: Eastern Kansas north into southern Ontario, across to Massachusetts, southward to the Gulf Coast, and into northeastern Mexico.

SIZE: 5 to 6 inches with a wingspan of 11 inches.

To Attract: Erect a nest box. Offer mealworms and suet.

Hummingbird	Wren	Sparrow	Starling	Robin	Dove	Crow
3¾"	4¾"	6"	8½"	10"	12"	18"

House Finch

Carpodacus mexicanus

■ **Year-round**

DESCRIPTION: The male house finch has a red forehead. The red wraps around the side of its head over the eyes. The throat and chest are red. The top of the head is brown. The upper-parts have brown streaks, and the wings display two narrow white wing bars. The chest and underparts have brown streaks. Occasionally the red on males is tinged with orange or yellow. Females and juveniles are dull brown overall with streaking on the breast and sides.

BEHAVIOR: A gregarious flocking bird in winter, the house finch is one of the more widely distributed backyard birds. It was originally from the West and was accidentally introduced to the East in New York in the early 1940s. During winter it will form mixed flocks, particularly with the American goldfinch and pine siskin.

SONG: A three-note rising warble ending with a very high, sharp note. Call notes are *chirps*.

HABITAT: Urban and suburban back-yards; parks, gardens, and open wood-lands; desert and wooded canyons.

NESTING: The female builds a nest in trees, shrubs, dense bushes, nest boxes, vines, and under building eaves, using grass, twigs, feathers, and other material. Two to six light blue eggs with black and purplish spots are incubated by the female for 12 to 14 days. Altricial young (born naked, eyes closed, and helpless) fledge within 19 days.

RANGE: Throughout the continental United States.

SIZE: 6 inches with a wingspan of 9 3/4 inches.

 **To Attract:** Offer black oil sunflower in tube or hopper feeders available at specialty nature stores.

Hummingbird	Wren	Sparrow	Starling	Robin	Dove	Crow
3 3/4''	4 3/4''	6''	8 1/2''	10''	12''	18''

House Sparrow

Passer domesticus

DESCRIPTION: The male house sparrow displays a black bib with a gray crown and cheeks. The upperparts include a chestnut nape bordered with a white stripe and a white wing bar. The back is buffy brown with black streaks. The underparts are gray. The female has a pale buffy eyebrow line and a plain gray chest with a striped black and brown back.

BEHAVIOR: The house sparrow hops along the ground as it forages. It gathers in flocks in winter. The sparrow is a loud, gregarious bird. It eats insects, seeds, grain, and spiders. It will glean insects from tires and grilles of automobiles in parking lots.

SONG: *Chirps* and repeated *cheeps*.

HABITAT: The house sparrow is the bird of the city. It has adapted well to urban landscapes after being introduced in New York City in the 1850s.

NESTING: Both parents build the nest, which is a rough hodgepodge of grasses, weeds, debris, twigs, and feathers. The nest is located in building crevices, nest boxes, vine tangles, and other sheltered areas. Three to seven green or blue eggs with gray and brown spots are incubated by both parents for 10 to 14 days. Altricial young (born naked, eyes closed, and helpless) fledge within 17 days.

RANGE: Across the continental United States and into Canada and Mexico.

SIZE: 6 inches with a wingspan of $9^{1}/_{2}$ to 10 inches.

 **To Attract:** Offer proso millet on platform or hopper feeders.

Hummingbird	Wren	Sparrow	Starling	Robin	Dove	Crow
$3^{3}/_{4}''$	$4^{3}/_{4}''$	6''	$8^{1}/_{2}''$	10''	12''	18''

Downy Woodpecker

Picoides pubescens

■ **Year-round**

DESCRIPTION: The downy woodpecker is the smallest woodpecker. Black and white overall, the male has a red nape. The back is white, bordered by black wings, with white spotting on the wings. The face has a black stripe through the eye and a black malar mark. The bill is short, stubby, and half the length of the head (back to front). There are black crosshatch markings on the outer tail feathers (not easily seen). The underparts are white.

BEHAVIOR: Downy woodpeckers forage in trees for insects and insect egg larvae. They will readily come to suet feeders. When establishing breeding territories, they drum on dead branches and other resonating objects to attract a mate and designate territory boundaries.

SONG: A short *pik* or *chik* call and a soft, high-pitched whinny.

HABITAT: All tree areas, especially suburban backyards.

NESTING: A cavity nester, it will excavate its own cavity and will use a nest box.

RANGE: Found throughout all but the southwestern United States.

SIZE: 6 1/2 inches with a wingspan of 11 to 12 inches.

 **To Attract:** Hang suet feeders and a good, formulated, nonmelting suet available at specialty nature stores. Erect a nest box sized for the downy woodpecker with an entrance hole of 1 1/4 to 1 1/2 inches.

Hummingbird	Wren	Sparrow	Starling	Robin	Dove	Crow
3³/₄''	4³/₄''	6''	8¹/₂''	10''	12''	18''

Tufted Titmouse

Baeolophus bicolor

■ **Year-round**

DESCRIPTION: The upperparts of the tufted titmouse are gray with a tuft that can be raised and flattened on the head. The bill is straight, short, and black. The underparts are white with rusty flanks. Feet and legs are gray-black.

BEHAVIOR: The titmouse is an active bird that forages in the trees for insects, insect larvae, spiders, seeds, berries, tree nuts, and acorns. It will cache seeds and nuts in the crevices of bark. It forms mixed foraging flocks with downy woodpeckers, juncos, kinglets, nuthatches, and other small songbirds in winter. The titmouse will take a nut or seed to a favorite branch, place it between its feet, and pound it open with its bill like a jackhammer.

SONG: *Peeto-peeto-peeto* whistled in a series. Call note is *see-nyahh* in a scolding tone.

HABITAT: Woodlands, parks, and suburban landscapes.

NESTING: The titmouse is a cavity nester. The female builds the nest with leaves, grass, moss, snakeskin, mammal fur, and hair. Four to eight white eggs with brown freckles are incubated by the female for 13 to 14 days. Altricial young (born naked, eyes closed, and helpless) fledge within 18 days.

RANGE: From the Gulf Coast states up to New England.

SIZE: $6\frac{1}{2}$ inches with a wingspan of $10\frac{3}{4}$ inches.

 **To Attract:** Erect a nest box with the entrance hole facing an easterly direction for morning sun.

Hummingbird	Wren	Sparrow	Starling	Robin	Dove	Crow
3¾"	4¾"	6"	8½"	10"	12"	18"

White-throated Sparrow

Zonotrichia albicollis

■ **Breeding**
■ **Year-round**
■ **Wintering**

DESCRIPTION: The white-throated sparrow has a distinctive white bib. It has crown stripes that are black or brown, with a similar eye line. The mandible is dark, and there are yellow lore spots in front of the eye. The back is a rusty brown with two white wing bars. The underparts are gray with light streaking on the flanks.

BEHAVIOR: The white-throated sparrow is primarily a ground feeder that gathers in mixed-species flocks in winter and individually or in pairs during the breeding season. It hops along, occasionally scratching among the leaf litter for seed and insects. If it is hidden in the underbrush or thicket, a visual response can usually be elicited with squeaky "pishing" sounds.

SONG: The mnemonics are "oh sweet Kimberly, Kimberly, Kimberly" or "poor Sam Peabody, Peabody, Peabody." Call note is a sharp *tseep*.

HABITAT: Thickets; weedy fields; shrubs, ground cover, and hedgerows; urban and suburban yards and gardens.

NESTING: The female builds a nest using grass, twigs, pine needles, moss, and softer plant materials for a liner. The female incubates three to six white and blue-green eggs. Altricial young (born naked, eyes closed, and helpless) fledge within 12 days and are fed by both parents.

RANGE: Northern states into Canada; during winter, from the Mid-Atlantic states to the Gulf Coast states.

SIZE: $6\,3/4$ inches with a wingspan of 10 inches.

To Attract: Scatter white proso millet, black oil sunflower, or cracked corn on a platform feeder near ground cover.

Hummingbird	Wren	Sparrow	Starling	Robin	Dove	Crow
3¾''	4¾''	6''	8½''	10''	12''	18''

Orchard Oriole

Icterus spurius

DESCRIPTION: A small oriole, the male features a black hood, back, and wings with a prominent orange shoulder and white wing bar. The bill is short and slightly curved. The mandible is two-toned: the upper mandible is black and the lower is blue-gray. The underparts and rump are dark orange. Females are olive-yellow with two white wing bars. Juvenile males look like females with a black throat.

BEHAVIOR: The orchard oriole is found individually or in pairs in the spring and in small family groups after the nesting season. It forages in trees and shrubs, feeding on insects, nectar, berries, and fruit.

SONG: A very vocal bird, with a rambling series of calls, chatters, and whistles. *Chuh-huh-huh-huh* chatter with loud whistles cascading into a slurred *wheer* ending.

HABITAT: Orchards; small woodland edges; suburban yards with trees and shrubs.

NESTING: The orchard oriole weaves a basket nest pouch hidden in leaves at the fork of a branch. The female incubates three to seven blue eggs with brown, purple, or gray splotches. Altricial young (born naked, eyes closed, and helpless) are fed by both parents and fledge within 14 days.

RANGE: Southeast and Midwest states, with lower densities occurring through the Mid-Atlantic states northward.

SIZE: 7 inches with a wingspan of 9 to 10 inches.

 **To Attract:** Put out oranges halves, grape jelly, and nectar in a feeder built for orioles. They will also take mealworms.

| Hummingbird | Wren | Sparrow | Starling | Robin | Dove | Crow |
| 3¾" | 4¾" | 6" | 8½" | 10" | 12" | 18" |

Baltimore Oriole

Icterus galbula

DESCRIPTION: There is no mistaking the male Baltimore oriole. It is the only bright orange-black oriole north of Florida. Its wing is black with a white wing bar. Females and young have random black markings on the head and throat. The upperparts are olive and the underparts are orange.

Orioles are Neotropical birds. They migrate to North America in the spring to breed and raise their young. They migrate south to the tropics in the fall.

BEHAVIOR: Orioles like to forage in the canopy of trees for a variety of insects and caterpillars. They will also eat berries and fruit. You can attract them with nectar feeders built for orioles.

SONG: A two-note whistle, *hue-lee,* with added chatter and occasional rattles.

HABITAT: Suburban yards with interspersed deciduous woodlots, and clearings and edges of these habitats.

NESTING: Female orioles weave an intricate nest of natural fibers, hair, yarn, string, wool, and grass into a basket shape. They hang the nest from a drooping deciduous branch, such as a willow. Four gray-white or light blue oval eggs with black and brown splotched scrawled marks on the large end will be brooded by the female. Altricial young (born naked, eyes closed, and helpless) are born after an incubation of 12 to 14 days and fledge from the nest within two weeks.

RANGE: Spring and summer throughout the Northeast, Midwest, and into the Southeast.

SIZE: 7 to $8\,^1/_4$ inches with a wingspan of $11\,^1/_4$ to $12\,^1/_4$ inches.

 **To Attract:** Plant red hot poker flowers, which orioles love. Hang oriole nectar feeders (4:1 ratio of water to sugar) and provide orange halves and grape jelly. Specialty nature stores are good sources of oriole nectar and fruit feeders. Place yarn, wool, string, and other natural fiber materials in a suet cage (cut into lengths of 5 to 7 inches). The orioles will pick from it for nesting material.

Hummingbird	Wren	Sparrow	Starling	Robin	Dove	Crow
$3^3/_4$"	$4^3/_4$"	6"	$8^1/_2$"	10"	12"	18"

Great Crested Flycatcher

Myiarchus crinitus

■ **Breeding**
■ **Year-round**
■ **Wintering**

DESCRIPTION: This bird has a crest that when raised gives the head a bushy appearance. The head and back are olive brown. The throat and chest are gray, which sets off the contrasting yellow belly. The tail and wings are rusty brown, most evident in flight.

BEHAVIOR: The great crested flycatcher likes to sit high in the canopy of a tree, usually on a dead branch that gives it good visibility for nearby flying insects. It will sally forth hawking an insect, often returning to the same perch. During the spring breeding season, males can be seen chasing females in courtship flights.

SONG: A sharp, whistled *wheep* followed by a long *berg* or *prrrrreeet.*

HABITAT: Large tracts of parks and suburban yards with tall trees.

NESTING: The great crested flycatcher is a cavity nester that can be attracted to a nest box placed high on a tree trunk or under a building eave. The female incubates four to eight creamy white eggs. Altricial young (born naked, eyes closed, and helpless) fledge within 21 days and are fed by both parents.

RANGE: Gulf Coast states north to Canada, and from the East Coast to the Midwest.

SIZE: $7\frac{1}{2}$ inches with a wingspan of 12 to 14 inches.

 **To Attract:** Erect a nest box 6 to 15 feet high on a tree trunk in a quiet part of the yard. Orient the hole facing east so that it gets sun in the morning but not all day long.

Hummingbird $3\frac{3}{4}''$ Wren $4\frac{3}{4}''$ Sparrow $6''$ Starling $8\frac{1}{2}''$ Robin $10''$ Dove $12''$ Crow $18''$

Summer Tanager

Piranga rubra

■ Breeding
■ Wintering

DESCRIPTION: The adult male summer tanager is the only all-red bird in North America. It has a yellow mandible. The female has a plain mandible, olive green upperparts, and orange-yellow underparts. Her overall appearance with the olive and orange overtones is a rich yellow. Juvenile males show patches of red and yellow.

BEHAVIOR: This is the most widespread and common of the tanagers. It frequents the upper canopies of trees as it forages for insects, bees, and wasps. The diet also includes fruit and berries. The summer tanager will catch a bee or wasp and whack it on a branch, removing the stinger before eating it.

SONG: A robinlike warble and whistled notes. Call note is *pikituck, pick-a-tuck.*

HABITAT: Riparian zones, particularly cottonwood in the West and Southwest. Pine and mixed coniferous and deciduous trees, primarily oak forests. Treed parks and suburban areas, especially near water.

NESTING: The female builds a nest using grasses, leaves, bark, and other soft plant material as a liner. The female incubates three to five blue eggs. Altricial young (born naked, eyes closed, and helpless) are fed by both parents and fledge within 14 days.

RANGE: Mid-Atlantic states, south to Florida, and west to Southern California.

SIZE: 7 3/4 inches with a wingspan of 12 inches.

 **To Attract:** Provide suet and peanut butter.

Hummingbird	Wren	Sparrow	Starling	Robin	Dove	Crow
3¾''	4¾''	6''	8½''	10''	12''	18''

Eastern Towhee

Pipilo erythrophthalmus

■ **Breeding**
■ **Year-round**
■ **Wintering**

DESCRIPTION: The male eastern towhee has a black-hooded head and black upperparts with rusty sides and white underparts. The female has a brown hood and upperparts with rufous sides and white underparts. The eye is red.

BEHAVIOR: The eastern towhee is a ground feeder. It takes a "one step forward, two steps back" approach. It flips up litter and uncovers insects and seeds. Towhees are skulkers, preferring to stay under cover among the thicket and undergrowth.

SONG: Sings a song that sounds like "drink-your-teeeeeeee." It is sung with two short notes and the *teeeeeeee* trilled.

HABITAT: Undergrowth, thickets, and tangles of cover; shrub edges in backyards; woodland streams.

NESTING: The nest is usually located on the ground and is made of twigs, grass, leaves, and other plant material. Two to six whitish eggs are incubated by the female for 13 days and the altricial young (born naked, eyes closed, and helpless) fledge within 12 days.

RANGE: Southern Canada down into the Midwest; eastern and southeastern states to the Gulf Coast states.

SIZE: 8 inches with a wingspan of 11 inches.

✓ **To Attract:** Leave undercover brush piles and low-growing shrubbery for foraging areas. Place proso millet on a platform feeder.

Hummingbird	Wren	Sparrow	Starling	Robin	Dove	Crow
3³/₄''	4³/₄''	6''	8¹/₂''	10''	12''	18''

European Starling

Sturnus vulgaris

■ Year-round
■ Nonbreeding

DESCRIPTION: The European starling is black overall. The feathers in breeding plumage have a green-purple sheen. The body shape is chunky with a very short tail. The European starling walks rather than hops. Its long, thin, pointed bill is yellow in spring and off-white to gray in winter. White spots cover its body in winter plumage. Juveniles are dull gray.

BEHAVIOR: This is a flocking bird in winter that can gather in the tens of thousands. The starling is a very gregarious, urbanized bird that has adapted well to the city, town, and countryside. It is non-native to the United States, introduced in New York in 1890. Its diet is extremely varied, including insects, mixed grains, and fruit.

SONG: A variety of whistles, gurgles, clatters, and twitters.

HABITAT: Urban and suburban landscapes.

NESTING: Starlings will nest in natural cavities, nest boxes, buildings, and other structural crevices, such as backyard grills, competing with native species. They will evict woodpeckers from cavities that they have constructed. Nest material is a wide variety of plant material, assembled in a random and shabby fashion. Four to eight blue-green eggs are incubated for 12 to 14 days by both parents. Altricial young (born naked, eyes closed, and helpless) fledge within 18 days. It has two to three broods per year.

RANGE: Throughout the continental United States and Canada. The starling is likely the most prolific and abundant bird on the continent.

SIZE: $8 \frac{1}{2}$ inches with a wingspan of $15 \frac{1}{2}$ inches.

 **To Attract:** Set out suet and seed feeders and erect nest boxes.

Hummingbird	Wren	Sparrow	Starling	Robin	Dove	Crow
$3\frac{3}{4}$''	$4\frac{3}{4}$''	6''	$8\frac{1}{2}$''	10''	12''	18''

Northern Cardinal

Cardinalis cardinalis

DESCRIPTION: The male northern cardinal is striking bright red with a red crest and a black mask around the eyes and on the throat under the bill. The bill is conical shaped and red. The female is duller olive brown on the upperparts with a buffy golden head with a crest and a large conical-shaped pink bill. The underparts are buffy brown and the wings show a red wash. Juveniles resemble females but with a black bill.

BEHAVIOR: Northern cardinals are found in pairs during breeding season. They form mixed foraging flocks in winter. They prefer trees and shrub edges with dense, low cover. Cardinals frequent parks, suburban backyards, and marshes and forests. They will eat insects, seed, fruit, and grain.

SONG: A loud song that includes whistles and gurgles, including the mnemonic "what-cheer, what-cheer." Call note is a *tchip*.

HABITAT: Woodlands and forest edges; farmland; parks and suburban backyards with shrubs, trees, and thickets of low cover; marshes.

NESTING: The female builds a nest of grass, bark, twigs, and other plant material, lined with hair and grass in a shrub or tree. Three to four pale greenish or bluish eggs with gray, brown, or purple spots are incubated 12 to 13 days by both parents, primarily the female. Altricial young (born naked, eyes closed, and helpless) fledge within 11 days.

RANGE: East Coast to the Midwest and down into the Gulf Coast states and Mexico.

SIZE: 7 1/2 to 9 inches with a wingspan of 12 inches.

 **To Attract:** Offer black oil sunflower seed in a hopper feeder.

Hummingbird	Wren	Sparrow	Starling	Robin	Dove	Crow
3 3/4"	4 3/4"	6"	8 1/2"	10"	12"	18"

Red-bellied Woodpecker

Melanerpes carolinus

■ **Year-round**

DESCRIPTION: The red-bellied woodpecker has black and white barring down the back. It has a red crown and nape with a pale buffy chest and face. The red belly for which it is named is not always seen but is low on its belly and between the legs when visible.

BEHAVIOR: This is a very vocal woodpecker that drums in the spring to establish a breeding territory. Red-bellied woodpeckers eat insects, seeds, suet, berries and fruits, and sap taken from sapsucker wells.

SONG: Loud repeated *churr,* and *chuck, chuck.*

HABITAT: Forests and forest edges; swamps; parks and suburban landscapes with trees.

NESTING: Both sexes excavate a cavity-nesting chamber. Three to eight white eggs are incubated by both parents for 11 to 14 days. Young fledge within 27 days.

RANGE: Northern and southeastern United States into the Midwest.

SIZE: 9 1/2 inches with a wingspan of 15 to 18 inches.

✓ **To Attract:** Offer suet, shelled tree nuts and peanuts, and hulled sunflower seeds.

Hummingbird
3 3/4''

Wren
4 3/4''

Sparrow
6''

Starling
8 1/2''

Robin
10''

Dove
12''

Crow
18''

American Robin

Turdus migratorius

- ■ Breeding
- ■ Year-round
- ■ Nonbreeding

DESCRIPTION: Perhaps the most recognized backyard bird in North America, the American robin is widely distributed throughout the continental United States. Although thought of as a harbinger of spring, the robin is found throughout the year in most of its range. It will migrate south of the snow line in winter when snow exceeds four inches in depth.

The robin features a brick-red breast. It has a yellow bill with a broken white eye ring. The throat is white with black striping. The back is gray. Juveniles when first fledging from the nest have a spotted chest and underparts; otherwise they resemble adults.

BEHAVIOR: Spring finds males fighting and defending territories that are made up of various neighborhood yards. Males will often fight their shadows in low windows in spring. They are often seen probing the yard for earthworms and other invertebrates. Robins switch to a fruit and berry diet in winter when worms are not available. Solitary or in pairs in spring, robins gather in large winter communal flocks.

SONG: A very vocal singer, often into the night with its repeated "cheerily cheer-up cheerio" phrase. Vocalizations vary with a whinny and sharp warning *tut-tut-tut*.

HABITAT: Urban/suburban lawns and yards with trees and shrubs.

NESTING: The robin builds a classic round grass nest with a mud bottom located in the fork of a tree. It will also use a nesting shelf. Robins usually locate their first nest in a conifer (it already has its leaves in early spring). A second nest and brood is raised in a deciduous tree that has leafed out by early summer. Occasionally, a third brood is raised. Three to seven sky-blue eggs are incubated by the female for 12 to 14 days. The altricial young (born naked, eyes closed, and helpless) fledge within 14 to 16 days.

RANGE: Throughout the continental United States.

SIZE: 10 inches with a wingspan of 14 to 16 inches.

✔ **To Attract:** Plant fruit- and berry-producing shrubs and trees that robins can use in spring and winter, such as mulberry, crabapple, pyracantha, and mountain ash. Robins will use suet if it is presented so that they can perch to reach it.

Hummingbird	Wren	Sparrow	Starling	Robin	Dove	Crow
3¾''	4¾''	6''	8½''	10''	12''	18''

Northern Mockingbird

Mimus polyglottos

■ **Year-round**

DESCRIPTION: The northern mockingbird is an overall gray bird with two white wing bars that become large white wing patches when seen in flight. The tail is long and has white outer tail feathers.

BEHAVIOR: The northern mockingbird is a fairly common bird in its range that forages in and around shrubs, trees, and edges of gardens and backyards. It eats insects, fruit, and berries. It vigorously defends its nesting area, attacking any animal, bird, or person passing nearby. It is often seen running on the ground and flashing its wings to flush insects.

SONG: The mockingbird is a mimic that sings and imitates other sounds and birdsongs. It sings repetitive phrases with a loud *tchack* call.

Mockingbirds will often sing all night during breeding season.

HABITAT: Suburban landscapes; parks, gardens, and farms. Well adapted to living in backyard habitats.

NESTING: Both parents build a nest in a shrub or tree with a variety of sticks, twigs, leaves, and string, lined with softer plant materials. Two to six bluish-green eggs spotted with brown are incubated by the female for 12 to 13 days. Altricial young (born naked, eyes closed, and helpless) fledge within 13 days.

RANGE: Eastern and southwestern United States into California.

SIZE: 10 inches with a wingspan of 13 to 15 inches.

 **To Attract:** Offer suet and dried fruits. Plant trees, shrubs, and vines that will produce persistent crops of berries and fruit.

Hummingbird	Wren	Sparrow	Starling	Robin	Dove	Crow
3¾"	4¾"	6"	8½"	10"	12"	18"

Blue Jay

Cyanocitta cristata

DESCRIPTION: Blue jays are very bright, flashy, and vocal birds. They have a crest that can be raised or lowered. The face and throat bib are grayish white with the neck adorned by a black necklace. The blue wings show a white wing bar. The blue jay has gray-white underparts and a blue back. Both sexes are similar in plumage characteristics.

BEHAVIOR: Blue jays have adapted to urban/suburban backyards and parks. They are very intelligent birds and are extending their range. They are most often found in pairs during nesting season and can be found in gregarious flocks in late summer. Blue jays are vocal birds who warn other birds when a predator, such as a cat, hawk, or owl, is present.

They are omnivorous but a large portion of their daily intake is acorns, seeds from pinecones, corn, fruit, and berries. They are opportunistic and will take eggs or nestlings. Carrion, insects, mice, meadow voles, other small mammals, small snakes, frogs, and small amphibians are included in a varied diet.

SONG: A loud *jayyy* and a *wheedle, wheedle.* It can mimic other birds, especially hawks.

HABITAT: Parks, backyards, and suburban landscapes with oak and beech hardwood trees.

NESTING: Both parents build a nest of twigs, grass, lichen, and other soft plant matter in the crotch of a tree. Three to seven pale greenish-blue eggs with dark brown marks are incubated by both parents for 16 to 18 days. Altricial young (born naked, eyes closed, and helpless) fledge within 17 to 21 days.

RANGE: Throughout the Northeast and Midwest where large canopy oak and beech hardwoods exist. Range is extending into the Northwest.

SIZE: 11 inches with a 16-inch wingspan.

✓ **To Attract:** Offer black oil sunflower seed in a hopper-style feeder. Blue jays will use suet and take peanuts in or out of the shell. A water feature with a heating element will provide a bathing area that they will use regularly.

Hummingbird	Wren	Sparrow	Starling	Robin	Dove	Crow
3¾''	4¾''	6''	8½''	10''	12''	18''

Mourning Dove

Zenaida macroura

DESCRIPTION: The mourning dove is a brownish-gray bird with black spots on the upper wing. Male doves show a pinkish tinge on the breast and a black spot on the cheek with a blue-gray crown. The tail is long and all of the tail feathers are tipped in white on the ends. The female is a faded brown. Juveniles have a scaled appearance.

BEHAVIOR: Males will aggressively defend breeding territories. Doves will form flocks after the breeding season. They feed on a variety of seeds and grains. Their wings make a whistling sound during takeoff.

SONG: A mournful coo repeated *cooo, cooo, cooo, cooo* by the male in breeding season.

HABITAT: Fields and agricultural areas; parks, gardens, and suburban backyards.

NESTING: The female pulls together a loose assortment of twigs that makes a flimsy platform in a tree or shrub. Two white eggs are incubated by both parents for 14 days. Altricial young (born naked, eyes closed, and helpless) fledge within 14 days. The young squab is fed crop milk, which is produced in the crop and regurgitated with seeds. Several broods are raised during the breeding season.

RANGE: Throughout the continental United States and into Canada and Mexico.

SIZE: 12 inches with a wingspan of 17 to 19 inches.

To Attract: Offer black oil sunflower seed, cracked corn, or proso millet on a platform feeder.

Hummingbird	Wren	Sparrow	Starling	Robin	Dove	Crow
3¾''	4¾''	6''	8½''	10''	12''	18''

Eurasian Collared Dove

Streptopelia decaocto

■ **Year-round**

DESCRIPTION: Larger than our native doves, the Eurasian collared dove is pale brown with a black collar on the back of its neck that forms a horseshoe shape. This is the definitive field mark separating this dove from native doves. During flight it shows white patches on its outer tail feathers.

BEHAVIOR: Found in and around cities, parks, and suburban areas, they are readily attracted to platform ground feeders and will eat a variety of grains and seeds, especially black oil sunflower, millet, and cracked corn.

SONG: Long and constant cooing *hoo-hoooo-hoo, cuk-KOOOO-cooo.*

HABITAT: City parks, suburban neighborhoods, and agricultural areas.

NESTING: The male gathers nesting material consisting of twigs and dry plant material, and the female builds the nest. Two white elliptical eggs are incubated by both parents. The young are fed crop milk, which is a mixture of partially digested food and fluid. They fledge from the nest within 20 days.

RANGE: This bird was introduced into Florida in the 1980s. It is quickly spreading its range into other continental states. It has been found as far west as Utah and north to Pennsylvania.

SIZE: 12 1/2 inches with a wingspan of 18 to 19 inches.

To Attract: Offer black oil sunflower, cracked corn, and millet on a platform feeder.

Hummingbird	Wren	Sparrow	Starling	Robin	Dove	Crow
3 3/4''	4 3/4''	6''	8 1/2''	10''	12''	18''

Common Grackle

Quiscalus quiscula

DESCRIPTION: Note the overall glossy black body with a purple iridescent sheen on the back. There is also a bronze-colored type whose back has a bronze contrast with the blue-black head. The eyes are a pale white-yellow; the bill is long, strong, and sharply pointed. The tail is long and has a crease down the middle, giving it a wedged shape.

BEHAVIOR: The grackle is common east of the Rocky Mountains, particularly in cities, suburban communities, agricultural areas, woodlands, and marsh wetlands. Grackles walk on the ground. The common grackle is a gregarious bird that gathers in large flocks in winter. They will nest in groups and forage together. Their diet is diverse and varied, including insects, caterpillars, spiders, worms, seed, crop grains, fruit, small mammals, eggs and nestlings, grubs, invertebrates, and small fish.

SONG: A sound like a rusty hinge creaking open with a gurgling added to it. A hard *chuk* note is also used.

HABITAT: Suburban backyards and parks; open areas and forest edges; farms and pasture lands; marsh wetlands.

NESTING: The female builds a bulky nest that includes twigs, grass, mud, feathers, and other debris that is lined with softer plant material and fibers. Four to seven light brown or green eggs with brown and lilac markings are incubated by the female for 13 to 14 days. Altricial young (born naked, eyes closed, and helpless) are fed by both parents and fledge within 20 days.

RANGE: Throughout the continental United States; especially common east of the Rocky Mountains and north into Canada.

SIZE: 11 to $13^{1}/_{2}$ inches with a wingspan of 17 to $18^{1}/_{2}$ inches.

 **To Attract:** Use hopper or platform feeders with cracked corn, proso millet, and black oil sunflower seed.

| Hummingbird $3^{3}/_{4}$'' | Wren $4^{3}/_{4}$'' | Sparrow 6'' | Starling $8^{1}/_{2}$'' | Robin 10'' | Dove 12'' | Crow 18'' |

Boat-tailed Grackle

Quiscalus major

DESCRIPTION: The boat-tailed grackle is a large, long-tailed, black bird. The male has an iridescent purple-black sheen in its breeding plumage. Females are plain with a cinnamon brown back and head. The breast and belly are a light to buffy brown. The tail and wings are dark brown. A pale brown line above the eye borders a dark line through the eye. Females are half the size of the male. Note the eye color: boat-tailed grackles in northeastern Florida and further north along the Atlantic Coast will have yellow eyes, while along the Texas and Louisiana coastal range their eyes will be dark.

BEHAVIOR: Boat-tailed grackles are omnivorous foragers, eating anything they can swallow, including invertebrates, tadpoles, frogs, seed, grain, fruit, and refuse scraps. They roost in large colonial flocks throughout the year.

SONG: A series of high, piercing, sharp notes with a series of rough guttural trills. The call note is a sharp *chek* with whistles.

HABITAT: In and around fresh, brackish, and saltwater marshes; open upland habitats; urban and suburban areas and farms.

NESTING: Nesting occurs in a marsh habitat. Boat-tailed grackles have a unique mating and harem-defense system called polygyny, where males take more than one mate. The female group nests in colonies; males compete for mates and defend the nesting colony. The dominant male breeds with many of the females. Nonetheless, his offspring only represent 25 percent of the juvenile offspring. The remaining offspring arise from breeding that takes place away from the colony and satellite males.

RANGE: Gulf Coast and southeast coastal states.

SIZE: 10 to 15 inches with a wingspan of 15 to 20 inches.

 **To Attract:** Set out platform feeders. Boat-tailed grackles will not use feeders with safflower and have difficulty using smaller tube-style feeders.

Hummingbird	Wren	Sparrow	Starling	Robin	Dove	Crow
3¾''	4¾''	6''	8½''	10''	12''	18''

Cooper's Hawk

Accipiter cooperii

■ **Breeding**
■ **Year-round**
■ **Nonbreeding**

DESCRIPTION: The adult Cooper's hawk exhibits blue-gray upperparts and light reddish bars on the chest and underparts. The undertail covert feathers are white. The juvenile has streaked underparts and brown upperparts. The tail is banded with a white terminal band. In flight, the tail appears rounded at the end and the head projects in front of the leading edge of the wing. Adult birds have a red eye.

BEHAVIOR: These accipiters are the 100-yard dash, high-hurdle runners of the bird world. They are built for short bursts of speed, cutting, wheeling, and making sharp turns in and around shrubs, trees, and other cover. They hunt and catch other birds on the wing. Cooper's hawks will also catch small mammals. They often use an ambush strategy, hunting from a perch.

SONG: Alarm call is a *keh-keh-keh* or a *kac-kac-kac* given near the nest.

HABITAT: Woodlands, parks, and backyards with trees mixed with woody shrubs.

NESTING: Both parents are active in nest building, incubation, and feeding of the young. A large nest is located in the crotch of a tree near the trunk. The nest is made with twigs and larger sticks and lined with wood chips and bark. Four or five bluish or greenish eggs with brown spots are incubated for 32 to 36 days. The semialtricial young (born with eyes open or closed, down covered, and nest bound until fledging) leave the nest within 34 days.

RANGE: Throughout the continental United States and into southern Canada.

SIZE: 14 to 19 inches with a wingspan of 28 to 34 inches.

Hummingbird 3¾''   Wren 4¾''   Sparrow 6''   Starling 8½''   Robin 10''   Dove 12''   Crow 18''

FEEDING PREFERENCES

OF FAVORITE BACKYARD BIRDS

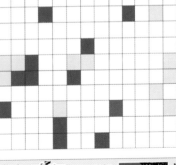

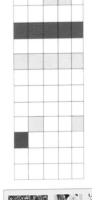

Birds

Perching Birds

1. Bluebirds
2. Cardinal, Northern
3. Chickadees
4. Finch, House
5. Finch, Purple
6. Goldfinches
7. Grosbeaks
8. Hummingbirds
9. Jays
10. Nuthatches
11. Orioles
12. Siskin, Pine
13. Titmouse, Tufted
14. Woodpeckers
15. Wren, Carolina

Ground Feeding Birds

16. Dove, Mourning
17. Juncos
18. Sparrow, House
19. Sparrows, Native
20. Towhees

Food Types

- Oil Sunflower
- Hulled Sunflower
- Striped Sunflower
- Millet
- Nyjer (Thistle)
- Cracked Corn
- In-shell Peanuts
- Shelled Peanuts
- Suet
- Safflower
- Mealworms
- Fruit
- Nectar

Legend:

- ■ = Most Preferred
- □ = Preferred

MEALWORMS

Millet

Reference Materials

Supplemental feeding

Some backyard birds are ground-feeding birds. Native sparrows, such as the dark-eyed junco, towhee, dove, quail, and pheasant, naturally feed on the ground (i.e., a flat surface). Others are considered perching birds, such as the colorful American goldfinch, house finch, and black-capped chickadee. These birds like to feed from a perching position.

Understanding a bird's preferred feeding style and behavior guides us toward the proper style of bird feeder selection. A platform feeder is an imitation of the ground that sparrows, doves, and quail will readily use. Scattering the right seeds on it, since these birds are seed eaters, will provide an attraction that they will soon come to enjoy—seed on a flat surface. A tube feeder with perches will attract perching birds: finches, chickadees, and goldfinches.

Positioning feeders at different height levels—hanging from tree limbs, on the ground, and in intermediate height areas—will provide birds with varying space dimensions that mimic natural feeding and foraging behavior. Place feeders where they can be easily watched and enjoyed as you observe the birds attracted to your backyard bird sanctuary. A nectar feeder placed in a flower bed around a patio area can provide delightful entertainment as you watch hummingbirds and orioles visiting the flowers for their nectar, as well as your sugar water.

Remember that there are more species of birds than just seed-eating birds. Provide sugar water in nectar feeders. There are a variety of feeder styles available that will enable you to present a wide assortment of food for the birds visiting your backyard bird sanctuary. There are feeders made to present mealworms, suet, fresh or dried fruit, jelly, tree nuts, and peanuts, in addition to a wide assortment of seeds. This variety of feeders and food assortment will help you attract a wide variety of birds.

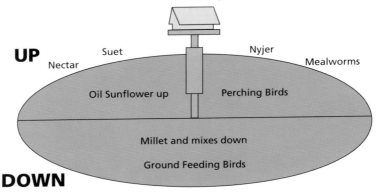

What Do I Feed Birds?
Where Do I Put My Feeder?

UP

Suet

Nectar

Nyjer

Mealworms

Oil Sunflower up

Perching Birds

Millet and mixes down

Ground Feeding Birds

DOWN

The Rule: Sunflower up. Millet Down.

The Question: Where do you want to watch birds from?

Warblers, vireos, and bluebirds will come readily to feeders offering mealworms. Woodpeckers and other insect-eating birds will be attracted to suet. Chickadees, finches, and siskins are just a few of the birds that will come to seed feeders. Orioles, robins, and mockingbirds are readily attracted to fruit, berries, and jelly.

Attracting and Understanding Hummingbirds

The hummingbird is a marvel of nature. You will never forget the first time you see one of these flying jewels visiting your backyard bird sanctuary.

Hummingbirds are attracted to and return to feeders that contain nectar resembling flower nectar. This nectar can be made at home with four parts boiling water to one part table sugar. Dissolve sugar in water and allow to cool to room temperature. Store for up to four weeks in a clean sealed jar in your refrigerator. Hummingbirds like fresh nectar, so only place enough nectar in your feeder that will be consumed in three days. Nectar sours in about four days when over 80 degrees F. Do not use red dye, honey, juice, fructose, artificial sweetener, brown sugar, or syrup in hummingbird nectar. These are dangerous to hummingbirds.

Nectar-producing flowers are very attractive to hummingbirds. Some of these that you may plant include the following: trumpet vine, columbine, honeysuckle vine, red penstemon, cardinal flower, bleeding hearts, bee balm, fuchsia, coral bells, and scarlet sage.

East of the Mississippi River there is only one type of hummingbird, the ruby-throated hummingbird. West of the Mississippi River there are several species, depending on your location and suitable habitat: Allen's, Anna's, black-chinned, broad-tailed, calliope, Costa's, and the rufous hummingbird. The rufous hummingbird is copperlike in color. The male is a big bully at the feeder. The black-chinned male has a dark, almost black head and throat. The broad-tailed male has a green head and garnet throat. The calliope is the smallest hummingbird in North America. The male has a garnet-streaked throat with a green head.

Mealworms for Birds

Mealworms can entice a bird to use a nearby nest box. They help an incubating female find food quickly, so her eggs are not left for long periods of time. Mealworms provide protein for nestlings, and they help birds survive during spells of severe winter weather, when food is hard to find. They are clean, easy to care for, do not carry human diseases, and are readily accepted by birds.

Keep mealworms in a refrigerator. Do not allow them to freeze; take them out every five to seven days. Allow them to warm up and start moving around (takes about one to two hours). Place cubes of apple $1/4$ inch in size in with them and leave for another one to two hours. Refrigerate again. Remove old apple cubes when you take them out for the next warming-and-feeding period and replace with new apple cubes.

In your backyard, place the mealworm feeder in the open, clearly within a bird's view. Place the feeder near existing feeding areas so that the birds will be able to easily find the new treat. Many birds are attracted to mealworms, including the chickadee, oriole, black-headed grosbeak, robin, cedar waxwing, jay, woodpecker, house wren, house finch, and goldfinch.

Protecting Birds from Cats and Other Predators

Place feeders where they are not within an easy leap of an ambush spot. I like to place ground feeders at least two cat bounds away from any cover. This provides the feeding birds an opportunity to detect and escape the cat. Cats are not native to this country. Birds have not evolved with domesticated cats, so they do not readily recognize them as dangerous.

Another method I use to provide added safety for the birds coming to my backyard bird sanctuary is to place a short garden fence with a large wire grid around the bird feeding area. The large grid opening in the fencing allows the birds to come and go easily. The short fence is easy for me to step over when refilling feeders. However, it is a barrier that the charging cat must navigate. This provides the birds with more opportunity to elude the cat.

Keeping a cat inside the house is the very best way to keep and enjoy a cat. They live longer lives when kept inside, avoiding accidents with vehicles and harassment from other critters, and they can safely enjoy watching birds through the window.

Bird Baths and the Importance of Water

A bird bath is perhaps the easiest way to provide the greatest diversity of bird species visiting the backyard. Many migrating birds will stop to

bathe and drink. Resident birds will soon learn of reliable local water features. They will visit the bath regularly.

When birds learn of a reliable open water source in winter, when all other water is frozen solid, they will "flock" to your backyard bird sanctuary. You will be delighted with the diversity and number of birds visiting your water feature. My wife called me recently one cold winter day to show me the twenty-five American robins using our bird bath. There were several more perched nearby, awaiting their turn at the "bird spa." You can keep your bird bath water from freezing with a heating element. If you are planning to purchase a bird bath, look for styles that incorporate a heating element that is controlled with an internal thermostat. If you already own a bird bath, you can buy a heating element that is designed for use in a bird bath. It is a good investment. The birds will be the benefactors. You will be too, just as Mom and I were as we enjoyed watching our visiting birds.

Regular bathing is important for the birds. They must bathe, clean, and preen their feathers to keep themselves aerodynamically fit. Clean feathers are better insulators that enable the bird to trap air. The air is heated by the body, which keeps the bird warm during those cold winter days and nights.

Water in a bath should have a depth ranging between $1/2$ inch and $1 1/2$ inches. Any deeper is of little use to birds. Birds prefer water at ground level, so the higher off the ground the bath, the less birds will use it. Fresh, clean water is attractive to birds, not dirty, algae-filled water. The more natural the water feature looks, the more birds will use it.

Remember:
Standing water is good
Dripping water is better
Misting water is great
Moving water is best

Birds are especially vulnerable while bathing. Wet feathers will slow their take-off and flight considerably. Therefore, birds are very cautious while bathing. Provide a safe bathing site for them and they will use it. A bath out in the open without any cover nearby (two to four feet away) makes a bathing bird vulnerable to attack from a bird of prey.

Pishing

Pishing is an onomatopoeic squeak, squeal, or stuttering slur emitted by a birder to lure a bird hidden from view into the open. Everyone is familiar with the famous saying: "A bird in hand is worth two in the bush." A birder would say "a bird in view in the bush is all I desire."

Often you catch a blur of movement in the yard as a bird flits into the cover of a nearby hedge or shrub. Some birds are natural skulkers, fox sparrows and catbirds, for example.

You wait but it will not come into view. The mystery bird is quiet, so there is no song to identify. You are not quite sure what bird it is. Yet you crave a view to satisfy your quest to know and identify it. Hence, you rely on your ability to pish, i.e., coax the bird out of the cover and into view.

Many birds will respond to alarm or mobbing calls out of curiosity. Chickadees, wrens, and nuthatches are particularly piqued by pishing. I use four types of pishing:

The first is a low sounding *pish-pish-pish,* as I force air against my lips with clenched teeth. The air pushes my lips open to make the pishing sound. Slow and low pishing in groups of three notes is usually sufficient.

My second style is a louder, more rapid series *pish-pish-pish,* with teeth slightly apart and lips closed. The force of air pushes my lips open, as if giving a kiss.

The third manner is to kiss the back of my hand while sucking air into my mouth. The loud squeak is repeated.

Sparrows respond best to a loud and sharp *chip* note. Hold your middle and index fingers against closed lips and give a high-pitched kiss. Repeat this kiss chip sound at one-second intervals for four or five notes.

Once you have lured the bird into view for identification, stop pishing. Don't overuse pishing, since you do not want to tax the birds or distract them from their daily routine.

Cover

Cover is the vegetation that exists in your yard that creates suitable habitat for birds. A key use of cover is for nesting. Besides feeding and bathing, birds need to have a safe place where they can make a nest and raise their young. Nesting cover can be shrubs, trees, vines, and other similar growth that gives the birds a structure to build a nest where they can safely lay eggs, incubate, and fledge their young. Some birds are ground nesters, such as pheasants and quail. Other birds build a nest off the ground, such as the robin and oriole.

Then there are the cavity nesters. Cavity nesters such as the woodpecker can drill and excavate a cavity in a tree. They will make a new cavity each year. Creating a cavity is part of the bonding ritual that the birds go through. Males show potential mates that they can acquire and defend a breeding territory. They will attract a female to their territory by showing existing cavities. The female visits and decides whether she will nest there. It is usually the female who builds and constructs the actual nest. Other cavity nesters will use old woodpecker holes or natural cavities. Some will excavate their cavities like the woodpecker. You can also erect a nest box to simulate the cavity. Erecting a nest box will give you the opportunity to provide suitable habitat for these interesting birds.

Nest Box Building

Nest boxes serve as a replacement of the natural cavity that cavity-nesting birds seek out. Placing nest boxes in suitable habitat enables cavity nesters to raise their young. The nest box also gives us an opportunity to enjoy the birds during this critical time in their lives.

Which bird will live in a particular nest box is determined primarily by the size of the entrance hole. Beyond that, there are recommended interior dimensions for the various species that make up the cavity-nesting birds. The following list includes some of the birds who are cavity nesters: chickadee; northern flicker; downy and hairy woodpecker; Williamson's and red-naped sapsucker; white-breasted, red-breasted, and pygmy nuthatch; juniper titmouse; western screech owl; house wren; eastern, mountain, and western bluebird; starling; house sparrow; tree swallow; American kestrel; and wood duck.

Remember that a nesting bird wants its nest to be secluded, out of the hustle and bustle of other birds, animals, and people. Don't locate your nest box next to your bird feeder or birdbath. Do not place a perch below the entrance hole, or other birds will use it to harass and worry the birds inside. A mother bird may abandon a nest if she is stressed in such a manner.

A nest box needs to be cleaned out in the fall after each nesting season. More than two broods may be raised within a season, so wait until fall to clean it out. Hang the nest box so that it gets morning sun. Place the entrance hole facing northeast, east, or southeast. The entrance hole should not receive afternoon sun. Place clean wood shavings or chips in chickadee and nuthatch nest boxes. Woodpecker boxes can be filled with shavings or chips so that they can "excavate" the box. This method prevents European starlings from entering a nest box.

Most boxes can be hung at "Grandpa's hoisting height." This is the height that I can lift up my grandkids so that they can see what is happening in the box without my needing to climb up a ladder with them in tow.

One particularly enjoyable nest box to place in your backyard bird sanctuary is the convertible nest box. It is a uniquely designed nest box that can be used by birds year-round. The nest box entrance hole located on the front panel of the nest box can be swiveled back and forth from the top (up) to the bottom (down) of the nest box depending on the season of the year. During spring the nest box entrance hole is placed in the top (up) position. The ventilation holes located high up on the side panels are placed in the open position. A small mesh wire platform is placed inside on the floor of the nest box. Hot air rises. This configuration facilitates free air flow through the nest box. There is a Plexiglas side panel that can be opened to inspect activity inside the nest box. You will delight when you open this panel and see a nest with eggs or young nestlings inside. After the nesting season is over in the fall, you reverse the entrance hole to the bottom (down) position on the front of the nest box. Next you close the vents on the inside panels and remove the old nest. It is important to remove the old nest from the nest box. It makes the nest box ready for new nest construction the following spring. Building a new nest is part of the bonding ritual of the breeding birds using the nest box.

Now the nest box is snug and ready for winter. There are two peg perches on the inside of the box that are raised up off the floor above the entrance hole that is now at the bottom of the nest box. These will serve as perches for winter roosting birds. Cold air sinks. Roosting birds perched on the two pegs will have their body heat trapped in the upper chamber of the nest box (remember that hot air rises). This arrangement will keep them warm and protected from the cold of long winter nights. The entrance hole has a metal strip around the outside edge so that squirrels or raccoons cannot chew the hole to make it wider, thus preventing them from gaining access to the eggs or young nestlings. There is an additional predator guard in place, as the entrance hole is two thicknesses of the faceplate board on the nest box. This prevents a raccoon from reaching his paw inside to grab the eggs or young nestlings.

Vegetation for Backyard Birds
Trees Used Primarily for Food
Abies sp. (fir)
> brown creeper, cedar waxwing, chickadee, finch, flycatcher, junco, kinglet, mourning dove, nuthatch, robin, western scrub and Steller's jay

Acer sp. (maple)
> American goldfinch, cedar waxwing, finch, grosbeak, pine siskin, robin, sparrow, vireo, warbler

Alnus italica (Italian alder)
> American goldfinch, chickadee, finch, mourning dove

Betula nigra (river birch)
American goldfinch, chickadee, finch, mourning dove

Carpinus betulus 'Fastiagata' (European hornbeam)
American goldfinch, finch, grosbeak

Celtis sinensis (hackberry)
cedar waxwing, mockingbird, oriole, robin, thrasher, thrush, titmouse, towhee

Celtus australis (nettle)
cedar waxwing, mockingbird, oriole, robin, thrasher, thrush, titmouse, towhee

Crataegus sp. (hawthorn)
blue, western scrub, and Steller's jays; cedar waxwing, flicker, oriole, pine siskin, robin, thrush, towhee

Ficus sp. (fig)
flicker, grosbeak, oriole, robin, warbler

Fraxinus sp. (ash)
cedar waxwing, chickadee, finch, grosbeak, pine siskin, robin, western scrub and Steller's jay

Juglans sp. (walnut)
flicker, oriole, sparrow, warbler, western scrub and Steller's jay, woodpecker

Liquidambar styraciflua (sweetgum)
American goldfinch, chickadee, finch, mourning dove, pine siskin, sparrow, towhee, woodpecker

Magnolia sp. (magnolia)
robin, thrush, vireo

Malus sp. (crabapple)
American goldfinch, cedar waxwing, finch, flicker, oriole, robin, towhee, warbler, western scrub jay, woodpecker

Quercus sp. (oak)
flicker, oriole, mourning dove, towhee, western scrub and Steller's jay, woodpecker

Picea sp. (spruce)
American goldfinch, cedar
waxwing, chickadee, finch,
mourning dove, pine siskin,
sparrow, woodpecker

Prunus sp. (cherry, plum)
American goldfinch, cedar
waxwing, finch, flicker, grosbeak, oriole, robin, sparrow,
thrush, towhee, vireo, western
scrub jay, woodpecker

Prunus caroliniana (Carolina cherry)
American goldfinch, cedar
waxwing, finch, flicker, grosbeak, oriole, robin, sparrow,
thrush, towhee, vireo, western
scrub jay, woodpecker

Prunus ilicifolia (holly leaf cherry)
American goldfinch, cedar
waxwing, finch, flicker, grosbeak, oriole, robin, sparrow,
thrush, towhee, vireo, western
scrub jay, woodpecker

Prunus lusitanica (Portuguese laurel)
American goldfinch, cedar

waxwing, finch, flicker, grosbeak, oriole, robin, sparrow,
thrush, towhee, vireo, western
scrub jay, woodpecker

Rhus lancea (African sumac)
California quail

Schinus mollis (California pepper)
cedar waxwing, flicker, robin,
thrush

Umbellaria californica (California bay)
Steller's jay, Townsend's solitaire

Shrubs Used Primarily for Food
Arbutus unedo (strawberry tree)
American robin, cedar waxwing,
western scrub jay

Arctostaphylos sp. (manzanita)
American robin, fox sparrow,
western scrub jay

Arctostaphylos uva-ursi (bearberry)
American robin, cedar waxwing,
sparrow, thrush, warbler

Elaeagnus sp. (Russian olive)
cedar waxwing, finch, flicker,

grosbeak, oriole, robin, sparrow, thrush, towhee, vireo, warbler, woodpecker

Heteromeles arbutifolia (toyon)
California quail

Ilex sp. (holly)
cedar waxwing, chickadee, finch, flicker, mourning dove, nuthatch, robin, thrush, towhee, vireo, warbler, western scrub jay, woodpecker

Ligustrum (privet)
cedar waxwing, finch, sparrow, towhee, wren

Mahonia sp. (Oregon grape)
cedar waxwing, mockingbird, robin, sparrow, towhee

Myrica californica (Pacific wax myrtle)
chickadee, flicker, towhee, warbler

Pyracantha sp. (firethorn)
cedar waxwing, flicker, nuthatch, robin, sparrow,

thrush, towhee, vireo, western scrub jay, woodpecker

Rhamnus californica (coffeeberry)
cedar waxwing, oriole, robin, thrush, warbler, western scrub jay

Rhus ovata (sugar bush)
California quail

Ribes sp. (gooseberry)
finch, flicker, robin, thrush, towhee, western scrub jay

Ribes californica; Rosa californica
(California gooseberry; California wild rose)
California quail, grosbeak, junco, pheasant, sparrow, Townsend's solitaire

Rubus sp. (blackberry, bramble)
cedar waxwing, finch, grosbeak, mourning dove, robin, sparrow, thrush, towhee, vireo, warbler, western scrub jay

Sambucus sp. (elderberry)
California quail, cedar waxwing,

finch, flicker, grosbeak, mourning dove, nuthatch, robin, sparrow, Steller's jay, thrush, towhee, vireo, warbler, western scrub jay, woodpecker

Symphoricarpos sp. (snowberry)
cedar waxwing, grosbeak, robin, thrush, towhee

Vaccinium sp. (huckleberry)
California quail, chickadee, flicker, grouse, robin, Swainson's thrush, waxwings

Viburnum sp. (honeysuckle)
cedar waxwing, grosbeak, robin, sparrow, starling, thrush, towhee

Vitis sp. (grape)
cedar waxwing, finch, mourning dove, robin, sparrow, thrush, western scrub jay

Grasses to Enhance Wild Bird Habitat

Ornamental grasses, especially native types, attract many birds. They are used for nesting materials, nesting sites, and seeds for food. There are many beautiful grasses to select from. Some of the birds that are attracted to grasses include meadowlarks, quail, sparrows, and finches. Here are just a few of the grasses that seem to be especially favored:

Andropogon sp. (bluestem)
Arrhenatherum elatius var. *bulbosum* (tall oatgrass)
Bouteloua gracilis (blue grama)
Briza sp. (quaking grass)
Cortedaria selloana (pampas grass)
Deschampsia sp. (tufted hair grass)
Elymus sp. (wild rye)
Festuca sp. (fescue)
Miscanthus sp. (maidenhair grass)
Muhlenbergia rigens (deergrass)
Panicum sp. (witchgrass)
Stipa sp. (needlegrass)

Annuals and Perennials Used for Food

Amaranthus sp. (amaranth)
Aquilegia sp. (columbine)
Aster
Calendula officinales (pot marigold)

Campanula sp. (bellflower)
Celosia sp. (cockscomb)
Centaurea cyanus (garden cornflower)
Chrysanthemum
Cirsium sp. (thistle)
Coreopsis sp. (tickseed)
Cosmos
Echinacea
Helianthus sp. (sunflower)
Limonium sp. (statice)
Myosotis (forget-me-not)
Nigella sp. (love-in-a-mist)
Papaver sp. (poppy)
Phlox sp.
Portulaca sp. (moss rose)
Rudbeckia sp. (black-eyed Susan)
Scabiosa sp. (pincushion)
Sedum spectabile (ice plant)
Solidago sp. (goldenrod)
Tagetes (marigold)
Verbena sp.
Zinnia sp.

Nectar-producing Plants to Attract Hummingbirds

Trees
Aesculus sp. (horse chestnut)
Alibizia julibrissin (silktree)

x Chitalpa tashkentensis (chitalpa)
Citrus
Crataegus sp. (hawthorn)
Melaleuca sp.

Shrubs
Abelia
Arctostaphylos sp. (manzanita)
Buddleia sp. (butterfly bush)
Chaenomeles sp. (flowering quince)
Correa sp. (Australian fuschia)
Diplacus sp. (monkey flower)
Feijoa sallowiana (pineapple guava)
Galvezia speciosa (Bush Island
    snapdragon)
Grevellia sp.
Heteromeles arbutifolia (toyon)
Hibiscus syriacus (rose of Sharon)
Lavandula sp. (lavender)
Jasminum sp. (jasmine)
Kolwitzia sp. (beauty bush)
Lantana
Ribes sp. (gooseberry)
Rosmarinus sp. (rosemary)
Trichostema (bluecurls)
Vitex agnus-castus (chaste tree)
Weigelia
Yucca sp.

Perennials/Annuals

Aguilegia sp. (columbine)
Agave sp.
Ajuga (bugleweed)
Alce sp.
Alstroemeria (Peruvian lily)
Althea sp. (hollyhock)
Antirrhinum (snapdragon)
Asclepias tuberosa (butterfly weed)
Castilleja sp. (Indian paintbrush)
Dahlia
Delphinium
Dianthus
Digitalis purpurea (foxglove)
Echium fastuosum (pride of madeira)
Fuschia
Gladiolus
Hemerocallis (daylily)
Heuchera
Impatiens balsamina (balsam)
Ipomopsis
Iris
Kniphofia (red hot poker)
Lilium
Lobelia cardinalis (cardinalflower)
Lupinus (lupine)

Marabilis
Monarda didyma (scarlet beebalm)
Nicotiana
Oenothera
Pelargonium
Penstemon (beard tongue)
Petunia
Phaseolus coccineus (scarlet runner bean)
Phygelius (cape fuschia)
Salvia sp. (sage)
Saponaria (soapwort)
Tropaeolum sp. (nasturtium)
Verbena
Zauschneria sp. (California fuschia)
Zinnia

Vines

Campsis radicans (trumpet vine)
Cestrum elegans (red cestrum)
Distictis buccinatoria (blood red trumpet vine)
Ipomoea
Lonicera (honeysuckle)
Tecomaria capensis (cape honeysuckle)

Creating a Safe Experience for Birds Visiting Your Feeder
—David J. Horn, Director of Research, Wild Bird Centers of America

In 1999, thousands of American crows died with the arrival of West Nile virus in New York City. The virus quickly spread, reaching the West Coast in 2003. As the virus spread from coast to coast, tens of thousands of birds died including hawks, jays, and chickadees. Fortunately for people who feed birds, West Nile virus is not known to be transmitted from bird to feeder to bird contact; rather, the predominant mode of transmission is from mosquito to bird.

There are, however, several diseases that birds can acquire at feeding stations if they are not properly cared for, and it is important for people who feed birds to create a backyard environment that is safe for our feathered friends. Follow the described steps recommended by the National Wildlife Health Center (www.nwhc.usgs.gov) to reduce the risk of disease to birds using your feeders.

First, provide birds with a large amount of space for feeding. Birds crowded onto a single feeder increase the likelihood of contact between sick and healthy birds and may increase a bird's stress level while feeding, making them more susceptible to disease. One solution would be to purchase feeders that minimize contact between birds. Overcrowding at feeders may also be alleviated by providing birds with other places to feed.

A second step is to keep the birds' feeding area free of a buildup of seed hulls and bird droppings by cleaning the area below the feeder. One way to minimize the cleaning needed would be to use no-waste seeds or seed mixes that contain hulled seeds, and to offer only the preferred seeds for the bird species in your area.

Third, purchase feeders that do not have sharp points or edges. Such feeders may cause bleeding or scratches on birds that can result in the transmission of disease.

Regularly cleaning your feeders is the fourth step you can take. Feeders should be washed approximately once a month with a solution of 10 percent bleach (one part bleach to nine parts water) by completely immersing feeders for at least three minutes and then allowing them to dry. Purchasing feeders that are made of materials that are easier to clean, such as metal and plastic, may also make cleaning the feeder easier.

Finally, store food appropriately and ensure that fresh seed is in your feeder. Use a rodent-proof container to store food, and avoid having wet, moldy, musty-smelling seed in your feeder. Providing feeders that protect the seed from the elements and placing seeds that birds in your area prefer should reduce the chance of seed getting wet or moldy.

In addition to the above steps, people who provide water to birds should scrub their bird bath and change the water in their bath several times per week to prevent mosquito reproduction and the possible spread of West Nile virus.

Bird feeding is a wonderful pastime and it provides those who feed birds with a greater connection to the natural world we live in. Providing a safe and clean feeding environment will allow you to enjoy our feathered friends while lowering the risk to birds of disease at feeders.

To learn more about additional ways to improve the bird feeding experience, download a copy of the 6 steps to turn your yard into a sanctuary for birds brochure on the Wild Bird Centers of America Web site (http://www.wildbirdcenter.com/cms/www_files/6ways.pdf)

Fun Bird Projects

A fun project for the individual or family is to keep a backyard bird list. Each time a new bird species arrives in my backyard bird sanctuary, I record it on my "backyard bird list." Over the last twenty-one years that I have lived in our present home I have recorded new birds visiting the backyard bird sanctuary. The list stands today at eighty-seven different bird species.

Over that same time period, I have continued to make improvements to the habitat. Trees that I planted twenty-one years ago have become substantial cover assets for the birds today. Nearly all of my plantings produce a crop of some sort. It might be crabapples, berries, grapes, acorns, or blossoms that produce. They also provide a harbor for insects, their larvae, and cocoons. The birds will enjoy foraging among the cover to discover what might be there for them to eat.

Nesting, loafing, and roosting cover is available for them too. There are several water features from the traditional pedestal bath to a mister, water dripper, and recycling pump that keep the water moving. The water dripper performs two functions: it moves water and replaces water lost through evaporation or splashing of bathing birds. Included in the water features are several rocks that I have placed to create structure and differing depth levels. Some birds like the robins will jump right into the deep end of the bath. Others like the American goldfinch like the shallow end of the bath. Chickadees like to pick up drops of water coming from the dripper. The pedestal bath is allowed to overflow into a ground-level bath below it, so that the doves, quail, and other ground-feeding birds can access the water. Present water and food at the level that mimics the bird's natural behavior. Doing so will reward you with birds flocking to your backyard bird sanctuary.

Additionally, I keep a list of when the different bird species arrive in my backyard bird sanctuary. This helps me to be prepared for those migratory species that I may only see for a short period of time. Lazuli buntings arrive in my backyard by April 1. I make sure that the platform feeder has ample white proso millet for them. April 15 brings a smile to my face while many others may be fretting and grimacing over their tax return. The hummingbirds are back. Nectar feeders are cleaned and hung with fresh nectar. May 1 will bring orioles. The mealworms, grape jelly, and orange halves are out and waiting for them. The red hot poker flowers are beginning to bloom. I have hung a ball of wool and cotton for nesting material that the oriole will pick at when making its basket-shaped nest in our cottonwood. The Bullock's oriole will find everything ready and the table set for his arrival. June is nesting and fledging time. Robins will be bringing their young onto the lawn where they will hunt worms. Young quail are following their mom through the scrub oak. They can leave the nest and begin following mom and foraging a few hours after hatching. July is a time for young to grow and stretch their wings. Some of the birds begin to molt. Goldfinches are late nesters and are bringing newly fledged young to the Nyjer feeders filled with those tiny black seeds bursting with oil. August and September begin to show early migration in some of the birds. Orioles will soon depart, as well as the hummingbirds. The Neotropical birds put on an extra layer of fat at my feeders in preparation for the migration that will take them far to the south, some as far as Central and South America. October arrives and I clean out the nest boxes so that they will be ready for use as winter roosting areas. The entrance hole is moved from the top of the box to the bottom. The air vents are closed and the old nest removed. Suet is placed in the feeders for the flickers and ruby-crowned kinglets that will winter in my yard. House finches eagerly take the black oil sunflower seeds I place in my tube or hopper-style feeders.

The spotted towhee arrives with winter's first snowstorm in November. His migration is one of elevation. Deepening snow higher up on the mountain forces this ground feeder down into sheltered valleys. My backyard is an ideal wintering area for him. My brush pile, low-growing shrubs, and Oregon grapevine tangle are ready to provide him the cover he desires, as well as areas to scratch about for seeds. Seed has been scattered under the brush pile for him to find. White-crowned sparrows arrive with the towhees. Dark-eyed juncos arrive soon after the towhees. Downy woodpeckers and black-capped chickadees form mixed foraging flocks with these sparrows. Together they will winter in the brush piles, hedges, shrubs, and thickets in the backyard. December shows that winter is here in earnest. Snow is deepening in the yard. I have shoveled a path around to the feeders from my garden shed where I store my seed in galvanized cans. Bright orange pyracantha berries are attracting cedar waxwings to the backyard sanctuary now. The grandchildren press their noses against the cold of the glass window as they watch the birds at the feeders. Quail and pheasant tracks are in my shoveled pathway. They use it so they can avoid slogging through the deeper snow. January is announced by the hooting of a great horned owl. A few nights later I hear the whinny of a screech owl. The owl breeding season will soon be here. My nest box for the screech owl has two inches of fresh wood shavings in it. There are two boxes set up in my scrub oak grove. The male will use one and keep watch over the female who will use the other. I have them placed so that he can see the entrance hole of his mate. Her box faces east so that she will have morning sun. He will receive the afternoon sun with his westerly facing roosting box. February is cold, yet there is a hint of warmer times not far off. Melting icicles hint of the spring thaw just around the corner. Black oil sunflower and Nyjer are favorites for the seed eaters. Suet provides energy for the insect-eating ruby-crowned kinglet that has remained in the backyard throughout the winter. Every once in a while I catch a glimpse of his neon red crown that he flashes. It is another hint that spring is not far away. Pheasant and quail march through the snow on my pathway to the ground feeders. The heated bird bath has lots of action throughout the day from birds who stop for a drink, as well as the robins and waxwings who bathe contentedly. March dawns and I hear the house finch singing as the morning sun warms the birds. His song signals that winter is loosening its grip and spring will soon prevail. Spring will bring the breeding season and new birds will soon arrive on their migration. Winter residents prepare to leave and the cycle begins anew.

Who needs a calendar to tell them what time of year it is? The natural rhythms and cycles let me know what time it is and what to expect next. I have reversed the convertible nest box so the chickadees will find it ready for their new nest. House wrens are singing. The flicker has started to drum on our wood-burning stove stack. The machine-gun staccato of his drumming wakes me this morning. My wife asks me, "Who is knocking at the door?" "Spring," I answer. "Spring is here."

Citizen Science Programs

The Cornell Lab of Ornithology and the National Audubon Society have a wonderful array of citizen science programs for the family or the individual bird lover. You can contact the Cornell Lab of Ornithology at www.birds.cornell.edu/. Here is a brief list of some of their programs:

- nest-box monitoring project
- informal science education
- continent-wide research
- proactive conservation

- information related to cavity-nesting birds
- online nest-box cam
- Project Classroom feeder watch

Contact the National Audubon Society at www.audubon.org. They have local regional chapters that you can consider joining. These chapters engage in a variety of local conservation projects that benefit birds and other wildlife. Audubon conducted the 107th Christmas Bird Count in 2007. These projects help scientists in learning about long-range trends in bird populations: whether they are shrinking, expanding, or remaining the same.

Birds are a key indicator species. They can act as an early-warning system when something is wrong in our environment. Other birding and conservation groups that can provide additional information:

- The Nature Conservancy (www.nature.org) is a wonderful national organization that promotes conservation and saving habitat. It has nature trails and has protected key species around the country with its important work.
- The American Birding Association (www.americanbirding.org) is an organization for those who want to become more serious in their study of birds.
- The American Bird Conservancy (www.abcbirds.org) maintains a Bird Conservation Alliance that helps groups further their knowledge and conservation work with birds.

Ruby-throated
Hummingbird
page 19

Carolina
Chickadee
page 21

American
Goldfinch
page 23

Carolina Wren
page 25

House
Finch
page 27

House
Sparrow
page 29

Downy
Woodpecker
page 31

Tufted
Titmouse
page 33

White-throated Sparrow
page 35

Orchard
Oriole
page 37

Baltimore
Oriole
page 39

Great Crested
Flycatcher
page 41

Summer
Tanager
page 43

Eastern Towhee
page 45

Northern
Cardinal
page 49

European
Starling
page 47

Red-bellied
Woodpecker
page 51

American
Robin
page 53

Northern
Mockingbird
page 55

Blue Jay
page 57

Mourning
Dove
page 59

Eurasian
Collared Dove
page 61

Common
Grackle
page 63

Boat-tailed
Grackle
page 65

Cooper's
Hawk
page 67

Backyard Birds across the country!

Soon to include all 50 states.
Available in stores nationwide or directly from

Gibbs Smith, Publisher
1.800.835.4993/www.gibbs-smith.com